AF605964

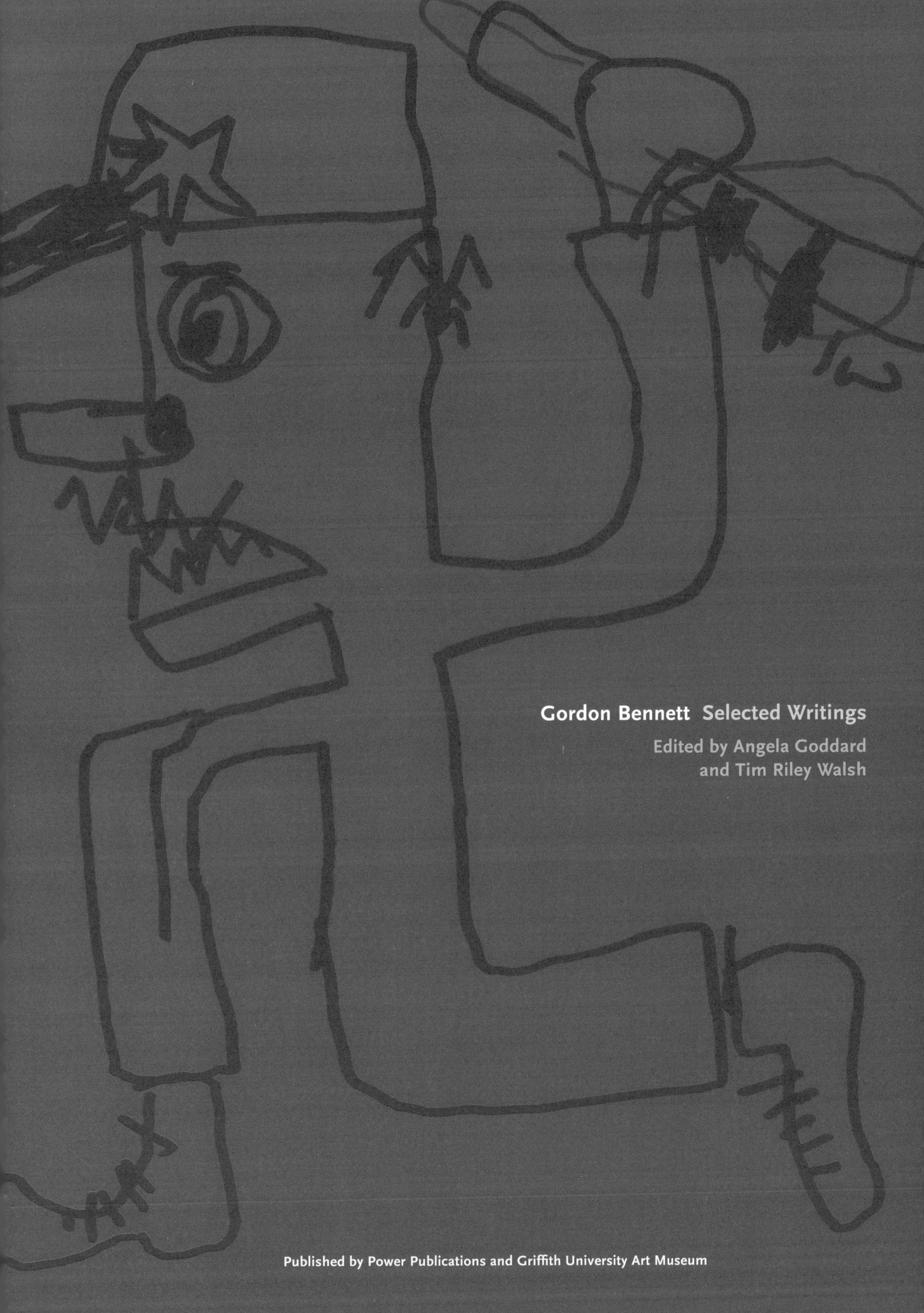

Gordon Bennett Selected Writings

Edited by Angela Goddard
and Tim Riley Walsh

Published by Power Publications and Griffith University Art Museum

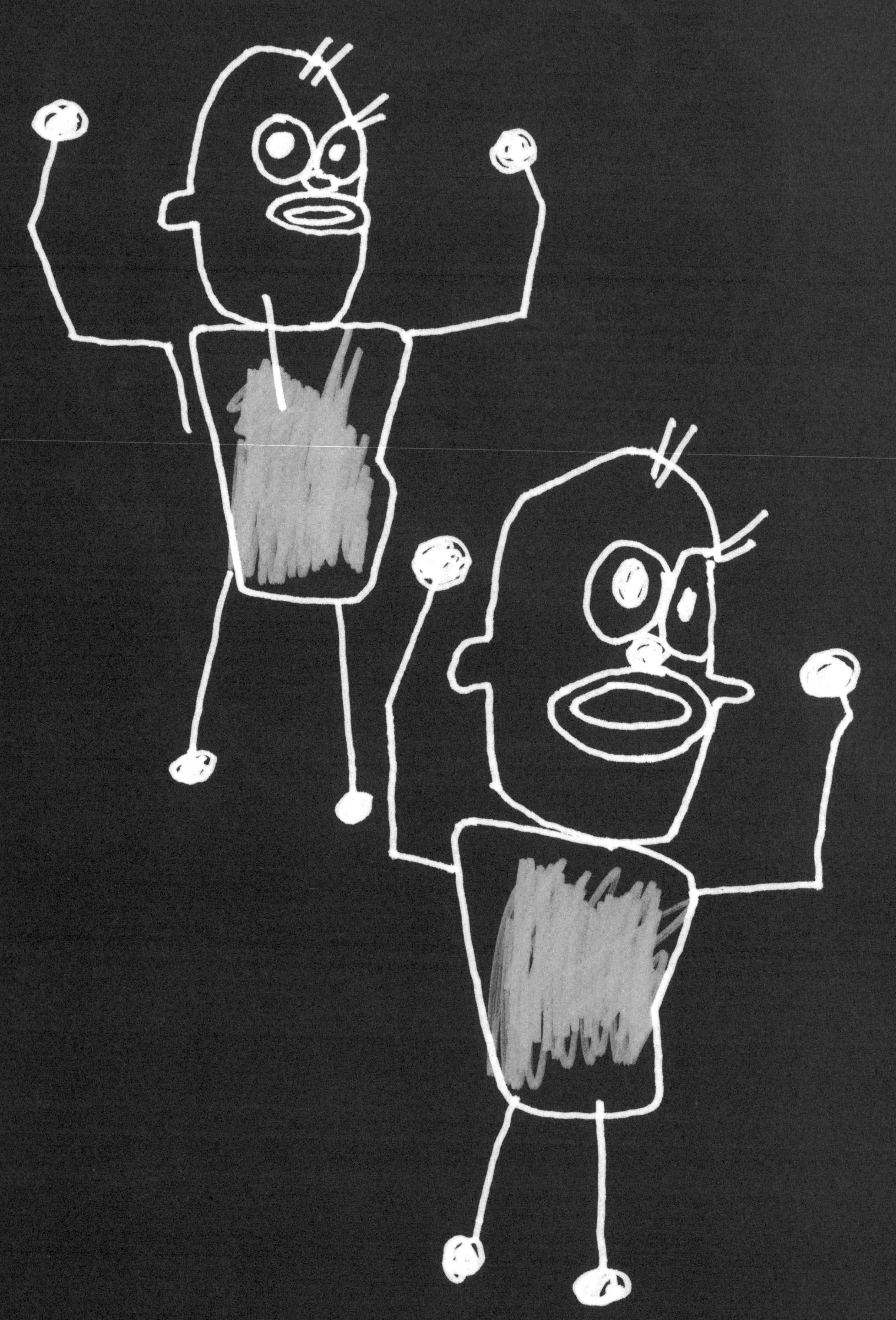

Contents

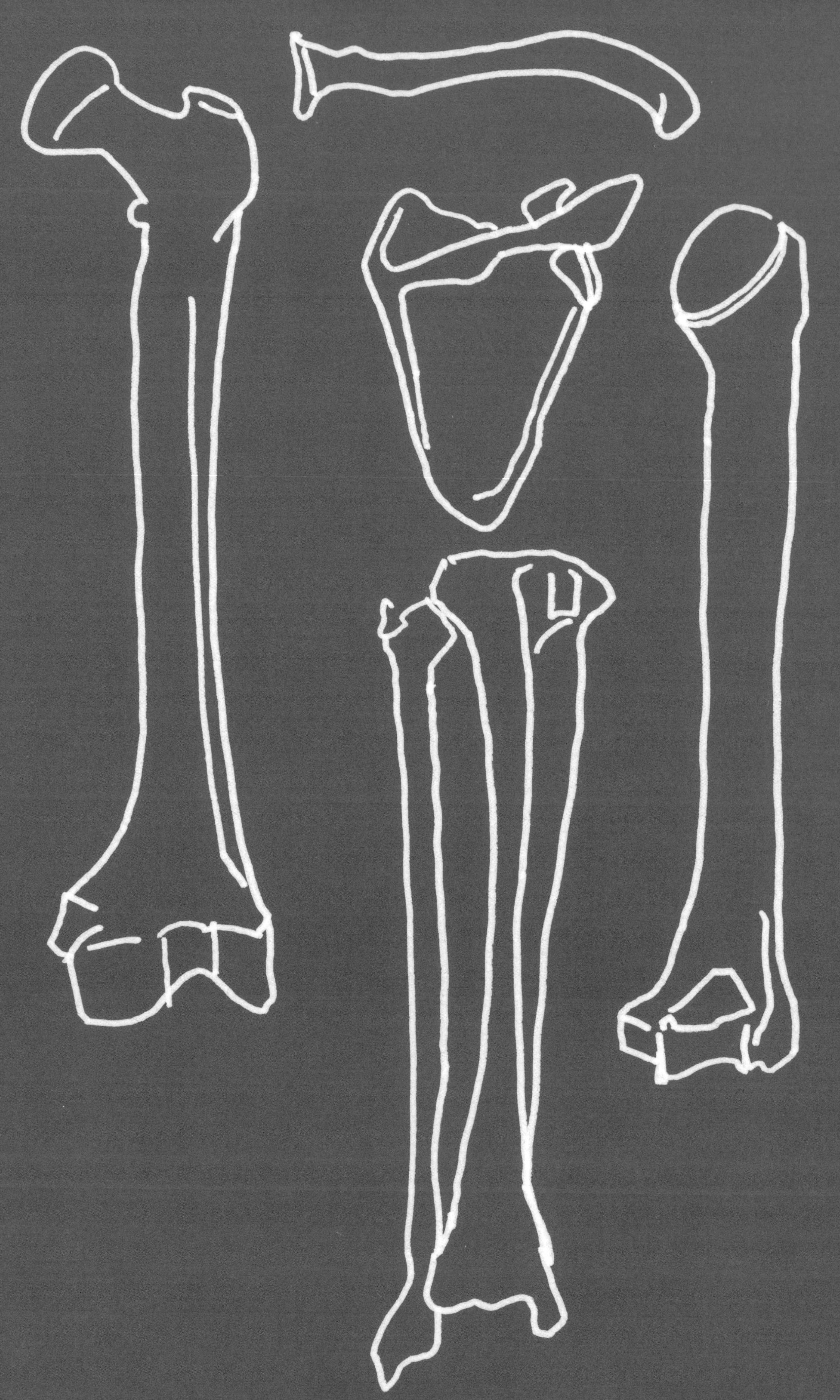

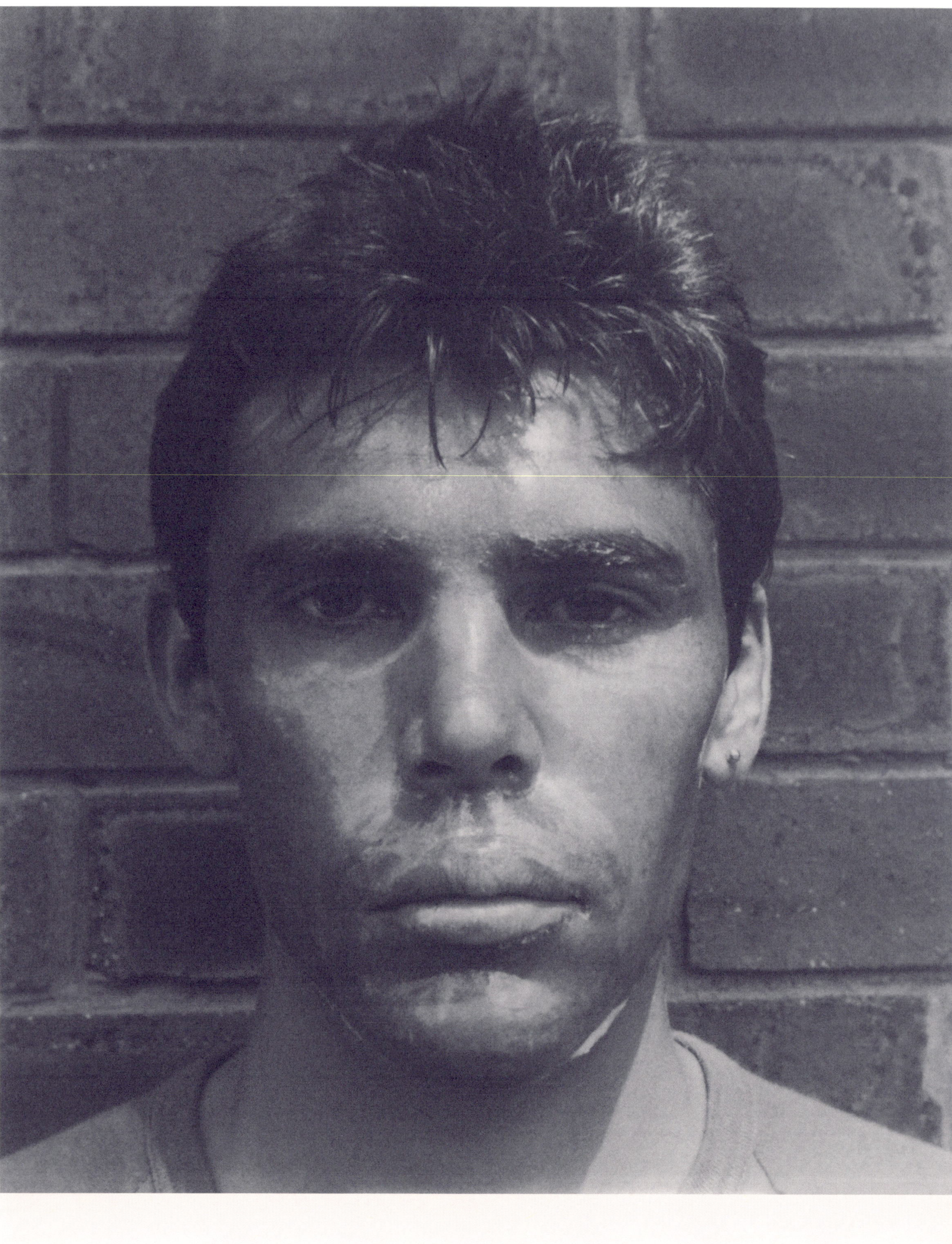

Editors' note:

Unless otherwise stated, all texts have been sourced from the personal archive of Gordon Bennett and are reproduced here in consultation with his estate. The majority of the texts are previously unpublished and therefore have not been through comprehensive structural or copyediting processes. As many of these papers are published posthumously, only minimal changes have been made to Bennett's writing. While original phrasing has been retained, changes to capitalisation, quotation marks, hyphenation, punctuation, and spelling have been made to unpublished materials for readability, accuracy and consistency, particularly to recurring terms such as those describing ethnic and cultural groups, art and political movements, events, artist names, and artwork titles. Any words that were previously underlined or bolded to indicate emphasis have been converted to italics. Editorial interventions that affect the interpretation of meaning or provide additional contextual information are placed in square brackets or explained in footnotes.

Bennett, like many writers from previous decades, did not always capitalise 'Indigenous' or 'Aboriginal', but in consideration of current usage, these terms have been capitalised throughout. Endnotes throughout this document have been standardised for stylistic consistency. While factual errors are discussed by the editors in footnotes, editors' notes appear in endnotes within square brackets.

In Bennett's 'Aesthetics and Iconography: An Artist's Approach', the style of punctuation follows the essay's reprint in Morgan Perkins and Howard Morphy's *Anthropology of Art: A Reader* (Oxford: John Wiley & Sons, 2006), 513–19. This changes the 1993 English version's use of > < and >> << in place of inverted commas and indented block quotes, respectively.

The interview between Pat Hoffie and Gordon Bennett included here has been transcribed from a satellite television broadcast recording from 1989. Subtle edits have been made to improve readability in the transcription's translation from spoken to written word.

Angela Goddard and **Tim Riley Walsh**
Editors

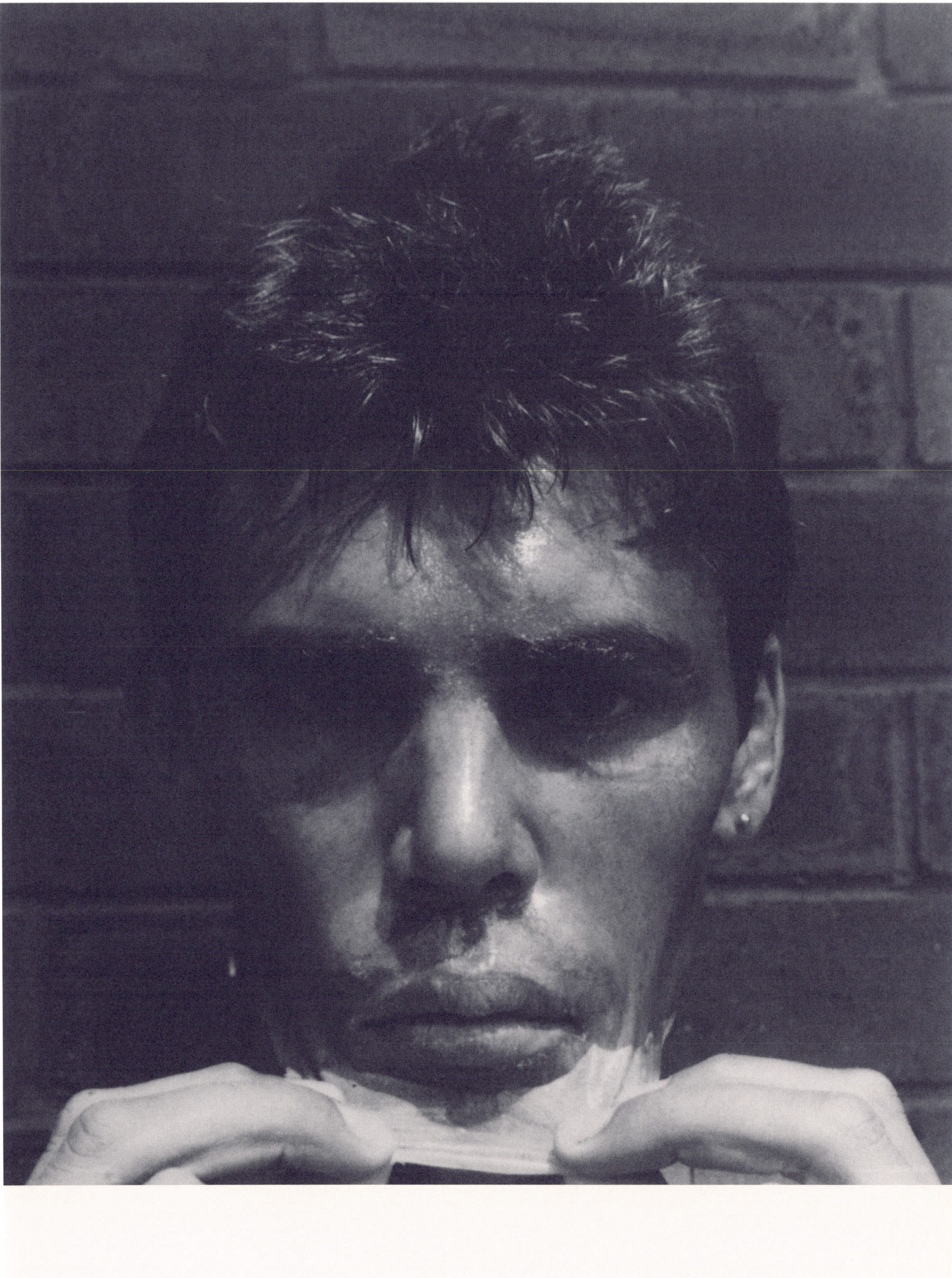

Foreword

Gordon Bennett was born in Monto, Queensland, in 1955. He enrolled as a mature-age student at the Queensland College of Art in 1986 and graduated with a Bachelor of Arts (Fine Arts) degree in 1988. Since his first major solo exhibition in 1989, his work has been at the forefront of contemporary Australian art. He passed away unexpectedly in 2014.

Much of Bennett's work interrogates Australia's colonial past and postcolonial present, including issues associated with the dominant role that white, Western culture has played in constructing our social and cultural landscape. He rejected racial stereotypes and categorisation as an Indigenous artist. Later, he created an alter ego who had a separate practice, John Citizen, whom Bennett considered to be 'an abstraction of the Australian Mr Average, the Australian Everyman'.[1] John Citizen also represented an opportunity to explore streams of thought that Bennett saw as outside his typical artistic remit. While Bennett's art is grounded in his personal struggle with identity as an Australian of Aboriginal and Anglo-Celtic descent, it presents and examines a broad range of philosophical questions related to perception and knowledge. This includes a focus on the role and power of language in shaping our understanding of these.

Although his work is internationally recognised, few know of Bennett's deeply insightful writing about his art, broader society, and the work of other artists. Much of it is difficult to access, being either unpublished or in obscure or even out-of-print sources. As the art gallery connected to Bennett's alma mater, we maintain a close relationship to his Estate, and so when Tim Riley Walsh commenced his thesis research in 2016 I was excited to turn my attention alongside him to Bennett's personal archive. While Riley Walsh's research has focused on what he theorises as Bennett's 'affective conceptualism', our parallel project, *Gordon Bennett: Selected Writings*, focuses on Bennett's own significant contribution to the discourse of art and marks the first time that this aspect of Bennett's intellectual project has been brought to light. This publication brings together selected essays, letters and previously unpublished writing, as well as transcripts from newly digitised recordings of early and largely unseen interviews. Revealing new knowledge and insights, this project amplifies Bennett's own voice on the subjects of race and identity in national and global contexts and reaffirms his ongoing role in the global focus on postcolonial issues in the twenty-first century.

Bennett passed away on 3 June 2014, but the interest in and ongoing relevance of Bennett's art are testament to the strength of his research-led practice, pioneering in its use of historical resources as a means to challenge the erasure of Indigenous Australian history and culture. Bennett emerged in a period dominated by postcolonialism, a theory that articulates the lasting impact and continued reverberations of colonisation. The legacy of Australia's colonial past continues to hold a prominent place in contemporary cultural debates—perhaps most recently apparent in commemoration and exhibition plans for the 250-year anniversary of James Cook's Pacific voyage. Bennett's artistic method of disrupting such attempts at erasure has had considerable influence on many of today's leading Indigenous Australian artists, such as Vernon Ah Kee, Tony Albert, Daniel Boyd, Karla Dickens, Megan Cope and Dale Harding, as well as valuable non-Indigenous artist-interlocutors he encountered during his life, among them Eugene Carchesio, Tim Johnson, and Imants Tillers. While the scope of this publication does not allow for a detailed examination of Bennett's considerable artistic influence, future publications are planned to further engage with Bennett's legacy.

A large body of writing has accumulated around Bennett's work over the last three decades, with many of Australia's leading art historians engaging with the issues and debates that his work reveals. Key contributions can be found in the work of Rex Butler, Kelly Gellatly, Bob Lingard, Terry Smith, and Simon Wright,[2] and, perhaps most significantly, in the seminal texts and essays of Ian McLean,[3] which arose from the close and fruitful relationship he had with Bennett. These texts have been a major vehicle to understanding Bennett's work. It is hoped that this publication will add to this body of knowledge, while foregrounding Bennett's own words and perspectives.

Through its focus on Bennett's voice, this publication reveals Bennett's art and life in new and insightful detail, describing at times the artist's methods and thoughts. An iterative quality is uncovered within Bennett's early writings, especially in the form of his early essays, such as in 1993's 'Aesthetics and Iconography: An Artist's Approach' (p. 27) and 1996's 'The Manifest Toe' (p. 37), where one can discern the artist creating a narrative around his work by returning to and repeating arguments made in the earlier text and building upon this. This is echoed in his painting practice, where he was building a lexicon of motifs that he often repurposed in new works, deepening their already existing meaning.

This publication also highlights the particular value that Bennett found in silence and withdrawal as artistic strategies. Bennett was conscious of how his position and cultural identity were co-opted into the arguments of others, especially regarding Aboriginality or postcolonialism. In 1992, he commenced the *Non-Performance* (1992–2014), a durational conceptual work conceived initially as a five-year project of non-participation in public events in Australia that extended to be international in 1994, and continued until Bennett's untimely passing. Early into its duration, he began to invite key academics and writers to be his interlocutors, especially McLean, who began writing on Bennett's work in 1993. By the end of the decade, this dynamic was firmly established, and Bennett stopped publishing his own words by 1999. From this point on, Bennett rarely conducted any interviews with the press, only occasionally responding via email (with the exception of the interview with the late curator William (Bill) Wright for the National Gallery of Victoria's survey catalogue in 2007, included in this publication, p. 135).

Although Bennett ceased publishing his writing, he continued to correspond with confidants and colleagues privately. Two eloquent letters dating from the early 2000s are included in this publication—one to McLean (2001) and one to Ihor Holubizky (2006). These

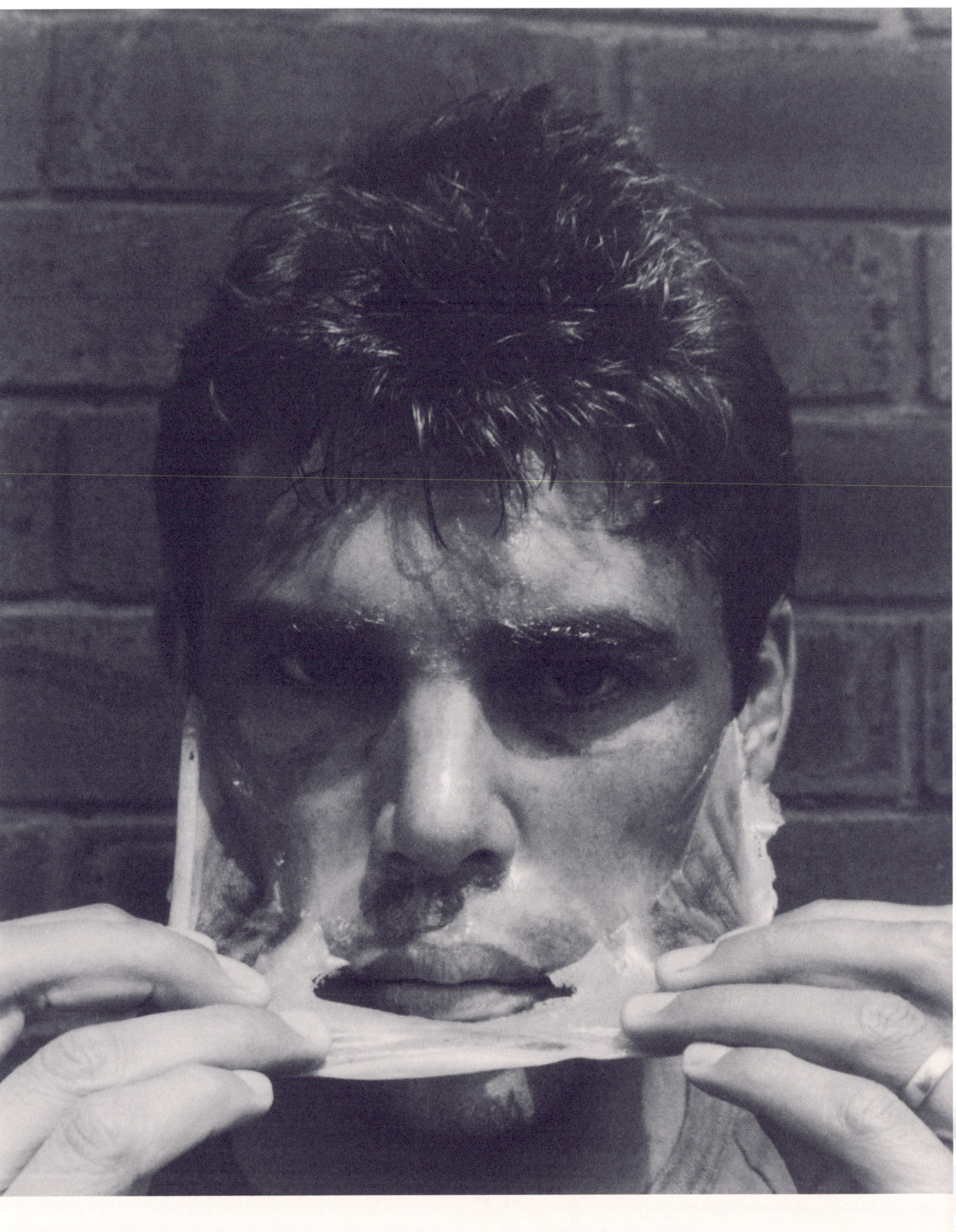

convey some of Bennett's thoughts on his 'Home Décor' (1995–2013) and 'Notes to Basquiat' (1998–2007) series, as well as his conceptualisation of John Citizen. Particularly significant insights can be found in his discussion of the synonymic word lists from the 'Notes to Basquiat' series and of Citizen's 'Coloured People' series (2000–08), which Bennett reveals as a response to engaging with the first generation American conceptualist Adrian Piper's (b. 1948) 1991 artist book *Colored People*.

Bennett's texts, letters and interviews are accompanied here by a contextual essay by Riley Walsh, in which he explores Bennett's relationship with writing. As Riley Walsh observes, 'Bennett's writing provided a crucial space for developing and testing his beliefs in a space of radical uncertainty.'[4] The anthology reveals a concentration of Bennett's publishing activity within the early years of his career, reflecting an impulse to formalise his ideas and ground his methodologies through a writing practice. Conversely, the introduction of the *Non-Performance* indicates the emergence of Bennett's wariness at his words being misunderstood.

Necessarily, this publication presents a selection, rather than an exhaustive collection, of Bennett's writing. Our selections were guided by close consultation with the artist's estate and with the shared goal of revealing new insights into Bennett's work. This publication is designed to be an accessible resource, engaging with themes addressed in upper primary and secondary school curricula, while at the same time providing rich provocations for both artists and scholars of contemporary Indigenous and Australian art and a general art audience.

Bennett's public position was one of resistance to strict identification as an Aboriginal artist: 'I have tried to avoid any simplistic critical containment or stylistic categorisation as an "Aboriginal" artist producing "Aboriginal art" [a containment that] misrepresents me and denies my upbringing and Scottish/English heritage.'[5] Bennett instead chose to identify as an Australian artist with Aboriginal and Anglo-Celtic ancestry. As non-Indigenous citizens of the settler-colonial society of Australia, Riley Walsh and I are acutely aware of our positions in the context of colonisation and the ongoing marginalisation of Indigenous people within this country. As such, this book is an attempt to centre Bennett's own voice in the context of his formative dialogues, even though he refrained from public discourse.

As well as partnering with the artist's estate, we received considered feedback from two anonymous peer reviewers and consulted closely with leading scholars on Gordon Bennett's work, with each exchange not only improving the project but also confirming it as a logical next step in the widening of knowledge and awareness of Bennett's contribution to the cultural life of the nation. As new contributors to this conversation, Riley Walsh and I are grateful for all the expertise, mentorship, and encouragement that has been so generously shared.

Our sincere thanks go to Leanne and Caitlin Bennett, the Estate of Gordon Bennett, and the artist's representatives, Josh Milani, Milani Gallery, Brisbane, and Irene Sutton, Sutton Gallery, Melbourne, for their enthusiastic support throughout the project's development. We owe deep gratitude, too, for the guidance and support provided by the co-publishers of this anthology, Power Publications, University of Sydney—in particular, Marni Williams and Mark Ledbury.

Being located in the Griffith University Art Museum and sharing a campus with the Queensland College of Art, where Bennett has long been recognised as an esteemed alumnus, I have observed the enduring relevance of his work to students, artists, and the wider public. This interest has only increased, and new scholars are continually emerging who will bring new interpretations of Bennett's oeuvre and powerful legacy to light. Our hope and intention are that Bennett's own words, highlighted in this publication, will assist in grounding and continuing these discussions.

Angela Goddard
Director, Griffith University Art Museum

Notes

1. William (Bill) Wright, 'Conversation: Bill Wright Talks to Gordon Bennett', *Gordon Bennett* (Melbourne: National Gallery of Victoria, 2007), 101.

2. Rex Butler, 'Two Readings of Gordon Bennett's The Nine Ricochets', *Eyeline* 19 (Winter/Spring 1992): 18–23; Kelly Gellatly, 'Citizen in the Making: The Art of Gordon Bennett', in *Gordon Bennett* (Melbourne: National Gallery of Victoria, 2007): 8–24; Bob Lingard and Fazal Rizvi, '(Re)membering, (Dis)membering : "Aboriginality" and the Art of Gordon Bennett', *Third Text* 26 (Spring 1994): 75–89; Terry Smith, 'Australia's Anxiety', in *History and Memory in the Art of Gordon Bennett* (Birmingham and Oslo: Ikon Gallery & Henie Onstad Kunstsenter, 1999): 10–21; Simon Wright, 'Into the Printout', in *Gordon Bennett: Out of Print* (Brisbane: Dell Gallery, 2004): 72–80.

3. Gordon Bennett and Ian McLean, *The Art of Gordon Bennett* (Roseville East, NSW: Craftsman House, 1996); Ian McLean, 'Probability, Rap and Coincidence: Notes to Basquiat', in *Gordon Bennett's Notes to Basquiat* (Sydney: Sherman Galleries, 1999); Ian McLean, 'Gordon Bennett's Abstract Art: The Aesthetics of Commitment and Indifference', in *Gordon Bennett: New Work* (Adelaide: Greenaway Art Gallery, 2004); Ian McLean, 'The Eternal Return of Irony: Gordon Bennett (1955–2014)', *Discipline 4* (2015): 170–82.

4. See Tim Riley Walsh, 'Uncertain Words: The Writing of Gordon Bennett', in this publication, page 187.

5. Gordon Bennett, 'The Manifest Toe', in *The Art of Gordon Bennett* (Roseville East, NSW: Craftsman House, 1996), 59.

23-1-90

I propose a more wholistic model of perception in daily life. Taking into account the role of you, the observer, in daily perceptions of events and activities. This necessitates an investigation into self, your conditioning & belief systems & how these effect a bias of ones point of view. Nothing is God given & natural.

Part One In his own words

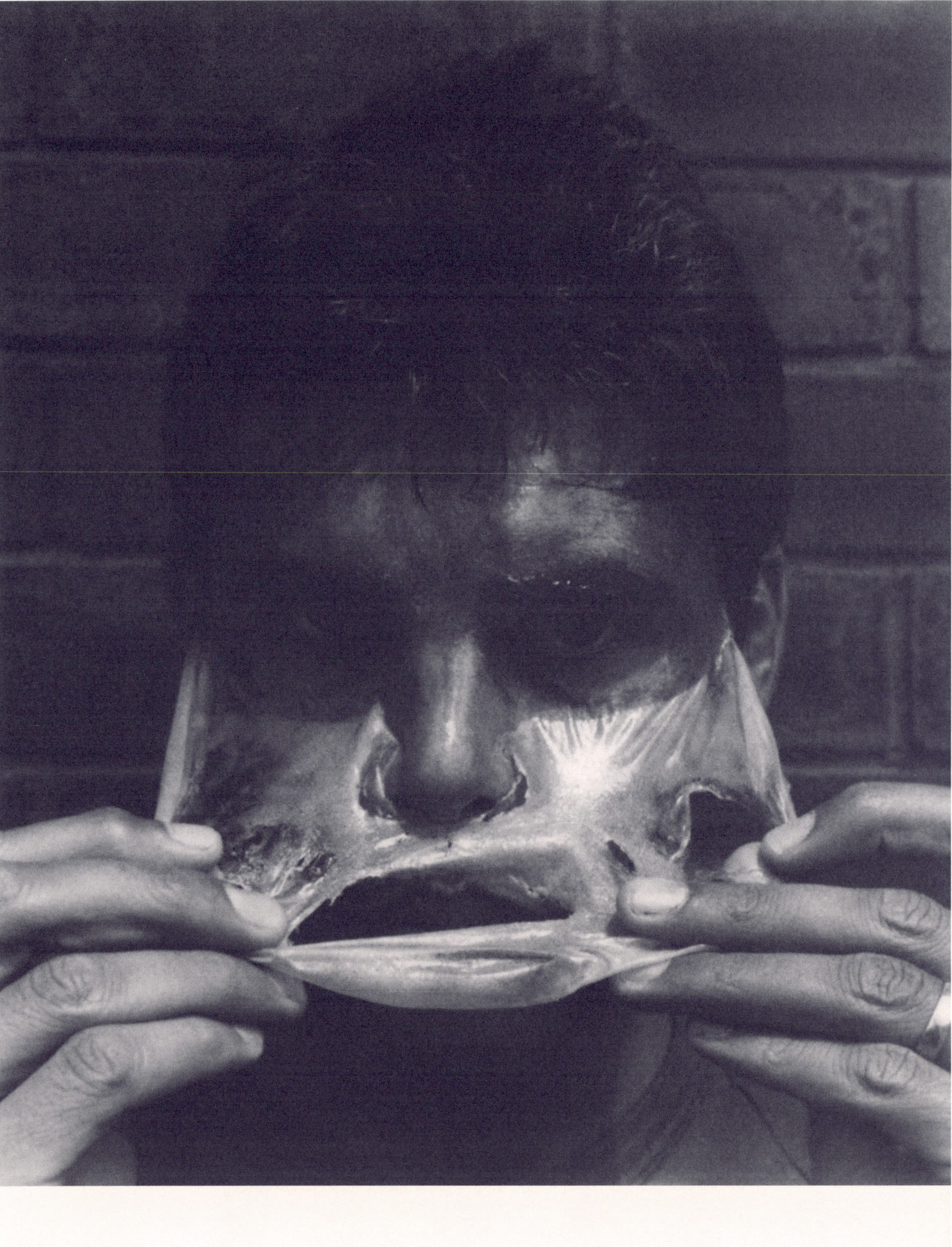

Essays and Artist's Statements

The majority of Gordon Bennett's published writing output takes the form of essays and shorter artist statements. These draw on a wide variety of sources, ranging from French West Indian psychiatrist and political philosopher Frantz Fanon (1925–1961) to the local *Courier Mail* newspaper, Bruce Elder's seminal history of colonial massacres *Blood on the Wattle* (1988) to John Berger's (1926–2017) *Ways of Seeing* (1971), as well as texts from fields including anthropology, psychoanalysis, and philosophy to support Bennett's thinking around and responses to identity, history, and colonisation.

Bennett also experimented occasionally with the essay format itself. His contribution to the 1992 exhibition catalogue for Camerawork's *Southern Crossings/Empty Land (Parts One and Two)*, 'Re-Writing History', is constructed entirely from short quotes spanning from 1824 to 1992. In a footnote, he explained his experimental text in the following way:

> I thought that rather than the usual didactic essay and the sometimes equally didactic, and sometimes obscure, artist's statement, I would write something that would basically allow others to speak for me. To this end I juxtaposed selected quotes from various sources ranging over almost the entire history of European presence in Australia. Included are quotes from former artist's statements I have produced. The usual teleological order of historicism is interrupted to open up the text for it is in the spaces between quotes that I believe the meaning to be most profound.[1]

For Bennett, history and theory were both personal and political. On one hand, he found his immersion in postcolonial and postmodern theories through his studies at the Queensland College of Art 'liberating'.[2] On the other, he was constantly called upon to relate his work to theoretical discourses during this early period, as well as wider understandings of Aboriginality and its position in Australian life. Such demands established a complex push and pull between Bennett's own interest in history and theory and the external pressure to take up a position in relation to these discourses, an added pressure for an artist quickly thrust onto a national and global stage.

The writings contained in this section reveal how Bennett's reading of theoretical texts fuelled his critical interrogations of institutionalised racism. He sourced postcolonial critiques from Fanon, Stuart Hall (1932–2014), and Homi K. Bhabha (b. 1949). He looked to Jean Baudrillard (1929–2007) for postmodern frameworks, and to Michel Foucault (1926–1984) and Roland Barthes (1915–1980) for poststructuralist ones. Books in his studio library include Fanon's *The Wretched of the Earth* (1961), Baudrillard's *The Evil Demon of Images* (1987) and *The Transparency of Evil* (1990), and Foucault's *This Is Not a Pipe* (1973) and collected essays edited by Paul Rabinow *The Foucault Reader* (1984), among many others. Bennett's long-form essays 'Aesthetics and Iconography: An Artist's Approach' and 'The Manifest Toe' demonstrate the breadth of his reading. Notably, theory is always intertwined with autobiographical observations, reinforcing the proximity of the intellectual and the personal in Bennett's writing and art.

The texts in this section were written across the 1990s, a period of significant social and political change in Australia. Important events that occured during this time include the 1992 Mabo decision, where Eddie Koiki Mabo (1936–1992) and the Meriam people of the Torres Strait successfully overturned the legal doctrine of *terra nullius* in the High Court of Australia. Also in 1992, Prime Minister Paul Keating's Redfern speech marked the first time an Australian political leader had publicly recognised the violent impact of white settlement. The *Native Title Act*, which established a legal process for Indigenous Australians to claim ownership of their lands, was brought in from 1993. But developments were not all positive. Despite her openly racist views, Pauline Hanson was elected to the Queensland Parliament as an Independent in 1996, and John Howard's *Native Title Amendment Act* of 1998, commonly known as the Ten Point Plan, repealed aspects of Native Title in response to the 1996 Wik decision whereby Native Title rights had been found to be able to coexist with some pastoral leases. All of these events formed a backdrop that influenced the tone and perspective of Bennett's words. While they may not be considered direct social commentary, his texts reflect on his art's relationship to wider Australian society and its history, along with his personal history.

In 1991, Bennett won the Moët & Chandon Australian Art Fellowship and spent eleven months in residence in Hautvillers, France, his first extended residency overseas. Confronted by the isolation of regional France and the language barrier, Bennett continued to make work about the Australian context. Even this far from home, he couldn't escape casual racism. In 'On Double Standards: An Other Perspective' (p. 85), Bennett recounts how, while on a train out of Berlin, he was subjected to derogatory comments directed towards Aboriginal and Torres Strait Islander peoples from a South American orchestra conductor.

The following year, in a deliberate gesture of refusal, Bennett announced the beginning of his ongoing *Non-Performance* work, which comprised the refusal to speak publicly within Australia, a 'performance' which he extended globally in 1994. Curator Kelly Gellatly later described this period of Bennett's life:

> [by] the mid-1990s, [Bennett] came to feel he was in an untenable position . . . the combination of his position (or as Bennett would argue, 'label') as an (urban) Aboriginal artist, and the subject matter of his work, seemed to ensure inclusion within certain curatorial and critical frameworks, and largely determine interpretation and reception . . . cultural and social structures surrounding perception, representation and identity that Bennett [aimed] to deconstruct in his work were ironically serving to pigeonhole him.[3]

In 1996, seemingly reflecting on this position, Bennett stated: 'I have resisted being a "spokesperson for my people"—since I do not have, nor do I seek, such a mandate—by declining to speak about my work.'[4] With *Non-Performance*, Bennett announced his retreat from explaining the complex subject positions he had long grappled with. After the publication in 1999 of an earlier-written essay 'Australian Icons: Notes on Perception', Bennett's published essay writing also ceased. From then on, apart from a few rare interviews, Bennett's artworks became his sole mode of communication with audiences.

Notes

1. Gordon Bennett, 'Re-Writing History', in *Southern Crossings/ Empty Land: In the Australian Image,* ed. Helen Sloan (London: Camerawork, 1992), 28–29.

2. Gordon Bennett, 'The Manifest Toe', in *The Art of Gordon Bennett* (Roseville East, NSW: Craftsman House, 1996), 27.

3. Kelly Gellatly, 'Citizen in the Making: The Art of Gordon Bennett', in *Gordon Bennett* (Melbourne: National Gallery of Victoria, 2007), 17.

4. Bennett, 'The Manifest Toe', 59.

Artist's Statement: *The Coming of the Light*

The Coming of the Light [1987, figure 1] deals with a questioning of faith; a crisis of belief. It relates specifically to the 1959 'Elias' series of paintings by the New Zealand artist Colin McCahon [1919-1987]. The words Will He Come / Let Be / Let Be / Will Elias Come To Save Him [featured in McCahon's work] were uttered by onlookers at Christ's crucifixion in response to his cry 'My God, my God, why hast thou forsaken me?'

This painting is thus a shared vision of McCahon's response and 1959 interpretation of this event. However, I have relocated the event to the fringe of a city—it being a concrete model for the perpetual growth of 'modernity' inherent in that ethnocentric notion of 'progress'. I have interpreted the event in terms of supplanting an Indigenous belief system with a Eurocentric model which is implied in the statement 'The Coming of the Light (to Illuminate the Savage Mind)'. The arm that holds the light also holds the noose and thus relates to a Judas betrayal.

Language is a key factor in this work. The ethnocentric boundaries implicit in such a categorising system are responsible for such widely accepted Eurocentric notions as the 'Savage', the 'Primitive', and for the perpetuation of a kind of street level 'Social Darwinism'. Words like 'Abo', 'boong', 'coon', and 'darkie', while composed of arbitrary basic units such as A, B, C and D, carry with them a weight of derogatory associations, built on outdated belief systems which, when directed at a group or individual over a long enough period, can produce a kind of claustrophobic box where self-esteem is stifled and suicide becomes a viable way out.

❖ This statement was originally published in *Balance 1990: Views, Visions, Influences*, ed. Janet Hogan (Brisbane: Queensland Art Gallery, 1990) and is reproduced courtesy of the Queensland Art Gallery | Gallery of Modern Art, Brisbane.

Artist's Statement: *The Persistence of Language*

This painting [*The Persistence of Language*, 1987, figure 2] began with three blank canvases and a number of cans of acrylic house paint which I had just managed to acquire for free. It was the first time that I had so much paint to splash around and I wanted to 'loosen' up my painting, which until then had been very constrained and tight. I began by placing two panels on the studio floor (at art college mid-late 1987). I only had enough room to walk carefully around the edges, so it was fairly cramped—the third panel was leaning up outside my space. I intended a diptych with the first panel being a tunnel and the other a prison cell with hanging figure—the third panel I had no particular plans for.

I poured paint directly from the can onto the canvas and using a large brush initially (4" I think and a 2"), I mixed the paint on the canvas, allowing the colours to swirl together—I enjoyed this immensely. The idea for the tunnel came from an English band called The The, a band that concerns itself with social issues. In fact, the lead singer/songwriter of the band had toured South America and had been so shocked by what he saw that he went blind for a short period (he did not want to 'see' any more!). The tunnel image was in a film clip I saw on television one night. A woman was strapped to a railway line, in a tunnel, her legs were apart, one on either rail facing the tunnel—the light of an approaching train could be seen down the tunnel which curved away to the left. This image was repeated many times and, I of course, related the train and tunnel image to the movie symbolism often used to suggest male sexual power and orgasm; i.e., a speeding locomotive erupting from a tunnel—very symbolic of patriarchal attitudes. When the train appeared finally, it was a toy train riding on a single track—this to me was very important as a symbol of *impotence*.

Such is the origin of the tunnel. The right panel was done virtually at the same time as the left—I moved from one to the other. I painted the faces in the cell window first, using a Chinese brush and ink, then painted around this to 'frame' the faces and create a 'window'. I then painted the hanging figure. After having done this first round of painting, I stood back to allow the paint to dry. I had a couple of dripping brushes in my hands so I went to the third panel and just simply attacked it for two reasons:

1. So as not to waste paint by washing all the excess down the drain.
2. So as to 'break the ice' with this panel—it helps sometimes to just get some paint on the surface.

This was a spur of the moment thing to do. When I looked at the marks I had made, I could discern two figures locked in struggle. I thought the one at the top looked like it had a wing, so I turned it into an angel. Thus, the central panel was created by 'accident' (I don't really believe in accidents though).

With the basics down, the rest was a process (a balancing process) of compositional, narrative and conceptual considerations over a period of time (possibly three days to one week, I don't really remember but I had other classes to go to and I was reading all sorts of things too). Somehow, I managed to get all three panels up together where I could see them properly—after deciding to expand my original idea of a diptych into a triptych. I used Chinese brush and ink to outline all the heads on sticks etc. I used a Janus head idea to link the first and second panels—it being a guardian of gates or passages (bit vague now on the finer points). I saw the left and centre panels as the unconscious—lower and higher consciousness respectively—with the third panel being a 'reality' (always the result of unconscious and conscious construction). The heads on sticks of course relate to words, which they are, but it is the conditioned associations that give them power; Aboriginal people are conditioned to believe (in a white context) that they are inferior—'stone age culture', 'primitive', 'savages' are all European categorisations. If one were to look closely at the treatment of black populations worldwide, one can see who the savages are. Actually, their treatment of their own is just as telling.

So the title 'Persistence of Language' relates to the persistence of the repetition in my head of the words I painted on the canvas and that relationship to the common usage persistently directed at Aboriginal people.

I think I've said enough about this work. There is always more as the elements combine to create new pathways of meaning—no closure is desirable or should be expected. Different people will extract different meanings from the work as they draw on their own past experience and conditioning (cultural) to read the painting. This is as it should be, but it is a danger that the viewer will attribute everything to the artist and his/her intent. A work of art should be a vehicle for self-knowledge, for both artist and viewers, and I think by owning one's perceptions/projections when reading or producing a work of art, then one is on the path of self-knowledge. To attribute all that one reads in a painting to the artist, I feel, is a kind of defence (though unconscious perhaps) and a barrier to self-knowledge. I've had some people attribute the weirdest things to me—when the reason they 'saw' what they did was because of their own personal experience. I must admit sometimes these experiences are interesting and indeed relevant because I am not always aware of why I use certain elements and so on. If I was, then I could not learn about myself, but I have been abused in the past by people who have read something in a work and then tried to make me responsible for it. That's strange, these people do not know themselves (and don't want to) but it's all part of the dynamics of life . . .

❖ This unpublished statement from June 1990 is from Bennett's personal archive. It was included in Bennett's correspondence with Judith Hugo, a volunteer guide from the Art Gallery of Western Australia (AGWA), Perth, who had written to him about *The Persistence of Language*, held in the AGWA collection (see p. 72).

Re-Writing History[1]

The best thing that can be done is to shoot all the blacks and manure the ground with their carcasses.

—**William Cox**, landowner, 1824[2]

It is now obvious that something has to be done with the Aborigines. There cannot be one law for them and another law for the rest of Australia.

—**B. L. Farnik**, 7 February 1992[3]

Unhappily hundreds of Aborigines have been killed and many of them are still so killed. Yet I have never heard of the execution of a Colonist for the murder of a native in Queensland.

—**Reverend Duncan McNab**, 1881[4]

I look on the blacks as a set of monkeys,[i] and the earlier they are exterminated from the face of the earth the better. I would never consent to hang a white man for a black one.

—**A letter to *The Australian***, 18 December 1838[5]

More rights for Aboriginals? Well, I think everybody, not everybody but many people in high places, have gone mad. I always maintain that if an Aboriginal came and held up his bare toe, they'd lick it. And you can write that if you like.

—**Sir Joh Bjelke-Petersen**, former Premier of Queensland, 1986[6]

I am an Indigenous Australian. My mother is an Indigenous Australian and her mother before that and so on for countless generations. My father was English. My work comes out of small town and suburban Australia. I was socialised into an essentially Anglo-Saxon Eurocentric society where attitudes to Indigenous people still seem entrenched at a Social-Darwinist level. From cocktail parties to backyard barbeques, to workplace parties and tea breaks predominately derogatory opinions about Indigenous people are exchanged with unquestioning ease and assurance.

—**Gordon Bennett**, artist's statement, 29 January 1992

A $50,000 settlement offer has been made to a public servant after claims of racial abuse by a Victorian State Minister. A conciliation hearing of the Equal Opportunities Board heard claims that an Aboriginal Affairs Department female advisor, Ms Trish Jones, a 41-year-old Aboriginal, had been subjected to racial taunts and abusive late-night phone calls from the Aboriginal Affairs Minister, Mr Brian Mier, while employed by the department. The hearing was also told that after Ms Jones left the department, Mr Mier shouted 'You black ...' and other racist remarks outside the home she rented in Prahran earlier this year. Friends and colleagues of Ms Jones said she moved house and sought psychiatric care after the incident.

—***The Sunday Mail***, 11 August 1991[7]

Relations between the first settlers and the Aboriginals were established, among other things, on the pretense that [Australia][ii] was unoccupied. This led to the legal fiction that for the purposes of British Law the colony was treated as being 'settled' rather than conquered. 'Settlement' meant that statute law of England to the date of acquisition and the common law, which was deemed to be certain and unchanging, were to be applied throughout the [country]. Had it been treated as 'conquered' English law would have provided for the continuation of the Indigenous peoples' laws with the reservation of the rights of the Crown to override those existing laws and to introduce new laws. 'Settlement' envisaged the introduction of English laws and customs as if [Australia] was *terra nullius*, that is, nobody's land.

—**Bruce Elder**, 1988[8]

[i] Bennett changed the quote from 'monkies', as it appears in Elder's text, to 'monkeys'.
[ii] Single square brackets used in these quotes indicate Bennett's intervention on original quotes. Double square brackets note interventions made by the editors of this publication.

I see much of my current work as History painting, not as a documentary History painting, but rather it is painting that investigates the way history is constructed after the event, always mediated by someone's point of view, a teleological one-point perspective that reflects a Eurocentric bias.

—**Gordon Bennett**, artist's statement, 29 January 1992

Major figures [in] our history will have to be reassessed—frontiersmen who lavished lead on neighbouring [Aboriginal] clans; selectors who notched the handles of their Colt revolvers as readily as they ring-barked rainforest trees; jolly swagmen who at night became far from funny shagmen when they staggered [to] blacks' camps. The high evaluation of explorers needs amendment. They were usually dependent on the expertise of their black guides; they followed Aboriginal paths, drank at their wells; slept in their gunyahs and were often passed on from clan to clan by people who constantly monitored their progress through a landscape the Europeans chose to call a wilderness.

—**Henry Reynolds**, 1981[9]

The land is already a narrative—an artefact of intellect—before people represent it. There is no wilderness. [[...An Aboriginal person moves]], not in a landscape, but in a humanised realm saturated with significations. Here 'something happened'; there 'something portends'.[iii]

—**Peter Sutton**, 1988[10]

Firstly, without condition or qualification Aboriginal culture is one of the world's most ancient and impressive cultures. Aboriginal cave art predates the famous cave paintings of bulls, horses and deer at Lascaux in the French Dordogne by nearly twenty thousand years. Evidence suggests that Aborigines developed religious beliefs and burial practices more than ten thousand years before similar ideas began to emerge along the Nile and in the Tigris-Euphrates delta.

—**Bruce Elder**, 1988[11]

They were nothing better than dogs, and [it was] no more harm to shoot them than it would be to shoot a dog when he barked at you.

—**Reverend William Yate**, 1835[12]

This Eurocentric bias was particularly evident in the bicentennial celebrations with the re-enactment of specific events (deemed important) by people in period costume and broadcast on television, reproduced in magazines and in advertising etc. The images being reproduced are a kind of selective memory reinforcing only those aspects of an even more selective history which I learnt in school like the majority of Australian children do. Thus during the bicentennial, people wondered why the Aborigines were protesting and not celebrating. Holes in one's education often lead to a lack of understanding.

—**Gordon Bennett**, artist's statement, 1989

In those days the full blood Aboriginal never got wages, just a shirt, trousers, boots and hat, and a stick of tobacco. That was their payment. And tucker. And any bad boys, say a boy with a bit of intelligence who stuck up for his rights, they would flog him. See, that was going on a long time. The Aborigines got that way they could not open their mouths.

—**Sandy McDonald**, 1920[13]

Perhaps the Aboriginal 'leaders' and their followers who occupied the old Parliament House in Canberra and propose now to approach the International Court might postpone their taxpayer-funded visit to deal with their peoples' greatest problem and really earn their right to posture on the national stage. Who is going to

[iii] Double brackets surrounding an ellipsis indicate that Bennett omitted text from an original quote without including an ellipsis in his text.

be the Aboriginal hero who says 'Liquor is killing our people and our culture'.

—**David Watts**, 7 February 1992[14]

I appropriate and recontextualise found images, or details of images, that have accumulated certain historical meaning over time. These fragments of visual 'History' are juxtaposed to construct visual texts that parallel the methodology of history but which aim to open up History to other perspectives and other meanings.

—**Gordon Bennett**, artist's statement, 29 January 1992

... the literal meanings, the visual devices, the aesthetic potential, and the social-contextual significance of Aboriginal art may each be distinguished in theory, they all interact in practice to constitute the total meanings of the works for Aborigines. Those who seek an understanding of the art need to approach it on all these fronts.

—**Peter Sutton**, 1988[15]

The Human Rights Commission has been asked to investigate a Queensland Parliament debate in which the former Aboriginal Affairs Minister, Mr Katter, was described as a 'gin jockey'. [[...]] On point of order Mr Katter claimed a disgraceful, racial comment was made to which [the Government Whip, Mr Prest] responded: 'I apologise to the dark girls'.

—***The Courier Mail,*** 22 August 1991[iv]

I got threatened. They were going to get the police up because I was forever fighting, swearing and everything, and I'd pelt stones at boys and hit them, and I'd be called out all the time. But they couldn't see that they were hurting me by just using 'boong' and 'coon'. I don't like them names. They all knew me name, they should've called me by me name. I'm not a bit of dirt.

—**Leonie Simpson**, 1979[16]

What of more recent, urban Aboriginal art? That which is promoted and labelled as such is still very social in its approach [[...]] A good deal of it is the art of identity assertion and of protest [...] and it is therefore no less social in intent than an Arnhem Land clan design.

—**Peter Sutton**, 1988[17]

A.O. Neville, a Western Australian Commissioner of Native Affairs, claimed in 1947 that he had a scientific solution to the 'Aboriginal problem'. Scientific research, he claimed, had revealed that skin pigmentation could be bred out of Aborigines in two or three generations. If he could only have the money and the legislative power to start a selective breeding programme he could, in a matter of sixty or seventy years, solve the 'Aboriginal problem' by breeding a race of white Aborigines.

—**Bruce Elder**, 1988[18]

A [Queensland][v] Government senior Aboriginal public servant has resigned, saying staff in the Premier's office made racist public remarks about her. [Reports] quoted a senior Queensland Government source critical of 'buppies (black urban professionals) from [the] West End who tried to live like whites and charged even more than consultants'.

—***The Courier Mail***, 22 August 1991[vi]

Western Desert [Aboriginal] art produces a finite design by subtraction—even quotation—from a potentially infinite grid of connected places/Dreamings/people, in which real spatial relationships are literally rectified and represented.

—**Peter Sutton**, 1988[19]

[iv] Where references are not provided in full by Bennett either directly after the quote or in the endnotes, they have been inserted by the editors as footnotes. Peter Morley, 'MP Reported to Racism Watchdog after 'Gin-Jockey' Jibe in House' *The Courier Mail*, 22 August 1991, p. 3.
[v] In his text, Bennett replaced 'Goss' with 'Queensland', presumably to cater to his international audience. He did not acknowledge this change.
[vi] Ed Southorn and Cheryl Thurlow, 'Senior Black Advisor Resigns: "Racist Remarks" by Goss Staff', *The Courier Mail*, 22 August 1991, p. 3.

The grid is a model of desert political geography. Subtractions from it reflect not only the time and space limitations of making selections for specific narrative purposes but also echo the technique of graded exposure.

—**Peter Sutton**, 1988[20]

My identity was shaped by the historical narratives of colonialism with all its romantic illusions and factual deletions. My Aboriginal identity was delineated by racist language such as Abo, Boong, Coon, Darkie and Nigger. I realised early in life that language directs the perceptions of its users giving them ways to categorise, analyse and reify experience. Thus one conceptual basis for my paintings springs from the correspondence of the first letter of each derogatory word to the first letters of the alphabet—A.B.C.D.

—**Gordon Bennett**, artist's statement, 29 January 1992

Chook Henry, he got a flogging from the coppers too. They gave him a hiding and when he was knocked on the ground they pissed on him. They were pissing on him ... I'm not the first bloke to get a flogging from the coppers here.

—Interview in **Mick Miller's** movie, ***Couldn't Be Fairer,*** ABC TV, 1987[21]

Mike Willesee is planning a new television program which he concedes is going to be a hard-sell. The theme is the History of Aborigines. 'It's the sort of thing that once it has had its run on television, it should be in the major libraries and teaching institutions of the world. It doesn't exist and it should. Travel around the country and take a look for yourself. There isn't a high standard of education, [[...]] there isn't a great rate of achievement among Aborigines.'

—***The Sunday Mail***, 1 December 1991[vii]

Stan Grant is the man with the hottest job in television heading Channel 7's new current affairs show *Real Life*. In a way Grant has a dual responsibility—to Seven and his people. He is the first Aborigine to anchor a prime-time program in Australia.

—***The Sunday Mail***, 22 December 1991[viii]

I am interested in the ethnocentric boundaries implicit in language as a categorising system. These boundaries are as invisible as the perspective lines that create illusionistic depth in Western painting. The illusion of a harmonious whole.

—**Gordon Bennett**, artist's statement, 7 December 1989

Evonne Cawley doesn't dwell on the times when she was the victim of racial prejudice, such as seventeen years ago when she was kicked out of a disco in Queensland because she was an Aborigine. She had won Wimbledon but no one recognised her.

—***The Sunday Mail***, 9 October 1991[ix]

But the way they are treated it would be a terrible thing to be an Aboriginal, wouldn't it?

—***The Sunday Mail***, 24 November 1991[x]

The grid is given an extradimensional parameter by labelling the corners A, B, C and D. These basic units of language enable a mind to construct a notion of the present, and its relationship to that present, but it also enables a mind to formulate notions of a past which also informs the experience of the present and projects speculations of a future and so on; a kind of psychic panorama.

—**Gordon Bennett**, artist's statement, December 1990

We replaced ecology with aggressive nineteenth-century exploitative capitalism. We built roads over sacred

[vii] 'Aborigines in Focus' *The Sunday Mail*, 12 January 1992, 3. The date Bennett included was incorrect.
[viii] Sandra McLean, 'Stan Had to Sit on the Story of His Life', *The Sunday Mail*, 22 December 1991, p. 11.
[ix] Bennett's quote here does not align with a particular article from *The Sunday Mail*, as the date provided is a Wednesday. An article about Cawley exists in *The Sunday Mail*, 6 October 1991, but this quote is not present in that particular article.
[x] Stephen Lamble, 'Racists Split Eumundi', *The Sunday Mail*, 24 November 1991, p. 18.

sites. We denied the land its spirituality. We killed off Aborigines with guns and poison and disease. We refused, through ignorance and arrogance, to see any tribal differentiation in those Aborigines who survived our insidious, long-term holocaust. Those Aborigines who survived were herded into reserves or 'allowed' to live in humpies on the fringes of towns. We took away their reason to exist and when, in their despair, they took to the bottle or simply threw up their hands in hopelessness and gave up on life, we had the arrogance to accuse them of drunkenness and laziness.

—**Bruce Elder**, 1988[22]

The cultures and values of Indigenous peoples have been positioned in contemporary Western culture through a process of Eurocentric observation which interprets and represents Indigenous peoples in terms of its own conventional and generally accepted beliefs and histories.

—**Gordon Bennett**, artist's statement, 29 January 1992

The Australian Aborigine is a doomed man ... it is too late to talk of preserving the Aboriginal race. It is and always was utopian to try and Christianise it. Rum and European clothes have ruined the people who half a century ago were temperate and naked. The Aboriginal race is moribund. All we can do now is to give an opiate to the dying man, and when he expires bury him respectably.

—***The Bulletin***, 1880[23]

In the first place, I do not think that it does injure their bodily health, more than allowing them to live in their wild state; and secondly, I do not think it inadvisable to Christianise them; for I would rather they died as Christians than drag out a miserable existence as heathens. I believe the race will disappear either way.

—**The Bishop of Adelaide**, Select Committee on Aborigines, 1860[24]

It is not a question of shoving a hard problem off to one side to be dealt with under 'tribal law' if that has any lingering credibility. It is not a question of black against white, but a breakdown in community living.

—**David Watts**, 7 February 1992[25]

I ask you dear Eurocentric reader when will 'you' look outside of your blinkers and see not 'Aborigines'—a European construct replete with centuries of your misguided notions of the 'primitive' and 'noble savage'—and see instead people? People with the same human needs as your own, that of self-respect and personal dignity.

—**Gordon Bennett**, artist's statement, 29 November 1991

Our wealth and lifestyle, the notion of 'Godzone' country, the much touted 'Aussie way of life', have all been achieved as a direct consequence of Aboriginal dispossession.

—**Bruce Elder**, 1988[26]

For many years white Australians have used Aboriginal words, symbols and designs to heighten their national distinctiveness and underline their separate identity. We can scarcely wonder if others judge us in this light and use our attitude to the Aboriginal historical experience as the acid test when they come to judge if white Australians have assimilated to the continent or are still colonists at heart. If we are unable to incorporate the black experience into our national heritage, we will stand exposed as a people still emotionally chained to our nineteenth-century British origins, ever the transplanted Europeans.

—**Henry Reynolds**, 1981[27]

Mr Keating [the Prime Minister] is wrong to support changes to the national flag. The flag in the corner is not just the flag of 'another' country; it is the flag of our mother country whose sons discovered Australia and made it. Would Mr Keating so despise his mother? The people who fought under this flag and the relatives of those who died for it will not calmly accept another.

—**H. M. Brownsdon**, 7 February 1992[xi]

About 5,000 Europeans from Australia north of the tropic of Capricorn died in the five wars between the outbreak of the Boer War and the end of the Vietnam engagement. But in a similar period—say the seventy years between the first [European] settlement in north Queensland in 1861 and the [[early]] 1930s—as many as 10,000 blacks were killed in skirmishes with the Europeans in north Australia. How do we deal with the Aboriginal dead? White Australians frequently say 'all that' should be forgotten. But it will not be. It cannot be. Black memories are too deeply, too recently scarred. And forgetfulness is a strange prescription coming from a community which has revered the fallen warrior and emblazoned the phrase 'Lest We Forget' on monuments throughout the land.

—**Henry Reynolds**, 1981[28]

The union flag and the subjects who arrived willingly or not, kick-started this country. This may have been to the distress of the Aborigines, but given the track record of other colonial empires of that period they came up with a lotto win. Our flag states very simply our origins as a nation and our geographic position. More importantly, it still serves as a shroud for many killed in wars supporting a somewhat chipped but otherwise rock-solid Westminster style democracy.

—**Frank Shubb** [[*sic*]],[xii] 7 February 1992[29]

I believe in the importance of history in informing one's sense of identity in the present and in that relationship to shaping one's perceptions for the future both on an individual level and on a national level since any nation is a collection of individuals.

—**Gordon Bennett**, artist's statement, 30 June 1991

Vicious bigotry and fears of racial violence are threatening plans for an Aboriginal and Torres Strait Islander arts centre and world-class tourist attraction in the Sunshine Coast hinterland town of Eumundi (Queensland). 'The sort of things that have been coming out are very, very embarrassing for any white man with any pride—I am very scared of going public in this town. If I am identified I will be labelled a "nigger lover" and that will make it very difficult for me in this town'.

—***The Sunday Mail***, 24 November 1991[xiii]

If identity is seen as an individual/collective self-image which has been defined to a certain extent by a succession of images that mirror a culture's sense of itself—as painting does—then I am naïve enough to believe that by interrupting a complacent sense of history, and therefore of identity, I can influence a change to a more open concept of culture. Perhaps a culture that is able to encompass and integrate multiple perspectives.

—**Gordon Bennett**, artist's statement, 29 January 1992

We came of age as a nation after World War II and were proud to fight and live under the Australian flag. It stands for all that is brave and good and free and true. Just because there is a union flag in one corner doesn't mean it is a British flag. It is the flag for me and I am glad I live under it. God preserve it from all bigots.

—**Joan Brown**, 7 February 1992[30]

[xi] H. M. Brownsdon, [[Letter to the Editor, *The Courier Mail*,]] 7 February 1992, p. 8.
[xii] Bennett misspells 'Shrubb' here.
[xiii] Stephen Lamble, 'Racists Split Eumundi', *The Sunday Mail*, 24 November 1991, p. 18.

I see the opening out of history as leading to a broader and deeper understanding of the world and of my identity as a human being. It is a holistic and integrative approach as opposed to a narrow Modernist linear approach.

—**Gordon Bennett**, artist's statement, 29 [[January]] 1992

❖ This text was originally published in *Southern Crossings/Empty Land: In the Australian Image*, ed. Helen Sloan (London: Camerawork, 1992), 21-29.

Notes

1. In my brief for this essay I was asked to write a personalised piece considering how Australia has been regarded as a European outpost and the effects this may have had on cultural production generally and on my work in particular. I was also asked to write a statement in regard to my work. After some consideration, I decided to approach both tasks from a different perspective in a somewhat experimental style. I thought that rather than the usual didactic essay and the sometimes equally didactic, and sometimes obscure, artist's statement, I would write something that would basically allow others to speak for me. To this end, I juxtaposed selected quotes from various sources ranging over almost the entire history of European presence in Australia. Included are quotes from former artist's statements I have produced. The usual teleological order of historicism is interrupted to open up the text, for it is in the spaces between quotes that I believe the meaning to be most profound. The method I have employed in some way reflects my art practice and serves to embed my work, and the work of other artists in my position, firmly in the Australian context.

[All changes in square brackets within the endnotes have been made by the editors of this publication.]

2. [William Cox cited in] Bruce Elder, *Blood on the Wattle: Massacres and Maltreatment of Australian Aborigines since 1788* (Sydney: Child and Associates Publishing, 1988), 42.

3. [B. L. Farnik] 'Letter [to] the Editor', *The Courier Mail* (a Brisbane-based Queensland newspaper) [7 February 1992, 8].

4. [Reverend Duncan McNab cited in] Elder, *Blood on the Wattle*, 122.

5. [A letter in *The Australian*, 18 December 1838, cited in] Elder, *Blood on the Wattle*, 72.

6. Sir Joh Bjelke-Petersen [cited] in Elder, *Blood on the Wattle*, 186.

7. ['Pollie in $50,000 Race Slur Row'] *The Sunday Mail* (a Brisbane-based Queensland newspaper) [11 August 1991, 3].

8. Elder, *Blood on the Wattle*, 187. [Bennett has replaced Elder's original use of 'Western Australia' for 'Australia', and 'state' for 'country'.]

9. Henry Reynolds, *The Other Side of the Frontier: Aboriginal Resistance to the European Invasion of Australia* (Ringwood, VIC: Penguin, 1982), [199-]200.

10. Peter Sutton, *Dreamings: The Art of Aboriginal Australia* (Melbourne: Penguin, 1988), 19 [Sutton quotes Stanner in the second half of this quote; see W. E. H. Stanner, *On Aboriginal Religion* (Sydney: Oceania Monographs, 1963), 227].

11. Elder, *Blood on the Wattle*, 199.

12. Reverend William Yate [cited] in Elder, *Blood on the Wattle*, 9. [Bennett has deleted an ellipsis that appeared before 'it was' in Elder's text and added parentheses around those two words.]

13. Sandy McDonald [cited] in Elder, *Blood on the Wattle*, 185.

14. [David Watts] 'Letter to the Editor', *The Courier Mail* [7 February 1992, 7].

15. Sutton, *Dreamings*, 14.
16. Leonie Simpson [cited] in Elder, *Blood on the Wattle*, 187.
17. Sutton, *Dreamings*, [29,] 32.
18. [Michael Howard cited in] Elder, *Blood on the Wattle*, 179. [Bennett misquotes Howard's 'sixty to seventy years' here.]
19. Sutton, *Dreamings*, 84.
20. Sutton, *Dreamings*, 86.
21. [Unnamed individual cited in] Elder, *Blood on the Wattle*, 184.
22. [Undated article from *The Sunday Mail* cited in] Elder, *Blood on the Wattle*, 8.
23. [Anonymous letter to the editor from *The Bulletin*, 1880, cited in] Elder, *Blood on the Wattle*, 175.
24. *South Australian Parliamentary Papers* [cited in Elder, *Blood on the Wattle*, 180–81].
25. [Watts] Letter to the Editor, 7.
26. Elder, *Blood on the Wattle*, 8.
27. Reynolds, *The Other Side of the Frontier*, [200].
28. Reynolds, *The Other Side of the Frontier*, 201.
29. [Frank Shrubb] Letter to the Editor, *The Courier Mail* [7 February 1992, 7].
30. [Joan Brown, Letter to the Editor, *The Courier Mail*, 7 February 1992, 7.]

Artist's Statement in *Southern Crossings/Empty Land: In the Australian Image*

Framing is a key component in my work. A photographer may point a camera in a certain direction and what is seen through the lens is framed. Elements such as composition, light and shadow etc. are considered in relation to the frame not only at the time of initial exposure but also at the time of processing. My painting has a strong relationship to photography. Not only do I choose an image as a photographer would choose a subject, but I then reframe the image, by re-photographing or by photocopying, as a photographer may crop an image during processing. I then project the image mechanically onto a canvas which involves framing the image in relation to the edges of the painting support. I then paint exactly what I see. As a painter I may thus be classified as a realist. However, since I paint in a darkened room at a range of around 12 inches from the canvas surface, I cannot see anything other than abstract marks, colours and shapes until I stand at a distance and turn on the light. Thus as a painter I may be classified as an abstractionist. Perhaps it may also be stated that as a photographer I am a painter since I replace the chemical action of the developmental process with the manual process of painting. But it would be equally true to say that as a painter I am a photographer since many paintings I do begin as photographs, and as everyone knows a 'real' painter never paints from a photograph. It is the frame I wish to subvert; that which classifies using a reductive one-point perspective in a world that has always existed in flux, where any absolutes exist only in the blind spots between the views offered by multiple perspectives.

—Gordon Bennett, 24 February 1992

❖ This text was originally published in *Southern Crossings/Empty Land: In the Australian Image*, ed. Helen Sloan (London: Camerawork, 1992), 43. Bennett also contributed a new work to the accompanying exhibition *Southern Crossings/Empty Land (Parts One and Two)*: *Untitled (Nuance)* (1992, figure 3).

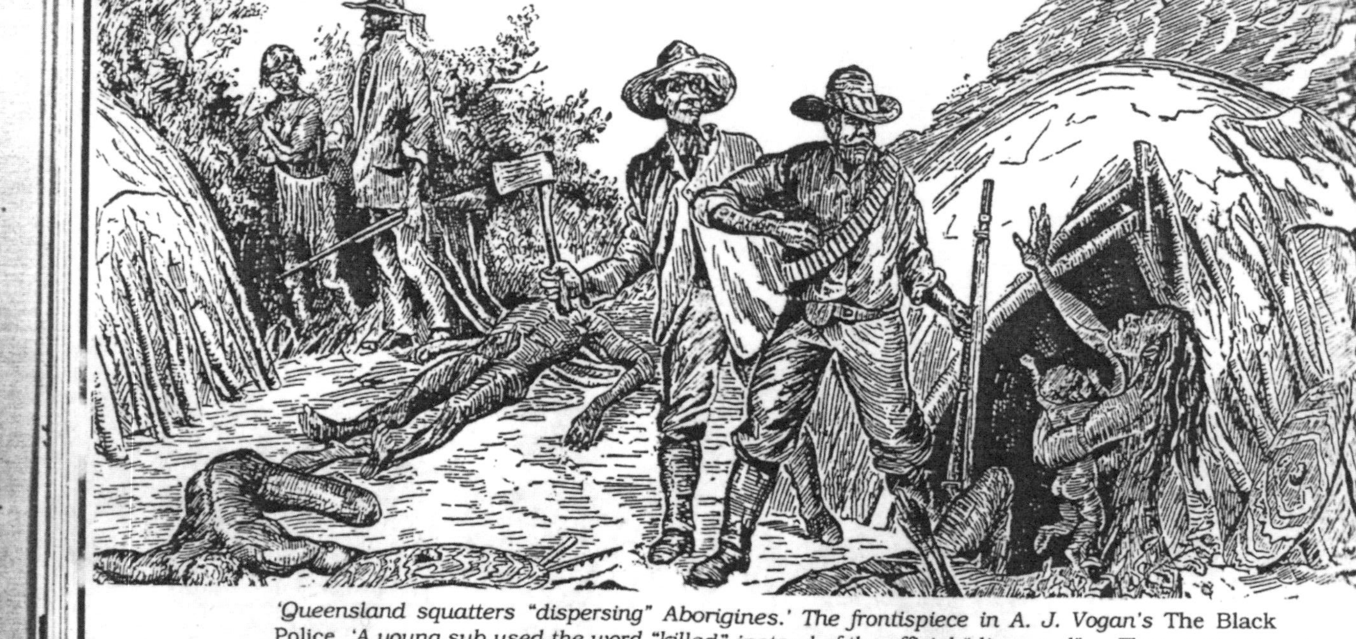

'Queensland squatters "dispersing" Aborigines.' The frontispiece in A. J. Vogan's The Black Police. *'A young sub used the word "killed" instead of the official "dispersed" ... The report was returned to him for correction ... The "sub" being rather a wag corrected his report so that the faulty portion now read as follows. "We successfully surrounded the said party of aborigines and dispersed fifteen, the remainder, some half dozen, succeeded in escaping ..."*

If the evidence of Charles Eden, who claimed that the native police loved to kill, is anything to go by, then the unreported massacre on Fraser Island would have involved anywhere up to one hundred innocent Aborigines. Eden wrote of the native police:

> It is a rash thing to rob a lioness of her whelps or a tiger of his prey, but I doubt if either would be attended with more danger than interfering between the troopers and their foes when once their blood is up. Then is the only time the officer loses his control over them.

Walker and Marshall were busily rewriting the history of their corps. Everyone on the frontier knew of the real brutality of the native police but the official records portrayed this band of licensed murderers as models of probity and conservatism.

There is a pointed story about these officially sanctioned lies in A. J. Vogan's book *The Black Police: A Story of Modern Australia.*

> A young 'sub', new in the force ... used the word 'killed' instead of the official 'dispersed' in speaking of the unfortunate natives left *hors de combat* on the field. The report was returned to him for correction with a severe reprimand for his careless wording ... The 'sub' being rather a wag corrected his report so that the faulty portion now read as follows. 'We successfully surrounded the said party of

Aesthetics and Iconography: An Artist's Approach

> *The best thing that can be done is to shoot all the blacks and manure the ground with their carcasses.*
>
> —William Cox, landowner, 1824[1]
>
> *It is now obvious that something has to be done with the Aborigines. There cannot be one law for them and another law for the rest of Australia.*
>
> —B. L. Farnik, 1992[2]

The above two statements, quoted from Australian newspapers 168 years apart, may seem like a strange way to introduce an essay on aesthetics and iconography but, given the strong social, political and spiritual aspects of a 'classical' Aboriginal aesthetic,[3] and as I proceed with my approach to the subject, I believe that their relevance will be revealed.

First and foremost, aesthetics is a rubric term with no simple universally accepted definition.[4] One dictionary gives the term's linguistic root as from the Greek: *aisthetikós* (perceptible by the senses), from *aisthesthai* (to perceive).[5] Therefore, it may be understood from the outset that aesthetics embodies the notion of perception; to thoroughly grasp or comprehend; to recognise a thing through the senses especially the sense of sight. Now this may seem such an obvious thing to point out, but to me it begs the question of how do we 'recognise' what we perceive?

Recognition seems to suggest having already seen a thing, it implies previous knowledge of the thing being observed, or at least an already given knowledge from which to base one's observation. Knowledge is something we gain during our lifetime. It allows us to understand the world of experience. However, knowledge is learnt experience and to be learnt it needs a vehicle for its transmission and indeed for its very structure. This vehicle is, of course, language.

Language is something we are all very familiar with, in fact at times it is a faculty that is so taken for granted that it seems an entirely natural phenomenon intimately and directly related to the world in which we live. In fact, it becomes all too easy to make the safe and simple assumption that language is a natural inventory of the world of experience.[6] However, it is not, it is never natural, as anyone who can remember the[ir] childhood experience of learning the alphabet, spelling and the structure of sentences can attest.

As a child I remember wondering when receiving demerits for the incorrect spelling of a word that I had spelt phonetically: why that spelling rather than this one? Why this sound rather than that? It was the threat of more demerits, and in the long run of physical punishment, that discouraged pressing the point too far. And so it is that as children we become socialised into a particular societal structure; a network of relationships to, and ideas about, the world that is constructed by language. Indeed, language may be seen as the cement that binds and maintains the social organisation of a particular society or cultural group.

Language defines the invisible boundaries or limits to the understanding of the world of experience. It does not constitute a natural inventory of the world, but rather language is a system of conventional and arbitrary sounds and symbols that represent the subjective human perception of it. Thus, a word does not represent an object in itself, it represents the image of the object reflected in the human mind.[7] In establishing this point of a conceptual gap or 'space' between language as a representational signifying sign system and the world of objects and sensation this system signifies or refers to, it is possible now to reintroduce the subject of aesthetics and, by extension, iconography.

Howard Morphy, in his article 'From Dull to Brilliant: The Aesthetics of Spiritual Power Among the Yolngu',[8] begins by establishing some broad definitions of what aesthetics is about. They are as follows:

> Aesthetics is concerned with how something appeals to the senses, in the case of paintings with the visual effect they have on the person looking at them. An aesthetic response concerns sensations or feelings that are evoked or caused in the viewer looking at a painting—a positive emotional response, one that can be associated with feelings of pleasure, but which is not necessarily interpreted to be pleasure. An aesthetic effect may be additional to some other kind of property of an object; for example, its communicating functions or practical properties. The aesthetic effect may be complementary to some other kind of property of an object or necessary to its fulfilling some other function. For example, an object may be aesthetically pleasing in order to draw a person's attention to it so that some other function may be fulfilled or message communicated. An aesthetic effect may arise out of the way some other purpose of the object is achieved; for example, through the perfect functional utility of a chair, the simplicity of an idea or the elegance of a solution to a problem.

These broad definitions are familiar enough to those schooled in the art practice and traditions of what may be termed a Western art perspective. Also within this perspective [are] other notions of aesthetics [that] exist defined by the equally broad classification of beauty. For instance, we may learn to experience a sunrise or sunset as beautiful, or the play of light across water. The experience and perception of nature is often expressed as beautiful, but all of these definitions have something in common and that is that they are all manifestations of learnt experience. We learn to 'recognise' beauty when we see it. Of course, there is room for disagreement within this culturally conditioned grid of classification. We may wish to argue our definition of what is beautiful over another's but ultimately it remains caught up in the system of representation that is language and thus reflects the experiential world of our particular society or language community.[9]

A person may wish to communicate a sense of nature's perceived beauty through art. As I am a painter I will restrict myself to the art of painting in particular. In order to represent a certain notion of the beauty of nature on canvas, a painter uses paint in a particular way: the paint is organised into areas of colour, areas of light to dark tones, areas of varying shapes and size in order to create a painting that is a reflection of the artist's perception of the landscape. In fact, the artist draws on a set of conventional visual signs and devices to represent an essentially subjective human perception of the world. The image produced does not represent the world itself but represents the image of the world reflected in and organised by the human mind. Thus, a visual sign or 'icon' may be understood as separated from the world of things by the same conceptual space as language.

The system of visual signs that constitute the iconography of a Western art tradition of representation can therefore be determined as functioning in a similar way to a language in its structuring of a visual world view. Implicit in the term 'world view', it should be noted, is the notion of ideology. Ideology, when understood as a body of ideas about the world that reflects the beliefs and interests of a cultural group or society, is reflected, maintained and reinforced by visual representation. Representation is in fact a powerful social instrument for the creation and maintenance of the world in which we live.[10] This applies equally to Australian Aboriginal societies as it does to any Western society; indeed, it applies to all societies.

My sense of aesthetics is that which was nurtured and developed within the structure of a Eurocentric world view. I was socialised into a Euro-Australian system of representation which included an art school education. However, my approach to aesthetics is to seek to extend my concepts of it and by extension to expand my concepts of representation.

There came a time in my life, in my sense of self and identity as an Australian, when I became aware of my Aboriginal heritage. This may seem of no consequence to the subject at hand, but when the weight of European representation of Aboriginal people as the quintessential primitive 'other' is realised, and perhaps understood as a certain level of abstraction involving a discourse of self and other with which we become familiar in our books and our classrooms but which we rarely feel on our pulses,[11] then it may be seen that such an awareness was problematic for my sense of identity. The conceptual gap between self and other collapsed and I was thrown into turmoil.

Michel Foucault talked of a concept of 'critical community' where something 'intolerable' is found in a system of identification. It is characterised as a refusal to participate in this system of recognition and thus 'problematises' identity and makes of 'subjectivity' an open and endless question, at once individual and collective.[12]

In Australia, the dominant system of identification begins with the 'discovery' of the continent by Captain James Cook. It continues with the 'exploration' and 'pioneer settlement' of a seemingly empty land. Today, the 'pioneer spirit' and a 'rugged outback image'[13] are still evoked as the identity all Australians share, even though the majority of Australians live in cities in one of the most urbanised countries in the world. I do not share this identity as I once did. My approach to the iconography that sustains it is deconstructive. This is not to deny the personal hardships of those European individuals who have been romanticised, indeed mythologised as heroes of Australian history but to expose other histories, other versions of settlement, of exploration and exploitation, and other systems of identification. I wish to reinstate a sense of Aboriginal people within the culturally dominant system of representation as human beings, rather than as a visual sign that signifies the 'primitive', the 'noble savage', or some other European construct associated with black skin.

Foucault maintained that a 'resistance' to a certain identity has an analytic role, related to a truth: it exposes what a particular strategy of 'power' is. It discloses something unseen and unacceptable in a form of identification, and exposes it to risk.[14] He thought that the historical construction of identity and the passion for identification should be a central issue.[15]

In 1835, the Reverend William Yate is quoted as referring to Aborigines as: 'nothing better than dogs, and [...] it was no more harm to shoot them than it would be to shoot a dog when he barked at you'.[16] Within the Eurocentric system of representation and identification of the Reverend Yates [*sic*], and others of the period, Aborigines were positioned as nothing more than dogs. Thus, it was justifiable to shoot us as we were not seen as human beings. It followed then that Aborigines had no culture, did not own the land but merely foraged as did the animals. These are all value judgements that were manifestations of the system of representation of the period, as embodied through language and iconographical sign systems.

When James Cook first set eyes on Australian shores, he already had a notion of the 'primitive'; it was just a matter of 'recognition' to position Aborigines as such in his mind. Cook also had his notions of culture and of landscape as property; it was only a matter of 'recognition' to see that Aborigines had neither. And so it was that Australia was declared *terra nullius* or empty land and became the 'property' of the English Crown.

Aboriginal cultures are among the world's most ancient and impressive cultures, incorporating a subtle, complex and rich way of life. Aboriginal cave art predates the famous cave paintings of bulls, horses and deer at Lascaux in the French Dordogne by nearly 20,000 years. Evidence suggests that Aborigines developed religious beliefs and burial practices more than 10,000 years before similar ideas began to emerge along the Nile and in the Tigris-Euphrates delta.[17] This, of course, points to a long tradition of cultural and self-representation through language and through art in the form of ceremonial dance and painting.

Aboriginal iconography is also a system of signs that represents not the world of things but again the image of the world reflected in the human mind. This system of signs cements the social organisation of Aboriginal societal structures as solidly as any European language, visual or otherwise. Therefore, given that the linguistic root of aesthetics is that which is perceptible by the senses, I would contend that the mental act of representation may be understood as an act of creative perception; and that is where the embodiment of a culture's aesthetic is located. In other words, the aesthetics of a culture are located not externally in an 'art' object, or in narrow definitions of aesthetic standards, but internally in the conceptual space between signifier and signified. As Foucault indicates, 'We should not have to refer the creative activity of someone to the kind of relation he has to himself, but should rather relate the kind of relation he has to himself to a creative activity.'[18] In this relation, a sense of 'beauty' could count as an important ethical category in how we as human beings might live. This would involve a type of critical 'passion' that would be non-racist, or anti-racist, in the particular sense that identity would not be the source of self-assertion and exclusion but the target of a questioning through which people might start to depart from the historical limits of their identifications.[19] This is not to say that identity will be lost but to say that it may be transformed, expanded to transcend narrow cultural and national boundaries of identification to encompass a sense of identity as more properly and correctly human.

This then is my approach to aesthetics at its most extreme, but within narrower definitions I locate my aesthetic approach within the more conventional notions of Western aesthetic, and iconographical traditions. My approach is however deconstructive in its orientation. I use strategies of quotation and appropriation to produce what I have called 'history' paintings. I draw on the iconographical paradigm of Australian, and by extension European, art in a way that constitutes a kind of ethnographic investigation of a Euro-Australian system of representation in general, but which has focussed on the representation of Aboriginal people in particular.

I foreground the use of perspective as fundamental to an Eurocentric world view. As the foundation of a system of representation, perspective produces an illusion of depth on an essentially flat two-dimensional surface by the use of invisible lines that converge to a vanishing point. The vanishing point may also be understood as the point from which these lines extend outward past the picture plane to include the viewer in the pictorial space; [they are] positioned as observer of a self-contained harmonious whole.

'Perspective has been called a systematic abstraction from the structure of [...] psychophysiological space'.[20] In its positioning of the viewer and in relation to the horizon, line perspective may be seen as symbolic of a certain kind of power structure relating to a particular European world view. The viewer is placed in a position of centrality to an ordered array of phenomenon which is rendered completely visible in a compressed symbolic configuration; particular inflections of knowledge are indexed allowing comparison, distinction, contrast and variation to be instantly legible.[21] It is an ideological fabrication, a powerful format of representation fixing relationships by which individuals represent themselves in their world of objects, their signifying universe, both a mirror of the world and a mirror of the self.[22] Aborigines caught in this system of representation remain 'frozen' as objects within the mapped territory of a European perceptual grid.

It has been said of Aboriginal art of the Western Desert that it produces a finite design by subtraction—even quotation—from a potentially infinite grid of connected places/'Dreamings'/people, in which real spatial relationships are literally rectified and represented.[23] My approach to quotation within the European tradition is to select images from Euro-Australian art history that have accumulated certain meaning over time, placing them in new relationships to other images. The images I select exist between the pages of art books and history books. Their unifying factor is the dot screen of their photomechanical reproduction and their iconographical relationships as points of reference on the Western cultural perceptual grid. By recontextualising images subtracted from this grid of Euro-Australian 'self' representation, I attempt to show the constructed nature of history and of identification as arbitrary, not fixed or natural but open to new possibilities of meaning and of identification.

In a sense then, this strategy can be understood as Aboriginal in firstly its subtraction, quotation from a potentially infinite grid of points or 'sites' of identification; and secondly in its exposure of the fact that images, as iconographical sites of reference, can have different meanings in different contexts. It has been established elsewhere that Western Desert artists employ a basic set of iconographical symbols such as curved and straight lines, concentric circles and dots which all have multiple meanings depending upon their context.[24]

My use of dots in some works, apart from their aesthetic potential, is in one aspect a reference to the unifying dot matrix of photographic reproduction and in another sense it is Aboriginal referential in the dot's relationship to the unifying space between cultural sites of identification in a landscape that is not experienced as separate from the individual, but as an artifact of intellect. In traditional Aboriginal thought, there is no nature without culture, just as there is no contrast either of a domesticated landscape with wilderness or of an interior scene with an expansive 'outside' beyond four walls.[25] This notion led me to conceive of the Eurocentric perceptual grid, with its sites of iconographical signification, as a kind of landscape of the mind—a psychotopographical map [figure 17] where sites, located in memory, represent the subjective human identification with the perceptual world.

By recontextualising images or fragments of images in particular relationships, I hope to create a certain turbulence in the complacent sense of identification with popular history. I desire to create a kind of chaos of identification where new possibilities for signification in representation can arise. This is an extended concept of art and of aesthetics in the sense of Foucault's notion of the kind of relation we have to ourselves as being a creative activity as put forward earlier. Furthermore, in this way, new relationships to others may be forged by the insights gained from the understanding and perception of 'nuance' that exists between any hard-and-fast definitions of identification.

Thus, I have returned to the approach to aesthetics that interests me most of all, which may be termed life as art. In this art, the aesthetic locus lies in the creative perception of nuance in the world that lies in between predetermined categories of thought and historically constructed identities. It is the art of a beautiful life or the ancient notion of a noble existence. An art of being or of making oneself free, in the sense of questioning the ways our own history defines us.[26]

My approach to iconography can best be expressed as an allegorical approach where images as sites of historical meaning are fragmented and recontextualised to form new relationships and possibilities for the generation of nuance. The conceptual gap between signifier and signified becomes most apparent in allegory and the real aesthetic enjoyment lies in the experience of interpretation, in the nuance of possible meanings.

In conclusion then, these approaches could be dismissed as utopian, and I would agree that they are utopian in focus but only in the literal sense of the word as 'no place', for if utopia were to come into existence it would be a stagnant and sterile environment, and that is never desirable. The path to 'no place' is one of attitude, a sensitivity to nuance and the possibilities of evolution toward a kind of ecological awareness in thought, and therefore in action. However, it is the path that is the key and not any final destination.

Perhaps this sense of attitude could be expressed in a less ideological way by referring to a work which, at the time of writing, is still in the early stages of development. It is to be constructed around a text that perhaps sums up my approach to aesthetics and iconography quite simply. The text is as follows:

> I am trying to paint the one painting that will change the world, before which even the most narrow minded and rabid racists will fall to their knees in profound awareness and spiritual openness thus recognising their own stupidity, at once transcending it to become [...] Of course this is in itself stupid and I am a fool, but I think to myself, what have I got to lose by trying?

The unexamined life is not worth living.
—Socrates

❖ This text was published in English in *Aratjara: Art of the First Australians* (Cologne: DuMont Buchverlag, 1993), 85-91, the exhibition catalogue that accompanied Bennett's involvement in the exhibition of the same name and year. Prior to this, the essay was originally published in German in the German art magazine *Art Vector*; "Ästhetik und Ikonographie: Die Annäherung eines Künstlers," *Art Vector,* vol. 10, no. 1 (June 1992): 11-16. *Aratjara* was first exhibited at the Kunstsammlung Nordrhein-Westfalen, Düsseldorf, from 24 April to 4 July 1993, before touring to the Hayward Gallery, London, and Louisiana Museum of Modern Art, Humlebaek, Denmark. Included in the exhibition was Bennett's 1990 painting *The Nine Ricochets (Fall Down Black Fella, Jump Up White Fella)*. The photocopy reproduced on page 26 includes the frontispiece from A.J. Vogan's *The Black Police* (1890), which Bennett appropriated parts of in *The Nine Ricochets*.

Notes

1. [William Cox cited in] Bruce Elder, *Blood on the Wattle: Massacres and Maltreatment of Australian Aborigines since 1788* (Sydney: Childs and Associates Publishing Pty Ltd, 1988), 42.
2. B. L. Farnik, Letter to the editor, *The Courier Mail*, 7 February 1992[, 7].
3. Peter Sutton, *Dreamings: The Art of Aboriginal Australia* (Ringwood, VIC: Penguin, 1988), 8.
4. Howard Morphy, 'From Dull to Brilliant: The Aesthetics of Spiritual Power among the Yolngu', *Man* 24, no. 1 (1989): [21].
5. *Collins English Dictionary*, ed. H. Collins (Glasgow: [Collins,] 1991).
6. Donald Preziosi, *Rethinking Art History: Meditations on a Coy Science* (New Haven: Yale University Press, 1989), 97.
7. Preziosi, *Rethinking Art History*, 98.
8. Morphy, 'From Dull to Brilliant', 21[-22].
9. Preziosi, *Rethinking Art History*, 97.
10. Preziosi, *Rethinking Art History*, 49.
11. Marianna Torgovnick, *Gone Primitive: Savage Intellects, Modern Lives* (Chicago: University of Chicago Press, 1990), 14.
12. John Rajchman, *Truth and Eros: Foucault, Lacan and the Question of Ethics* (New York: Routledge, 1991), 102.
13. Stanthorpe Art Gallery Society Incorporated in a pamphlet advertising the Stanthorpe Heritage Arts Festival held in February 1992. The major sponsor is the Heritage Building Society which is a Southern Queensland Finance and Investment company. Stanthorpe is a medium to large township situated close to the New South Wales/Queensland border. It is a major agricultural centre of the region.

14. Rajchman, *Truth and Eros*, 102.
15. Rajchman, *Truth and Eros*, 108.
16. [Reverend William Yate cited in] Elder, *Blood on the Wattle*, 9.
17. Elder, *Blood on the Wattle*, 199.
18. Rajchman, *Truth and Eros*, 98 [cited in *The Foucault Reader*, ed. Paul Rabinow, 351].
19. Rajchman, *Truth and Eros*, 108.
20. W. J. T. Mitchell, 'The Pictorial Turn', *Artforum* 30, no. 3 (March 1992): 91; in referring to the 1924 essay 'Perspective as Symbolic Form', by Erwin Panofsky.
21. Preziosi, *Rethinking Art History*, 66.
22. Preziosi, *Rethinking Art History*, [67-]68.
23. Sutton, *Dreamings*, 84.
24. Sutton, *Dreamings*, 91.
25. Sutton, *Dreamings*, 18.
26. Rajchman, *Truth and Eros*, 109.

Artist's Statement: A Non-Apology

Dear friends,

Some people have come to regard any expression of an Aboriginal history, point of view or experience as some kind of 'guilt trip', designed to make non-Aboriginal people feel bad about Australia's past. In fact, some conservative politicians dismiss such expressions or any support for an Aboriginal perspective as part of a 'guilt industry'. I feel saddened, and not a little disgusted, that Aboriginal people are expected by some people to keep quiet about our experience, quiet about our history.

This exhibition,[i] as with all of my work, is intended, among other things, to foster empathy and understanding, never guilt, which I believe to be irrational. I admit sometimes my methods can be heavy-handed, but that is the way I am working through my own experience of thirty-seven years of a non-Aboriginal historical education and my experience in a non-Aboriginal world where I hear almost daily the derogatory opinions directed at Aboriginal people.

I believe it is important for all Australians that an Aboriginal historical experience be recognised as an integral part of Australian history. For every statement regarding a 'pioneer spirit' there is an equal Aboriginal spirit of stoicism in the face of overwhelming adversity, for every explorer's journey of discovery there was an Aboriginal excursion into an alien world.

Some people want to dismiss the past with regard to an Aboriginal experience as if it bears no relation to the present or for that matter the future (but of course they see it differently when applauding 'our' pioneer spirit). They naively say let's forget the past and get on with the future. My only response to that is 'lest we forget'. Should we forget the experience of a people who fought for their country and way of life against overwhelming odds, a people who are still fighting, indeed fighting for something as basic as our human dignity? In a country that reveres the 'fallen warrior' in monuments right across the land, why should it be that Australians who bled on their own soil be excluded? In a country that celebrates its past with a national public holiday, why is it that for Aboriginal people the past should be forgotten?

Please ask yourself why is it that some people require Aboriginal silence?

❖ This unpublished text, dated 13 February 1993, is from Bennett's personal archive.

[i] According to Leanne Bennett, this text accompanied Bennett's Sutton Gallery exhibition 'A Black History', 13 February to 10 March, 1993.

Artist's Statement: 'Bounty Hunter' Series

This polyptych [from the 'Bounty Hunter' series, figure 5], produced in 1991, has a kind of 'narrative' content. The first panel, which is titled *Valley of Dry Bones (To the Sound of Cicadas)*, depicts a young black youth sitting on the ground surrounded by bones which have been exposed by erosion. In the background is a church which is placed so that the perspective lines used to construct the A B C blocks converge to the vanishing point at the front door. The 'sky' consists of a decorative pattern of red crosses. [Creating this,] I had in mind illuminated manuscripts and the works of the so-called 'Italian Primitives' which depicted biblical and religious themes, and which often include scenes of extreme violence.

The A B C blocks refer to the role of language in constructing one's world view and the role it plays in the construction of history and national/individual identity. These blocks may have multiple meanings. In one sense, they symbolise childhood with reference to the acquiring of language and thus the socialising process of cultural initiation ... the acquiring of knowledge, but a knowledge that is biased in its perspective. On the sides of the blocks, I pasted photocopies of images appropriated from an Australian history book. They are details of larger images which focus on specific things such as sight/perspective and mapping. The lower image on block C depicts two Europeans gazing across the landscape; the woman is pointing at something beyond the frame, surveying the landscape of the new territory. The image on block A depicts a ship at anchor with a view of the landscape divided into grid sections and fenced. The two images combined may be interpreted as referring to the mapping of the landscape with the imposition of the grid of Western cultural and philosophical beliefs 'floating' out across it, perhaps like a net.

On top of the blocks stands a photocopied image of a cemetery angel. I sometimes use the number three, as in three blocks, or as in 'ABC' and three-point perspective, to refer to the 'holy trinity'. I took the photograph of the angel myself—I have taken many photographs of such cemetery sculpture—and the reference to the 'sound of cicadas' is in one sense a way of asking the audience to be aware of other sensory perceptions when looking at the work as a way of 'defining the moment' or 'being there'. In another sense, it refers to my experience of taking the photograph, of being alone in the cemetery with only the loud noise of cicadas and the summer heat to keep my thoughts company while I pondered the headstones and statuary that marked the death, and life, of people I never, and would never know. The silence of angels. The cultural hopes, beliefs, deeds and aspirations of people set in concrete, while they, and their memories, crumble into dust and become part of this land.

I chose the image of an angel holding a finger to her lips in a gesture of silence perhaps in reference to a work I once did titled *You Know You Mustn't Say* [1988] in which the angel of Fra Angelico's *The Annunciation* (1438-45) holds up a finger to silence an unseen companion behind a wall of thorns while surrounded by a text, partly painted out, which detailed the memories of an Aboriginal man who witnessed the forced removal of his parents from their land. They were taken away in chains. The words 'You Know You Mustn't Say' issue from the angel's lips. Perhaps this angel is the angel of history who asks silence of the black youth.

The Valley of Dry Bones is the title of the last image in this polyptych and is also a biblical reference which perhaps serves as the beginning and the end of the work's overall 'narrative', a kind of parenthesis. In the last image of the work, a black youth, perhaps the same youth as in the first image but now older, utters the words 'Come from the four winds, O Breath, and breathe upon these slain, that they may live.' The speech bubble and text is an appropriation from a work by Colin McCahon titled T*he Valley of Dry Bones* (Nov 1947). I simply photocopied the speech bubble and then cut and pasted it into my own context.

I am no theologian so I can't say a lot about the biblical reference. I was drawn to McCahon's image intuitively and later I was given a text about the 'valley of dry bones' biblical context which I felt supported my intuitive appropriation. I can't relocate that text at the time of writing. I remember it was to do with the Jewish people returning to their country from exile,[1] and that the words in the speech bubble were spoken. In any case, the last image of this work depicts a now politicised youth, no longer willing to keep silent and perhaps calling forth that which has been suppressed for so long ... the bones now speak, the skeletons in the closet of Australian history and national identity have been given breath and they add their voice to the narratives of Australia.

The images that lay between the parenthesis of *The Valley of Dry Bones* tell only part of the story that was silenced. Each one refers to events that were documented as taking place, though they are not specific in the sense of actually documenting a particular event. All the events I used as my departure point can be found in the book *Blood on the Wattle: Massacres and Maltreatment of Australian Aborigines since 1788* by Bruce Elder [Sydney: Childs and Associates Publishing Pty Ltd, 1988].

❖ This unpublished text, dated 12 March 1996, is from Bennett's personal archive.

Notes

1. I remember it was something about the reclaiming of their country—so my intuitive response was about land rights, *terra nullius* and the fight for justice and human rights.

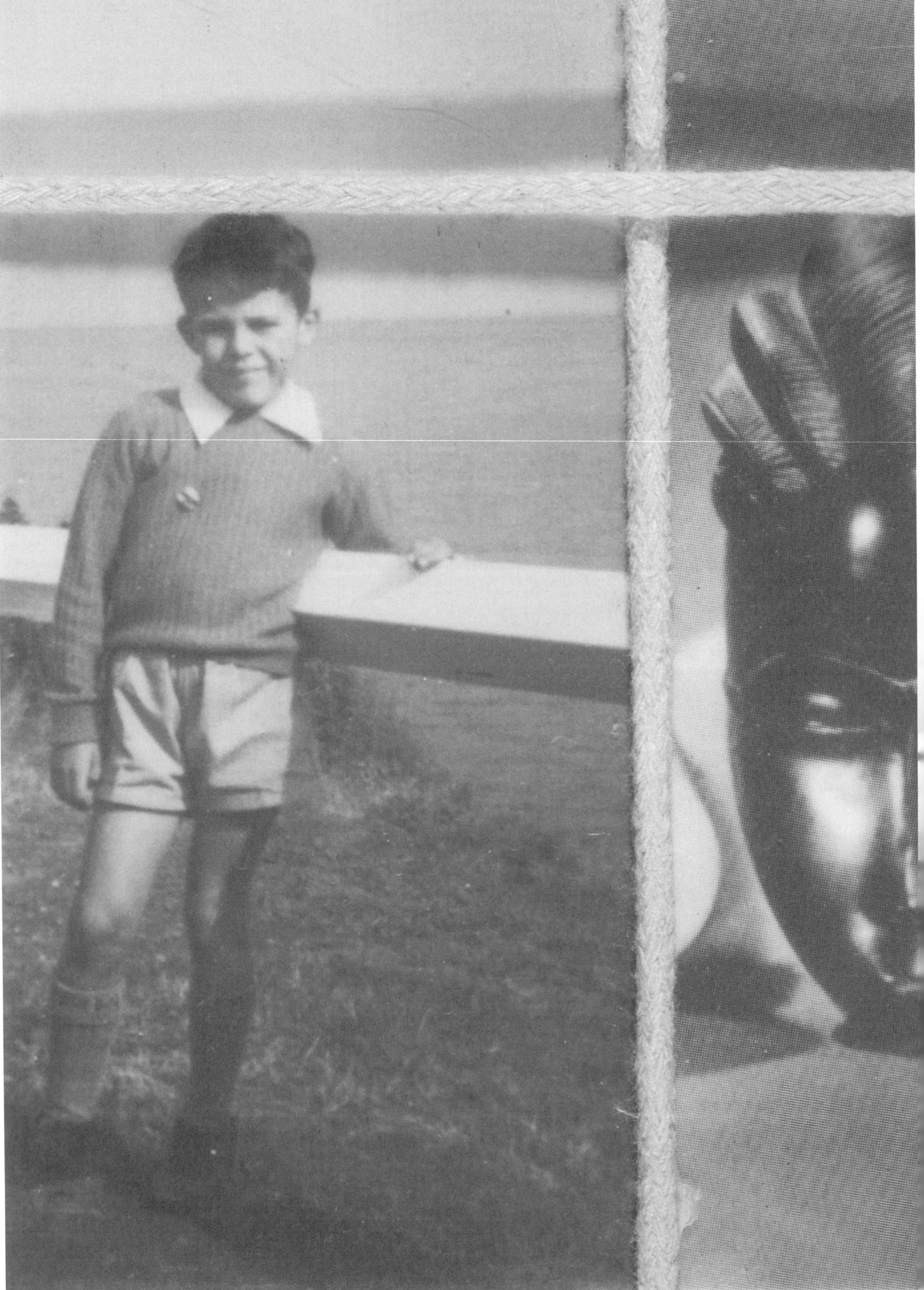

The Manifest Toe

> *More rights for Aboriginals? Well, I think everybody, not everybody but many people in high places, have gone mad. I always maintain that if an Aboriginal came and held his bare toe up, they'd lick it. And you can write that if you like.*
>
> —Sir Joh Bjelke-Petersen, Former Premier of Queensland, 1986 [1]

> *So instead of everyone wearing bowler hats and speaking pidgin English we face peoples clinging to their own heritages, traditions, languages, and styles of selfhood, insisting that they be written into history as themselves, and that their picture of us, with elements we might not relish, be written into that history too.*
>
> —Thomas McEvilley [1981][2]

Prologue:

There came a time in my life when I became aware of my Aboriginal heritage. This may seem of little consequence, but when the weight of European representations of Aboriginal people as the quintessential primitive 'Other' is realised and understood, within discourses of self and other, as a level of abstraction with which we become familiar in our books and our classrooms, but which we rarely feel on our pulses;[3] then you may understand why such an awareness was problematic for my sense of identity. The conceptual gap between my sense of self and other collapsed and I was thrown into turmoil.[i]

It is the collapse of the conceptual gap between the binary opposites of self/other, civilised/savage, sophisticated/primitive, or perhaps more appropriately its gradual disintegration and my process of integration, that forms the substratum of my life and work. Consequently, I am interested in psychoanalysis, particularly in the kind of radical analysis that interprets the so-called norms of society as repressive illusions and which regards analysis as a preparation for the analysand to get outside them once and for all. The aim of radical analysis is to foster the strength to deal with the effects of such a break—rejection, hostility, fear and anxiety—and to live creatively with the diversity of meanings outside set judgements.[4]

Michel Foucault was a thinker whose critical analysis of 'systems of thought', and how they maintain their hold over us, articulates what has been a central issue for me; there is nothing 'natural' or given about our membership in social groups. He asked the question 'how [do] we *recognise* ourselves as a society, as part of a social entity, as part of a nation [or] state?'[5] If I were to choose a single word to describe my art practice it would be the word *question*. If I were to choose a single word to describe my underlying drive it would be *freedom*. This should not be regarded as an heroic proclamation. Freedom is a practice. It is a way of thinking in other ways to those we have become accustomed to. Freedom is never assured by the laws and institutions that are intended to guarantee it. To be free is to be able to question the way power is exercised, disputing claims to domination. Such questioning involves our 'ethos', our ways of being, or becoming who we are. To be free we must be able to question the ways our own history defines us.[6]

Antonio Gramsci [1891-1937], an Italian thinker and anti-fascist activist imprisoned by Mussolini, wrote that the starting point of critical elaboration is the consciousness of what one really is, and is 'knowing thyself' as a product of the historical process to date which has deposited in you an infinity of traces without leaving an inventory.[7] An 'infinity of traces without an inventory', those few words best describe for me an identity, a concept of self, which involves a process of creative flux—a remembering of experience, knowledge and history from the many diverse culturally relative, dismembered, and repressed fragments, an ever flowing process that is alive with possibilities, and which confuses and flows through and around the conceit 'I am'.

[i] In 1994, Bennett presented a paper titled 'The Non-Sovereign Self: Diaspora Identities' at a London conference organised by the Institute of International Visual Arts (INIVA) and hosted at the then Tate Gallery, London. This paper would become the basis for Bennett's 1996 'The Manifest Toe', with both texts sharing a close similarity in content and style. For this reason, the former text has not been included in this publication. See 'The Non-Sovereign Self: Diaspora Identities', *Global Visions: Towards a New Internationalism in the Visual Arts*, ed. Jean Fisher (London: Kala Press in association with INIVA, 1994), 121-130.

A Personal History

The passing of the *Aboriginals Protection and [the] [R]estriction of the Sale of Opium Act* in 1897 was the Queensland Government's first major involvement in the lives of the colony's Indigenous peoples. This Act was the first comprehensive protection and segregation Act in Australia and resulted in the Queensland Government exercising wide-ranging control over the lives of individual Aboriginal and Torres Strait Islander people. The Act was not replaced until 1939, with the creation of two Acts: the *Aboriginal Preservation and Protection Act* and the *Torres Strait Islanders Act*.[8]

A subtle policy shift occurred at this time from one of protection and segregation, that had characterised the period since 1897, to one of 'protection and preservation' that was to characterise the period from 1939 to the next major piece of legislation in 1965. The 1939 Act, however, meant little change for Aboriginal people and, in fact, meant that the Director of Native Affairs was given increased powers in relation to Aboriginal property, Aboriginal Courts, police and jails, and this increased power was also extended to Superintendents on reserves.[9]

My mother was born in St George in 1934 and was subject to the provisions of these Acts, as was her mother and her people. Grace Bradley grew up on Cherbourg reserve in south-east Queensland, 240 kilometres northwest of Brisbane. As an orphan from the age of five, she never really knew her own mother and father, or her mother's country, language or customs, as all cultural manifestations of the various Aboriginal groups present at Cherbourg were officially forbidden. Grace is reluctant to talk of her life at the 'dormitory', a home for young girls and women, but has told me a little of the raids on garbage bins, and on the superintendent's orchard she and the other children would go on to supplement the dormitory diet, and of the practice of shaving [girls'] heads for punishment.

At the dormitory domestic science school, my mother was taught domestic skills and was sent to work for a middle-class family. After proving that she could live successfully with 'white' people for a period of three years, she was able to secure an official exemption permit to leave the mission. The decision to grant an exemption was based on the ability of the person to manage their own affairs and their disassociation with people of their own race.[10] She went to live in the nearby town of Monto, 125 kilometres west of Bundaberg in south-east Queensland, and managed to secure a job as a domestic at a local hotel. While working at the hotel she met my father, an Englishman working as a foreman electrical linesman for a large British construction company contracted by the Queensland Government.

I was born in Monto on 9 October 1955. At that time, my mother still had to carry with her the official exemption certificate that gave her a limited freedom from the 1939 Act, and from the reserve. I say limited freedom because this 'dog tag', as Aboriginal people referred to it, could be revoked at any time and had to be produced on the demand of any police officer. My mother lived in fear of me being taken from her. I don't doubt for a second that she wanted for me a life that she had never had; a life that would never know the environment of a regimented institution. I was raised in a cultural climate where my mother was not even a legitimate citizen until I was twelve years old. It should be understood that it was not until 1967, the year my brother Bradley was born, that Aborigines were given the right to be counted in the national census as Australian citizens; this was accomplished through a national referendum.

Our family moved often, never settling in one place for long. Part of the reason for this itinerant lifestyle was my father's job erecting high tension electrical towers taking electricity to Queensland country towns. In the four years after I was born, we covered a lot of territory, living mostly out of caravans. I don't remember any of it however, and I look at the photographs of myself as a child as if it were someone else [figure 4].

I've been told that I used to like wandering off by myself exploring the countryside, much to the distress of my parents. At some point, my father joined the Australian army and we moved to Melbourne in 1959-60.

In Melbourne, the itinerant lifestyle persisted, as indeed it would for another eighteen years. At first we lived in inner-city Richmond, then at the beach in suburban Frankston and Mornington where my earliest childhood memories begin. Eventually we moved to Sunbury, a country town approximately 34 kilometres west of Melbourne, where I began my first two years of primary school. I did well in reading and comprehension, and I have vague memories of finger painting, but I think that may have been kindergarten in Mornington. I remember that I was also good at running away from school and was punished often for doing so.

Both my parents enjoyed reading; indeed, my mother educated herself to a large extent as she received only a limited education at Cherbourg. I don't know much about my father's education except that, late in life, he once confided to me that he had aspirations of going to art school. He often said how he would make elaborate stages out of cardboard and put on puppet shows for his seven brothers and sisters. His father was a Sergeant Major in the British army and had served in colonial India. My father was in the Sea Cadets when he was fifteen or sixteen, and when World War II started, he lied about his age to join the navy. Art school aspirations were left far behind.

My father died in 1987, during my second year of art college. We disagreed on many things, including his sometimes racist beliefs about Aboriginal people and cultures. I talked with him about it before he died and came to understand this as a reflection of his European upbringing, and of the attitudes of the broader so-called 'mainstream' community during his life in Australia. I have nothing but respect for him in that he stayed by us, and looked after us to the best of his ability, sometimes working up to three jobs at a time, along with my mother who worked as a domestic, and in a clothing factory, in order to support us and make ends meet.

I grew up a shy introverted child, self-conscious and timid. I grew used to my own company and tight family circle and developed an active and creative imagination. The itinerant lifestyle we led was not conducive to forming lasting relationships with people. I don't remember any Aboriginal faces as I grew up and I never considered myself any different from my peers. At primary school from grades three to six, having moved again to a school in the small town of Diggers Rest about four kilometres closer to Melbourne than Sunbury, I proved to be a good runner, high jumper and long jumper. This brought the approval of both school and peers at inter-school sport carnivals.

I was an average student and did well in English, Art and Social Studies. In fact, my Social Studies books were often used as examples of student work by the school principal, who also taught grade three through to grade six, all of us in the same room. Grades one and two were in an adjoining room with their own teacher. I had given up running away from school by the time I reached grade three, but I remember going for long walks across the surrounding paddocks with only the sheep for company.

We stayed in Diggers Rest until I began secondary school in Sunbury. My father was out of the army by then and we ran a family business. It was a Mobil service station and we all pitched in to help. My mother cooked and served tables in the attached café/restaurant. In the afternoon and on weekends I served behind the counter and did other general duties like chopping wood for the kitchen stove. We had our first television set. I was eleven years old and my mother was pregnant with my brother when we moved once again. This time it was back to Queensland and another Mobil service station in Nambour in the Sunshine Coast hinterland, just north of Brisbane. It was early 1966 and I remember that we moved twice in four years within Nambour itself.

Sometime during my last years at Nambour High School, I painted a small painting which now seems quite prophetic in that I had used text, one-point perspective, abstract and figurative elements as well as hard-edge geometry, coupled with more painterly aspects, and a content that is concerned with alienation and race relations [figure 7]. I remember that I tried to disguise the text by leaving out some of the letters to avoid the usual criticism from my parents of 'why don't you paint normal paintings instead of weird ones[?]'. The text was meant to read 'Men hate Men' and the 'B' and 'O' referred to the threat of nuclear holocaust.

Art was my best subject at high school, followed by Geography and English. I remember that I was interested in the work of [Hieronymus] Bosch [1450-1516] and [Pieter] Bruegel [the Elder, 1525-1569] and I suppose that I was indeed influenced by such 'weird' painters. I was also amazed by the work of Jackson Pollock [1912-1956] and did my own versions of his style, none of which survive. I had a dislike of the illusion and 'rules' of perspective, and for representational art, preferring to work with my imagination and an idea as a point of departure. However, art classes at school were quite 'dry' in that there was a focus on remembering by rote particular dates and architectural styles.

I completed secondary school to junior level and soon after left Nambour for Brisbane at age fifteen for an apprenticeship as a fitter and turner, following my father's advice to 'get a trade'. In 1970 there was little work around for young school leavers in Nambour, so rather than wait to go on the dole I applied for a job in Brisbane. I was successful and moved into an inner-city boarding house where I lived for the first year of my apprenticeship. I was caught shoplifting a paint set from a major department store later that year. My family moved down to the outer northern suburbs of Brisbane soon after; I think they feared I was going off the 'rails'.

I finished my apprenticeship in 1975 and promptly left my trade behind to join the Australian Telecommunications Commission (Telecom) as a trainee line serviceman. At this time, I met and fell in love with Leanne and we were married in 1977. Eventually, I came to a point where I had reached the limit of promotional avenues available for what I thought were my capabilities. I saw only years of drudgery ahead of me doing the same thing day to day and finally decided to leave job security behind and go to art college. It was not an easy decision to leave Telecom. At first, I studied acupuncture for six months at night school before deciding that I didn't want to continue down that path. Acupuncture did increase my appreciation of Taoism however, and I guess I chose to try that particular profession as my way out of Telecom because I already had an interest in the martial arts, which I took up shortly after being attacked and beaten with a pick handle by a drunken 'white' man in 1978. I was later drawn to the philosophical aspects of the martial arts more than the physical side.

I finally settled on art as my way out. In 1985, after taking art classes at night for two years, I took my portfolio and applied for entry to art college as a 'mature age' student. Thankfully, I was accepted into the second Brisbane college I applied to, after being refused entry to one other. I began art college in 1986.

The Voyage Out

The process of assimilation into the dominant colonial culture of Euro-Australia was completed over at least three generations of my mother's family. The experiences of my great-grandmother and grandmother may never be known, but it is a fact of my life that this process of assimilation was completed by my mother and inherited by me. My upbringing was overwhelmingly Euro-Australian, with never a word spoken about my Aboriginal heritage. I first learnt about Aborigines in primary school, as part of the Social Studies curriculum. The history I was taught was the history of colonisation. A school history primer, written in 1917, reads in its opening passage:

> When people talk about 'the history of Australia' they mean the history of the white people who have lived in Australia. There is a good reason why we should not stretch the term to make it include the history of the dark-skinned wandering tribes who hurled boomerangs and ate snakes in their native land for long ages before the arrival of the first intruders from Europe . . . for they have nothing that can be called history. They have dim legends, and queer fairy tales, and deep-rooted customs which have come down from long, long ago; but they have no history, as we use the word. When the white man came among them, he found them living just as their fathers and grandfathers and remote ancestors had lived before them . . . Change and progress are the stuff of which history is made: these blacks knew no change and made no progress, as far as we can tell. Men of science may peer at them and try to guess where they came from, how they got to Australia, how their strange customs began, and what those customs mean; but the historian is not concerned with them. He is concerned with Australia only as the dwelling-place of white men and women, settlers from overseas. It is his business to tell us how these white folk found the land, how they settled in it, how they explored it, and how they gradually made it the Australia we know today.[11]

By the 1960s, when I began third grade in primary school, very little had changed. In the two-room school in Diggers Rest, I learnt that Aborigines had dark brown skin, thin limbs, thick lips, black hair and dark brown eyes. I did drawings of tools and weapons in my project book, just like all the other children, and like them I also wrote in my books that each Aboriginal family had their own hut, that men hunt kangaroos, possums, and emus; that women collect seeds, eggs, fruit and yams. The men also paint their bodies in red, yellow, white and black, or in feather down stuck with human blood when they dress up, and make music with a didgeridoo. That was to be the extent of my formal education on Aborigines and Aboriginal culture until art college.

I can't remember exactly when it dawned on me that I had an Aboriginal heritage. I generally say that it was around age eleven, but this was my age when my family returned to Queensland, where Aboriginal people were far more visible. I was certainly aware of it by the time I was sixteen years old after having been in the workforce for twelve months. It was upon entering the workforce that I really learnt how low the general opinion of Aboriginal people was. As a shy and inarticulate teenager, my response to these derogatory opinions was silence, self-loathing and denial of my heritage.

Over the fifteen years I spent in the workforce, and as I listened to the majority of my peers and workmates talk about the 'abo's', 'boongs' and the 'coons', as Aborigines were usually referred to, I felt more and more alienated. On the surface I would sometimes smile, maybe nod my head to indicate that I was participating in the general conversation, that I was part of the group, trying to fit in as best as I could. The thought never crossed my mind that they might be wrong, or that I should, or even could, challenge these opinions.

Quite apart from being shy and inarticulate, all the education and socialisation upon which my identity and self-worth as a person—indeed, my sense of 'Australianess' and that of my peers—had as its foundation the narratives of colonialism. I had never thought to question those narratives and I certainly had never been taught at school to question them . . . only to believe them. Neither had I thought to question the representation of Aborigines as the quintessential 'primitive Other' against which the 'civilised' collective 'Self' of my peers was measured.

Aborigines are imagined by 'white' Australians within a powerful and seemingly inescapable whirlpool of 'civilisation' and 'savagery' which engage European representations of Aborigines in a type of tautology. Being a negative transgressive image of civilisation, the grotesque formulation of the 'savage' lacks any positivity—whether paraded in the masks of the noble, comic, or ignoble. All are found in the same exotic places and with the same dark skin—expressions of the same semiotic formula by which the colonised have another's struggle for identity thrust upon them.[12] The dominant myth of Australia was the history of exploration and colonisation; the spirit of the explorer, the pioneer, and the settler was a spirit all Australians could share in. Such was the unproblematic sense of national identity I was taught to believe in. This Australian identity that so effectively colonised my mind and body was presumed to be a white experience, informed as it was by the colonial diaspora of an essentially Western culture.

I had been taught to believe in this identity and its foundations; everyone around me seemed to believe it too, and everything I saw on television or read in the newspapers also reflected it. Living in the northern suburbs of Brisbane with Leanne, our main concerns were chasing the 'Australian dream' of buying and eventually owning our own house and raising children, bringing them up within the social structure and culture with which we ourselves had grown up. But, my growing feelings of alienation became intolerable.

It's important to understand that the position people hold in this society and the jobs they perform play an important role in the conceptions they form of themselves. The centre of it all is their job and corresponding social position. Their identity, or sense of continuity in their experience at any moment, is in being someone somewhere performing a task, moving along a given life-cycle from child to adolescent, student, trainee, young parent, experienced worker, expert, parents whose children have left home, grandparents, senior citizens, and so on unto death.[13]

Happiness, satisfaction, contentment and such emotions are dependent on accepting the terms of the life pattern you have chosen. You must invest in the chosen path and believe totally in that investment before you can reap the benefits and see the value of your life experience. What do you do though, with the frustration suffered in conforming to that life pattern? What do you do if the values promised for your labour are not forthcoming; you do not feel happiness, satisfaction, or great comfort in the sacrifice? What happens if even the money, or greater golden symbols, cannot compensate for what you feel you have lost?[14]

After fifteen years in the workforce, my dignity and self-esteem were through the floor. Leanne and I were only two years away from owning our own house, but any satisfaction I felt was hollow. Leanne wanted to have children, but I didn't feel I could cope with the responsibility of parenthood. I didn't want to bring a child into the world to grow up in the same atmosphere of institutionalised racism I was experiencing. My experience was similar to that of Adrian Piper, a conceptual artist of African-American descent with a fair complexion, who writes:

> Blacks like me are unwilling observers of the forms racism takes when racists believe there are no blacks present. Sometimes it hurts so much we want to disappear, disembody, disinherit ourselves from our blackness. Our experiences in this society manifest themselves in neuroses, demoralisation, anger, and in art.[15]

The early 1980s were a time of great personal growth for me, a time of learning to believe in myself as a person and a time of reconstructing a self-image distorted by the 'mirror' of racist beliefs. I understood the need to stop denying and repressing my Aboriginal heritage. I found the courage and self-confidence to quit my safe secure job and go to art college.

The Voyage In

At art college, I somehow felt that I belonged. It was a haven, a world of ideas, theories and concepts ranging from the chemical structure of paint to the socio-psychological and political structure of human societies and cultures. It was the Humanities electives that interested me most of all: Communication Theory, which taught me how to think critically, and Art History (which I duly noted positioned the rock art of 'primitive' man as its foundation, 'progressing' through the Renaissance to modernism) were compulsory subjects for the first year. However, it wasn't until my Postmodernism elective in second year that I really understood the full implications of what art college could mean for me.

I found the information I was absorbing liberating. I use the word 'absorbing' on purpose in order to establish a point on my relationship to theory. My interest in theory has been integral to my art, but I soon found that I could not verbalise my intuitions and understanding of the theories I was being exposed to. I could write well enough to demonstrate my understanding, and I was a straight honours student, but to talk theory was just beyond me; I was still that inarticulate teenager who had retreated into silence many years before. I found the language in which I was most articulate to be the visual language of painting, and it was through painting that I found a voice. Postmodernism was only one of my second-year electives. I did two other electives in that year: Art Therapy and Personal, Interpersonal and Creative Development. The next year I chose as my electives Aboriginal Art and Culture, and Classicism.

The Aboriginal Art and Culture elective opened my mind to the complexity and sophistication of the many and varied Indigenous Australian cultures, part of which was my own heritage, but which part? I didn't feel comfortable with depicting X-ray fish or kangaroos. I wanted to explore 'Aboriginality', if only to heal myself, but I felt that for me to paint fish and kangaroos and the like would have been like painting empty signs of this thing called 'Aboriginality'.

Aboriginality, I soon discovered, was an ephemeral thing, something that could not be adequately pinned down to a set of particular characteristics although many people, both black and white, still try. I see one of its manifestations as a kind of strategy, born out of a necessity, to conceive of a collective Indigenous Australian identity that is in its essence non-white. This was supposed to give someone like me something seemingly solid to cling onto, a kind of life raft to keep from going under. I was told by many Aboriginal people that Aboriginality is in the heart. I interpret this as an underlying 'truth' that cannot be verbalised, save to say that it is an essence of shared experience, of pain and of loss and of the struggle to maintain human dignity in the face of a colonial onslaught that, as the [French West Indian[iii]] postcolonial thinker Frantz Fanon observed:

> ...is not satisfied merely with holding a people in its grip and emptying the native's brain of all form and content. By a kind of perverted logic, it turns to the past of the oppressed people, and distorts, disfigures, and destroys it.[16]

There are sound strategic reasons for investing in essentialist versions of Aboriginality because, in many ways, it's all we have, while white Australia has all the material and institutional support. However, I would contest the concept of Aboriginality being nothing more or less than a strategic logocentre for whatever purposes such a stratagem may be gainfully applied.[17] While I would concede that a strategic logocentre may be one of the manifestations that Aboriginality can take, I would also point to this kind of essentialist identity as being the object of what Fanon once called a:

[iii] In the original text, Bennett incorrectly identifies Fanon as Algerian.

> passionate research . . . directed by the secret hope of discovering beyond the misery of today, beyond self-contempt, resignation and abjuration, some very beautiful and splendid era whose existence rehabilitates us both in regard to ourselves and in regard to others.[18]

While I do not wish to underestimate the importance of such an essentialist identity for many people, I soon realised that everything I knew about Aborigines, everything I was finding out about my heritage in my art college elective Aboriginal Art and Culture was filtered through a European perspective, through the canons of anthropology and ethnography: those 'men of science' who peered at Aboriginal people and made judgements based on an assumed cultural superiority predicated on such binary definitions as 'civilised' and 'savage', 'self' and 'other'. Euro-Australian power, knowledge and Aborigines are mutually constitutive—they produce and maintain one another through discursive practices which have become known as 'Aboriginalism'.[19]

'Aboriginalism' has been characterised by an overarching relationship of power between coloniser and colonised. This renders Aborigines as inert objects who have been spoken for by others. Furthermore, Aboriginalism essentialises its object of study: Aborigines are manufactured in ontological or foundational terms as an essence which exists in binary opposition to non-Aborigines, and which is not subject to historical change.[20] The so-called 'mixed bloods' or 'detribalised remnants' have been considered unworthy of serious anthropological consideration since (they) lacked the prestige attached to the classic field-work enterprise which typically involved living intimately for one or two years with people who are isolated from the modern world.[21] The traditionalist studies of anthropology and ethnography have thus tended to reinforce popular romantic beliefs of an 'authentic' Aboriginality associated with the 'Dreaming' and images of 'primitive' desert people, thereby supporting the popular judgement that only remote 'full-bloods' are real Aborigines.[22]

Aborigines are thus still being cast and recast as the living embodiment of the 'childhood of humanity', that which is the evidence of the 'progress' of history and of Western culture. Today, popular primitivism enforces an expectation for contemporary Aboriginal subjects to display or demonstrate evidence of their authenticity, either by asserting an essentialist position (I am Aboriginal), or by being knowledgeable (I know everything about the kinship systems of Arnhemland [*sic*]), as if Aboriginal culture were some kind of endowment.[23] Furthermore, such expectations are based on a myth of an Aboriginal culture that is both static and homogeneous, which is none other than the reified binary 'Other' of the hidden 'norm' that is white and Western.

Aboriginality is no life raft for me. It remains too problematical to identify with and leave unquestioned. After all, it was this very same problem of identification that drove me to bail out of my previous life in the first place, and I wasn't about to provide a foil for anyone to affirm that colonial identity I myself had rejected. I decided that I was in a very interesting position: My mind and body had been effectively colonised by Western culture, and yet my Aboriginality, which had been historically, socially and personally repressed, was still part of me and I was obtaining the tools and the language to explore it on my own terms. In a conceptual sense, I was liberated from the binary prison of self and other; the wall had disintegrated but where was I? In a real sense I was still living in the suburbs, and in a world where there were very real demands to be either one thing or the other. There was still no space for me to simply 'be'.

I decided that I would attempt to create a space by adopting a strategy of intervention and disturbance in the field of representation through my art. I was acutely aware of racist stereotypes and the power/

knowledge relationship that governed the historical representation of Aborigines within contemporary Australian culture. Cultural identities are the points of identification, or suture, which are made within the discourses of history and culture—not an essence, but a positioning.[24] Identities come from somewhere, have histories, and like everything which is historical, they undergo constant transformation. Far from being eternally fixed in some essentialised past, they are subject to the continuous 'play' of history, culture and power. Far from being grounded in a mere 'recovery' of the past, which is waiting to be found, and which, when found, will secure our sense of ourselves into eternity, identities are the names we give to the different ways we are positioned by, and position ourselves within, the narratives of the past.[25]

At first my painting was characterised by an overt expressionism informed by theory. My first interest in a theoretical basis for my painting came from theories on postmodern deconstruction and strategies of appropriation as well as the 'grotesque'. I quoted in an essay for my Classicism elective in 1988 a passage from *The Critical Idiom: The Grotesque* by Philip Thomson:

> The characteristic impact of the grotesque, the shock which it causes, may be used to bewilder and disorient the spectator, jeopardise or shatter their conventions by opening up onto vertiginous new perspectives characterised by the destruction of logic and regression to the unconscious—madness, hysteria or nightmare. Thus the spectator may be jolted out of accustomed ways of perceiving the world and confronted by radically different and disturbing perspectives.[26]

I did a painting in early 1988 that depicted a decapitated Aboriginal figure standing over Vincent van Gogh's bed [*Outsider*], with red paint streaming skywards to join with the vortex of Vincent's starry night. It was exhibited at the inaugural Adelaide Biennial of Australian Art in 1990. After the exhibition opening, I was subjected to a racist verbal attack in a crowded Adelaide restaurant by a woman who stated that she 'could not handle' my painting. At first, I was devastated and returned to my hotel, but later I decided that this attack was at least evidence that a painting can have an effect. However, by this time I had already moved towards a 'cooler', more overtly conceptual approach, though which retained elements of the grotesque as a strategy of 'Turning Around'.[27]

In the Aboriginal Art and Culture elective at art college, I also learnt something of the hidden history of colonial Australia, of the outrageous violence perpetrated in the name of 'civilisation'. Through the reading lists, I discovered such historians as Henry Reynolds [b. 1938] who, far from being the kind of historian described previously in the 1917 school history primer, was interested in addressing the imbalance of Australian history by describing life on the other side of the frontier.[28] Reynolds also acknowledges the major contribution made by Aboriginal people in the exploration and development of Australia, information that was new to me.[29] For me, this kind of information served to strengthen my developing critical awareness of a 'politics' of representation. The ways in which black people and black experiences were positioned and constructed as subjects in the dominant regimes of representation were the effects of a critical exercise of cultural power and normalisation. Aboriginal people were constructed as different and other within the categories of knowledge of 'Western' culture by those regimes. They had the power to make us see and experience ourselves as 'Other'.[30]

In 1988 Australia was in the grip of bicentennial celebrations that saw various re-enactments of one sort or another, including the 'tall ships' event that saw a group of sailing vessels set out to retrace the journey of the 'first (European) fleet' to Australia. Aboriginal groups declared a year of mourning. I began to use illustrations out of old social studies and history textbooks by way of critical intervention in the seamless flow of images that I plainly saw was designed to reinforce the popular myths and 'common sense' perspective of an Australian colonial identity and 'pop' history. I had in mind to create fields of disturbance which would necessitate re-reading the image, and the mythology. For example, I foregrounded perspective because its discursive underpinning of the colonialist field of representation exposed the ideological framing of the observing subject and the observed 'object' within a Eurocentric power structure. By disrupting this field of representation, I hoped to implicate the observing subject in the production of meaning, not in order to affirm the subject but in order to stimulate thought, and the possibility of exceeding the historical parameters that frame it.

As the foundation of a system of representation, perspective produces an illusion of depth on an essentially flat two-dimensional surface by the use of invisible lines that converge to a vanishing point. The vanishing point may also be understood as the point from which these lines extend outward past the picture plane to include the viewer in the pictorial space, positioned as observer of a self-contained harmonious whole. Perspective has been called: 'a systematic abstraction from the structure of (...) psychophysiological space'.[31] In its positioning of the viewer and in relation to the horizon line, perspective may be seen as symbolic of a certain kind of power structure relating to a particular European world view. The viewer is placed in a position of centrality to an ordered array of phenomenon[iii] which is rendered completely visible in a compressed symbolic configuration; particular inflections of knowledge are indexed allowing comparison, distinction, contrast and variation to be instantly legible.[32] It is an ideological fabrication, a powerful format of representation fixing relationships by which individuals represent themselves in their world of objects, their signifying universe, both a mirror of the world and a mirror of the self.[33] Aborigines caught in this system of representation remain 'frozen' as objects within the mapped territory of a European perceptual grid.

The *Collins English Dictionary* defines perception as: 'to thoroughly grasp or comprehend; to recognise a thing through the senses especially the sense of sight'. To me, this begs the question of how do we *recognise* what we perceive? Recognition presupposes having already seen a thing, it implies previous knowledge of the thing being observed, or at least an already given knowledge from which to base your observation. Knowledge is something we are taught, and also gain by experience during our lifetime. Knowledge is learnt experience and to be learnt it needs a vehicle for its transmission and indeed for its very structure. This vehicle is language.

Language is something we are all very familiar with; in fact, at times, it is a faculty that is so taken for granted that it seems an entirely natural phenomenon intimately and directly related to the world in which we live. In fact, it becomes all too easy to make the safe and simple assumption that language is a natural inventory of the world of experience.[34] However, it is not, it is never natural, as anyone who can remember the childhood experience of learning the alphabet, spelling and the structure of sentences can attest. As children we become socialised into a particular societal structure, a network of relationships to, and ideas about, the world that is constructed by language. Indeed, language may be seen as the cement that binds and maintains the social organisation of a particular society or cultural group.

Language defines the invisible boundaries or limits to the understanding of the world of experience. It does not constitute a natural inventory of the world, but rather language is a system of conventional and arbitrary sounds and symbols that represents the culturally relative subjective human *perception* of it. Thus, a word does not represent an object in itself, it represents the image of the object reflected in the human mind.[35] I am interested in this conceptual gap or 'space' between language as a representational signifying sign system and the world of objects and sensation this system signifies or refers to.

[iii] Bennett uses 'phenomenon' here whereas Preziosi's text states 'phenomena'.

In 'representational' painting, a painter uses paint in a particular way. The paint is organised into areas of colour, areas of light and dark tones, areas of varying shapes and size in order to create a painting that is a reflection of the artist's perception of the landscape. In fact, the artist draws on a set of conventional visual signs and devices to represent an essentially subjective human perception of the world. The image produced does not represent the world itself but represents the image of the world as reflected and organised by the artist's mind. Thus, a visual sign or *icon* may be understood as separated from the world of things by the same conceptual space as language. The system of visual signs that constitutes the iconography of a Western art tradition of representation can therefore be determined as functioning in a similar way to a language in its structuring of a visual world view.

Implicit in the term 'world view', it should be noted, is the notion of *ideology*. Ideology, when understood as a body of ideas about the world that reflects the beliefs and interests of a cultural group or society, is reflected, maintained and reinforced by visual representation. Representation is in fact a powerful social instrument for the creation and maintenance of the world in which we live.[36] This applies equally to Australian Aboriginal societies as it does to any Western society; indeed, it applies to all societies.

Soon after graduating from art college in 1988, I painted a series of works which I called 'Australian Icon: Notes on Perception' [1988–90]. I began by selecting a detail, or reduced section, of a reproduced historical image, specifically a painting of Captain James Cook. I photocopied the selected part, enlarging it and then projecting it onto a piece of paper. I saw this as a kind of ritual practice that in a sense replicated or even parodied the selective process of a teleological historical perspective. I painted the image in the quick gestural brush strokes of what may be termed a Western art tradition. I then inserted dots in the spaces between the brush strokes, some of which were created by the photocopy enlargement process, in what may be referred to as an Aboriginal art tradition. I combined Cook with an image of an Aborigine's head in classical 'noble savage' pose with face uplifted (taken from a beer coaster), and enclosed in a box-like structure created by perspective lines that converged to a vanishing point in the centre of Cook's eye.

The resultant image I related to as a kind of 'mapping' of two of the major icons of my cultural socialisation. I called the work *Australian Icon (Notes on Perception No. 1)* [1989]. I continued the series with images and details of nineteenth-century photographic postcards that staged Aboriginal people in supposedly 'natural' environments [figures 13 and 14]. By re-contextualising these images, I gave them new meaning by placing them in another time and place and in new relationships to the present with its different sense of world view and the benefit of a critical distance to the time in which they were produced. I called these works *Australian Aborigines (Notes on Perception)* and assigned each its own number. These works relate to the 'evolution' of an Aboriginal stereotype; i.e., what a 'real' Aborigine looks like. Everyone could, and still can no doubt, 'picture' an Aborigine in their mind's eye and this picture has become the internalised icon against which contemporary Aborigines are measured.

The method of gestural brush strokes and dots in the works on paper combine at close range to obscure the image. The image is dissolved in brush strokes and dots until one steps back a short distance from the surface to find the image 'reveals' itself. This is important in that it is essentially one's mind that constructs the image out of the mass of data which is paint on a surface perceived by the organ of sight. What the mind constructs is based on the past learnt experience of cultural conditioning and culturally relative knowledge.

Australian Icon (Notes on Perception No. 6) is a detail from a larger work depicting a ship in a storm. Which particular ship is unimportant. It is its *shipness* that is important. Up close to the image, it is difficult to determine anything except paint on a surface. At a distance, the ship will appear as the mind recognises and constructs it. The observer sees a sailing ship because of the mind's perception of 'shipness'; i.e., the image resembles what a sailing ship is supposed to look like based on previous experience of sailing ships, or images of them. What the image of a ship means to the observer is relative to that person's cultural associations as to their purpose and historical context, etc. In relation to Australian history, and particularly so soon after the bicentennial as it was painted in 1989, a ship is very likely to be interpreted in relation to the 'first (European) fleet', or even Captain Cook's *Endeavour*. I chose an image of a ship specifically to evoke the romantic narratives of adventure, danger, exploration and discovery that form a major part of the mythology that informs an Australian 'mainstream' identity. Of course it could just as easily have been interpreted as a slave ship, but is not as likely to have been interpreted in that way given its Australian context—even though many of the convict ships that made the journey to Australia were in fact [former] slave-ships.

It has been said of Aboriginal art of the Western Desert that it produces a finite design by subtraction—even quotation—from a potentially infinite grid of connected places/'Dreamings'[iv]/people, in which real spatial relationships are literally rectified and represented.[37] My approach to 'quotation' within the 'mainstream' European tradition is to select images from Euro-Australian art history that have accumulated certain meanings over time, placing them in new relationships to other images. The images I select exist between the pages of art books and history books. Their unifying factor is the dot screen of their photomechanical reproduction and their iconographical relationships as points of reference, or 'sites', on a Western cultural perceptual grid. By recontextualising images subtracted from this grid of Euro-Australian 'self' representation I attempt to show the constructed nature of history and of identification as arbitrary, not fixed or natural, but open to new possibilities of meaning and of identification.

In a sense then, this strategy has its parallels in the art of Aboriginal people from the Western Desert in firstly its subtraction, quotation from a potentially infinite grid of points or 'sites' of identification; and secondly in its exposure of the fact that images, as iconographical sites of reference, can have different meanings in different contexts. It has been established elsewhere that Western Desert artists employ a basic set of iconographical symbols such as curved and straight lines, concentric circles and dots which all have multiple meanings depending on their contexts.[38]

My use of dots, apart from their aesthetic potential, is in one aspect a reference to the unifying dot matrix of photographic reproduction and in another sense it is Aboriginal referential in the dots' relationship to the unifying space between cultural sites of identification in a landscape that is not experienced as separate from the individual, but as an *artefact of intellect*. In traditional Aboriginal thought, there is no nature without culture, just as there is no contrast either of a domesticated landscape with wilderness, or of an interior scene with an expansive 'outside' beyond four walls.[39] This notion led me to conceive of the Eurocentric perceptual grid, with its sites of iconographical signification, as a landscape of the mind—a 'psychotopographical'[40] map where sites, located in memory, represent the subjective human identification with the perceptual world.

I use postmodern strategies of quotation and appropriation to produce what I have called, as an ironic strategy, 'history' paintings. I draw on the iconographical paradigm of Australian, and by extension European, art in a way that could constitute a kind of 'ethnographic' investigation of a Euro-Australian system of representation in general, but which has focused on the representation of Aboriginal people in particular. By recontextualising images, or fragments of images, in particular relationships I hope to

[iv] Bennett has incorporated quote marks around Dreamings here, whereas Sutton does not.

create a turbulence in the complacent sense of identification with pop history, and create a kind of chaos of identification where new possibilities for signification in representation can arise; in this way, new relationships to others may be forged by the insights gained from the understanding and perception of 'flux' and 'nuance' that exist between any hard-and-fast definitions of identification.

In 1990 I began referring to Jackson Pollock's work extensively by making paintings using a pastiche of his signature dripped paint style and then 'floating' images within the painted field where they could be brought into differing relationships. I was interested in the way in which people often imagined that figures were lurking in Pollock's 'abstract' fields. It seemed to me to be like 'cloud gazing' where a person may perceive recognisable shapes within the shifting formations of clouds. It felt to me to be an obvious extension of the 'Notes on Perception' series. I also regarded that the implied extension of Pollock's matrix out past the frame and field of representation was important in referring to my selections of images as 'sites' on a potentially infinite grid.

In 1991 Thomas McEvilley seemed to confirm my intuitive approach to Pollock's painted field by interpreting Pollock's drip painting as:

> . . . assert(ing) flux and indefiniteness of identity as qualities that can be found in the world. This tautological interface between form and content is not a mystical attempt to unify opposites. It simply means that a work demonstrates a type of reality by embodying it. Thus abstract art, far from being non-representational, is, in effect, a representation of concepts; it is based on a process like that of metaphor, and overlaps somewhat with both iconography and representation.[41][v]

I thought of Pollock's position as one of the last modernist 'heroes'. I was also interested in how art history, the narratives of North American colonialism, and the notion of 'primitivism' had positioned him in the establishment of an 'American style' of art by tracing his development to his birth in the American west and his interest in Navaho ground painting. This is a story that has been played out many times and is equally relevant to Australia. Quite apart from Pollock's probable genuine interest in Navaho ground painting, we have the myth of the sophisticated and civilised 'white' artist who discovers something of value in the art of 'primitive' indigenes and brings it back to enrich the lives and cultivated sensibilities of 'real' artists and 'ART'. Meanwhile, the poor natives fall from grace, their primitivist purity—circumscribed by the recurrent belief that the qualities of 'primitive' or chronologically early cultures are superior to those of contemporary civilisation[42]—are hopelessly contaminated by contact with 'civilisation', they descend to the level of producing 'quaint' folk art, craft or 'airport' art produced only for commercial gain with inauthentic materials and motives.

I can't say how often I've heard that banal argument, let alone defended myself against it, and other institutionalised racist platitudes and misapprehensions. Institutionalised racism has been described as a racism practised and controlled by an institution or society; it includes actions controlled by the norms, rules, or customs of an institution or society.[43] The West, it seems, is the self-declared leader of history, guiding the peoples of the world towards an Hegelian sunset. Voyages of plunder and conquest were recorded as 'voyages of discovery', undertaken, supposedly, as altruistic attempts to lead other peoples toward history's culminating spiritual realisation. My life experience, and that of my mother, has led me to utterly reject this idea of progress, and I can only agree with Thomas McEvilley when he suggests that: '. . . at the heart of Modernism was a myth of history designed to justify colonialism'.[44]

The modernist period was dominated by the seventeenth-century German idealist philosopher Georg

[v] In McEvilley's text, 'demonstrates' is italicised for emphasis.

Wilhelm Friedrich Hegel [1770-1831]. Hegel's belief was that history had an internal direction and goal, and that 'progress' was, in effect, a law of nature. Entranced by this faith, the Western nations felt that history was on their side, that it was taking them where they wanted to go—to the vaguely conceived spiritual culmination which Hegel had written about. History was more like Providence, really, benignly watching over and guiding.[45] The formation of the idea of progress in art in terms of the spiritual advancement of humanity was the fuel of the transcendental modernist stream that ran through the works of Kasimir Malevich [1879-1935], Wassily Kandinsky [1866-1944], Piet Mondrian [1872-1944], Yves Klein [1928-1962], Lucio Fontana [1899-1968], Mark Rothko [1903-1970], Barnett Newman [1905-1970] and many others.[46]

As it has been developed by historians, at least in the post-Enlightenment period, history has a linear sense of time and records the past of 'civilised' literate peoples and their 'progress' towards the present. In the nineteenth century and much of the twentieth century, this historiography was an important means of teaching people to know themselves as citizens of bourgeois society and the nation-state. In this conception of the discipline, 'illiterate', 'savage' Aborigines had no history, just as they had no future place in the Australian nation founded in 1901: they were a dying race doomed to disappear. Thus, history in Australia began not with Aborigines but with the arrival of the Europeans.[47]

When Captain James Cook first set eyes on Australian shores, he carried with him his cultural baggage that positioned him and his culture at a point along the teleological perspective lines of history. It was just a matter of *recognition* to position Aborigines as 'primitives', 'savages' and therefore as 'ahistorical'. However, such beliefs have been proven to be nothing more than the distorted mirror reflection of European societies. The history of the theories of 'primitive' societies is the history of an illusion, as much an illusion as the construction of three-dimensional space on a two-dimensional surface.

The theory of 'primitive' society is about something which does not and never has existed. Hardly any anthropologist today would accept that a 'classic' account of 'primitive' societies can be sustained. On the contrary, the orthodox view is that there never was such a thing as 'primitive society'. Certainly, no such thing can be reconstructed now. There is not even a sensible way in which one can specify what a 'primitive society' is. The term implies some historical point of reference. It presumably defines a type of society ancestral to more advanced forms, on the analogy of an evolutionary history of some natural species. But human societies cannot be traced back to a single point of origin, and there is no way of reconstituting prehistoric social forms, classifying them, and aligning them in a time series. There are no fossils of social organisation.[48]

In the '[W]elt' series of paintings [figures 6a and 6b], which I began in France in December 1991, I overpainted a Pollock drip style underpainting with black. This created a surface which looked remarkably like an illustration of the scarified back of an African slave I later saw reproduced in a book about the representation of blacks in the nineteenth century; the title of the triptych was *A Typical Negro* (1863).[49] I drew on the conventional European cultural associations of 'blackness' which positioned the colour itself as representing the polarised qualities of life in the binary equations white/black, light/dark, civilised/savage, self/other, etc.

In these works, I also made reference to Malevich's abstract, or non-objective, 'Black Square' and 'Cross' formations, and Lucio Fontana's cut canvases. The term 'abstract' usually means to generalise, or to universalise, attributes that may be seen as common to one and all. It is usually seen as being opposite to the representation of a specific thing as opposed to the representation of an 'essence' that is rather common to many things. Thus, representation and abstraction are usually seen as opposites. My concept and use of abstraction in these works is closer to the spirit of McEvilley in the representation of concepts so that 'a work demonstrates a type of reality by embodying it'.

Malevich's *Black Square* [1915] may be seen as a representation of the concept of the human spirit. Being Russian, his abstract works are sometimes related to as icons in a similar vein to the great religious icons of Byzantium. However, Malevich was most certainly trying to get beyond the medieval denominational religious confines of such icons to a kind of spiritual 'essence' that was common to all humanity. I certainly have no quarrel with that, and I admire Malevich very much, but it is clear that in reality black and Indigenous peoples, as people considered ahistorical—trampled, enslaved, exploited and discarded, their lands confiscated and wealth plundered over five hundred years of colonialism—were not to be joining Europeans on their great journey to that glorious sunset and spiritual culmination waiting for humanity just over the horizon line.

My intention was to imbue such commendable spiritual aspirations with a little physical realism. With the '[W]elt' pieces, I wanted to convey the wounding of the human spirit, its scarification [with] the overpainted modernist trace of a Pollock skein as [a] metaphor for the scar as trace, and memory, of the colonial lash. On some of the works in the series, I used text created by laying down beads of red paint, overpainting in black and then cutting into the raised bead to reveal its red interior. The texts so created were metaphors for the inscription of the black body as *Tabula Rasa*—as the darkness which is 'illuminated' by 'the coming of the light': the so-called civilising force of European colonialism that created, cast and inscribed the objectified black body and mind as its 'Other'. It is generally acknowledged that, at least since the Enlightenment, the category of the 'self', and the group, is fashioned through the construction of an Other, which is outside and opposite, and that the making of an identity rests upon negating, repressing, or excluding things antithetical to it.[50]

It may be argued that in taking this position I am portraying black people as victims. This was indeed my intention and I wanted to not only 'play the victim' but to take it further and use that energy to advantage by not resisting, or trying to display strength, but to show pain and how much it hurts, even to the extent of self-mutilation. In this I am drawing on Aboriginal funeral ceremonies in which ritualised public displays of grief and mourning can involve blood-letting and cutting one's own body. Lucio Fontana's cut canvases and the ceremonial scarification of initiation rights common to both Aboriginal, and some African peoples, were both factors in making these works. My interest in Taoism is also significant in the sense of utilising a strategy of least resistance, which uses an aggressor's energy by turning it to one's own advantage, rather than opposing a force directly, better to intercept obliquely, or roll with it turning the opposing energy around for your own advantage.

The 'grotesque' remains as a theoretical subtext in these and other works that show decapitated and otherwise mutilated Aboriginal bodies 'polluting' the otherwise serene quality of colonial images depicting 'peaceful settlement' of the Australian landscape. All these works have their genesis in historical 'fact' in that they respond to actual recorded events or appropriate already existing imagery. My strategy in depicting 'victims' was partly a subversive one and partly acceptance of actual events and my own experience. While it is true that Aboriginal people did fight long and hard for their land—indeed the fight is still being played out through the courts—I was always more interested in questioning the field of representation, and the cultural conceits it embodied, rather than creating Aboriginal 'heroes' of the resistance, and there are many resistance fighters to choose from to challenge the white myths of 'peaceful settlement'. I abhor violence, and I have little compulsion to glorify it in any case, so I thought of the depiction of violence as a way to disturb firstly the complacent acceptance of Australia's sanitised history, and secondly, through the shock of that disturbance, to 'jolt' the spectator 'out of accustomed ways of perceiving the world' and perhaps foster empathy and understanding of contemporary issues that affect all of us as human beings.

Epilogue

Like many artists during their lifetime, I feel my motives have been misunderstood. I'm not one for saying what art should or should not be, but I do believe art can function to expand one's consciousness, to act as a catalyst perhaps, to exceed the boundaries of language and how it defines and limits our understanding of the world in which we live. However, my work has been met with accusations of 'moralising' and of being 'heavy handed' which I find quite disturbing, particularly given that I am quite often only recirculating already existing images. The implication in such criticisms seems to be that these images should stay buried, that perhaps some people, with misplaced feelings of guilt, rather than recognising the obvious alternatives of empathy, compassion and understanding, feel that they cannot 'handle' my paintings, or is it their own feelings, or the truth of a nation born out of near genocide, they cannot handle?

Many people want to dismiss the past in regard to an Aboriginal experience, as if it bears no relationship to the present, or for that matter to the future—but of course they see it differently when applauding 'our pioneer spirit'. They naively say we should forget the past and get on with the future. My only response to that is 'lest we forget'. Why should we forget the experience of peoples who fought for their country and way of life against overwhelming odds, people who are still fighting, indeed fighting for something as basic as human dignity? In a country that reveres the 'fallen warrior' in monuments right across the land, why should it be that Australians who bled on their own soil be excluded? In a country that celebrates its past with a national public holiday, why is it that for Aboriginal Australians the past should be forgotten?

I believe it is important for all Australians that an Aboriginal historical experience be recognised as an integral part of Australian history. For every statement regarding a 'pioneer spirit' there is an equal Aboriginal spirit of stoicism in the face of overwhelming adversity, for every 'explorer's' journey of so-called discovery there was an Aboriginal excursion into an alien world. The historian Henry Reynolds has written:

> In the long run black Australians will be our equals or our enemies. Unless they can identify with new and radical interpretations of our history they will seek sustenance in the anti-colonial traditions of the third world. If they are unable to find a place of honour in the white man's story of the past their loyalties will increasingly dwell with the 'wretched of the earth'. But if the Aboriginal experience is to be woven into new interpretations of Australian history changes will be necessary. We will have to deal with the blacks as equals or they will see our sudden interest in their history as merely another phase of our intellectual usurpation of their culture and traditions. We must give due weight to the Aboriginal perceptions of ourselves and they will not be flattering.[51]

Many people, it seems, have come to regard any expression of an Aboriginal point of view or experience as some kind of 'guilt trip' designed to make non-Aboriginal people feel bad about Australia's past. In fact, some politicians dismiss such expressions as part of a 'guilt industry'. I feel saddened, and not a little disgusted, that these people expect Aboriginal people to keep quiet about our history, quiet about our experiences. And to those who dare break the 'white blanket' of silence are directed the emotional accusations of 'moralising', as if morality is a dirty word and has no place in art. The history of Western art and its relationship to the church and so-called 'high culture' should indicate, to even the most ignorant, that morality has always been a driving force in art; particularly in colonial art, and it is even more evident in the representation of Aboriginal peoples.

Certainly, 'white' Australia has proven itself to be a master of moralising; my own experience confirms that much. It seems that any expression of an 'Aboriginal' perspective, or critique of colonial narratives and myths—both romantic and 'scientific'—is derided by some people as 'the guilt industry'. Alternative views are also dismissed by labelling them in a derogatory manner as 'politically correct'[52]—even to the extent of the Queensland Government, in 1993, pulping Year 5 primary school readers that dare to deviate, or offer alternatives from the conventional line and myth of 'peaceful settlement'. The shrill cries of such derision always seem to drown out the real issues, and any form of rational discussion and examination of them. Aboriginal children go to school too. Brave indeed is an Aboriginal child who stands up in class and gives confidently their point of view from a 'place of honour in the white man's story of the past', when the very instruments of their education marginalise, not only their point of view, but their ancestors, and even their own experience. I guess pulping books that dare to tamper with 'white' myths is far more subtle, and at least more ecologically sound, than burning them?

While I'm sure that such irrational and emotive forms of 'defence' are great for 'white' Australian social cohesion and bonding, it does tend to make a mockery of Australia's moralising to other countries on human rights; not to mention the myths of 'a fair go', and 'free speech'. It is clear that history involves a rearrangement of the past which is subject to the social, ideological, and political structures in which historians live and work. It is also clear that history has been and still is, in some places, subject to the conscious manipulation on the part of political regimes that oppose the truth. Nationalism and prejudices of all kinds have an impact on the way history is written and taught to our children.[53]

I have never started out to do a 'political' painting. If my work is political then that is because of the politics of my position and the cultural climate in which I live and work. I didn't go to art college to graduate as an 'Aboriginal Artist'. I did want to explore 'Aboriginality' however, and it is a subject of my work as much as colonialism and the narratives and language that frame it, and the language that has consistently framed me. Acutely aware of the frame, I graduated as a straight honours student of 'fine art' to find myself positioned and contained by the language of primitivism as an 'urban Aboriginal artist'. While some people may argue this has been a quick road to success, and that my work is 'authorised' by my 'Aboriginality', I maintain that I don't have to be an Aborigine to do what I do, and that 'quick success' is not an inherent attribute of an Aboriginal heritage, as history has shown, nor is it that unusual for college graduates who have something relevant to say. Being aware of my positioning I have often used it as a 'strategic logocentre' in response to a society that seeks to transfix me with the patronising and conceited gaze of those who only seem able to think in terms of the conventional and 'common sense' binaries of the 'noble' or 'ignoble' savage.

Thus (sm)othered, I embarked on a critique of the foundations of this and other stereotypes of 'Aboriginalism'. I am very aware of the boundaries of critical containment within the parameters of 'urban Aboriginal art', and have so far worked within these boundaries to try and broaden, extend, and subvert them. The reality is, however, that I never really had much choice; and I have been faced with my work not entering some collections on the grounds of it being not 'Aboriginal' enough, to being asked to sell my work through stalls at cultural festivals, to being described, along with two other artists, in the catalogue of a recent Australian exhibition in New York as 'Urban Aboriginal Artists' whose 'most peculiarly Australian characteristic of their work is the lesson they carry from their bush-dwelling cousins'.[54] Such is the politics of my position.

I am fortunate that there are people who have the awareness, inclination and ability to understand my work and who are involved in similar critical projects within their own fields. I have consistently drawn succour from these people through reading and responding intuitively in my work; while at the same time being driven by the continued negative stereotyping of Aboriginal people through the mass media and in general conversational contexts in which I find myself. The recent Royal Commission into Aboriginal Deaths in Custody, Commissioner Elliott Johnston QC, expressed his shock at the constancy of non-Aboriginal Australia's treatment of Aboriginal people as if they were inferior. He identified the 'pinpricking domination, abuse of personal power, utter paternalism, open contempt and total indifference with which so many Aboriginal people were visited on a day-to-day basis'.[55]

I have tried to avoid any simplistic critical containment or stylistic categorisation as an 'Aboriginal' artist producing 'Aboriginal Art', by consistently changing stylistic directions and by producing work that does not sit easily in the confines of 'Aboriginal Art' collections or definitions. At the same time, I have resisted being positioned as a 'spokesperson for my people'—since I do not have, nor do I seek, such a mandate—by declining to speak about my work. I am close to abandoning my project altogether in an attempt to avoid banal containment as a professional Aborigine, which both misrepresents me and denies my upbringing and Scottish/English heritage.

In the face of institutionalised racism, I have considered leaving Australia so my daughter can grow up without having to face a life circumscribed by it. There may be nowhere on this planet where racism doesn't exist, but at least it won't be so close to the bone; it won't be felt on her pulse. I don't want to experience the first time she comes home in tears because of racist taunts, and I don't want to have to tell her that it's just their ignorance and insecurity that makes them say racist things because I don't think ignorance can be an excuse any longer.

One of the long-term goals for my work is to have my paintings returned to the pages of textbooks from which many of the images in them originated, where they may act as sites around which a more 'enlightened' kind of knowledge may circulate; perhaps a knowledge that is understood from the outset as culturally relative, which is not to say that this relativity should be feared as an attack on a culture's system of values, but to recognise the equal validity of the values and basic humanity of others. This would involve a kind of critical awareness in thinking that would be anti-racist, or non-racist in the sense that identity would not be the source of self-assertion and exclusion, but a target of a questioning through which people might start to depart from the historical limits of their identifications.[56]

One question might be: 'can we today invent a free discourse that would take up again the question of the art of living, through an activity of thought which would not base its way of speaking truly on any given positive knowledge about ourselves or our world, or any theory of government presumed to be final or sufficient, a critical philosophy that in questioning such knowledge and such theory, would open new possibilities in what we might become?'[57][vi]

Bain Attwood, a lecturer in History at Monash University, has written in his introduction to the book *Power, Knowledge and Aborigines*:

> The domain of Aboriginal Studies has . . . started to change in theoretical terms. Two inter-related developments can be pinpointed. First, Aborigines are viewed as socially constructed subjects with identities which are relational and dynamic rather than oppositional (in the binary sense) and given. This challenge to essentialism and the teleological assumptions embedded in Aboriginalist scholarship

[vi] Bennett has slightly misquoted Rajchman here: 'or any theory of government' is 'or on any theory of government' in the original; 'presumed to be final or sufficient' is 'presumed to be final and sufficient' in the original.

> involves historicising the processes that have constructed Aborigines, thus revealing how Aboriginal identity has been fluid and shifting, and above all contingent on colonial power relations. This approach necessarily involves a new object of knowledge—Ourselves, European Australians, rather than Them, the Aborigines—and this entails a consideration of the nature of our colonising culture and the nature of our knowledge and power relations to Aborigines.[58]

This means opening up 'the locked cupboard of our history' where the crimes we have 'perpetrated upon Australia's first inhabitants' have lain hidden, and coming 'to terms with [the] continuing Aboriginal presence'.[59]

In the end, I am aware that the quest for freedom from frameworks becomes simply another framework. The self remains relative, and cannot escape into the absolute. Modern scientific thought, finally, has evolved a composite view of the self as a shifting ripple in the Heraclitean river.[60] I once read a book by Hermann Hesse, in the early 1980s, called *Siddhartha* [1922] about a man's search for enlightenment. He eventually found it through his reflection in a river, not a still pond; and he didn't fall in love with his own reflection as did Narcissus. What he saw was a 'panorama' of the past, the present, and the future in a state of ever-flowing flux with his 'self' but one moment in that cyclic continuum. If we think of Australia as Narcissus-like, obsessed with its self-image, gazing into the mirror surface of a still pond, then perhaps my work may be understood as one of many disruptions sending ripples across its surface.

❖ This text was originally published in Ian McLean and Gordon Bennett, *The Art of Gordon Bennett* (Roseville East, NSW: Craftsman House, 1996), 9-62.

Notes

1. Bruce Elder, *Blood on the Wattle: Massacres and Maltreatment of Australian Aborigines since 1788* (Sydney: Childs and Associates Publishing Pty Ltd, 1988), 42.
2. Thomas McEvilley, 'Enormous Changes at the Last Minute', *Artforum* 30, no. 2 (October 1991): 87.
3. Marianna Torgovnick, *Gone Primitive: Savage Intellects, Modern Lives* (Chicago: University of Chicago Press, 1990), 14.
4. Martin Stanton, *Outside the Dream: Lacan and French Styles of Psychoanalysis* (London: Routledge and Kegan Paul Ltd, 1983), 25.
5. John Rajchman, *Truth and Eros: Foucault, Lacan and the Question of Ethics* (New York: Routledge, 1991), 101.
6. Rajchman, Truth and Eros, 111-12.
7. Antonio Gramsci, [*Selections from the*] *Prison Notebooks* [*of Antonio Gramsci*], trans. and ed. Quintin Hoare and Geoffrey [N]owell Smith [London: Lawrence & Wishart, 1971], 324.
8. *Community and Personal Histories*, Department of Family Services and Aboriginal and Islander Affairs, 3.
9. *Community and Personal Histories*, Department of Family Services and Aboriginal and Islander Affairs, 7.
10. *Community and Personal Histories*, Department of Family Services and Aboriginal and Islander Affairs, 6.
11. Walter Murdoch, *The Making of Australia: An Introductory History* (Melbourne: Whitcomb and Tombs, 1917), 9. This was one of a series of Australian history school books written by Murdoch. The others were entitled *The Struggle for Freedom* and *The Australian Citizen*. The first chapter of *The Making of Australia* is called 'The Unknown Continent', and facing the title page is a drawing of Cook landing at Botany Bay and raising the British flag.
12. Ian McLean, 'Colonials Kill Artfully', *Papers on Academic Art: Papers of the Art Association of Australia* 3,

ed. Paul Duro (Canberra: AAANZ, 1991), 60.
13. Stanton, *Outside the Dream*, 2.
14. Stanton, *Outside the Dream*, 1.
15. Lucy Lippard, *Mixed Blessings: New Art in a Multicultural America* (New York: Pantheon Books, 1990), 43; see also Adrian Piper, 'Flying', *Adrian Piper* (New York: Alternative Museum, 1987), 23-24.
16. Frantz Fanon, 'On National Culture', in *The Wretched of the Earth*, trans. Constance Farrington (London: Penguin, 19[90]), [169.]
17. Stephen Mue[c]ke, 'Lonely Representations', in *Power, Knowledge and Aborigines*, ed. Bain Attwood and John Arnold (Melbourne: La Trobe University Press, 1992), 42.
18. Fanon, 'On National Culture', [169].
19. Bain Attwood, 'Introduction', in *Power, Knowledge and Aborigines*, ed. Bain Attwood and John Arnold (Melbourne: La Trobe University Press, 1992), ii.
20. Attwood, 'Introduction', xi.
21. Gillian Cowlishaw, 'Studying Aborigines', in *Power, Knowledge and Aborigines*, ed. Bain Attwood and John Arnold (Melbourne: La Trobe University Press, 1992), 24.
22. Cowlishaw, 'Studying Aborigines', 25.
23. Mue[c]ke, 'Lonely Representations', 40.
24. Stuart Hall, 'Cultural Identity and Diaspora', in *Identity: Community, Culture, Difference*, ed. Jonathan Rutherford (London: Lawrence and Wishart, 1990), 226.
25. Hall, 'Cultural Identity and Diaspora', 225.
26. Philip Thomson, *The Critical Idiom: The Grotesque* (London, Methuen and Co Ltd, 1972), [58].
27. Lippard, 'Mixed Blessings', 199-242. 'Irony, humour, and subversion are the most common guises and disguises of those artists leaping out of the melting pot into the fire. They hold up mirrors to the dominant culture, slyly infiltrating mainstream art with alternative experiences—inverse, reverse, perverse. These strategies are forms of tricksterism, or "Ni Go Tlunh A Doh Ka"—Cherokee for "We Are Always Turning Around ... On Purpose"—the title of a 1986 travelling exhibition of American artists organised by Jimmie Durham and Jean Fisher. Those who "are always turning around on purpose" are deliberately moving targets, subverting and "making light of" the ponderous mechanisms set up to "keep them in their place".' [Ibid., 199-200]
28. Henry Reynolds, T*he Other Side of the Frontier: Aboriginal Resistance to the European Invasion of Australia* (Ringwood, VIC: Penguin, 1982).
29. Henry Reynolds, *With the White People: The Crucial Role of Aborigines in the Exploration and Development of Australia* (Ringwood, VIC: Penguin, 1990).
30. Hall, 'Cultural Identity and Diaspora', 225.
31. W. J. T. Mitchell, 'The Pictorial Turn', *Artforum* 30, no. 3 (1992): 91; [Mitchell was] referring to the 1924 essay 'Perspective as Symbolic Form' by Erwin Panofsky.
32. Donald Preziosi, *Rethinking Art History: Meditations on a Coy Science* (New Haven and London: Yale University Press, 1989), 66.
33. Preziosi, *Rethinking Art History*, [67-]68.
34. Preziosi, *Rethinking Art History*, 97.
35. Preziosi, *Rethinking Art History*, 98.
36. Preziosi, *Rethinking Art History*, 49.

37. Peter Sutton, *Dreamings: The Art of Aboriginal Australia* (Ringwood, VIC: Penguin, 1988), 84.
38. Sutton, *Dreamings*, 91.
39. Sutton, *Dreamings*, 18.
40. The term 'psychotopographical' I found in a text that I have since been unable to relocate. It was referred to as a now 'discredited' concept which to me seemed to be a perfect irony. It felt right to use this 'discredited' term as a title for paintings that were exploring a Eurocentric perspective.
41. Thomas McEvilley, 'On the Manner of Addressing Clouds', in *Art and Discontent: Theory at the Millennium* (New York: McPherson and Company, 1991), 81.
42. *The Macquarie Dictionary* (New South Wales: The Macquarie Library, Macquarie University, 1991), 1402.
43. *Psychology Today: An Introduction* (Del Mar, CA: CRM Books, 1972), 729.
44. Thomas McEvilley, 'Father the Void', in *Art and Discontent: Theory at the Millennium* (New York: McPherson and Company, 1991), 171.
45. McEvilley, 'Father the Void', 170.
46. McEvilley, 'Art History or Sacred History?', in *Art and Discontent: Theory at the Millennium* (New York: McPherson and Company, 1991), 149.
47. Attwood, 'Introduction', ix.
48. Adam Kuper, *The Invention of Primitive Society: Transformations of an Illusion* (London: Routledge, 1988), 7.
49. Albert Boime, 'The Revulsion to Cruelty', in *The Art of Exclusion: Representing Blacks in the Nineteenth Century* (London: Thames and Hudson, 1990), [73].
50. Attwood, 'Introduction', iii.
51. Reynolds, *The Other Side of the Frontier,* 199.
52. Political correctness and anti-political correctness are two sides of the same coin. Both tend towards censorship of language that may give offence to, on the one hand so-called 'minorities', and on the other to the so-called 'mainstream' (read: 'white' backlash). Either way, dissent is punishable by censorship. With the anti-political correctness lobby in defence of the old order of things, claiming constriction of 'free speech' as their moral platform, and clouding real issues of inclusion and empowerment by turning any debate into a debate on political correctness per se. Is the term 'peaceful settlement' as opposed to 'invasion' any less a 'sensitive phrase' than 'differently abled' is to 'cripple' or 'ethnic cleansing' is to 'genocide'? The trouble with the fiction of free speech is that so-called 'minorities' don't have much access to the mass media, and do not generally have the 'right of reply' to offensive or racist cultural commentary that the idea of free speech might imply. When issues are reported in the media it is usually by a member of the 'mainstream', to a presumed 'mainstream' audience, and framed within the perspectives and cultural prejudices of the 'mainstream'. The fact is that there are no Aborigines with a regular 'opinion' column in our newspapers, but there is a surplus of non-Aboriginal commentators only too willing to censure those views and criticism of 'white' myths they feel offended by. Mark O'Connor, in his argument against the term 'invasion' in *The Courier Mail* of February 1994, said that: 'Aborigines may well be offended by talk of their homelands being "discovered" by others; but they do not have the right to ban the term'. And with that the argument was turned to a debate about political correctness and censorship. My point is that for the Queensland Government to pulp year five readers that used the term 'invasion', and for 'mainstream' commentators to so thoroughly denounce the term—and the different perspective it supports in a land of free speech—in such a vehement way is most certainly censorship of the very kind the anti-politically correct lobby decries. O'Connor describes a politically correct state as one where: '... dissent is punished—

whether by jail, or more subtly by ostracism or denial of promotion—until *officially approved* views prevail' (my italics). Sounds like an Aboriginal, and other 'minority', experience to me. I don't consider my work as 'politically correct' in any sense of the term and I reject the reductive, polarised and artificial binary space the semantics of the argument, and the argument over semantics, enforces. I would argue my position as searching for a balance and would place myself in the space between 'oppositional' cultural politics. Not a 'fence sitter', which is a term relevant only to a simplistic binary framework, but an agitator for a holistic world view that can experience the world from multiple perspectives, from a position of empathy and ethics, an 'aesthetic' of rethinking the ancient question of 'ethos'. John Rajchman, in his book *Truth and Eros: Foucault, Lacan, and the Question of Ethics* (p. 144), describes Ethos as: 'how to be "at home" in a world where our identity is not given, our being-together in question, our destiny contingent or uncertain: the world of the violence of our own self-constitution'.

53. Jacques Le Goff, 'Preface', in *History and Memory*, trans. Steven Rendall and Elizabeth Clama[n] (New York: Columbia University Press, 1992), xi.

54. Daniel Thomas, 'Land versus People', [in] *Antipodean Currents: Ten Contemporary Artists from Australia* (New York: Guggenheim Museum Publications, 1995), 36. While I respect Daniel Thomas and believe that this comment was made with no racist intentions, I nevertheless feel that this gross kind of reductionism misrepresents all of the artists concerned.

55. Frank Brennan, 'Land Rights Make Room for Self-Rule', *The Australian*, 31 July 1995, 11.

56. Rajchman, *Truth and Eros*, 108.

57. Rajchman, *Truth and Eros*, [130-131].

58. Attwood, 'Introduction', xv. One should note however that much Australian Anthropology remains 'cautious, conservative and ... basically unfashionably empiricist' (J[ohn] Morton, 'Crisis, What Crisis?': Australian Aboriginal Anthropology, 1988', *Mankind* 1 (1989): 7), although some innovative work exists, e.g. J[eremy] Beckett, ed., 'Past and Present[: the construction of Aboriginality' (Canberra, ACT: Aboriginal Studies Press, 1988)]; [Barry] Morris, 'Domesticating Resistance[: The Dhan-Gadi Aborigines and the Australian State' (New York: Berg, 1989)]; J[ulie] Marcus, ed., 'Writing Australian Culture: Text, Society and National Identity,' *Social Analysis* 27, 1990. Furthermore, while the ingredients of a post-Aboriginalist History are evident in the historiography of the last two decades or so, there is little sign of well-theorised and well-executed work of this nature, but see (Bain Attwood's) *The Making of the Aborigines*, and K[laus] Neumann, 'A Postcolonial Writing of Aboriginal History', *Meanjin* 51, no. 2, [1992]: 277-98. (For helpful discussion of post-Orientalist history, see G[yan] Prakash, 'Writing Post-Orientalist Histories of the Third World: Perspectives from Indian Historiography', *Comparative Studies in Society and History* 32, no. 2 (1990): 383-408.) And in prehistoric archaeology, there has been little change in reconceptualising Aboriginality, but see [Tim] Murray, 'Tasmania and the [Constitution of] Dawn of Humanity', *Antiquity* [66, no. 252 (1992): 730-43], for a consideration of this.

59. Bernard Smith, *The Spectre of Truganini* (Sydney: Australian Broadcasting Commission, 1980), 10, 44; as quoted by Attwood ['Introduction', xv].

60. Thomas McEvilley, '"I Am" Is a Vain Thought', in *Art and Discontent: Theory at the Millennium* (New York: McPherson and Company, 1991), 115.

Artist's Statement: *Eddie Mabo (after Mike Kelley's Booth's Puddle, 1985, from Plato's Cave, Rothko's Chapel, Lincoln's Profile)*

Behind every cave … there is, and necessarily must be, a still deeper cave: an ampler, stranger, richer world beyond the surface, an abyss behind every bottom, beneath every 'foundation'.

—Friedrich Nietzsche[i]

When thinking about Eddie Mabo, I realised that I could not think of him as a real person. I could not know him in the way his family and friends knew him. I could only 'know' him through his image in the newspapers, through what was written about him and his role in overturning the great white lie of *terra nullius*.

Like most Australians, I only know the Eddie Mabo of the 'mainstream' news media, a very two-dimensional 'copy' of the man himself, a mere 'shadow'. The name 'Mabo' seemed to whip up fear and hysteria in many non-Aboriginal Australians who seemed to think that land claims would be made on their backyards. I am still disgusted by the lies that were told by opportunistic politicians who played on the public's fear and ignorance. Australia's racist underbelly remains exposed. The image and name of Mabo seemed to me to take on the qualities of a demigod, to many a symbol of joy, of hope and justice, yet able to strike fear into the hearts and minds of others.

In making this work [*Eddie Mabo (after Mike Kelley's 'Booth's Puddle' 1985, from Plato's Cave, Rothko's Chapel, Lincoln's Profile) No.3*, 1996, figure 8], I decided to use a newspaper image of Eddie Mabo and some of the headlines from the many newspaper articles I collected about the 'Native Title' furore, and furore it was indeed! People seemed to go mad. Wild claims were made about what Native Title would mean and the headlines screamed about a 'Nation Divided'. I couldn't help but think that justice hurts sometimes, and that the mask of Australia as a just and egalitarian nation had slipped a little more.

To me, the image of Eddie Mabo stood like the eye of a storm, calmly asserting his rights while all around him the storm, a war of words and rhetoric, rages. I chose to use an image by the American artist Mike Kelley [1954–2012], an artist I admire, because it seemed to fit perfectly in a number of ways. The image of the edge of a city I related to a work I did in 1987 called *The Coming of* [*the*] *Light* [figure 1] which was how some Indigenous people of the Torres Strait referred to the coming of the missionaries. In this work, the arm that holds the 'light' (of Enlightenment) is double-sided and also holds a noose that hauls a black man out of a box by the neck. I referred to the work being about a crisis of belief and a questioning of faith; a deconstruction of Western perspectives that I feel intuitively intersects with Kelley's work of 1985, though I was unaware of Kelley at the time, but I don't have the space to follow these threads and elaborate. In any case, the work should remain open, and I have an abiding aversion to providing the 'author's voice' as final arbiter of meaning (courtesy of Roland Barthes and John Berger).

The black man in *The Coming of the Light* is portrayed as [a] victim, but Eddie Mabo is the direct opposite, and as such may represent a reversal and inversion, a mirror image of the latter work, perhaps it is 'other'? But that is my speculation. The image of the city is changed also. In another work I did in 1987 called *Perpetual Motion Machine*, I depicted the edge of the city as ploughing onward, steam-rolling over a huddled group of Mimi Spirit figures while a group of white heads bang together suspended by strings from the doors of their houses like the steel balls of some executive toy. Now the city is disintegrating at its edge, the balance of the 'Perpetual Motion Machine' is upset, and from now on any 'forward' motion may involve a more careful process of negotiation.

❖ This unpublished statement, dated 2 February 1996, was written to accompany Gordon Bennett's series of works on Eddie Koiki Mabo.

[i] Nietzche's text reads in full: 'whether behind every cave in him there is not, and must necessarily be, a still deeper cave: an ampler, stranger, richer world beyond the surface, an abyss behind every bottom, beneath every "foundation"'. Friedrich Nietzsche, *Beyond Good and Evil: Prelude to a Philosophy of the Future*, trans. Helen Zimmern, originally published in 1886, http://www.gutenberg.org/files/4363/4363-h/4363-h.htm, accessed 5 June 2019.

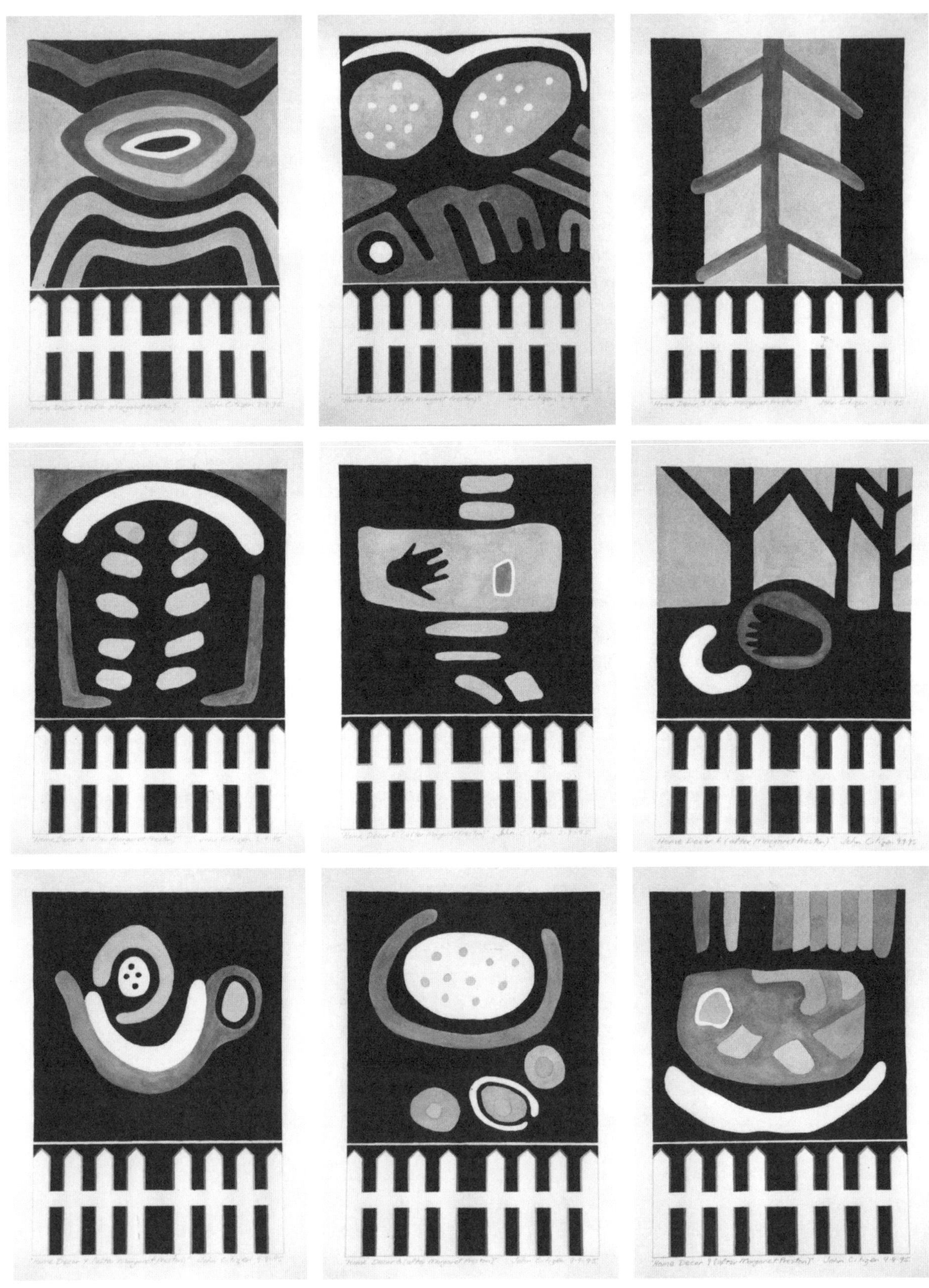

Home Décor (Preston + De Stijl = Citizen)[i]

These works [figures 9 and 10] are picking up on some of the issues I explored in a set of watercolours on paper I produced in 1995 [opposite] which used small details from works by Margaret Preston—specifically, the 'Aboriginal' works from the 1940s and 1950s.

Initially, I began by using the appropriated detail as a starting point for paintings that were primarily concerned with formal issues but which also played with the possibility of a perceived narrative, a narrative that is suggested by the relationships of the various elements in the work but which did not actually exist. I am interested in the play between the figurative and the abstract in these works. I am also interested in exploring the cross-cultural issues that these works may provoke, particularly the issues surrounding Preston's advocacy of appropriating 'Aboriginal art' as a means to develop an 'Indigenous' style of Australian modern art, while, at the same time, being dismissive of Aboriginal cultures and peoples. This is an obvious issue, which is extremely relevant to our times and national identity, but not the only issue I am interested in.

The idea of style interests me also. De Stijl (the style) was based on a multidisciplinary approach that embraced all aspects of formal creation and aimed at universality. I am also interested in Mondrian's Theosophic concepts which led him to create an abstract visual language in order to represent the universal harmony that would result from the resolution of the antitheses between the masculine and the feminine, the static and the dynamic, and the spiritual and the material. While such a resolution would be nice, I am more interested in the dynamic/static interplay between the binary opposites of abstract/figurative, black/white, good/bad, right/wrong, inclusion/exclusion to name a few. Here I am merely adding to Mondrian's list some of the binaries that preoccupy me at present.

Within the modernist grid of Mondrian's spiritual universality and Preston's stylistic utilitarianism, I hope to further explore a history of ideas, the history of events and the spaces between the binary opposites that form their foundation, and which form our sense of ourselves. After all, there must be some utility in exploring the common ground between self and other.

I must reiterate that these are works in progress and my ideas and ability to express them are not yet fully formed, and I don't really expect them to be; they will surface during the making of the work. The thing that stimulates me most of all is the possibility of a meaningful dialogue in a visual language and the implications that may arise from this for contemporary life and society.

❖ This unpublished text (c. 1996) is from Bennett's personal archive.

[i] This short artist's statement relates to the 'Home Décor' series of Bennett's, the first group of which he produced between 1995 and 1998. The original text is undated, with a rough estimate of c. 1996 based on his description in the letter of work from the same series from 1995 (see opposite page).

they admired and respected each other's ability, and became firm friends.

Cook's second lieutenant was Zachary Hicks and his third John Gore, who had been with Wallis in the *Dolphin*. When the *Endeavour* sailed from Plymouth on August 26 1768 she had on board a total of 94 people comprising 71 crew, 12 marines and 11 supernumeraries.

On her way south she stopped briefly at Madeira to take on fresh food and wine, and again for 24 days at Rio de Janeiro. Here Cook struck trouble with the Portuguese viceroy, who could not believe that such a scruffy-looking vessel as the *Endeavour* could be a British warship, or that men would sail thousands of miles merely to make an astronomical observation. He concluded that she must be a smuggler. As a result only Cook and officers and men on duty were allowed ashore, and all food had to be bought through an agent.

The next stop was at the Bay of Good Success, so named by Cook, on the east coast of Tierra del Fuego at the southern tip of South America. Banks led a party inland to look for new plants. The result was disastrous. The artist Buchan had an epileptic fit, the party was caught overnight in a blizzard and two of Banks's servants, both negroes, although they had drunk most of the rum supply nevertheless froze to death.

Cape Horn was rounded in good weather, and on April 13 1769 the *Endeavour* anchored in Matavai Bay, Tahiti. The place and the people were all that Wallis had said of them and more. Cook was delighted and Banks felt that he was in "a perfect Arcadia". Spike nails, hatchets and other trade goods were bartered for hogs, vegetables and fruit, and a small fort was built ashore to keep thieves away from the observatory tent and the scientific instruments it housed.

The transit of Venus was observed on June 3 from three different points, but although the weather was good the various timings differed considerably. Cook sailed round the island in a pinnace and charted it with his usual painstaking accuracy, while Banks and his people had a busy time collecting rare and unknown plants. From the natives Cook

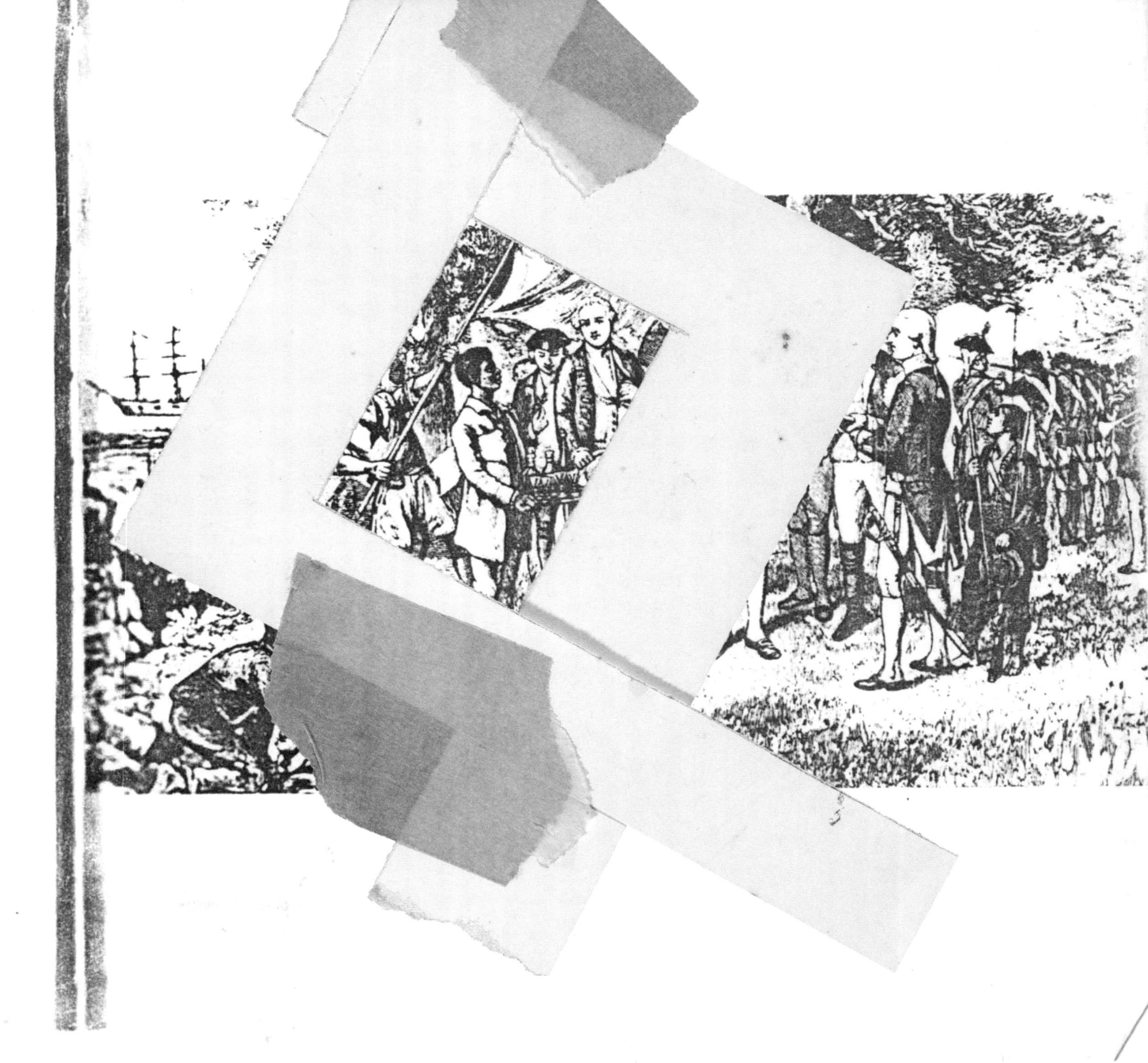

Cloud Gazing

> There is not even a sensible way in which one can specify what a 'primitive society' is. The term implies some historical point of reference. It presumably defines a type of society ancestral to more advanced forms on the analogy of an evolutionary history of some natural species. But human societies cannot be traced back to a single point of origin, and there is no way of reconstituting prehistoric social forms, classifying them, and aligning them in a time series. There are no fossils of social organization.[1]

In 1990 I began referring extensively to Jackson Pollock's work by painting pastiches of his signature dripped-paint style. I then 'floated' images within the painted field, bringing them into diverse relationships. I was interested in the way in which it is often imagined that figures lurked in Pollock's 'abstract' fields. This seemed like 'cloud gazing' in which a person perceives recognizable shapes in the shifting cloud formations. I was also interested in the relationships between Pollock's work, Navaho ground painting, and Australian Aboriginal ground painting as acts of cultural significance in the ceremonial reinforcement of spiritual and cultural mores.

Further to these significant reference points, Pollock seemed to embody the modernist/colonialist ideals of heroic exploration: a concept of linear progression as well as acts of colonisation: Picasso takes from African art what he wishes to use with little regard for its meaning or context, as does Pollock in relation to Navaho ground painting. Regardless of Pollock's real or fancied appreciation of Indigenous cultures—and my considerable respect for him as an artist—his reference to Indigenous sand painting was appropriated by others, lending to his work as an authentically 'American' reference point without regard for the actual position that European cultural perspectives have imposed on the Indigenous cultures of the so-called 'new world'. Here we have the myth of the sophisticated and civilised 'white' artist who discovers something of value in the art of 'primitive' indigenes and brings it back to enrich the lives and cultivated sensibilities of 'real' artists and 'Art'. Meanwhile, the poor natives fall from grace and their primitivist purity—circumscribed by the recurrent belief that the qualities of 'primitive' or chronologically earlier cultures are superior to those of contemporary civilisation[2]—is hopelessly contaminated by contact with 'civilisation' whereafter they descend to the level of producing 'quaint' folk art, craft or 'airport' art for only commercial gain with inauthentic materials and motives.

This is a story that has been played out many times and is equally relevant to Australia. In fact, the myths of popular 'primitivism' in relation to contemporary Australian Aboriginal art, and the notions of the 'spiritual' and the 'authentic', are still widely used to exclude and marginalise the work of artists of Aboriginal descent. Given these insights into the use and abuse of the notion of 'primitivism' in the project of modernism, it is useful to place it in context with the 400-year period of the African slave trade which began in the mid-fifteenth century. One of the most grotesque inconsistencies in the development of the Americas was the idea that a utopian enterprise could be founded on the backs of slaves or on the genocide of Indigenous peoples.[3]

In a series of works I began in France in December 1991, I overpainted a Pollock drip-style underpainting with black. This created a surface which looked remarkably like an illustration of the scarified back of an African slave I later saw reproduced in a book about the representation of blacks in the nineteenth century; the title of the triptych was *A Typical Negro* (1863).[4] With this '[W]elt' series I wanted to convey the wounding of the human spirit, its scarification; the overpainted modernist trace of a Pollock skein serving a metaphor for the scar as trace, and memory, of the colonial lash.

The painting *Possession Island* [1991, figures 11a and 11b], also produced in France, depicts James Cook claiming possession of Australia from an offshore island he named 'Possession Island'. The painting is about *perspective*; it's about a certain European perspective or way of seeing that has historically positioned people with dark skin as inferior, primitive, savage, fit to perform certain kinds of labour only within an expanding European world, etc. As I mentioned earlier, Europeans first began enslaving Africans in the fifteenth century. Thus when Cook arrived in Australia, he and his party already had very fixed ideas about black people, which they imposed on Indigenous cultures and people. The black person is only represented in the 'history' painting in a predetermined role; that is, as a servant/slave or 'possession'. As the foundation of a system of representation, perspective produces an illusion of depth on an essentially flat two-dimensional surface by the use of invisible lines that converge on a vanishing point. The vanishing point may also be understood as the point from which these lines extend outward past the picture plane to include the viewer in the pictorial space, as observer of a self-contained harmonious whole. Perspective has been called 'a systematic abstraction from the structure of ... psychophysiological space'.[5] In its positioning of the viewer and in relation to the horizon line, perspective symbolises a certain kind of power structure relating to a particular European world view.

The black person enters the space of the painting (a European space) from behind. Footprints mark his journey—a reference to Australian Aboriginal painting of the Western Desert. He either enters the space of European representation in his new role or he enters not at all. He is the only black person in the scene and is thus also an 'island' surrounded by a sea of white culture/people. His black skin is associated/identified with a black rectangle, an *abstraction*. The rectangle is a kind of void, as is the black body in a sense, to be filled by European knowledge of the world. European understanding of the world is here depicted in an abstract/conceptual way as a grid. The grid, delineated by language, and referred to by the basic alphabetical units of A, B, C, D, is *mapped* onto the void and by association onto the black body. The black body can thus only exist in representation, within the context of this painting, as a prisoner of the grid—caught in its web—and it has no choice except to fall into the void, through the pit created by the perspective lines—disappearing from the scene altogether.

Men with Weapons (Corridor) [figure 12] was painted in July 1994. It incorporates a Pollock-style drip underpainting, some of which is overpainted in black. Over the black 'scarified' surface I painted two diagrams of 'mirrors'. They show how to represent the reflection of an object in a mirror according to the rules of perspective. I painted two mirrors facing each other which, in reality, would have the effect of infinitely multiplying the reflection of an object placed between them. The perspective lines create a kind of corridor between them receding into the illusionistic depth of the painting to the 'horizon' line. On either side of this corridor are the figures of white 'settlers' (in simple binary terms, 'civilised'), and the figures of Aboriginal people ('savage'). Each is a reflection of their other. Based on the illusion of the primitive, European colonialism has created, cast and inscribed the objectified black body and mind as its 'Other', as the darkness which is 'illuminated' by 'the coming of the light', so-called civilisation; for it is generally acknowledged that, at least since the Enlightenment, the category of the 'self', and the group, is fashioned through the construction of an Other, which is outside and opposite, and that the making of an identity rests upon negating, repressing, or excluding things antithetical to it.[6] But the two facing mirrors complicate this simple binary and make it more complex, reflections of reflections and so on.

If identity can be seen as an individual/collective self-image which [h]as been defined, to a certain extent, by a succession of images that mirror a culture's sense of itself, as in the examples of painting, then I am naïve enough to believe that by interrupting a complacent sense of 'pop' history, and therefore of popular concepts of identity, I may affect a change towards a more open, tolerant and just society. Cultural identities are the points of identification, or sutures made within the discourses of history and culture; they are not essences, but positionings.[7] Identities come from somewhere; they have histories and, like everything which is historical, undergo constant transformation. Far from being eternally fixed in some essentialised past, they are subject to the continuous 'play' of history, culture and power. Far from being grounded in a mere 'recovery' of the past, which is waiting to be found, and which, when found, will eternise our sense of ourselves, identities are the names we give to the different ways we are positioned by, and position ourselves within, the narratives of the past.[8]

❖ This text was originally published in *Breaking Borders* (Winnipeg: St. Norbert Arts Centre, 1997), 37–42.

Notes

1. Adam Kuper, *The Invention of Primitive Society: Transformations of an Illusion* (London: Routledge, 1988), 7.
2. *The Macquarie Dictionary* (Sydney: The Macquarie Library, Macquarie University, 1991), 1402.
3. Albert Boime, ['Preface'], in *The Art of Exclusion: Representing Blacks in the Nineteenth Century* (London: Thames and Hudson, 1990), xiii–xiv].
4. Boime, ['Revulsion to Cruelty', in *The Art of Exclusion*, 73].
5. W. J. T. Mitchell, 'The Pictorial Turn', *Artforum* 30, no. 3 (1992): 91; [Mitchell was] referring to the 1924 essay 'Perspective as Symbolic Form' by Erwin Panofsky.
6. Bain Attwood, 'Introduction', in *Power, Knowledge and Aborigines*, ed. Bain Attwood and John Arnold (Melbourne: La Trobe University Press, 1992), iii.
7. Stuart Hall, 'Cultural Identity and Diaspora', in *Identity: Community, Culture, Difference*, ed. Jonathan Rutherford (London: Lawrence and Wishart, 1990), 226.
8. Hall, 'Cultural Identity', 225.

Australian Icons: Notes on Perception

In 1988 I began to paint the series 'Notes on Perception' [1988–1990] after seeing a reproduction of a painting by Yala Yala Gibbs Tjungurrayi [c. 1928–1998]. I was fascinated by the shimmering quality of the untitled work which was achieved with just black, white and red ochres. I decided that I would do a work on paper using a similarly restricted palette of red oxide, white and Paynes grey.

The paintings of the Western Desert Aboriginal people are topographical in that they depict the landscape and events that happened within it. Most paintings contain information about the relationships between people, land and Dreamtime beings and events. Traditionally ceremonial paintings contain information concerning the beliefs and laws by which order and continuity of Aboriginal societies are maintained. In other words, they are vehicles for a socialisation and cultural conditioning process. A sense of one's identity and place in the world is thus constructed and maintained.

In thinking about my own cultural conditioning, in the so-called 'mainstream' of Australian culture, and how it was given continuity and reinforced by similar means—such as images, myths, stories in books, on television and at school—I reflected on how much my mind seemed to me like a landscape with the stream of my conscious, rational self traversing it and passing by the various sites of knowledge, images and memories that informed my sense of identity and my 'place' in the world I live in [as] a kind of 'psycho-topographical' map.

Since I had a strictly Euro-Australian upbringing and education, I came to learn about Australian history and Aborigines with a Eurocentric bias and perspective. This Eurocentric perspective was particularly evident in the 1988 bicentennial celebrations. Throughout these celebrations, specific events that were deemed important were re-enacted by people in period costume and broadcast on television, reproduced in magazines, commemorated in books, and so on. The tall ships event is a case in point. The images of ships became important because they recalled the 'romance' of adventure and danger faced by the First Fleet, and the opening up of the 'New World' of unexplored territories for 'settlement' and exploitation.

Thus, images of ships were being widely reproduced and contributing to the effect of reinforcing this nation's colonial identity; but what about the full story? The images being reproduced were a form of very selective memory that served to reinforce an even more selective history which I and most 'mainstream' Australians were taught in school and which was an unchallenged part of the mindset of popular culture. Thus, during the bicentennial celebrations, people wondered why the Aborigines were not celebrating, but protesting. Holes in one's education often lead to a lack of understanding.

I began the series 'Notes on Perception' by selecting a detail, or reduced section, of a reproduced historical image; specifically, a painting of Captain Cook. I photocopied the selected part, enlarged it and then projected it onto a piece of paper. I saw this as a kind of ritual practice that in a sense replicated, or even parodied, the selective process of a teleological historical perspective. I painted the image in the quick gestural brushstrokes of what may be termed a Western art tradition. Then, in the spaces between the brushstrokes, I inserted dots (some of which were created by the photocopy enlargement process) in what many people refer to as an Aboriginal art tradition. I combined Cook with an image of an Aborigine's head in classical 'noble savage' pose with face uplifted (from a beer coaster), and enclosed it in a box-like structure created by perspective lines that converged to a vanishing point in the centre of Cook's eye.

The resultant image I related to as a kind of psycho-topographical 'map' of two of the major icons of my cultural conditioning. I called the work *Australian Icon (Notes on Perception No. 1)*. I continued the series with images and details of nineteenth-century photographic postcards that staged Aboriginal people in supposedly 'natural environments'. By re-contextualising these images, I gave them new meaning, placing them in another time and place and in new relationships to the present with its different sense of world view and the benefit of a critical distance to the time in which they were produced. I called these works *Australian Aborigines (Notes on Perception No.* [2, 3, 4, and so on]*)* [figures 13 and 14].

These works relate to the evolution of an Aboriginal stereotype—that is, what a 'real' Aborigine looks like. Everyone could, and still can, 'picture' an Aborigine in their mind's eye, and this picture has become the internalised icon against which contemporary Aborigines are measured. This is an ongoing problem for many people whose skin is never quite dark enough, or hair never quite curly enough, to satisfy some observers who feel that their stereotype overrides another person's self-definition.

The method of gestural brushstrokes and dots in the works on paper combine at close range to obscure the image. The image is dissolved in brushstrokes and dots until one steps back a short distance from the surface to find the image 'reveals' itself. This is important in that it is essentially one's mind that constructs the image out of the mass of data, which is paint on a surface perceived by the means of sight. What the mind constructs is based on the past learnt experience of cultural conditioning and culturally relative knowledge.

Australian Icon (Notes on Perception No. 6) is a detail from a larger work depicting a ship in a storm. Which particular ship is unimportant. It is its 'shipness' that is important. Up close to the image it is difficult to determine anything except paint on a surface. At a distance the ship will appear as the mind recognises and constructs it. The observer sees a sailing ship because of the mind's perception of 'shipness'—the image resembles what a sailing ship is supposed to look like based on previous experience of sailing ships, or images of them. What the image of a ship means to the observer is relative to that person's cultural associations as to their purpose, historical context, and so on.

When viewed by an observer familiar with Australian history, a ship is very likely to be interpreted in relation to the First Fleet, or even Captain Cook's *Endeavour*, especially when the image was produced in the year after the bicentenary, as was *Notes on Perception No. 6*. From the 'Notes on Perception' series of works on paper, or 'drawings' as they may be referred to, I selected particular images for larger works on canvas. The ship image in *Australian Icon* (1989), the same as in *Notes on Perception No. 6*, was chosen specifically to evoke the romantic notions of adventure, danger, exploration and discovery that forms a major part of the mythology informing an Australian 'mainstream' identity. This series is part of an overall body of work that is dealing with the deconstruction of my 'mainstream' Australian identity, as it was constructed through the culture in which I was born and raised, and its relationship to my 'Aboriginality', which was an inheritance through my mother's lineage—but also an identity constructed solely within the parameters of a Eurocentric perspective.

I believe this process I have undertaken to be relative to the greater Australian context of black and white relationships, insofar as I am a measure of 'mainstream' Australia, given the shared environment of Anglo-Celtic cultural conditioning, and the socialisation process of my upbringing and my experience of, and even participation in, the racially biased beliefs of popular Australian culture.

❖ This text was originally published in *Double Vision: Art Histories and Colonial Histories in the Pacific*, ed. Nicholas Thomas and Diane Losche (Cambridge: Cambridge University Press, 1999), 252-56. This text is reproduced courtesy of Cambridge University Press.

no one position is right over another. Life must be treated as an interactive system, an ecology. This is progress & as a creative response to life & living it is also art.

JB. 23-1-90

This results in a wider frame of reference from which to understand the the world at large, to

Canvas 66 x 54 ins. (167 x 137 cm)

Part Two In response

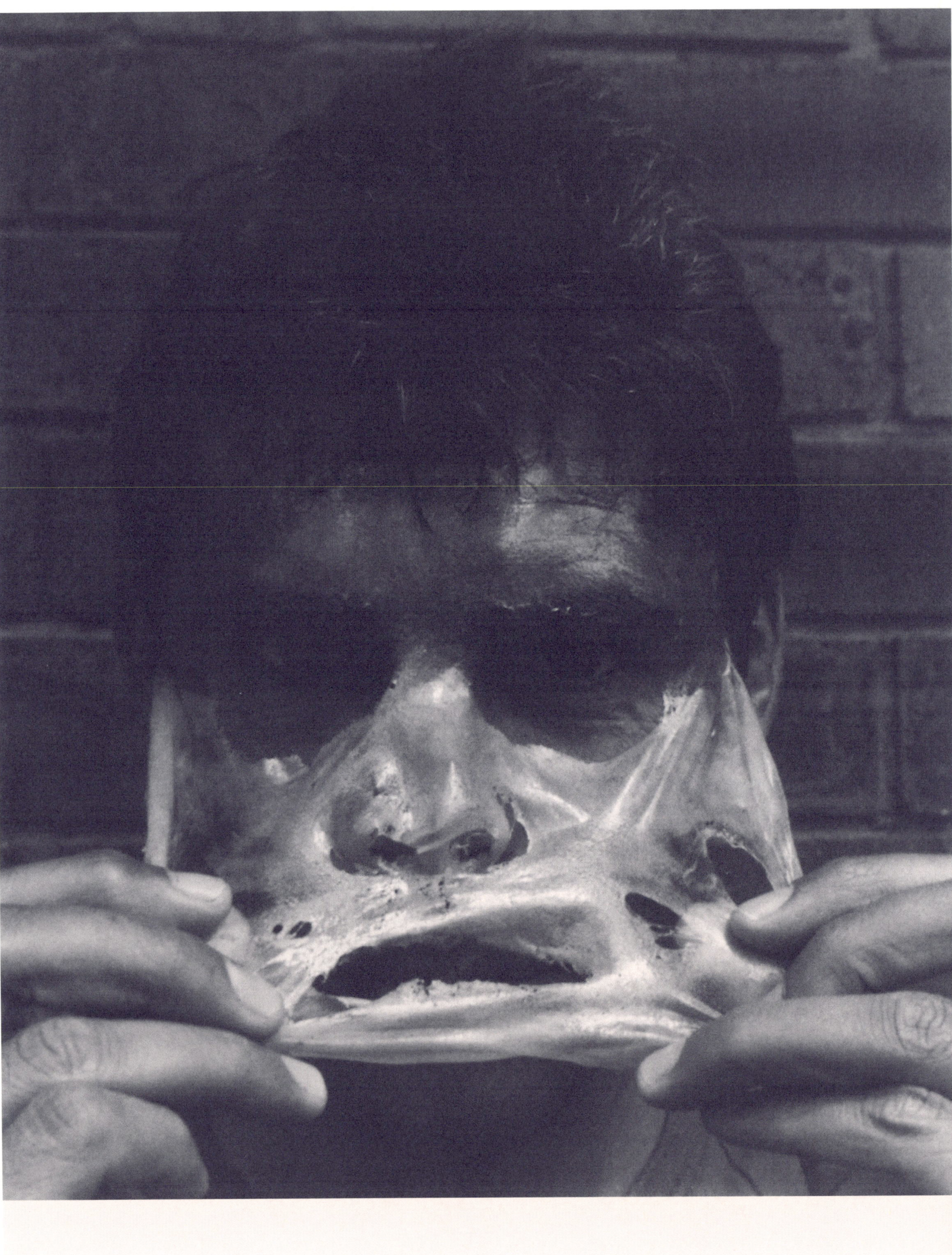

Letters

Gordon Bennett wrote letters for two very different reasons. On the one hand, the letter format provided a direct, even confrontational mode of public address to critics and detractors. On the other, it provided a more intimate means of communication, as seen in his private correspondence, which also included faxes and emails.

Sometimes, the addressee was a specific figure within the art world, such as the Australian artist Mandy Martin (b. 1952), as seen in Bennett's 'On Double Standards: An "Other Perspective"' (p. 85). In this letter to the editor, published in *Art Monthly Australia* in 1992 and written in response to Martin's article 'Diary from the Centre' from two issues prior, Bennett critiques the harsh double standards at work within the Australian art market for Indigenous artists.

Bennett also uses the personal directness of handwritten letters to great effect as a component of his series of watercolours 'Home Sweet Home' (1993–94) [p. 88, figures 22 and 23]. Works in this series juxtapose scenes of graphic domestic and sexual violence and its concealment behind Australian 'larrikin' behaviour, with handwritten letters responding to these traumatic themes.

Another effective use of the letter format within an artwork draws on Bennett's exchange with Latvian-Australian artist Imants Tillers (b. 1950). Bennett's conversation with Tillers is evident in a 1993 work that is made up of three parts (figures 18–21): *Ricochets*, which includes nine wall-mounted photocopies on canvas board of the two artists' correspondence and exchange of works via fax, as well as a copy of *Eyeline* (vol. 19, Winter–Spring 1992) featuring Bennett's *Resurrection (Bloom)* (1990) on the cover, hung on the left; *Manifest Destiny (A Painting for the Distant Future: 2001)*, 289 canvas boards, with the top board featuring a photocopy of Tillers' painting *Manifest Destiny* (1991) stacked in a single pile beneath *Ricochets*; and *Window onto a Shadow Universe*, nine wall-mounted photocopies on canvas board with an image of Giorgio de Chirico's *Greetings from a Distant Friend* [*Salutations d'un ami lointain*] (1916), hung on the right. The faxes describe the artists' creative conversation, including Tillers' curious suggestion of telepathic exchange. Presented by Bennett as a 'proposed collaboration' with Tillers, the work was first exhibited in 1993 in the group exhibition *Commitments* at the Institute of Modern Art, Brisbane, before being posthumously displayed in 2016 in *Black, White and Restive* at Newcastle Regional Art Gallery.

Conversely, Bennett's unpublished letter to John Laws from 1994 [p. 90] is a challenge to the popular talkback radio announcer, pointing out his duty to discuss Australia's institutionalised racism in broad public terms. The arguments Bennett presents here remain pertinent to continuing debates regarding memorials to Indigenous warriors and leaders in Australia. This perspective also recalls the influence of the Australian historian Henry Reynolds on the young artist's work, in particular Reynolds' 1981 text *The Other Side of the Frontier*.

Bennett's private correspondence also provides insight into his personal thoughts and feelings. On his introduction to the Australian scriptwriter Nadine Amadio in 1992 as part of pre-production for *Black Angels: A Widening Vision*, a 1994 documentary film on Bennett, the artist responds by letter with wariness [p. 75]. Reacting to Amadio's purchase of a book critiquing the Derridean theory of deconstruction, of which Bennett was a proponent, he responds with a tone of admonition, describing the necessity of his critical methods in light of a culture of ingrained racism. Over the course of their correspondence, however, Amadio opens up about her experience of misogyny—a reflection that Bennett empathises with, responding in kind with a deeply personal analysis of his upbringing and self-image.

Insights into Bennett's personal life and his sources of inspiration are also gained as part of a series of letters from the same year, addressed to fellow Brisbane artist and frequent collaborator Eugene Carchesio (b. 1960) [p. 82]. Bennett shares his recent discovery of the work of Belgian poet and artist Marcel Broodthaers (1924–1976), which he encountered in a solo exhibition at the Galerie National de Jeu de Paume, Paris. Recounting Broodthaers' 1968 act of relinquishing his role as an artist to become the 'director' of a new 'travelling museum', Bennett describes his desire for a conceptual 'non-action' where he will commit to a period of silence for five years. This idea would become the basis of his 1992 essay 'Re-Writing History' and the beginning of his *Non-Performance*.

In some cases, Bennett takes up the right of reply to published criticism, as seen in an unpublished letter from 1995 addressed to Sue Smith, the art critic for *The Courier Mail* [p. 92]. Bennett responds to Smith's negative review of Bennett's exhibition 'BLACK: Fear of Shadows', of the same year at Bellas Gallery, Brisbane, challenging what he saw as her misreading of the layered references of his work and advising her to review later works of his with a more considered analysis.

One of Bennett's later examples of correspondence is his published 'Letter to Jean-Michel Basquiat' [p. 101], written in 1998, ten years after Basquiat's death, to accompany the first exhibition of Bennett's *Notes to Basquiat* series (1998–2007, figures 27 and 28) at the Gramercy International Art Fair in New York City. Perhaps the most powerful singular piece of writing produced by Bennett, the letter is emotive and open, empathising with the influential American artist of Haitian and Puerto Rican descent and what Bennett describes as their shared experience of their 'separate' worlds' efforts to 'exclude, objectify, and dehumanise the black body and person'.[1] Bennett frankly outlines his strategies for appropriating and emulating Basquiat's distinctive style to capture the 'language' of the New York context, but also acknowledges their connection as 'human beings in the world of material existence'.[2]

With the exception of Bennett's letter to *Art Monthly Australia*, the transcripts provided here are taken from copies in Bennett's personal archive, and have been reproduced in consultation with his estate.

Notes

1. Gordon Bennett, 'Letter to Jean-Michel Basquiat', in *Gordon Bennett* (Sydney: Sherman Galleries, 1999), 4.

2. Bennett, 'Letter to Jean-Michel Basquiat', 4.

Letter to Judith Hugo, 7 June 1990

Dear Judith,

Thanks for your letter and my apologies for the delay in answering it. I received your letter a day or two before flying out of Australia bound for the van Gogh exhibition in Amsterdam. We spent four weeks in Holland, which was great, but meant I could not do anything about replying to you until now.

I have written some notes[i] on *Persistence of Language* [1987, figure 2] that I hope will answer some of your questions. I tend to ramble a bit and I don't pay strict attention to grammar and spelling when writing such notes so please ignore such things.

What you said about Gauguin[ii] is interesting; I would resist any notions of an artist as a spiritual leader but I would not reject it outright either as I do believe in the search for self-knowledge and awareness of the world around us and our relationship to it. As for his notions of uncontaminated cultural purity, well I must reject that on the grounds that such notions were created by 'noble savage' theories (Rousseau, etc.) and involve dangerous cultural preconceptions that are as debilitating as any other preconceptions about Aborigines or others. Culture is dynamic and interacts with new input to evolve when on an equal exchange level but when it is attacked as inferior by another culture or isolated (kept 'pure') as a museum exhibit that is when real problems are created. (Sorry I started to ramble on that one.) Any reference to Gauguin's Jacob and angel [*Vision after the Sermon (Jacob Wrestling with the Angel)* (1888)] was really an afterthought on my part (it should be remembered that the story is biblical in the first place) but then I am always amazed at how images 'appear' to me and how relevant they turn out to be. I usually go intuitively with an image and only later do I think about interpreting possible meanings. (But then I work in other ways too!)

The tabloid interpretation of the 'window' in the right-hand panel is an appropriate one and probably the 'urbanisation' effect too, but I wouldn't say that those interpretations are the only ones—many white people (people in general, in fact) suffer the destructive effect of urbanisation—to say that Aborigines can't live in an urban environment because of, say, an inherent genetic or psychological need for the 'bush' wouldn't be appropriate but that kind of an interpretation could be gleaned by embracing the 'destructive effect of urbanisation' line, and would be the 'other' side of a romantic 'noble savage' philosophy. (Ramble, ramble, ramble!)

I hope my notes and comments are helpful to you and the other gallery guides. You have a difficult job. I'm about worn out, so I won't say much about the Albert Namatjira work [*Valley of the Ghost Gums* (1989)] except that I thought of the angel as being ashamed of the actions of its creators. I say creators because I see an angel as a manifestation of the spiritual but from a European perspective, since angels etc., belong to European creation myths, etc. I thought of Albert's wounded spirit, the misinterpretation of his motives for painting *his country* in a 'Western' style (as one jerk artist said, 'a hack Hans Heysen style'), the reverence of his work for its monetary value (the barcode—its commodity value), etc.

Thanks for your interest and kind comments.

Warm regards,

G Bennett

❖ This previously unpublished letter, dated 7 June 1990, is from Bennett's personal archive. Bennett wrote in response to Judith Hugo, a volunteer guide from the Art Gallery of Western Australia (AGWA), Perth, after Hugo had written to Bennett regarding *The Persistence of Language* (1987), which is held in the AGWA Collection.

[i] See p.16 for these notes.
[ii] In the original, Bennett spelled 'Gauguin' as 'Gaugin'.

Self Portrait, 1991

Floating throbbing violence staring red glowering embers—that dismember internal organs—I envision my brain slowly turning, racing its own shadow through streaming tunnels of vacuous excrement in the abstract land of mind—turning slowly, turning slowly, ever slowly elated in the burning fire of castrating dragons, I sing—'Having a wonderful time wish you were here'—gleefully giggling to a hideously unnamed joke.

All the best, Gordon

❖ This text is transcribed from a postcard work entitled *Self Portrait* (1991, figure 16) that was sent by Bennett to his Brisbane gallerist, Peter Bellas. Bellas was Bennett's first gallerist and a close friend. Bennett secured representation from Bellas Gallery in 1989, one year after graduating from art college.

Letter to Gary Lee, 7 April 1991

Dear Gary,

Thanks for the letter and the congrats! We've decided to leave for France on 11 July 1991 for our twelve months 'holiday' (and a holiday it shall be!). I'm not planning any huge 'debut' exhibitions or to try and 'sell' my work to any galleries overseas. I will do some work, however, watercolours and collage maybe, in portable format but I take the line that I am at a very early stage in my development as an artist and to pretend anything else can only lead to disaster. You know it's uncomfortable to be perceived as a tall poppy when one is still only a seedling. Anyway, I'll be looking at a lot of art and catalogues and reading, etc. I have my own developmental curve that I am following (an intuitive one).

I am glad you shredded your paper on the use of Aboriginal imagery if, as you say, it had degenerated into a comparison between the work of Lin [Onus] [1948-1996] and myself. I consider Lin a friend and would hate to be set up in opposition to him for good or bad. I do admire his skills as an artist and consider him a pioneer of so-called 'urban Aboriginal artists'. I have no problem with his use of little machines as painting aides and in fact I find that conceptually interesting. I myself use projectors and I'm sure you're aware Gary that painting and drawing aides have been used since I don't know when. Many people seem to object to the use of such devices out of some romantic notion that the artist should paint and draw everything by hand, that the 'art' is in fact the technical skill of hand crafting (my neighbour thinks using a projector is cheating—an interesting notion when examined carefully—but then he's a mechanic; I wonder should he be using an electronic tuning device instead of tuning a car the old way, by ear?).

As for the rrark (is that how it's spelt [*sic*]?)[i] that Lin uses, well I guess with his involvement with people in Maningrida and their artistic interaction and permission for use he has, I believe, been given, there is not really much room for accusations of misuse. If I were to use rrark, then I think there would be definite case insofar as I have not had (nor am I likely to [have]) the same interaction Lin has; also, I have no conceptual 'handle' or reason for using it. It would be an *empty* sign of Aboriginality for me, as would the use of kangaroos, fish, crabs, birds, etc.—all empty signs for a culture that is not of my experience and the reassertion of which my work is not about. (One of *the* hardest points for me to get across given the current understanding of 'Aboriginal art' and 'Aboriginal artists'.) I think Lin's use of rrark is an intelligent use and is never a mere 'sign' of Aboriginality.

So, enough of that. Gary, you must tell me what you find simultaneously disturbing and appealing in what you called my Rover Thomas [1926-1998] series. You know areas of colour delineated by dots do not a Rover Thomas make! I thought I would get abused for painting over Hans Heysen [1877-1968] prints, it

[i] Bennett misspells 'rarrk' here, but his spelling has been retained for authenticity, given his query regarding its spelling.

being seen as a very aggressive thing to do, which I guess it was in a way. (I thought of it as a conceptual repossession of landscape in one way—almost a land rights claim on the pictorial representation of landscape and history?) I guess, deep down, I expected an attack on the somewhat tenuous (which is really the case) relationship to Rover's work from the more irrational among us. However, when it came, and so quickly, I was not really ready for it and found it deeply disturbing. I feel I understand and yet don't understand such a rabid willingness to attack on the part of some 'urban' Aboriginal people. I see it as primarily a psychological problem, of low self-esteem and a still deeply felt shame, which has been ingrained, of being Aboriginal. It's like an abused dog will attack anyone that makes a move towards it as it expects to be beaten again (not a good analogy) I know I still suffer from this affliction and must constantly be vigilant lest I go for someone's throat. Do you know what I mean Gary? It's like we've come to expect exploitation and abuse to the level that we unconsciously look for it and consequently find it, sometimes in unlikely places. Of course, I could be wrong about all that (maybe the real reason for such, sometimes unwarranted attacks is just something as simple as plain stupidity). However, I notice such things in myself and part of my work at least is involved with examining and analysing how this shame has been induced into me and people like me (of mixed descent) through the ethnocentric bias of a Euro-Australian cultural socialising process. It's kind of an exorcism of the personal, but with a relationship to the general since the socialising process acts on us all in similar ways. While I sit in class and feel shame as Aboriginal culture is taught in the terms of a primitive society, etc., little Johnny beside me may feel superior and become more complacent in his acceptance of cultural superiority (as an example). Different reactions to the one lesson but it's the lesson that is not questioned. The notion of the primitive is not questioned. I want to question such things. I don't know what answers will come up; I just want to broaden people's consciousness and my own (I don't want to assert Aboriginal culture over any other and I don't want to reinforce 'Western' Euro-Australian culture either—I guess an ideal convergence of cultures with ecology and an understanding of connectedness to all things would be a culture worth asserting over all others). I think I'm rambling a bit now, sorry, it always happens when I write letters—my mind starts to wander and speculate. Basically, I have a strong *intuitive* sense of purpose to what I do that I cannot explain in words to my own complete satisfaction.

I thought I might enclose a photo of a work from this series [of] Hans Heysen overpaintings [figure 17]—one I have kept for myself—[which] are all based on a simple idea (which is hard to articulate, however). There is an inner 'oval'-shaped area encompassing a Heysen image of a pastoral scene. This is overpainted in a series of transparent washes of umber and alizarin red to give it a kind of Rothkoesque colourfield effect, a spiritual colour saturation, veiling the romantic nostalgia of Heysen's pastoral image. Two seated white figures frame this image. Here there is a juxtaposition between flatness and depth, the flatness of Aboriginal Western Desert paintings (and of modernism's paint on a surface, flatness of abstraction) (these paintings were originally titled *Abstractions*). The white figures are of course depicted using the abstract symbols of desert painting which denote seated figures. Two seated white figures framing a romantic pastoral image which acts as a cultural site (it could easily be a concentric circle [Bennett included a drawn diagram here], an image that in Euro-Australia acts as a site for an 'Australian' cultural identity. A sanitised site, by the way, a generalised abstracted site. The outer 'oval' (i.e., the second row of dots surrounding the inner image) contains four cells with the letters A, B, C and D, one in each. The first four fundamental building blocks of the English language from which a Eurocentric world view is built and able to be transmitted (i.e., as history or whatever). Language lies outside our conscious understanding of the world; i.e., we don't see it but without it, what kind of consciousness would we have? Language is an integral part of our experience of the world. That's basically the story of this painting and others like it: the dark space in which the two cells, one within the other, 'floats' can be seen as an unconscious void, an empty landscape of the unknown, containing this known part, this site of constructed identity. I call these psychotopographical landscapes.

Well Gary, I've raved on enough for now. I could ramble on forever trying to capture every nuance of meaning that arises in my mind but I feel that if a painting like this can disturb simply by the juxtaposition of two depictions of landscape, thus reinforcing an Aboriginal alternative view over a European one then it's a success (that's putting it in rather oversimplified terms!) I hope you know what I mean.

❖ This previously unpublished letter, dated 7 April 1991, is from Bennett's personal archive. Bennett wrote in response to Gary Lee, a project officer for the Aboriginal Arts Unit, Australia Council for the Arts, who was corresponding regarding Bennett's 'Psychotopographical Landscape' series (1990-91).

Letter to Nadine Amadio, 5 January 1992

Dear Nadine,

Thanks for your letter. By now you should have received Leanne's Christmas card and know that we will be travelling in April and May of 1992. June looks like the best month. I am fairly certain that I will be exhibiting in a group show of Australian artists in Paris in June sometime. It's being curated by an Amsterdam gallerist (an expatriate Australian) for SPADEM, which is a Parisian-based group that looks after artists' rights. (NAVA is an Australian equivalent). SPADEM is opening a new gallery space in Paris to help its members who are not associated with a commercial gallery. This will be its first show.

Up until June I will be very busy, painting, writing and travelling (actually, I feel a little over committed). I've enclosed a photocopied text that was sent to me by a curator from Düsseldorf whom I have recently met. The text points to a world 'movement' (for want of a better word) of which I realise I am a part (and others in Australia engaged in the kind of 'deconstruction' I am). Which brings me to something I wish to discuss with you. That word 'deconstruction' which points to particular theories, mostly about literature, about which you seem a little worried, which in turn worries me. It worried me that you had thought it necessary to purchase a book on 'against deconstruction' which you had stated you intended to give to me. I wonder why? Have you read a book on 'deconstruction' previously? If not, why not? I don't wish to explain my motives for working the way I do in the context of a theory—I don't work that way. My work comes from a need to understand the world I'm living in, not from the need to illustrate a theory, which my work may have a relation to.

My work comes from a suburban environment, where attitudes to Aborigines are entrenched at a Social Darwinist level. From backyard barbeques to workplace Christmas parties and morning tea breaks, derogatory opinions about Aborigines are exchanged with the same unquestioning ease and assurance as the knowledge that the sun will rise in the east every morning. This complacent belief in a 'white' cultural and even human superiority is based on many 'accepted' though now seen to be false premises. It is however reinforced daily by biased newspapers, television reports and by racist jokes and anecdotes, etc. Primitive, savage, stone-age, dark skin/dark mind, heathen are just some of the concepts, past and present that need to be addressed. And that inform my thinking (just the tip of an iceberg). These concepts are much of the basis for the 'backyard opinions' I mentioned earlier—all of them over the past 204 years have been used by a supposedly moral and civilised society to justify the theft of land and the murder and degradation of a people whose many faceted and diverse cultures were equally complex and sophisticated in organisation (and far less brutal, I might add) as any European culture—though very different. Being different should never be seen as an excuse to position anything as inferior—in my opinion. As far as the romantic belief of the 'pioneer spirit' goes, well I think it needs to be 'deconstructed' for a truer picture to evolve, that of thieves and murderers—those who didn't actively participate in genocide supported it by non-action. Of course, this is a gross simplification, as gross a simplification as the general belief that Aboriginal cultures are stone age and primitive but I wanted to make a point—that there are other histories, other points of view and references that constitute Australian history and therefore Australian identity. It's no good building an Australian 'image' on a lie: The romantic fiction of a 'pioneer spirit' because even a cursory glance at the new emerging histories of Australian 'settlement' (a misleading word indeed) reveals the emptiness of such an image. Such an image hides the truth and hiding the truth harbours guilt. Guilt seems to generate two phenomena: 1. a sympathising sentimental smothering effect which ends up paralysing everyone involved; or 2. a reactionary feeling of not being responsible for the past which seems to generate the same kind of attitudes from that past that led to the genocide and ethnocide in the first place. Guilt is getting Australia nowhere. I think the truth of history needs to be told to generate an understanding of the present so we can all get on with a better-informed concept of the future. I guess that on one level I am saying a very basic 'look this is what happened and is still happening, 'we' have suffered and are still suffering from 'your' ignorance and savagery. 'We' are human beings! Get off 'our' backs and let 'us' live a life of dignity as equals. Some of 'us' wish to practice a culture that is different from 'yours', some of 'us' wish to compete alongside 'you' in contemporary Australian culture. This should be achievable in a multicultural society like Australia. 'We' don't need 'your' myth of a 'pioneer spirit', 'we' have a true spirit of survival and a will to live, otherwise 'we' would have been long gone—this is based on the truth of 'our' beings which is battered everyday by 'your' prejudice, 'your' attitudes and psychological and physical violence towards 'us', but 'we' live and I for one demand my personal dignity in the face of your overpowering prejudice!' (I use here the words 'you' and 'your' towards a Euro-Australian audience in general—'we + us' = Aboriginal people.

Sorry for the 'stream of consciousness' writing but I am good and angry. I've had too many conversations with ignorant people here (not French people though). I had 'Aborigines produce nothing, but just live off the state' from a Venezuelan orchestra conductor on a train out of Berlin—(30 million dollars generated by Aboriginal art and culture last year is not nothing)—the same person described the cold in New York at least 'took care' of the poor. He complained the weather was too good in South America! It worries me when people such as a conductor of symphony orchestras thinks this way, given the circles in which they would move. He considered himself French and not Venezuelan—another example of cultural cringe from a 'colonised' country?

Another incident involved Lord and Lady Portman, friends of the Duke and Duchess of Kent, visiting Moët. We were invited to dine with them. Hossein Valamanesh and his wife Angela and son were there, also. Lord Portman kept complaining about all the black West Indians who 'didn't want to work' and who were just 'bludging off the state'; he even said that sure they used to work in the colonies (bought as slaves) but that was under the whip. Again, given the circles in which this man associates I wonder is that the prevailing attitudes?—the man himself inherited property from a great-grandfather in the Middle Ages so was born wealthy. This is an attitude to colonialism I am finding everywhere it seems. The sweat off black backs and of Indigenous peoples that built the various empires and made Europe fat and wealthy is conveniently forgotten in a 'white'-only historical 'continuum'. Indigenous peoples everywhere are pushed aside after their 'usefulness' is over and then even blamed for their inability to 'assimilate' (that great myth), outsiders in their own lands or, in the case of many African peoples, outsiders in strange lands due to the slave trade. Many of the people I have spoken to have been from New Zealand and the perception of Māori people is no better there in spite of the myth of New Zealand's 'enlightened' engagement with Māori culture.

Well Nadine, enough of this, I could go on with pouring all this out, but I don't want to dump all my exploding passions on to you. I had to say something though as it is all bottled up with little outlet. You see, I have never seen art as decoration for someone's wall. I think art has a social function, it can serve as a catalyst to an expansion of one's consciousness to encompass other perspectives and broaden one's understanding. However, it does require an audience to participate, to want to know. I'm starting to 'rave' again here, so I'll stop.

I would like to recommend a book to you. It would give you a 'picture' of the relevance of my work to the broader context of 'deconstruction' and 'decolonisation'. (now don't get worried about that one). It's by Lucy R. Lippard, *Mixed Blessings: New Art in a Multicultural America* (New York: Pantheon Books, 1990). I hope you are willing to read it as a way of placing my work into a broader context and out of the context or 'negative?' relationship you seem to have with this theory called 'deconstruction'. I worry that you have an 'agenda' or a plan for the film and I wonder what it is, however loose it may be. I realised there must be some sort of agenda when I felt that I wasn't giving the 'correct' answers to certain questions being asked that day at Sydney['s] [Art Gallery of New South Wales].

I am thankful that the film will be a serious one and feel that you are open to my input. I would not have agreed to do it otherwise. I want to be sure of your understanding of what my work is about. I'm certain you can understand this. The reason I did not want the Channel 10 documentary was because of the focus on 'entertainment'. They could not believe it when I said I did not want to do it. [And] kept at me saying how it would benefit me. I am a serious artist and my work is of a serious social and philosophical nature. I did not want it to become thirty minutes of entertainment between the news and *Neighbours* or whatever. I don't want to be trivialised, lost in the soup of commercial televisions need to produce 'good television' with its focus on entertainment (and ratings) rather than to inform. That was my main reason for refusing Channel 10. I don't like the bias of reporters and television and, for that matter, newspapers. I'll give you an example of what I mean. During Expo ['88] at Brisbane, there was a street march that culminated in an Indigenous cultural festival held at a nearby park to the Expo site. Leanne and I were there for the march, which was peaceful, and for the cultural activities, which included singing and dancing, art displays, etc., from various Aboriginal and Islander groups. On returning home, we turned on the television for the *7.30 Report* (ABC) and were confronted by a well-known TV reporter on location at the park reporting on the fact that 'nothing was happening'; i.e., no violence, no confrontation, which is what they obviously wanted to report on. Instead of reporting on a peaceful cultural festival which was well attended by both black and white, we—the 'informed' people who watch the ABC—were told nothing was happening but to stay tuned because as soon as something did happen, we would know 'all' about it! We were disgusted, and this goes on and on (as I do, it seems).

OK, this time I'll finish off Nadine. I needed to get this off my chest (about any possible 'agenda' Juniper [Films] has) I'm not questioning anybody's integrity or 'sinister' intentions but wish to make clear that sometimes a 'bias' can be present and not be noticed. (The commercial network people never stopped assuring me of their serious intent but with the qualifying 'if it's entertaining so much the better'.) Well I didn't trust them, but I do trust you.

Well, I hope you are well as we are—and I must apologise for my scrawl and constant mistakes (like that!) but I'm tired and when all this anger surfaces, as it has done while writing this letter, I get excited and make mistakes as it all pours out. Leanne's across the table correcting mistakes I have missed.

I am trying to get a retrospective catalogue organised through Moët as they have a budget for such things—so if it all goes well, it should be ready for June. I have a show in London in late May [*Southern Crossings* at Camerawork] that I'm very concerned about as it is a photographic-based show and I am frustrated by my isolation here. We may have a three-week trip to Amazonia in South America in February too, but it's not confirmed yet. So I'm very busy but it keeps me occupied out here in the country. OK, enough for now I'll say goodbye and all the best from Leanne and myself. I hope you can get Lucy Lippard's book.

Warm regards,

Gordon and Leanne x

Letter to Nadine Amadio, 28 January 1992

Dear Nadine,

Thanks for your letter, I feel we know each other a little better now. It was interesting to have an insight into your 'formative' years and I found myself reflecting on how really easy my own early years really were, sometimes I just can't understand why I get so angry when my own personal situation of growing up seems to have been so easy. I think that when compassion was handed out, I came back for seconds but then other times I think I'm just a masochist who somehow enjoys torturing myself with things over which I have no control.

I guess I have always been in my own world of thought. I grew up shy and mostly alone. I invented playmates and always had a strong imagination, but I also was very sensitive. Perhaps too sensitive for my own psychological health, I don't know. I am still trying to find out, I think. I am still going through my 'baptism of fire'. I hope to have integrated many things about my life so far and to have learnt something about 'acceptance' before I become a father. I don't want to teach my children anger, but rather a love of life and learning, to foster their growth as themselves rather than what I think they should be (an extension of myself?). Of course, I was taught to be a perfectionist by my father and as with most perfectionists, I can never reach perfection and so see myself as never quite good enough (as I grew to believe my father saw me as never good enough). I don't want this for my children. I hope they can teach me many things about life. I believe that when they come (I know they will because I feel ready to accept them) that they will be the children I need to do this—it's a spiritual notion that sees everything in the world as having a purpose—the people I meet who upset me most are my best teachers with the lessons I most need to learn. At the moment, I have built a wall of resistance to them and their lessons and so I seem to meet more of them. Of course, this may be nonsense, but I think what I'm saying is about attitude if nothing else, an attitude to learning, an openness to experience. However, these will be my hardest lessons because my problem is I am not open to many things (I screwed this letter up at this point, Nadine, because I felt like such a hypocrite talking about openness in the light of my experience in France). I have discovered I am very suburban in attitude, very resistant to change and not very happy with myself at all—my perfectionist sense of failure is dominant at the moment. I have felt under extreme stress at times, so much so that I have developed a problem with my heartbeat, which is at times very irregular and in fact skips beats, which is quite alarming to myself and Leanne.

Although we are in the country, I seem to have attracted a lot of attention—I seem dogged by the spectre of success—a funny thing to say, isn't it? Unlike many artists, I have not tried to promote myself here at all, but I find myself trying to apply the brakes more than attempting to accelerate along this 'success' road. So part of my stress problem is related to feeling a little out of my depth over here—art here is big business and is produced on an industrial scale that I just could not keep up with nor do I think I would wish to. I don't know—I think the real benefit of my European experience will come months after I return to Australia and can relax in my own surroundings, where I don't feel so isolated. I am questioning many things—not least myself but then I have always done that.

Well in regard to Juniper Films, below are some dates for you to work with—

1. 29 March our mothers arrive in France
2. 21 April we begin a European tour (dates are set and paid for)
3. 16 May we arrive back in Hautvillers
4. 18 May I go to London (with Leanne) for five days to install an exhibition at Camerawork
5. 23 May I return to Hautvillers
6. 4 June—opening of a group show of Australian artists in Paris, which I am in with six paintings
7. Mid-June sometime we leave for Australia.

That's our itinerary. We should have time from 1 April until 19 April [...] which looks good for Juniper, I think? Our mothers will be here, but I don't think that's a problem; in fact, I think they would enjoy the film making process—a behind-the-scenes treat for them. I hope to have all my work done before they arrive on 29 March, so as to have 'free' time and thus be much more relaxed than I am at present.

I hope the above dates are good for you and Juniper. I find your idea of me talking to Umberto Eco [1932-2016] very intimidating. It would be great, of course, but I feel very inferior to a person of his standing—I've read *The Name of the Rose* [1980], though I don't remember if I finished it. I've also read [Eco's] *Foucault's Pendulum* [1988]. Both [are] fascinating novels but unfortunately my memory is so bad that I would not be able to talk to him about them, I think. My 'problem' is I'm extremely intuitive in my understanding of things—I read, yes, but I can never recall specifics—ideas click and come out in my work convincingly enough to satisfy more 'rational' thinking critics and observers. But I cannot regurgitate ideas verbally very well in relation to sources. This is why I avoid talking theory, whether it be 'deconstruction' theory or otherwise—I avoid lectures and panel discussions on art practice, etc., because 'rational argument' is required. Intuition is a devalued thought process in a so-called rational world. It is, however, the basis for spiritual knowledge, I believe, which can never be understood rationally. I think the closest science can come to a[n] understanding is through ecology and chaos theory. (Fritjof Capra, I think, could understand and more recently perhaps David Bohm.) Anyway, I don't know—I always get weird around very intelligent people. I feel inferior, of course. Do you know Umberto Eco personally? I would like to meet him, I think. I can't see why he would agree to talk to me at all, but I'm open to it.

I remember Eco's book *Foucault's Pendulum* for its effect it had on me. I was involved with so-called 'New Age' thought many years ago. It was an 'opening' and a revelation to me that I needed at the time—it led to other ideas and philosophies many of which Umberto Eco talks about in that book and I remember being disturbed very deeply by it. Art college shook the foundations of many of my newfound 'new age' beliefs—beliefs that were instrumental in my leaving Telecom for territories unknown. I came out of art college not knowing what to believe anymore—I still don't, and I think that *Foucault's Pendulum* (probably the first book I could manage to actually read right through after leaving college) caused me to shed the last vestiges of 'New Ageness' I might have had left, all I have left is doubt I think. I would like to talk to Eco, but as a student to a teacher and with much humility on my part. I can't say that I remember ever reading anything by him on aesthetics, etc. I would like to—especially since I am to write an essay on 'Aesthetics and Iconography' for an upcoming exhibition in Düsseldorf of Aboriginal art (called *Aratjara—Australian Aboriginal Art*[i]). I find this task of fourteen pages quite daunting, especially since I have little resource material here in the French countryside. I always found writing essays difficult. (I left school at fifteen and never really learnt how to write one). At college, I was dumped into it at a startling pace. I could understand the theory on my intuitive level (helped by the fact of my previous readings in psychology and indeed by my readings on spirituality too), but putting that into the rational context of language was pure hell for me. Of course, I always got H, H+ or at worse C+ for my essays—I'm a perfectionist after all, and I had something to prove too. This essay on 'Aesthetics and Iconography' is currently hanging like a cloud over me. It's due by the end of March and I am currently trying to read what I can.

Well then, Leanne is happy and sends her best wishes to you. I don't know how she stays so happy living with me, she is a source of great strength to me always but I worry where she gets her strength from, certainly not from me. People say we complement each other because we are so opposite in personality. I see how she complements me, but I don't really know how I complement her at all. Sometimes I feel she would be better off without me. I have this neurotic need to be told I'm OK all the time since I am never satisfied in myself that I am—this is a manifestation of my perfectionism again and my conditioning as a child and young adult. I always feel I am walking on quicksand; paintings, I sometimes feel, are like stepping stones in a way that give me something solid to my life—a life filled with doubt. I've revealed a lot about myself in this letter Nadine, perhaps even portraying myself as the cliché of the 'disturbed artist' (it's funny how I'm drawn to Munch, van Gogh and Pollock, but then I am also drawn to many others who don't fit the popular notions of disturbed). In fact, I sometimes feel like a cliché, like my life is a movie rerun (the first time I thought this was when I was thirteen or so). I found your letter very rewarding in its honesty—thank you—your experiences must have [a]ffected you deeply—sexism is of course the same as racism and equally abhor[r]ent. As a male, I find this another disturbing influence or rather 'inheritance' of my conditioning, one which is all too easily reinforced by advertising and daily life, etc. I find some hip hop music by black bands such as Niggers With Attitude [*sic*] (NWA) really disturbing in its anger against women, advocating rape but also just plain violence—their main audience is the white middle-class youth of America. I wonder if it is really NWA's 'attitude' or is it a marketing ploy by record companies with no ethics, like advertising companies it seems. (Women sing in the band.)

I was amazed by the content of your first collage. In the 1950s, this was a very strong thing to do (as it would be today). It seems to be a method of social criticism that turns things around by forcing people to confront the language and attitudes that constitute the problem. I employ this method myself and I sometimes suspect this is NWA's real attitude—that of displaying openly these gross attitudes—I don't know. With my work, what sometimes saves it from reinforcing racist attitudes is the fact I am Aboriginal. With your collage you being a woman does the same thing—it would not be read as a critical response if a man had done it. The shock of confrontation is fundamental—like holding up a mirror so these people can see themselves. I've recently done a small painting in black and Prussian blue. It's of a cross [illustration of painting inserted]; down the centre of the cross, I 'wrote' words in cadmium red using a syringe so that when [the] paint dried, it left raised 'welts' or beads of paint. I painted over these words in a flat vinyl paint, a Prussian blue. I then cut into the beads of paint, making small slashes to reveal the red paint. The words are thus made up of cuts into the 'skin' of the paint. They read: 'Whip me', 'Beat me', 'Spit on me', 'Piss on me', 'Kill me', 'Burn', 'Scatter my ashes' [figures 6a and 6b]. Do you recognise your collage in another form? My

[i] The exhibition's correct title was *Aratjara: Art of the First Australians.*

painting is still a 'history' painting in that the whipping, killing and burning did happen; the spitting, beating and pissing on still happens to Aboriginal people. It refers to an experience not unlike crucifixion, I think.

To change the subject now, I thought you might like to know that the director of Channel 10 is coming to Epernay in February—I don't know why but I am suspicious, perhaps needlessly. Moët seems very interested in having Leanne and I present when he arrives—Jonah is coming in February too, I suspect at the same time. I have not said that I will be here in February as I have been waiting on confirmation of my participation in an artists' workshop in Amazonia, South America, in February. The workshop looks like not coming off, so I guess I'll be in Epernay when this person arrives. We have not been told why he is coming to Epernay but both Jonah and Moët seem very keen for us to be here. You know Jonah very well, perhaps you can draw him out on it—as I said, I am probably being very paranoid needlessly, but it is strange that after all the fuss about a documentary on Channel 10 that now we have the General Manager arriving. Moët is talking about dinners etc., and tours of course, which may be interesting; certainly it will be appetising—the restaurants are superb.

It's late Nadine, and I find I have written another marathon letter. I hope I have said something in it. I didn't talk about my paintings much, perhaps because I am tired of it having just written another statement (for the Paris show I'm in). I'm tired of trying to say the same things in different ways. I may enclose the statement; I am a bit concerned about it actually, but I felt the need to begin it the way I did—with 'I am an Indigenous Australian, my mother is Indigenous Australian and her mother before that and so on for countless generations'. I find I am being drawn into not wanting to be labelled as an 'Aboriginal artist' making 'Aboriginal art'. They are narrow categories fraught with much stereotyping, even hype, and I find myself shying away from it and stating 'I am an artist who is Aboriginal' as a turn-around strategy or so I thought. I find myself questioning is this the case or is it really the same as the many years of denying my Aboriginality—do I not want to be seen as Aboriginal again? I ask myself. It is a dilem[m]a, one of many I face because of my position—perceived to be between two cultures of very different kinds but feeling I belong to neither anymore—an outsider (and yet, I am firmly rooted in Euro-Australian culture but perceived by many as that 'other'). It's an interesting position to be in from a detached perspective, but it's a turmoil when one goes from an 'us' and 'them' situation to an us and them situation all locked into one mind, but subject to strong external force from both sides of the fence. So much for signing off! It used to be that I could not put two words together, but now it seems I can't shut up!

Thanks again Nadine, and I look forward to your next letter—Oh, I must say that I'm excited by most paintings, etc., I have seen. I am always open to influence in my painting, it's that attitude to art that I wish to integrate into my life (life is art—art is life), an attitude to creative living—I think this was Joseph Beuys' [1921-1986] aesthetic; it's a fine goal to strive for, but perhaps my problem is I strive too much and should just relax and let it happen.

Warm regards,

Gordon and Leanne too xx

❖ These previously unpublished letters are from Bennett's personal archive. Bennett wrote to Nadine Amadio, who worked as a scriptwriter for Juniper Films, an Australian production company, and was developing a documentary on Bennett and his art. The film was released in 1994, titled *Black Angels: A Widening Vision*. Bennett's January 1992 correspondence with Amadio functioned as an opportunity for the scriptwriter to understand the artist's practice and philosophy prior to filming, which commenced during Bennett's Moët and Chandon residency in France.

Letter to Eugene Carchesio, 28 February 1992

Dear Eugene,

I thought I would write you a real letter this time Eugene, since you're the only person who keeps in touch anyway. I've enclosed a set of fifty business cards I made for you. I hope you like them. In France they have these business card machines, in shopping centres, railway stations etc., where you insert thirty francs, select a design, and print your own business card. I did some for myself (just a 'straight' card with Bellas Gallery on it).

A couple of weeks ago, I went to see the Marcel Broodthaers retrospective on in Paris. I really liked it a lot and I have since gotten many ideas through reading a catalogue I bought of his work. One of his ideas that really struck a chord was his 'museum'. I've photocopied some extracts from the catalogue for you to read rather than me trying to reiterate it all. Intuitively, I immediately thought of the 'museum of silence'. Marcel's museum existed in obscurity, a non-place; it was a conceptual museum set against the usual organising tendencies of what we know as museums. Museums organise, classify, label and present the result as part of a continuous historical narrative. This 'illusion' of history informs ou[r] present identity as human beings; actually, it probably doesn't get that far—I think it stops short of 'humaness' and gets stuck in Europeans, Americans, Australians, etc. (national identities, materialist identities bound up with the narratives of colonialism). But I'm moving off my original track. We saw the Moët catalogue the other day and your three little works looked very beautiful among all the rest. The patterns [that] I saw as mandalas I saw as [being] about transcendence of self and of identity in the silence of the museum (and I guess museums are about silence, contemplation and knowledge—though I think the 'museum of silence' is about *Gnosis*). Thus, I see your work as pointing toward a centre (to put it crudely, but can it be put any other way with words?). 'I too am a disciple of silence', though that may be hard for some people to believe. My strategy has been to point out what the centre is not, what identity is not, especially for Aboriginal people (because as any metaphysician will tell you, a healthy identity is first necessary before any identity can be transcended). And the attitudes too many people have towards Aborigines is demeaning to their own spirits, let alone to us. I see my work a bit like Ad Reinhardt's [1913-1967] or rather his attitude of refining by defining what (art) is not. I seek to define what identity is not. I don't know if I'm making sense and I'll get to the weather later! Perhaps it's like my back to the centre, circulating around it, [with] us on the periphery.

Anyway, I had in mind a project, a 'non-action' of say, five years duration, to begin when I return to the old country (and it is my old country). Over this five years, I intend to say nothing about my work other than what I have already said in the past (it has become a matter of saying the same things in different ways anyway, so nothing will be lost in this practice). This silence will lay the foundations of a 'museum'—you see, I want to build one. This museum will of course be a 'regional' museum in that I am circling a centre. Now this really brings me to the point. I want to know if it's OK with you to call my museum 'The Museum of Silence—Regional' or something like that. I remember we played with this idea together in the past. This project will be of necessity be a loose collaboration between us. I haven't thought it all through yet but I'm thinking of the body of work I produce in my 'silence' as building the museum. Statements will constitute quotes by other people and myself juxtaposed or ordered in particular ways—I've set down some 'functions' of the regional museum:

1. To collect information, historical or contemporary, and re-distribute it in newly constructed forms, not in a teleological sequence but crossing back and forth across time.

2. To collect and order.
3. To collect and re-order.
4. To collect and disorder.
5. To disrupt the 'chatter' of a complacent historical continuum and create silent spaces for thought.
6. To listen to the wind.

These practices have been part of my painting, but I want to extend them into other areas. It's all at a very preliminary stage so far, so let me know what you think of the name idea—'The Regional Museum of Silence' or 'Regional division' or 'Aboriginal art department' (every museum should have one, ha!). Well, I don't know, perhaps another title entirely would be more appropriate. Marcel Broodthaers had many 'departments'.

Well, it's been warm lately and the sun was out today. By warm, I mean 15° max and 5° min. We went swimming in Reims (heated pool, of course). I told you I'd get to the weather! It's so boring though, all I can think about is the Museum. I hope I still have the energy for it all when I get back (only three-and-a-half months!). I feel like I'm waiting for my release from solitary confinement sometimes.

There are many things I can't put into words about this Museum project—and I guess it's best not to—it's a long-term project that should be open to development and meaning will be generated in an accumulative fashion—intuitively and even autonomously. It will be bigger than both of us, of course, and perhaps even dissolve such notions as centre and periphery, past, present and future, black and white? I liked your idea of using the vacant office space below Bellas [Gallery] as a 'site' for exhibitions—it could be like a large scale 'mini-MOCA'—lots of possibilities there and one fluorescent light could illuminate the whole space easily—great for night shows through that big window—like a giant shadow box? (I can share the power bill and cost.) But these are only possibilities and need never be realised—it should be more spontaneous, I think.

That's about all for now in the continuing saga of life by remote control in France. We have to go to Paris within two weeks for a 'research' trip on museums that I think will be good to have in a film that a film company is producing soon—more about that another time. Leanne is well and happy. We are both a bit disappointed that we will miss the Moët opening in Brisbane—we'll have to have a glass to celebrate here instead. Hope all is well with you and Liza, Eugene, and that the publicity for the Moët machine wasn't too bad—part of the project I'm thinking of is no more interviews, especially with the media. I could say it's 'a period of mourning' in silence. Anyway—did you get those couple of watercolours? Bye for now.

Best wishes,

Gordon. Leanne says hi.

Letter to Eugene Carchesio, 2 March 1992

Dear Eugene,

Just received your letter this morning as I was preparing an envelope to post all this. Thanks for the watercolours—I know just what to do with them and as soon as I finish this I'll go and do it and maybe send them back for your contemplation. Glad to hear you received the watercolours I sent—I was a bit worried. You sound a bit down in your letter—I hope you are OK. Perhaps it is the music and the rain. A symphony of sorrowful songs in every drop. It's nice to know the plants enjoy it. Rain and sunshine and all that lies between—the grand cycle of our ecology (and we humans like to think we are somehow separated from nature!). Sadness and happiness and growth and mowing the lawn on Sundays (now, I don't know why

I added that, I just can't help myself). I like the notion of 'not expecting anything'; it speaks of openness and of flux but still accommodates other things—like setting out on a path with a goal in mind but not being concerned with the expectation of arrival. You know, I tried not to expect anything here in France, much to the annoyance of the press and others who wanted me to predict how I would change, react and develop like I was a fortune teller in a side show; it's been difficult and a real learning and growth process and much of what I learnt about myself has been hard to swallow. It's easy to sit in the suburbs and wax lyrical about openness to the world and then I c[a]me here and found it so hard to put words into practice. To accommodate so much change all at once was a kind of trial by fire. I found out just how 'suburban' I am (not so much in my thought processes, but in my actions, the actuality of my experience). This experience has led me to consider many things—as yet, I have no answers. But yes, I am looking forward to living in Brisbane again with my cat on my lap (I really miss her) and our own backyard and the sun (and the rain). And yet even while saying that, I feel just a little twinge of regret at leaving France—I think because it's the beginning of spring here and I remember how pleasant the summer was, weather wise, although I hated being here at first. Still, we *are* counting the days 'till we leave for home. It will be months before the benefits of this trip and stay overseas will be fully realised (if it can be put that way). I don't think I could ever leave Australia permanently (unless things got really oppressive). I would never be so 'provincial' in leaving for career motives, to be near the 'centre' of the art world as perceived by so many Australian artists, and as demonstrated by last year's New Zealand Moët winner Julia Morison [b. 1952] and John Hurrell [b. 1950] (and Stephen Bambury [b. 1951] before that) who have all moved to France permanently—and Susan Norrie [b. 1953]. I realised Australia is my centre and I am in no way a provincial artist.

I've been going on a bit about that, I've been thinking a lot about how Australia is still a colonial outpost. I've enclosed a copy of my 'statement' for a catalogue being produced in relation to an exhibition I'm in, the exhibition is called *Southern Crossings* and is at a place called Camerawork in London. It's on in May. The essay/statement I did is in the style I've been contemplating for future statements from 'The Regional Museum of Silence' (Department of Angels) I hope you like it.

It's been so gloomy here through the winter months. I thought I was going mad sometimes. It doesn't really rain here, it just drizzles all day, and it's cold, and it's grey and all the landscape is brown and frozen. It didn't snow, which would have brightened things up. I've been keeping really busy with painting but not as much as I would like to do—there seems to be so much paperwork to do what with a diary to keep and receipts to sort and even letters to write, and statements and essays, etc. I'm working harder here now than I was in Brisbane, but then there really is not much else to do here. We can't visit anyone [...] I've got a text to write for a catalogue being produced for a[n] exhibition in Düsseldorf next year. It's on 'Aesthetics and Iconography' and I'm a little worried about my ability to do it well (especially since my research material is extremely limited). The show is called *Aratjara—Aboriginal Art from Australia*. After I've done that, a film crew arrives in April and our two mothers. Then in April/May, we go with our mothers on a European bus tour, in June a group show in Paris, and our mothers leave. We follow shortly after (about 14 June), so keeping busy. Well now I've raved on a bit, but I've filled another page so as not to waste paper (?!). I've started saving all our plastic spring water bottles for an installation I'm thinking of (picture a blue plastic bottle carpet spread over the gallery floor, reflecting light and with labels reading *eau de France* and *source st cyn la source*); it looks good in my head anyway. I hope Moët can ship them back for me! OK, bye again, and say hi to Liza and anyone else you can think of.

Warm regards,
Gordon

❖ These previously unpublished letters are from Bennett's personal archive. Eugene Carchesio was Bennett's friend and frequent collaborator. Both artists continued corresponding and making art during Bennett's stay in Hautvillers, France, from 1991 to 1992, as part of his winning the 1991 Moët and Chandon Australian Art Fellowship.

On Double Standards: An 'Other Perspective', 1992

I followed Mandy Martin's 'Diary from the Centre' ([*Art Monthly Australia*], no. 45) with interest at first but then with rising disgust as I saw [Indigenous artist and grandson of Albert Namatjira] Hermann [sic] Malbunka's [1939-2013] initiative slated as 'a particularly bad example (of) Robert Smithson's heritage'. How on earth can this ground 'painting', whatever its purpose, seriously be associated with any 'heritage' from [American conceptual artist] Robert Smithson [1938-1973]? I thought, that's just too silly for words, but then I read on, and lo and behold I find that 'money is the biggest issue for Aboriginal people'. This was just too much! How dare Mandy Martin judge the Malbunkas on their right, in the late twentieth century, to earn a living by attracting the tourist dollar (instead of suffering for their 'art', like all good artists should)?

This 'holier than thou' hypocrisy by Martin is patently obvious in her betrayal of playwright Marilyn Bray's private disclosure to her concerning the motivation for writing another play, in a blatant judgement of not just Ms Bray but all Aboriginal people!

I was reminded of an art student who interviewed me for her assignment on 'Aboriginal art'. One of her first questions was: 'Do you make Aboriginal art for the money?' How many contemporary artists would get a question like that if not for the prejudice of opinion against 'Aboriginal' art and artists—an extension of the racism that permeates contemporary Australian culture like a cancer? A prejudice that is fostered by ill-considered remarks, like Mandy Martin's, which lump all Aboriginal people and their art together as one homogenous whole. A prejudice that is fostered in art schools by the generalised accusations of 'tourist' or 'airport' art!

The same art student 'borrowed' a tape I had made of our conversation, promising to return it once she had written her assignment. Later I discovered she had handed the tape in as part of her assignment! She had ripped me off in the grand Euro-Australian tradition. Should I judge all Euro-Australian art students, and by extension artists, by her example? Should I judge all Euro-Australian art ... by what I can see in weekend markets, tourist stops, motel/hotel rooms and yes, even in airports (I find the same kitsch here in Europe)? Is the tradition of nostalgic Australiana painting representative of all Euro-Australian art? Of course not!

Mandy Martin goes on to describe how the patterning and design in 'Aboriginal art' becomes more 'explicable from the air'. A revelation indeed when one considers that earlier in the piece Martin relates how exciting certain Aboriginal people's first attempt at 'landscape' was! It's painfully obvious that Ms Martin is unable to shift her perspective on landscape painting away from the 'pretty(ness)' of the MacDonnell Ranges and the grand operatic panorama of her Eurocentric, and no doubt saleable, vision! (Not to mention the 'pretty dingoes'—babies beware!)

Martin's narrow, blinkered outlook is very nicely counterpointed by the paternalism of Jennifer Isaacs' writing about the same ground 'painting' project by the Malbunkas in the article following 'Diary from the Centre'. Isaacs condescendingly points to a 'prevailing attitude that Aborigines should be allowed to make their own mistakes'. It seems that earning a living by exploiting one's culture, in Hermann [sic] Malbunka's case at least, is to be considered a mistake? Is the $30 million a year (*The Courier Mail*, 4 August 1990) generated by tourists' interest in Aboriginal culture and art (some of which comes from the sale of books on 'Aboriginal art') considered a mistake? The only mistakes made are when this money doesn't find its way into Aboriginal pockets. I can see how letting Aborigines make their own mistakes in this case can be very convenient and indeed lucrative.

It seems that Aboriginal people are now seen as not only lazy dole-bludging parasites (as I was informed by a Venezuelan orchestra conductor on a train out of Berlin), but also as money-grubbing producers of tourist kitsch!

In the case of playwright Marilyn Bray, who dared confide to Mandy Martin that money was a motive for writing a play (a blasphemy that any pure (white) artist would never ever consider for a moment, I'm sure!), I would like to point out that Anselm Kiefer [b.1945], 'perhaps the greatest living artist' (*Art Monthly* [*Australia*], same issue), employs thirty people in his workshop. This is a European tradition that I am not criticising, but merely wish to point out that art in Europe and America is big business (as if you didn't know) and is produced on such an industrial scale that to deny that money is not a consideration is just plain ludicrous. A visit to any European art fair would shatter even the most hard-core romantic's illusions.

I ask, when will the hypocritical double standards and paternalism, first introduced by the missionaries and now perpetuated it seems by such judgemental 'pure at heart' artists such as Mandy Martin and others, ever cease? I ask you, dear Eurocentric reader, when will 'you' look outside of your blinkers and see not 'Aborigines'—a European construct replete with centuries of your misguided notions of the 'primitive' or 'noble savage'—and see instead people? People with the same needs as your own, that of self-respect and personal dignity which for some of 'us' is gained by earning what should be a respectable living, by the general standards of contemporary Australian culture, but which it seems is still 'qualified' by the double standard of those who would require of Indigenous Australians high ideals they themselves can never attain.

Gordon Bennett, Artist-in-Residence
Moët & Chandon, Hautvillers, France

❖ This letter was originally published in *Art Monthly Australia* 47 (1992): 26-27. This letter is reproduced courtesy of *Art Monthly Australasia*.

Letter to Michael O'Ferrall, 5 June 1992

Dear Michael,

Thanks for your letter, it was good to hear from you. I think your observations on Australia as a lost orphan is very apt. There is a definite quality of not letting go of the apron strings of 'Mother' England—I wish Australia would take a leap into adulthood (or at the very least adolescence!), but I'm being too cynical. It would be nice though if the explorer would let go of the pole; however, after eleven months in this exotic world, I know how hard that is to do.

[...]

The *Confess Conceal* show sounds good. Thanks for all the details; sounds like hard work to me. I'm glad I'm not a curator! I find it tough enough being an individual artist, let alone organising a bunch of artists for anything other than a barbeque.

[...]

Back on the writing subject. I wrote a fourteen-page essay for an exhibition catalogue—*Aratjara—Australian Aboriginal Art* curated by Bernhard Lüthi in Düsseldorf. I've enclosed a copy of it for your information [p. 27]. It's being published first in a new German art magazine called *Art Vector* (in German) with six black-and-white reproductions [of Bennett's work]. It was very tiring to write this essay, but it seems to be paying off at least—the subject was aesthetics and iconography. Germany seems to me a much more exciting place for art than France. I saw a Mike Kelley show—same opening night as [Jeff] Koons [b.1955] and also a [Georg] Baselitz [b.1938] show up in Cologne—Bernhard Lüthi showed us around. I saw the two large [Joseph] Beuys retrospectives at Knefeld and Düsseldorf too.

I like Baselitz for some perverse reason—I'm always drawn to so-called 'expressionists'; of course, I have to be careful in which circles I say that if I don't want to attract howls of derision. The 'school of cool' is very powerful in Brisbane and elsewhere too—very anti-gesture, anti-emotion, and they think that's intelligent. Seems to me very stupid to polarise emotion/intelligence. It's like saying the day is better than the night, you need both for the function of the world and all the changing light in between. Some people can only think in such gross 'binary oppositional' terms. Baselitz's sculpture is so raw and 'dumb' that I'm drawn to them; perhaps I might like to use them as a starting point for something of my own later. [...]

❖ This previously unpublished letter is from Bennett's personal archive. Michael O'Ferrall (1945-2013) was the Curator of Aboriginal and Asian art at the Art Gallery of Western Australia, Perth, and author of an essay on Bennett's work 'On Other Perspectives' included in *Gordon Bennett, Paintings 1987-1991* (Epernay, FR: Moet and Chandon, 1992), n.p.

Letter to Peter Bellas, 1993

Dear Peter,

Following is a copy of a fax I intend to send to Galerie Boomerang regarding [the] show *Who's Afraid of Black, Red & Yella?* After all the discussions I had with Bernhard Lüthi and other artists in Düsseldorf concerning the race bias in art exhibitions regarding artists 'of colour' etc, I believe it would be stupid of me to show in an ethnographic museum. That would demonstrate to people that I know my 'place'. It also serves to pigeonhole me to the extent that I would be even more susceptible to being Aboriginal first and an artist second. An ethnographic museum positions race, culture, art in that order. Thus, the viewer enters with preconceptions about race, culture, art of an 'other'. As you know, I only 'know' Western culture and operate immersed (swimming) in this culture while exploring its representations of the 'other' namely Aboriginal (which I know of only through a Western representation). To 'other' myself for the sake of a show in Rotterdam would be a mistake given the contextualising site of an ethnographic museum.

G.B.

❖ This previously unpublished letter is from Bennett's personal archive.

Letters from 'Home Sweet Home' series, 1993–94

Shadow monsters from the id 27-4-94

Please excuse me, I don't mean to offend. I was just remembering the many years I've spent living in the suburbs. All the parties I've been to, the barbeques, the discos and pubs, etc. I've seen a lot of violence in my time people drinking and becoming aggressive, punching out walls or each other. I've heard about the rapes, the murders, the robberies and general assaults. I've been the victim of violent assaults myself, several times. In fact, I learnt to feel unsafe in crowds of people and sometimes I'm still unable to enter a crowded room. I feel like an outsider sometimes, and even a victim. I see and hear all this violence in this society, but I see and hear another kind of violence that is just as prevalent. It's the psychic violence directed towards Aboriginal people and it disables and scars just as much as the physical violence that is perpetrated daily in the general non-Aboriginal community. I remember the abuse I've heard about us being drunks, violent, unable to look after our children, immoral, lazy, bludgers who can't seem to look after themselves, and more, much, much more, too much more. It seems to me that Aboriginal people are the dumping ground for all those human traits the non-Aboriginal community can't seem to accept in their own behaviour; all that is savage, uncivilised, and even primitive (by their own definition) in their own behaviour, as can be seen in the daily newspapers and on TV. It's like all that is repressed, pushed away to be unconsciously dumped onto Aborigines as the black shadow monsters from the id.

G Bennett 4-04PM

Suburban boyz have brown eyes too 22-9-93 11-47AM

Please excuse me, I don't mean to offend but I was remembering some of the things my friends would do as teenagers—somethings I guess a 'shrink' would call 'ego development'. I used to hear about this thing called 'chucking a brown eye'. It was performed as a kind of expression, usually out of speeding car windows aimed at no-one in particular. While I never actually participated myself (perhaps I was ashamed of my bum—I don't know), I did see it performed a few times. However, the extent of my participation never went as far as exposing myself. I did indulge in the yelling of certain statements out of car windows. Some of these statements were aimed at the male partners of pretty girls walking along the street. 'Fuck her mate, we did!' or 'Spit her out mate, you never know where she's been!' were two of the most popular. Everyone would break up in laughter. If a lone girl was unlucky enough to be on the street when we drove by, she would get 'drop your pants', accompanied by loud wolf whistles and howls of laughter. I don't recount these teen memories with any fondness; in fact, I am very ashamed of some of the things I did in order to fit in with my peers, and like any young person I did so want to fit in. I guess it was the same for many teenagers growing up in the suburbs of Brisbane. I feel compelled to add that I'm not talking about Aboriginal teenagers here, all my friends were 'white'—I was the only boong on the block.

G Bennett 12-05PM

Bathtime 22-9-93 11-25AM

Please excuse me, I don't mean to offend but I was recently reading a book on child abuse, and its [e]ffect on the victim in later adult life, and came across some case studies of women who sexually abuse their male children. It said how in most cases the general public didn't really consider this type of thing as abuse; rather, they thought that the child had somehow 'got lucky', that the abuse was somehow an initiation into manhood and not really abuse of a small child's trust and innocence at all. I became furious. I couldn't understand. It's different with a girl it seems. It's a terrible violation of a child's trust if a father acts in a

sexual way with her, but for a mother to act sexually towards a small boy is somehow a lucky break. How can an adult male speak about these things to his peers, his friends, I began to ponder. How can he relate the feelings of anger that seem to come from nowhere and for no reason, or the feelings of wanting to punch or attack a person he is talking to in a conversation, a feeling that can switch just suddenly into an urge to kiss that person, or worse, to put his dick in that person's mouth, all urges that feel beyond his capacity to control, let alone understand? How does the abused child, as an adult male, talk about such feelings to his male peers? What reaction does he get: a clap on the back, have another beer, and an exclamation—'shit mate, I didn't get my first until I was fifteen years old!'
G Bennett 11-45AM

A little healthy competition 23-9-93 10-13AM

Please excuse me, I don't mean to offend. I was remembering something about my teenage years, the so-called 'ego development' years, that seems to me to sum up this culture's obsession with competition. I think it was called a wanking competition; twenty cents in the middle and whoever can ejaculate the furthest wins. I'm not sure how it went, I never participated myself. I can only speculate as to how one would rise to the occasion. Twenty cents never seemed like much incentive to me, so I guess there was some other, more obscure incentive to win. I suppose the size of one's penis had something to do with it. One or two centimeters in length might just make the difference, provided the trajectory was a constant. But how to get an erection in the first place was the baffling question. Twenty cents would not work for me. Perhaps an element of imagination was required. Did the participants see in their 'mind's eye' a naked woman for instance? If so, what did she look like and was it someone known to the participant, a classmate, a friend's sister or maybe a movie star? I guess I'll never know. I couldn't bring myself to ask. Nobody ever asks why. The object of the whole thing seemed to be to get as many sticky coins as possible. I suppose the closest I ever came to understanding the whole principle was in seeing who could piss the highest on the urinal wall, but there was never any money in that.
G Bennett 10-36AM

Murder/Suicide 22-9-93 11-15AM

Please excuse me, I don't mean to offend, but I keep seeing and hearing all this violence on television. I don't mean the stuff in the movies, but what's on the news. You know, those people who seem to explode, who go out and get a gun and start shooting people. The ones who disturb me the most are the guys who shoot their families before shooting themselves, like they've got the right to take the wife and children with them, like so much property. Why can't people seek help before it gets to that stage? I guess I do know why men don't ask for help. You can't really get beyond the couple of beers and a pat-on-the-back stage of so-called mateship. To admit you can't cope or need help is seen as weakness. It's much easier to bail out, pull the pin, maybe even take a few of the bastards with you. It's a scandal that therapy costs more than a gun, but then I guess a therapist has to earn a living too. It's more important to maintain the illusion of the 'great Australian dream' than to maintain your mental health, right? Or perhaps use your wife or children as scapegoats? A living hell on a quarter acre block.
G Bennett 4-44PM

Home sweet home 30-9-93 10-37AM

Please excuse me, I don't mean to offend. I was just reflecting on the 'great Australian dream'. Leanne and I own our house in the outer northern suburbs of Brisbane. We saved like crazy to pay it off. All that

time getting up in the morning and going to work, coming home, going to work, coming home, going to sleep and getting up again, like clockwork toys. Spending weekends in the garden, mowing, maintaining the house. We put a lot of time and effort into it—but for what? So I could go to the backyard barbie with the neighbours, have a sense of community, have children, get drunk, watch TV. I think it was the barbeques that got to me in the end. The party talk both at work and around the neighbourhood. The subject of Aborigines always came up. It was then that I felt an outsider. I could not fit in. The bloody boongs, the fucking coons, abo's, niggers—put them in a house and the first thing they do is burn it down. Try and imagine what it's like, sitting quietly, listening to this shit while your stomach turns in knots—try to fit in, keep the peace; after all, you live right next door, right? Who needs to be a target for all that bullshit—life's tough enough as it is. So, there I sit, in a quiet rage, hoping no-one will notice my tan, my nose, my lips, my profile, because if I start trouble by disagreeing, then that would be typical of a damn coon wouldn't it?
G Bennett 10-54AM

A little discipline 22-9-93 12-56PM

Please excuse me, I don't mean to offend but I've been seeing and reading about the level of child abuse in this society and I am quite shocked by the severity of some of the cases. I don't understand why a person would give birth to a baby and then wrap it in plastic and throw it in a garbage bin. To treat a life like so much garbage. I find I cannot condemn such a person completely. I feel more sadness than righteous about such events. I don't know why. Perhaps it's because I do feel that I understand cycles of violence. I hate to hear our neighbours in the suburbs yell at their children. They say things they wouldn't say to their dogs. It's usually accompanied by physical violence too, as if verbal abuse was not enough. Why must discipline be interpreted as violence and abuse? Is there a difference between being treated like garbage through abusive language and physical violence (masquerading as discipline) and being wrapped in plastic and thrown into a garbage bin? You may think there's a world of difference. I'm not so certain. How can a person explain the compulsion to hurt an innocent child—would anyone listen? How does an abused child interact, as an adult, with their own children, especially when the abuse has been repressed, forgotten, or even accepted as normal parenting? How is one to understand the compulsion to hurt a child? I'm no expert, I can't explain it, but when I see the results on television or read about it in the newspapers or I hear the abuse floating across the fence at home, I feel like screaming. Fleeting memories of abuse rattle in my head also. I feel compelled to add that all my neighbours are white. I'm the only nigger in the neighbourhood.
G Bennett 2-52PM

❖ This text is transcribed from the letters that comprise part of Bennett's series 'Home Sweet Home' (1993-94, figures 22 and 23).

Letter to John Laws, 3 June 1994

Dear John Laws,

I am writing in response to your article in the *Sunday Telegraph*, 29 May [1994], page 38, entitled 'Beware the White Supremacists'. Thank you for your comments regarding this issue. It is a fear of mine that these people are coming here and bringing their insane hatreds with them. They will find many people who are willing to listen to them, unfortunately.

You are dead right when you say that 'much of the Aboriginal discrimination (racism) is institutionalised'. It starts in schools with the way Australian children are educated in Australian history and Aboriginal culture (singular!). I know this from my own experience as an Aboriginal person, able to pass for white, educated in 'mainstream' Australia. In the workforce from age fifteen, I listened to all the derogatory remarks and racist opinions being circulated around until I could not bear it anymore and quit my job to study art. I was able to understand their racism, though I could not bear it, as ignorance of Australian history, Aboriginal cultures and the role Aboriginal people played in the founding of modern-day Australia.

There was a strong belief that 'settlement' was a peaceful process and that Aboriginal people were weak or too stupid to fight for their land. There was no recognition of the role Aboriginal people played in 'opening' up this country by guiding and aiding the white explorers or the role we played in the pastoral industry under appalling conditions. We should be respected for all of these roles, but we are not. Jackie Jackie was an Aboriginal hero who saved a white explorer's life. Is he remembered for this? No, he is the butt of racist jokes.

All this is to say that Aboriginal 'problems' are white Australia's problems too. During the bicentennial, many people I know genuinely did not understand why Aborigines protested. Indeed, they thought we should be grateful! Given the history of abuse, murder and maltreatment, including the psychological abuse I understand so well, there is no reason to feel grateful except to those people who genuinely felt for us as human beings—it is with sadness that I feel these people to be a minority. It seems that only these people who understand the human needs of self-esteem, pride, confidence and humility can accommodate the full version of Australian history—the 'good' with the 'bad', so to speak—and still be proud Australians. Others, it seems, need Aboriginal silence and for Aborigines to 'forget the past'—even though we still labour under the same kinds of prejudice imported in 1788—in order to be proud of our 'pioneer spirit'. In a country that reveres the 'fallen warrior' and has monuments across the land emblazoned with 'Lest we forget', Aboriginal silence and forgetfulness is a strange recipe for racial harmony. Let's not forget also that Aboriginal people fought overseas too—only for less pay and in fact 'illegally' as we weren't even considered citizens!

Mr Laws, all I am trying to say is that a monument to an Australian who fought and died defending their land, who bled on their own soil, will not be offensive to the kind of Australian who is not prejudiced by ignorance. It will only be offensive to those people who you identify as 'falling over themselves to denounce Indigenous people'; to those blinded by hate and ignorance. Would it be so divisive to recognise that Aboriginal people fought long and hard for our country, and are still doing so, but through the courts? Is it so divisive to recognise that our 'pioneers' were not such pure at heart individuals and that savagery is a *human* trait rather than a racial one? Is it so hard to recognise that the European 'settlers' can also be seen as 'invaders' by acknowledging the other side of the frontier where there were pioneers of a different race coming to terms with equally new circumstances and harsh realities?

After such a fine start to your article, I was very sad to see it degenerate into sarcastic remarks in inverted commas. Do you think that silence and non-recognition of Aboriginal history (which is the missing half of a *mature* Australian history) will foster harmony or rather just perpetuate the problems of white ignorance and thus fuel the blind hatred of those who denounce us? Why would a monument to Pemulwuy [1750-1802] be so offensive? Here was a man who fought tremendous odds with inferior weapons and became very respected as a clever and brave adversary at the time. He was an underdog, a rebel who never gave up until he was killed. He deserves to be remembered by us and respected as an Australian by those who revere the fallen warriors of our nation.

There cannot be 'reconciliation' without recognition of both our fight for our country and our aid in its development. There can never be reconciliation while ignorance is fostered. This is not to 'pick at old wounds' but to heal wounds that have festered. Please, try and understand that.

I find it very offensive when people say that Aborigines did not fight for our country or when people say that we, as a people, actually came up with a 'lotto win' when we were colonised by the English rather than someone else. It is a fact [that] 10,000 Aboriginal people died in skirmishes north of the Tropic of Capricorn in north Queensland alone in the seventy years between 1861 and the early 1930s. Compare this figure to the 5000 Europeans from the same area who died overseas in the five wars between the Boer War and the end of the Vietnam War—a similar time period. This country was taken by force. There is no doubt about it. Why is white Australia so reluctant to admit this? To me, your sarcasm was most offensive and your compassion and recognition of Aboriginal peoples' burden of discrimination is severely compromised by your last few assertions in your article. You have a lot of power through your media access, please use it to foster understanding rather than fuelling the ignorance of those you are obviously at pains to distance yourself from. Please take my comments as positive criticism, as most of what you said I agree with. I just could not understand the way your comments seemed to reverse towards the last few paragraphs. Please try and understand.

Yours sincerely,

Gordon Bennett

❖ This text is transcribed from a previously unpublished letter from Bennett's personal archive. Bennett wrote to John Laws following the publication of Laws' article 'Beware the White Supremacists', *The Sunday Telegraph,* 29 May 1994, 38.

Critiquing the Critic: An Open Letter to Sue Smith (Art Critic for *The Courier Mail*), 11 May 1995

Dear Sue Smith,

Thank you for reviewing my show. Any publicity is good publicity, or so the story goes. It is unfortunate that you missed the point of most of the work entirely. To demonstrate this publicly, as you have done, must be embarrassing for you. At least it would be if you could realise your mistakes. Please talk to me about the work in future. You have only demonstrated your own prejudices (which was the point of the 'mirror' works in one sense, but not of the mirror lined boxes!). This is obvious in the way you have both described and interpreted the work.

First of all, the work *Aborigine Painting (White Obelisk) The Inland Sea*[i] is not the 'piece de resistance' [*sic*] of the show, as you described it, nor is it 'earnestly historical' as you interpret it—describing myself as a 'history painter' is an ironic strategy. It is meant to be, and is, 'overblown', i.e., overly dramatic, even stupid. [I]t is about mock heroics, hence the use of [Roy] Lichtenstein's mock expressionist brush stroke throughout the exhibition (perhaps you are unaware of the rivalry that existed between the 'Abstract Expressionists' and the 'Pop' artists?). The Aborigine squatting quietly in the corner has more to do with stereotype than the theme of the historical 'search for the inland sea' (which is a very overblown historical narrative!), a point you obviously missed in regard to your expectations of, and search for, a theme of 'oppression', and your need to classify me as both 'Aboriginal' and 'urban Aboriginal' artist. As for the 'heavy morass of obscure academic references', I put academic references in my work as a means to provoke thought, even to exceed stereotype, both among those viewers who would not find Kant and Hegel et al. 'obscure', and among those who may be interested enough to find out more for themselves. You seem to be neither.

Furthermore, as far as 'contemporary answer to historic masterpieces' goes, I am no more interested in mythologising, documenting, or dramatising colonial Australian narratives of 'exploration', and so-called

[i] According to Leanne Bennett this work was subsequently retitled by Bennett to *Big Baroque Painting (The Inland Sea)* (1995).

'settlement', than I am in creating a 'masterpiece'. After all, my source for the 'early explorer in a boat' is a primary school reader in *comic strip*-form, which is hardly the stuff of historical masterpieces!

History painting, you seem to be saying, has a set of clearly defined qualities in order to be successful, but you do not suggest what your conception of 'successful' would be? Surely you could not be referring to the 'social and moral' qualities of a colonial Australia which still refuses to cut the apron strings from mother England? Given the shameful attitudes to Aboriginal people and such realities as a still rising deaths in custody and mortality rate! Also, given my reality as an artist of Aboriginal descent educated and working in a postcolonial climate, I can only say that to criticise my work with such preconceptions says more about you and your attitude than it does about my painting! And this from someone expecting themes of oppression? Shades of Arthur Tunstall!

Finally, the only thing I could lay claim to having in common with [Théodore] Gericault's *Raft of the Medusa* [1818–19] is to be critical of colonial ambitions of exploitation at the expense of human life, which was one political aspect of that work, and maybe a 'large eccentric and sprawling composition' or two.

Now to the really malicious part of your review, 'Sophomorically silly floor sculptures' indeed! The only thing sophomorically silly was your literal and intellectually vacuous interpretation of these works. First of all, you seem to have missed the relationship between each floor piece and the paintings they were located directly in front of. Obviously, they dealt with negative stereotyping of Aboriginal people but they go beyond a simplistic 'chastisement', and the rather stupid 'you are "white" so you must be responsible too' inference such a chastisement may invoke in the simple-minded.

Short of spoon-feeding you all together, I can tell you that the work refers to the reductive (literally 'box-like' or 'packaged') nature of stereotype, the kind of effect such stereotypes can have on the human spirit of real people (i.e., the quotes from victims of such racist abuse in the paintings, and the fact that a 15-year-old girl was expelled from a Mackay high school only last month for exacting her own sense of justice on another student for similar racist abuse—abuse that went unpunished by school authorities), and the prevalence of such views in regard to the fact that such blatantly racist advertising could ever have been created with impunity in the early part of this century, to the facts of an Aboriginal persons memory of such abuse in the 1970s and the facts of those views and beliefs today as the attitude of Arthur Tunstall, the Mackay high school, and the debate on racism in football attest.

You also neglected the obvious references to psychoanalysis in the paintings associated with the boxes and in the works on paper. Psychoanalysis for me is never 'art theory' or 'obscure academic reference', or the subject of a humorous stereotyping—as found in cheap magazines of the kind Richard Prince [b. 1949] uses—but is a way I have come to exceed the debilitating [e]ffects of racism on my spirit. The interiors of the boxes suggest a far more complex contents than the racist exterior surface could ever imply or allow.

With the mirror lining, I intended a metaphor for complexity and the indescribable (with language) 'reality' of the human mind with its constant flow of thoughts, knowledge, memories of the past, experience of the present and imaginations of a better future (hopes, desires and fears, reflections of/on self and that relationship to history, philosophical speculations and [analyses of] the realities of 'being-in-the-world'; as the work on paper allude to!). The clues are there, throughout the show, for those who wish to spend the time and make the effort to find and connect them.

Those who 'expect' to find only what their preconceptions can allow will undoubtedly look into the mirrored box, as you have, and only see themselves ('the true face of racism'? That is not for me to say, nor would I if I thought it so!), perhaps they too might spend the rest of their time looking for what they consider to be 'leaden paint' and 'stiff drawing', based on an aesthetic that I remain defiantly opposed to and actively subversive of. I disagree with Jules Olitski [1922-2007] who, like myself and Sue Smith, has neither a monopoly on truth nor the last word on painting!

Which brings me to the 'rarefied air of 1920s Constructivist-style abstraction'. My works are indeed characterised by 'clumsy carpentry' and in some cases a 'cluttered composition'. I am glad that you at least noticed that much. Unfortunately, you gave these works the same superficial and 'sophomoric' interpretation as you did with every work you mention in your review. These '(re)Constructions' do indeed refer to Constructivism, a reference that cannot be avoided even if I myself were to be totally ignorant of art history. However, they are no more intended to resurrect such a 'style', or the philosophical climate and aspirations of the 'high' modernism of that period (as the '(re)Construction' of the titles may imply to the superficially inclined—thankfully, even you didn't go that deeply into it!), than they are intended to be well crafted.

These works too must be read in relation to the other works in the exhibition as indeed the other works must be read in regard of these constructions and in regard of my ongoing oeuvre (without the stereotype of an 'Aboriginal' art as it currently stands—at least in your mind). If you had taken note of the psychoanalysis aspect of the other works in the room, one of which includes a (re)Construction, and also talked with me about the work, inarticulate as I am, then it may have dawned on you that these works are about picking up the pieces of lives and cultures shattered by the very philosophies of modernity, colonialism and enlightenment that was the climate which gave succour to and birth to Constructivism in the first place. Rather, I relate these works to the Dadaists and Kurt Schwitters [1887-1948], but that is probably a bit of 'obscure academia'.

In any case, the point is that these works are 'poor' in the sense of the materials used and the way they are 'cluttered' by things that don't quite fit properly—in fact, scraps of timber that I found lying around building sites. Even the pieces that were left over after making the misshapen geometric forms were used in the works. While some aspects of the work refer to 'newness' and 'modern' industrial materials, such as the screws with their shiny surfaces, they are used in a way that is 'poor' and they remain exposed and misaligned. The construction and poor 'clumsy carpentry', as you observed, and the 'skew' nailing of old bent and rusty nails, which are not as visible as the screws, but which are equally awkward, is meant as a metaphor for the piecing together of cultural and family relations, and histories, much of which is filtered and distorted through a European 'mirror' image of ourselves.

Aboriginal psychologies have been colonised equally as much as our landscape and modes of self-representation (painting included). [Hence], the 'clumsy' and 'cluttered' compositions, the not-quite-'right' feel, which it seems I successfully achieved. 'Diminished' is a good word to describe these works, but not in the way you meant it. Rather in a sense that refers to the effects of a colonial 'enlightenment' on the people it purports to have 'uplifted'. These are 'coats of arms' (I won't spoon-feed you on that one), that we make do with, and add to, in order to go forth into the world and wear with what pride we can muster. As such, they must bear the brunt of the ignorance, the sniggering, and the fully blown racism of those puffed up individuals and groups, who in their ignorance still subscribe to a kind of Social Darwinism that glorifies destruction and murder as the 'price of progress'.

The painted supports for these (re)constructions are in fact the backdrops from the 'Video Performance' *D.U.H!* [1994] which was later painted black and used as a floor piece in my Sutton Gallery exhibition in Melbourne last year titled *Mirror Mirror (The Inland Sea)*. The video of *D.U.H!* was shown as part of the total installation which involved the viewer having to walk on the black paintings in order to view the work. (See *Art and Australia* 32, no. 3 for information on that work.)

So, even the support for these constructions has been thoroughly walked on. I did not repaint them or clean them in any way prior to using them. The past, the present and the future are interwoven as they are in the reality of everyday existence. The experience of being walked on is 'remembered' by the material. It carries the traces into its future, the present reality of tomorrow. The suit in the next room was also made from this material as was the object in the video you described, not surprisingly, as 'baffling'—although the 'box' in this work was made before the *D.U.H!* video and so was not walked on; it was, however made to my body specifications as was the suit on the wall next to it.

The video you found so 'baffling', as well as the rest of the work in the exhibition which you dismissed as 'slight offerings' and as a 'side show' were all integral to the overall show, each referring to the others, a point you so patently and painfully failed to grasp. I don't know how you managed to see a scowl on my face when my head was totally covered, except for eye slits, by white bandages. That fact coupled with the way in which the images totally obliterate my head most of the time certainly 'baffles' me and says much about your powers of observation.

The point of the piece, in part at least, is the field of representation that is the television screen. This work is a digitally manipulated and enhanced video performance. It was a studio-based event with the intent of producing a work to be viewed on a television or video screen—a medi[um] which reflects and shapes the culture of our nation and provides a 'window' through which to view the culture of others (a quote from the government's 'Creative Nation' policy document).

I am interested in the field of reproduction that is the television screen and how it mirrors the culture in which it operates. The screen is in perpetual flux and may be seen as a 'tabula rasa' until it receives a signal that stimulates the dot matrix into constructing identifiable images in what appears as a seamless flow.

The notion of guilt refers to a repressed Australian history which denies Aboriginal people any dignified position in the cultural heritage of Australia; first as a people who fought, and are still fighting, for their country but also as a people who both explored the encroaching colonial culture and who acted as guides and laboured in the service of the colonists only to be denied the fruits of such labour.

The work aims for a cathartic response and seeks to invoke a fluid notion of identity as 'sites' which flow through the conscious mind, informing and constructing our sense of self—a remembering of experience, knowledge and history from many diverse dismembered and repressed fragments.

I wish to explore the spaces between illusory opposites of black/white, civilised/savage, right/wrong which have excluded Aboriginal people from becoming an essential element of Australian identity, a vital expression of who we all are ('Creative Nation' again). I seek the positivity in deconstructing an *Australian* identity which excludes and measures itself against the mirror reflection of a constructed Aboriginal 'other'. Thus, the use of Lichtenstein's *Mirror No 6* of 1971 in the paintings and titling of those works as 'Mirrors'.

I hope this letter has cleared up your misunderstanding of my work and those individuals of the viewing public who may actually believe what you say! As for most of the viewing public, and those who have commented to me on the work in this exhibition, your comments are better described by your own words: Sophomorically silly.

I must congratulate you on your turn of phrase, even though I found some of them quite malicious and hurtful in their intent. However, I do invite you to review further exhibitions of mine but please do try to make an effort to understand, and do try to do some research, or at least talk to me!

Yours sincerely,
Gordon Bennett

❖ This previously unpublished letter is from Bennett's personal archive. Bennett wrote to Sue Smith following the publication of her review of his 1995 exhibition *BLACK: Fear of Shadows* at Bellas Gallery, Brisbane. Bennett references this body of work in his interview with Christopher Chapman on page 126. Smith's article is reprinted below:

> Followers of urban Aboriginal artist Gordon Bennett, a self-described 'history painter', will know what to expect from his latest show. There are a few diversions, but Bennett mainly continues to address issues of Aboriginality, racism and cultural history. On view are some works on paper, a couple of sophomorically silly floor sculptures (read the rude racists' words, and properly chastened, look into mirrors to discover the true face of racism!), a surprising series of wall sculptures (geometrical plywood reliefs whose rarefied air of 1920s Constructivist-style abstraction is unfortunately diminished by cluttered compositions and clumsy carpentry) and a video of baffling 'performance' in which the artist stalks about grim-faced while cracking a bullwhip. These slight offerings are, however, but a sideshow to the main event: the paintings, which may appear (depending upon your point of view) either as works of suave post-modernity or of tediously pedantic intellectualism. Previously, the tenor of Bennett's best work has been one of wry intelligence and savage anger, focusing on the ways in which popular culture, our mythologised history, and even the structures of high art itself, have all at times been used as agents of racist social conditioning. His most powerful earlier paintings have tended to appeal to the mind and the heart rather than to the eye, to be formally simply but devastatingly effective. But this latest work is becoming increasingly baroque and self-conscious in its complexity, perhaps too long shackled to an arid post-modernist methodology. There is also the added problem that Bennett's limited technique seems to be unequal to his new epic ambitions. Take, for instance, the piece de resistance [*sic*] of this show, a large, eccentric, sprawling composition, entitled, *Aborigine Painting (White Obelisk) The Inland Sea*. Whatever passions the theme of oppression might conceivably arouse in the viewer are quickly snuffed out under the heavy morass of obscure academic references (including an early explorer on a boat, appropriations from modernist painters Roy Lichtenstein and Jackson Pollock, skulls and bones, an Aboriginal elder, dot painting, and the Aboriginal colours of red, yellow and black). Earnestly historicist, stiffly drawn and leadenly painted, this overblown museum piece seems in some respects intended as a contemporary answer to such earlier historic masterpieces as Gericault's *The Raft of the Medusa*, but lacks the dynamic intertwining of aesthetic, social and moral qualities which is the essence of successful history painting in any era. In concentrating so hard on history, Bennett seems to have forgotten, as the American painter Jules Olitski once remarked, that 'What is of importance in painting is paint'. Sue Smith, 'Heavy Hand Snuffs Out Art's Impact', *The Courier Mail*, 11 May 1995, 32.

Letter to Lucienne Fontannaz, 17 August 1995

Dear Lucienne,

Thanks for the fax. In the 'Relative/Absolute' series [1991-92; figure 24] I was thinking about the relationship between language and the object 'in the world' that it describes or refers to. The signifier and the signified.

I was thinking of the relativity of language and the idea of the absolute—as in 'complete; perfect'. Or as in free from limitations, restrictions, or exceptions—unqualified. For instance, the word water, the sound of the word itself as it is spoken, does not mean water, is not water the element itself, but is an arbitrary noise, an abstract sign that refers to, but is separate from, water itself. Whether you call it *aqua, nukou, l'eau, gulli* or whatever, it is still a thing that is life sustaining—a thing that exists with the same properties under different names (arbitrary signifiers).

I was musing on the relationships between such basic human traits, or of just 'being' when I did these works. I was looking for what connects things rather than what makes things different. I was thinking what is fundamentally the same in France and in Australia or anywhere—man, woman, child, fire, water, air (the sky), earth (the circle), etc. The relativity of language, and also its reductive properties are brought into question (I hope). I guess the 'absolute' may be referring to the spiritual, essential qualities of the signifieds in question. (Like Plato's cave perhaps—where our words describe only shadows or abstract effigies). A *relative Absolute*, however, may be when we describe one man/homme as 'civilised' and another as 'savage'. So, the opposite is also true in these works in that any absolutes we have may be entirely relative—culturally relative. So you may be right in your interpretation that homme does not act as an appropriate signifier for an Aboriginal man, but I think I was aiming at the opposite view—that homme is as appropriate as any other name for 'man'. The name being arbitrary and relative (which is not about privileging one language over another, rather it exposes their equal relativity) while the object (external) remains the same.

There is a wealth of philosophical debate about the relationship between signifier and signified, the internal mind and external 'world of things', etc. They all come into play as these works aim to raise questions about language, relativity and absolutes etc. It doesn't aim for a definitive statement or closure. I can say that I was thinking of making connections beneath the level of reductive language. Please don't quote any of this scribble![i]

Yours sincerely

Gordon Bennett

P.S. Water is a good metaphor in that a stream may flow through many countrysides and be called many things, but it remains essentially the same. Languages change, countries change, politics change but the stream keeps on flowing in its cyclic journey to the ocean, clouds, rain back to stream etc.—duh!

Did you notice the *auras* around the central 'icons' in these works—they fascinate me! They are about *icons*, signifier, signified.

❖ This previously unpublished letter is from Bennett's personal archive. Bennett wrote to Lucienne Fontannaz, the Swiss-born curator of the 1995 group exhibition *Lingo: Getting the Picture* at the then City Gallery, Brisbane (now Museum of Brisbane) as the exhibition included a number of works from Bennett's 'Relative/Absolute' series.

Letter to Rose Johnson, 3 October 1996

Dear Rose,

Thanks for your letter. Please find in the following pages my responses to your questions. Please grant me one favour in return. I would appreciate if you did not catalogue me as an 'Aboriginal' artist. I am trying to escape this adjective as it is not relevant to my work—only to stereotype.

Given my cultural heritage and development as a person within an Australian context, I must point out how such a reductive adjective is not appropriate. It denies my Anglo-Celtic heritage—which is what I grew up with and which was the culture into which I was socialised. I refuse to dump 'one' culture for another as I have refused to deny my Aboriginal cultural heritage. I remain Anglo/Celtic/Aboriginal, but I don't believe

[i] Though Bennett expresses here his desire for this text to remain unquoted, the letter has been included in this publication in consultation with the Estate of Gordon Bennett. This decision was based on its valuable contribution to understanding Bennett's perspective on his 'Relative/Absolute' series.

any artist should be identified by race.

I hope I have answered your questions adequately …

a) Region, clan, totem, etc., are not relevant

b) There are twelve works in all. They are a set. The title is 'How to Cross the Void' [1993].
The works have a satirical edge but [are] tempered by humour (black humour—no pun) leaning towards the 'grotesque'.

c) Yes, some works have been realised, namely—

1. *Culture Bag*—exhibited in:
   a. *The Colour Black and Other Histories*—Bellas Gallery 1992
   b. *A Black History*—Sutton Gallery 1993
   c. *Painting History*—Contemporary Art Centre of [South Australia] [and] Drill Hall [Gallery], Canberra, both 1993
2. *Apostle of Silence*—exhibited a[t]
   a. The Ninth Biennale of Sydney; The Boundary Rider—Sydney 1992
3. *Created by Flux*—exhibited as *Self Portrait (Ancestor Figures)* [figure 26]
   a. The Ninth Biennale of Sydney: The Boundary Rider—Sydney 1992

All of the works are after pages in my ideas notebook [figures 25 and 26]. The idea and its poetic resonances with the politics of identity are foregrounded rather than the aesthetic of an 'artful' etching.

d) Poetics is never clear, but ambiguous which increases the possibilities for meaningful engagement and demands the viewer to think. My work endeavours to provoke thought. River stones are 'sculpted/shaped' by the flow or passage of water over time. If the river, or passage of time is seen as a history of events which affects/sculpts cultures which in turn sculpts individuals (and vice/versa)—clues are given to this metaphor by other elements in the work—then the individual stones may be seen as metaphors for culture and for individual people as 'products' of the historical/cultural flux and passage of time—the past, the present, the future, all exist as potential elements in the lives of individuals—sometimes rocks/individuals [do] affect the course of the river/history and usually the river/history affects the shape of individuals/rocks. Rocks can weigh things down as cultural and historical baggage can do ('culture bag'—'memory').

By sealing river stones in lead, they become isolated from the processes that created them. They are 'frozen' in the state in which they were isolated. Whether this be Aboriginal cultures isolated by anthropological/ethnographical study and frozen into 'authentic' and its opposite (inauthentic, creole, etc.), or migrant cultures which bring their cultural practices with them and pander to their 'traditions' here, while back in the mother country 'tradition' evolves and changes—the results are similar.

By placing such cultural baggage, memories, traditions, abstract representations or whatever in the 'culture' [drawer] of one's 'dressing' table, an individual may accumulate points/sites of reference or identification. They dress themselves. The metaphor continues with what is placed in the 'history' [drawer], memories (cultural and personal/individual), 'knowledge' (learnt, experience, lies/truths whatever are accumulated as sites of identification)—some may get buried to be later found, some may be disregarded or stay buried. The top drawer is closed (Self) because who truly 'knows' themselves—we are in the abstract here—there is our face reflected in the mirror (but backwards and distorted).

We associate with the photographs/images/memories of our families/ancestors on the wall arranged around the mirror—some we may have never met—they are abstractions—we may only 'know' them from memories of them told to us by our parents/uncles/aunts, etc.—this may give us a sense of historical continuity—our family line/history, but they remain faces/abstractions on a flat photographic surface. The watercolours are abstract paintings which refer to Malevich and other 'transcendental' modernists—I am making a juxtaposition of two kinds of abstractions which may be more connected than is first apparent. Malevich refers to a spiritual icon, an abstraction of pure spirit perhaps, of human spirit beyond culture, race, etc. (though I am not sure it can ever be divorced from his cultural context—that's another story). So too the images of our families relate to our spirit, to where we came from, our line, our history—the flow of time, faces reflected in the river. I could write a novel about this series alone. It may be a truism or a cliché, but a picture is worth [a] thousand words. All the works in the series interact on one level or another. Whether it be the futile effort to escape into the 'purity' of Malevich's square or abstract spiritual world (*Blue Retreat*—the colour blue should perhaps be seen as a reference to Yves Klein's [I]nternational [Klein] Blue or a spiritual blue of the sky or water) or the bludgeoning effect of cultural imperialism (*Tribal Object*) or the pain inflicted by such imperialism (*Culture Bag*) or the escape to the spirit by suicide (*How to Cross the Void*) or to final 'equality' as an 'angel' once one has passed through into the abstract (but with the edge of futility or 'fat chance' that is present in *Blue Retreat, Non Swimmer* and *Ask a Policeman*).

f) I am influenced by everything and everyone in one way or another.[i]

I hope this helps you out, Rose.

Best wishes,

Gordon Bennett

❖ This previously unpublished letter is from Bennett's personal archive. Rose Johnson, a student at Flinders University, Adelaide, had written to Bennett as part of her research into the 'How to Cross the Void' series.

[i] If there was a question labelled 'e' in Rose Johnson's letter, Bennett appears not to provide an answer for it in his response.

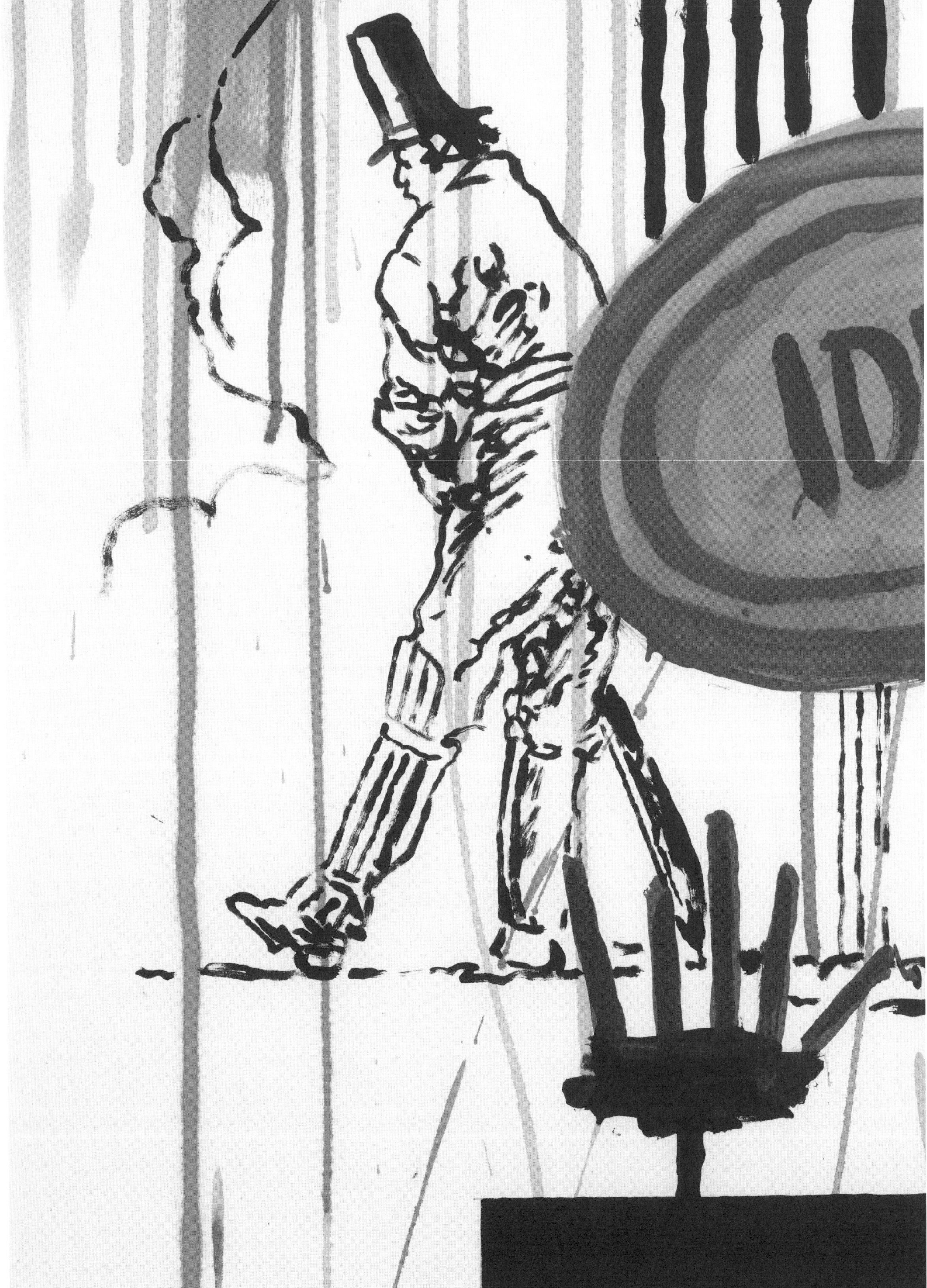

Letter to Jean-Michel Basquiat, 29 April 1998

Dear Jean-Michel Basquiat

1988, the year you died, was my last year at art college in Brisbane. I was aware of your work through art magazines at the time but there were no books on your work available. You were one of a small group of 'Black' role models. At the time, my biggest influence would have been Komar and Melamid [Russian-born American conceptualists who have a joint practice; Vitaly Komar, b. 1943, Alexander Melamid, b. 1945], and theoretically semiotics and postmodernism were my main interests. I saw an exhibition of Komar and Melamid's in Brisbane in 1988. I found their ability to paint in any 'style' they chose, and indeed to use styles of painting as a language or system of signs to make what amounted to visual texts, incredibly intelligent and conceptually stimulating. Since then, I have pursued my own path of conceptual painting based on the semiotics of 'style' and paint application, images and text, historical and contemporary juxtaposition. I am of a mixed heritage, being Scottish, English and Indigenous Australian. Brought up, educated and socialised as a 'white' Australian, I became acutely aware of racist stereotypes and the power/knowledge relationship that governed the historical representation of Aborigines within contemporary Australian culture. I wanted to explore my Indigenous heritage and how it was inherently intertwined with the history and reality of colonialism. I found the avenue of 'appropriation' art within the conceptual framework of postmodernism to be the most suitable way of pursuing my interests.

In 1994 I purchased a book on your work published as a catalogue to a 1992 exhibition at the Whitney.[i] I was drawn once again to the semiotic and painterly fields of your work and particularly to the layered lines of your drawing of the human figure. I guess it spoke to me of the traces of different experience and layers that make us the individuals we are and the histories of shared experience and levels we can relate to each other [on] as human beings in the world of material existence, even though we may be separated by cultural context, time and space.

I was excited to find in the essay 'Welcome to the Terrordome: Jean-Michel Basquiat and the "Dark" Side of Hybridity' by Dick Hebdige, in your book, a reference to Stuart Hall, which I have included in my own past efforts to 'explain' myself—it reads:

> Cultural identities are the points of identification, or suture, which are made within the discourses of history and culture—not an essence, but a positioning. Identities come from somewhere, have histories, and like everything which is historical, they undergo constant transformation. Far from being eternally fixed in some essentialised past, they are subject to the continuous 'play' of history, culture and power. Far from being grounded in a mere 'recovery' of the past, which is waiting to be found, and which, when found, will secure our sense of ourselves into eternity, identities are the names we give to the different ways we are positioned by, and position ourselves within, the narratives of the past.[1]

I found the essays on your work to be very enlightening in many ways, particularly in relation to issues of race and identity, and I found many similarities in your experiences and my own life experiences. Of course, there were/are huge differences also, but when the opportunity arose to show my work in New York, I decided to attempt to communicate with some of the 'language' of the New York context, via the appropriation and referencing of your work, to highlight the similarities and cross-connections of our shared experience as human beings living in separate worlds that each seek to exclude, objectify and dehumanise the black body and person.

To some, writing a letter to a person posthumously may seem very tacky and an attempt to gain some

[i] Richard Marshall, ed., *Jean-Michel Basquiat* (New York: Whitney Museum of American Art, 1992).

kind of attention, even 'steal' your 'crown'. That is not my intention, I have had my own experiences of being crowned in Australia, as an 'urban Aboriginal' artist—underscored as that title is by racism and 'primitivism'—and I do not wear it well. My intention is in keeping with the integrity of my work in which appropriation and citation, sampling and remixing are an integral part, as are attempts to communicate a basic underlying humanity to the perception of 'blackness' in its philosophical and historical production within Western cultural contexts.

The works I have produced are 'notes', nothing more, to you and your work, posthumously yes, but importantly for me—living in the suburbs of Brisbane in the context of Australia and its colonial history, about as far away from New York as you can get—these are also notes to the people who knew you and your work, those who carry you with them in their memories and perhaps in their hearts.

Another quote in the Dick Hebdige essay I found I connected with was by Greg Tate, which reads: 'To be a race-identified race-refugee is to tap-dance on a tightrope'. You lost your balance, I feel I can understand why. Jean-Michel Basquiat, I salute you.

Gordon Bennett

❖ This letter originally accompanied the exhibition of the first works from Bennett's 'Notes to Basquiat' series (1998-2007), displayed at the Gramercy International Art Fair, New York City in 1998 (figures 27 and 28). In 1999, the letter was published in the exhibition pamphlet for Bennett's solo exhibition at Sherman Galleries, Sydney: *Gordon Bennett* (Sydney: Sherman Galleries, 1999), 4.

Notes

1. Stuart Hall, 'Cultural Identity and Diaspora', in *Identity: Community, Culture, Difference*, ed. Jonathan Rutherford (London: Lawrence and Wishart, 1990), 225[-26].

Letter to Ian McLean, 'Notes to Basquiat: Modern Art', 4 April 2001

This series uses as a starting point a painting I did in October 1999. It is based on a watercolour I did from one of the photographs of Jackson Pollock painting (by Hans Namuth [1915-1990]). I did the watercolour some years previously, but I forgot to date it. This image dominates the canvas [figure 30]. The image of Pollock hovers over a 'canvas' which he is 'painting' (something like in Namuth's photos). Pollock's 'canvas' is represented in perspective, thereby reintroducing the perspective diagram into the otherwise 'flat' paintings of the 'Notes to Basquiat' series. The image Pollock 'paints' is a late work—'The Dying of the Light' period, as the book on Pollock I have puts it (*Jackson Pollock*, by Ellen G. Landau, Harry N. Abrams Inc., New York, chapter 11). Actually, this is the same period as *Blue Poles* [1952].

The Basquiat samples relate either to Pollock or Native American imagery. Pollock was stated by Basquiat as an 'influence', as was Cy Twombly [1928-2011] and Picasso (in a book on Basquiat—can't remember exactly where offhand). [i] Basquiat was also described as identifying with the disenfranchised. So, I started by doing more watercolours from Namuth's photographs and then scanning them into the computer, as part of my overall 'library' of images, my bank of 'samples'. I also sampled some of Pollock's older work, before the 'pinnacle' of his drip paintings. The early works became part of the under painting or background for the perspective and Pollock figures. Once I have all the images, I think I need I then start 'mixing' or 'remixing' the images into new works.

The 'Notes to Basquiat' series are a kind of communication to Basquiat, much like this letter is to you,

[i] According to Leanne Bennett, this was in Richard Marshall, 'Repelling Ghosts', in *Jean-Michel Basquiat* (New York: Whitney Museum of American Art, 1992), 15.

only pictorial. In the previous works, I was 'speaking' about history, culture, violence, identity and stereotypes, etc. I think the name of my Sydney show in 1999 was *Notes to Basquiat: One Tense Moment (Episode 2)*. I was communicating a sense of tension, like a fit almost (the brain wave pattern diagram I used in many of these works, including the first Pollock watercolour-derived work, was of a kind that is normally found in children—theta waves—but when found in an adult is indicative of extreme emotional stress). This related to the idea of Basquiat being described as 'walking a tightrope' since he was a 'race identified, race refugee'.

The notion of emotional stress can also relate to Pollock—who was seeing a 'Jungian' therapist at one time and was very interested in the unconscious and the 'collective unconscious'. I think primitivism is connected to these things too. So, I was interested in emotional tension in this series, about how it related to Basquiat and how it relates to myself in an autobiographical sense. And now how it relates to Pollock, his position, rise and fall, emotional tension. Actually, this was the same kind of relationship I have with van Gogh—[see] *Outsider* [1988]. And Edvard Munch, those seemingly pained expressions on the faces of the many figures I have done—not to mention that famous still photo from *Battleship Potempkin* ... 'Pure' anguish. Pollock also represents a kind of arrival of modernism to Australia, a 'coming of age' as a documentary I saw frames it (described below). This notion of the arrival of modernism to Australia via *Blue Poles* is why I called the show *Notes to Basquiat: Modern Art*.

Even though I am trying for this emotion thing, I am doing it in a non-emotional way, in the sense of the paint. It is not expressionistic painting; rather, it may look like an expressionist work at first, but on closer inspection, one can see that the paint is applied in a fairly labour-intensive way[, s]tarting with a traditional base coat of burnt umber etc., with up to three to four top coats. This is to de-emphasise the emotional tension attributed to the expressionist brushstroke. Perhaps to get around any stereotyped expressionist reading of the work and indicate that there is more to it.

Appropriation is part of it, but I find that classification lacking in describing the work, there's more to it. I like the concept of sampling and remixing much better. Especially because Basquiat liked jazz and was in his own rap band, he would have been aware of sampling surely? The concept of syncopation, a jazz (musical) device was known to him as evidenced in some of his work (syncopation was a big reference in my Melbourne show of 2000).

Pollock too liked jazz and often painted while listening to it. A point could be made in relation to Pollock's 'action painting' as a dance. Certainly, the Namuth photos suggest stills of Pollock's 'dance'. I think the idea of the shaman has a relationship here too. The idea of a 'primitivist' authenticity to Pollock's work, the shaman's ritual dance or ceremony (Navaho sand painters). Also, the 'primitivist' underpinning of modern art via Picasso. (Pollock did drawings while working through Picasso based on *Guernica* [1937]—the anguished expression of the (abstracted) horse and figures. I have used some of these in the paintings I have done.)

In 1999 I did three shows. The Bellas show was called *Notes to Basquiat: One Tense Moment*, the Sherman show was *Notes to Basquiat: One Tense Moment (Episode Two)*, and a small show at Sutton [was] called *Notes to Basquiat: One Tense Moment (Episode Three)*—I may be wrong about that subtitle on the last one. The term 'episode' related to the brain wave pattern of emotion[al] distress. Perhaps a psychotic episode of sorts—in some works, there were references to anti-depressants, etc., and cannabis, as well as internal organs etc. (X-ray imagery) [figure 29]—it's a real mix! I was playing with the idea of the new millennium, all that fear and apprehension, as well as the looking back on history, etc. A 1, 2, 3 build up to the end—tension. I guess, I titled the shows so as to make a 'poem' of sorts—a kind of work which no one will notice until they read a CV.

The Sutton show in early 2000 was called *Notes to Basquiat (Samo) Another Millennium*. The major painting in the show was called *Notes to Basquiat: Psychopathic, Syncopation, Sycophantic, Symphony* after a 'poem' I wrote. The Bellas show in 2000 was called *Notes to Basquiat: Subtext*. I guess this was referencing the reading of the work as what's underpinning the visible imagery as much as the cultural references, also a layer of text and nuances of interpretation (meaning). The major work in the show was called *Notes to Basquiat (Samo) Twenty First Century*. I was referring to more of the same in the new millennium—SAMO, Basquiat's street signature, fit my attitude to politics, cultural change etc. (always motivated by the Zeitgeist).

You know, the 'Home Décor' series [figures 9 and 10], the large paintings, was a kind of reaction to [right-wing politician] Pauline Hanson and [former Prime Minister] John Howard. That series became like basket weaving, something to do, a way of keeping going until I felt better, when I felt like just stopping work altogether—[t]he idea of political and cultural context for my work is seriously overlooked in its reading. At a time when cultural stereotype and denigration snapped back in place tightly, why wouldn't I use 'grotesque' black primitive [Margaret] (Preston) figures tangled in the grid of 'high' modernism? The tightness of the paintings, all those taped edges, and woven through with more 'organic' curves and painterly elements to form an overall composition. Also, I was kind of reviewing my own work in the context of new images and possible 'meanings'. It kept me in the 'game' at least. Eventually, I felt really bored with the taping; basket weaving was never really an appealing form of therapy for me.

So, all that brings me to the urge to 'communicate' ('link parabole', as Basquiat indicates in his work) with 'someone' from somewhere else, outside of Australia. I chose Basquiat because I felt an affinity with his work and life. I also felt this way with van Gogh, Pollock, Munch, but this was always on a more emotional level. With Basquiat, it is different in that I relate to his cultural issues of identity, what he had to live with in the sense of cultural stereotype, etc. I had done work with Basquiat imagery as far back as 1994—*Ideal (Basquiat and I)* [figure 15], acrylic on paper. The first group of works were on paper [figures 27 and 28] and done in response to my dealers want[ing] me to do a show for the Gramercy Park Hotel Art Fair in New York City [in 1998]. I wanted to translate my work into American, so to speak. As well it felt really freeing to do this, probably because there was no more taping (except now with the perspective, I am taping again—but then this is a kind of sub-series as I won't continue with talking to Basquiat about Pollock after this).

Well, I guess one point of the show then, part of the impetus for it, was a documentary on the purchase of *Blue Poles* by the Whitlam Government [in 1973], the controversy generated by its purchase—emotional tension, fear of change (is it Art?), even a symbol of a certain 'coming of age' culturally as discussed in the documentary. The arrival of *Blue Poles*, the Whitlam Government, the Aboriginal [T]ent [E]mbassy, and land rights are all historically linked. Even if only by the fact of what the Whitlam Government was doing at the time (and the response of the Australian people of the times). *Myth of the Western Man: White Man's Burden* [1995] was featured in the documentary as well. I guess I felt an opportunity to reference this work, kind of revisit it and expand on it in some way—I think I have mentioned the [Georg] Baselitz idea of: any idea, even a bad one, is a good point of departure for a painting. Anyway, I thought this was a good idea.

I think the documentary was made as an anniversary of *Blue Poles*' purchase. That probably makes this show a response to that anniversary also, and an anniversary of land rights legislation, the Tent Embassy and an Aboriginal Cultural 'Renaissance' if not assertion. I think some of the first paintings were coming out of Papunya around then also. Another 'poem' I wrote and have used in the work (like *Notes to Basquiat: Myth of the Western Man*) reads: 'Conjunction Apposition Cluster Juxtaposition'. In the work is a conjunction of references to historical events, images, and ideas. The text is a kind of mantra for the process and execution of the work. Not just my work but also Basquiat's. This is one of the connections I make with his work. I suppose it's a conceptual 'bent' that I find interesting and similar to my own processes of 'bricolage' (oohh, nice use of the art speak term and reference to the 'hybrid' nature of the work—there I go again ...). The term 'hybrid' may even refer to the mixing of painting 'styles' in my work, from expressionist brush stroke to spray paint. It all adds to the mix and contributes to the aesthetics of the composition in a physical and a metaphorical sense.

Other text I have used refers to representation through allegory to parable. I am using word lists made from a thesaurus, so the words are linked by nuances of meaning [figures 31 and 32], something like the work is linked via links of meaning, history, cultural sameness or indeed differences but with links of sameness (for example, the idea of primitivism as relevant to African, Native American or Aboriginal cultures within a Western cultural context). This is all non-linear intuitive thought processes at work here, I guess, which result in paintings. There is no conclusion reached by the work, just a process being kept in play. Thoughts, images, ideas, etc. The text reads something like spoken word lyrics or poetry. Poetry doesn't seek closure on its meaning. I think it seeks to go beyond the words on the paper into a world of metaphor, allegory, images and ideas in order to say 'something'.

So ... poetry, lyrics, syncopation (music—a beat—rapping), a remix. All part of it. I wish I could get away with a statement like Emily Kngwarreye [1910-1996] and say the work is about a 'whole lot, everything'. I think I have said that before. Back to jazz ... [I] found some information on the use of the word 'Cherokee' in a painting of Basquiat's called *Charles the First* (1982). The word is printed on a yellowish field in blue. The word is circled in blue and what look like feathers are above it. Below is a blue crown. I took the word to refer to Native Americans, which I guess it does given the feathers but it also refers to a 'standard pop tune' by Ray Noble, which was revised by Charlie (Bird) Parker—a favourite jazz musician of Basquiat's—as 'Ko—Ko' and again as 'Marshmallow'. This is indicated as evidence of the futility of origins. A happy coincidence indeed—a conjunction of sorts? My source for this information is a manuscript for a [forthcoming] book by Greg Dimitriadis and Cameron McCarthy called *The Work of Art in the Postcolonial Imagination*. The chapter is called 'Three Postcolonial Painters: The Pedagogies of Bennett, Roche-Rabell and Basquiat', which is Chapter 5, page[s] 174-75.

Other word list[s] refer to: Population through Citizen through to Colonist and Indigine. Sign through Totem to Symbolism and Writing. Original through Ideal to Canon and Norm. Portrayal through Imagery to Cartography and Hypsometry (the measurement of elevation in relation to sea level?!—perhaps understood in regard to an artist's elevation and positioning in relation to some 'base' line or canon?). There are a couple of references to racist Australian brand names like Abo Brand—lists I used in the first works on paper of this series—as well as animal brand names as in Possum Brand etc. (although that particular work is not in the show). There is a repeated reference to 'Animism' in many of the works. Also called 'Panpsychism'. I list the protagonists of the concept from [Empedocles] through Schopenhauer to Schiller and de Chardin. I got these names from my little *Handbook of Philosophy*.[i]

I remember in art college we learnt that the naming of football teams etc. after wild animals was a form of animism. I guess the same can be said for the naming of products after Australian native species. At the heart of this then is a kind of cultural and identity appropriation, like boomerangs used to indicate an authentic 'Australianess' or the use of Native American cultures as authentically 'American'. It works both ways though, doesn't it? So mix it up I say. Blur the edges, blend the borders—I think this is why I am

[i] Antony Flew, ed., *A Dictionary of Philosophy* (London: Pan Books, 1984).

interested in the aesthetics of the edges of things. The 'Panorama' paintings [1991-93] were of the water's edge where it soaks into the solid earth, it permeates the earth and there is an area between where the water stops and the earth begins (so my name is mud). A poetic series of work. That part of both, 'in between' space is important.

All the text, like the images, are done in at least two layers of different colours. The text is usually black over brown, which gives it a slightly blurred effect, or maybe it's my eyesight. Most things in the work have this slight variation of colour at the edge of it. It all adds to the aesthetics.

The images and text can connect into various relationships but may just as easily break down. Somehow like the expressionist painting, which is not really just an expressionist painting according to the conventions of the language of painting but a painting that on closer inspection is something more. Always something more. I suppose I aim to confuse, to destabilise and just as much to connect, but to connect through a feeling of uncertainty and unstableness. I think. The text can get inside a person's head. A viewer will invariably recite the text in their minds. Like poetry, only this is 'illustrated' with images that may serve to multiply the interpretations possible so as to say 'something'. So, I think it's about associations, something like poetry or music but with word and image. Even something like a psychological test in order to find out more about one's self, at least an invitation to think, like most art? Of course, the invitation is often turned down (and I am guilty of that too). So, like Homer Simpson I say 'eh, what can you do?'

When and if I make another video, it will be more like a rap music video with spoken word lists and weaving samples from my work through it for the visuals. I have a 'court jester' type hat in red, black and yellow I could wear too and maybe dance a painting to 'life'. I like the Harlequin and Court Jester (Fool) idea a lot actually. A kind of shaman in a postmodern backhanded sort of way.

The paintings in the show are meant to bounce off each other—one big painting in many parts. So the show is an installation using paintings on (polished?) white walls in a traditional manner. In this case, Pollock's image is seen in different painting positions, framed by each painting, something like movie stills. The references to his body moving suggests the ritual of painting, the 'action' of it. I hope people notice these things—I guess this is about something more than what one thinks one sees again, or what one thinks one will see (urban Aboriginal art, for instance). I was thinking I would like to hire a hip hop/rap DJ for the opening, but I think they have a neighbour issue about noise.

Some of the samples I have used are some of the 'poles' from *Blue Poles*, *Totem Lesson 2* [1945], *Bird* [c. 1938-41], [*The*] *Moon Woman Cuts the Circle* [1943], *Stenographic Figure* [c. 1942], *Lone Rider* [c. 1934-35] (an early work showing the influence of Thomas Hart Benton and romantic ideals of the 'old West'), some details from sketches showing the influence of Picasso—the minotaur and figures derived from *Guernica*, other stick-like figures that resemble rock art figures, and later drip painting works for the perspective areas.

The Basquiat samples are a bit more obscure except for *Charles the First*, perhaps because I have been working with him for longer and we've become 'mud'. My totemic/spirit figures were developed through Basquiat's drawing. And through him to Picasso—believe it or not but I am getting really interested in what I can do with layered abstract figures and hope to explore this more in two works on paper shows in Melbourne and Brisbane.

The John Citizen 'Coloured People' series are different, but in some way the same [figure 33]. At least, they are meant to mock (I suppose) the idea of people identified by their colour, by their surface. My 'people', taken from the social pages of *The Courier Mail*, are multicoloured (they are usually people photographed at openings of one cultural event or another). [Henri] Matisse [1869-1954] is a reference in these work[s]—*Madam Matisse (The Green Stripe)* [1905]—and someone suggested Max Beckman[n] [1884-1950] in regard to the heavy black outlines. In any case, I have thought of them as images of 'party people' under coloured lights at a dance party, maybe on E, and full of love and happiness taken away by the music, the beat. A kind of 'to hell with it all, let's party' cathartic dance ceremony enacted every weekend. While the figures are all different colours, they seem to be more the same, more connected, than separated by colour. I called the series 'Coloured People' as a kind of 'dumb take' on Adrian Piper's work called *Colored People* [1991], a book where she coloured the black-and-white photographs of people with what appears to be coloured crayon.[i] The book is divided into colour sections such as 'Scarlet with Embarrassment' and 'Green with Envy'. A kind of 'dumb take' on a literal translation also. So I wanted to say something the same, but different.

How did I start talking about that? Oh yeah, figures. My samples in the paintings are of rock art like figures and/or totemic/spirit figures. Also some little houses that go with the population/citizen text. I did little houses like that in the paintings in which I used Mimi spirit figures. I got into trouble with that, so I have developed my own 'spirit' figures through Basquiat. I still like to reference those rows of houses though. Most of us live in them. I guess that's enough for now, so I'll sign off.

Best wishes,

Gordon Bennett

P.S. Think of Edvard Munch's *Puberty* [1984-95] in relation to the 'shadow' for the Pollock figures. All that red looming over the figure—alter ego, shadow, blood, violence, car crash, etc.

❖ This previously unpublished letter, dated 4 April 2001, is from Bennett's personal archive. Ian McLean was a frequent interlocutor with Bennett.

Letter to Ihor Holubizky, 2006

[Gordon Bennett:] Dear Ihor, I have tried to answer your questions. I am not sure how to define John Citizen so the results are a little weird, but don't mind me, it's sometimes just my sense of humour.

To answer the questions ...

[Ihor Holubizky:] *1. How can I identify John Citizen in the biographical-background aspect of my writing?*

To expand. Biographies 'demand' a date and place of birth—a career trajectory that positions the work being exhibited. Not what I demand, but to respect the needs and positive curiosity of the viewer and the reader.

1. John Citizen CV with birth date and list of exhibitions. There is no 'life story' type of Biography other than that of Gordon Bennett up to the date of John Citizen's first exhibition.

2. Would it be appropriate to describe John Citizen as a parallel practice of Gordon Bennett? Rather than an assumed 'identity'.

The latter could be misread as a device or strategy for its own sake. Meaning, John Citizen has thought—makes work—and so does Gordon Bennett.

2. You could describe it as one or the other, or both at the same time. It would not necessarily be a misreading only the precedence of one over the other for sake of argument, it is open to interpretation.

[i] Adrian Piper, *Colored People: A Collaborative Book Project* (London: Book Works, 1991).

3. I do not intend to include a checklist biography in the catalogue, but [it] will include a paragraph summary for each artist. Is it appropriate to identify Gordon Bennett's practice—but equally, to highlight John Citizen exhibitions?

The two have been muddled a bit—the recent example being the Three Colours *[2004] exhibition. The last work in the Gordon Bennett checklist is, correctly, John Citizen. But the distinction is not quite clear in the texts. Funnily enough, laid out as parallel columns. Which is very clever.*

3. There goes John's CV. It is appropriate to mention both. I don't know what to say for a paragraph summary. John Citizen is always becoming, and while that is happening, he likes a pleasant surrounding, nice furniture, nice paintings, backyard pool. John is quite hedonistic and enjoys modern technology, especially his computer, Playstation and television. He enjoys making home DVDs, and learning new software. He likes to paint and draw, which he has plenty of time for as he is an 'invalid' pensioner. He started to make art soon after the 'accident' and he got his computer with the 'compensation'. John enjoys reading too. He sometimes collaborates with the artist Gordon Bennett.

4. Can I suggest that Gordon Bennett poses identity questions—and that John Citizen answers them, or answers back ... without being (necessarily) burdened by the discourse of identity[?]

5. Following No.4—can I then suggest that the 1996-1997 'Home Décor' works are Gordon Bennett and John Citizen coming together to discuss the problem?

And that 'Coloured People'—the suite—is John Citizen's thought on the subject[?]

I am not trying to be clever, not asking the artist(s) to do my work—but I feel that I have a dialogue with both—one that the viewer—in Canada, unaware of either—can enter into with clarity—as much as can be mustered in the realm of galleries and curatorial practices.

John Citizen and Gordon Bennett are equal. First and foremost. Whether they are separate and equal is a question that need not be answered at this moment—no need to rush to judgment. They are both alive and well, and doing what they need to do.

Regards,
Ihor

4. You could say that, for arguments sake, and it could be said that it is John's birth, or rite of passage, or the splitting of Gordon Bennett away from his Aboriginal artist 'naming', in as much as what does the term 'Aboriginal' mean, what signs stand for it within a Western context and discourses on 'Identity'? Some people dumb it down to my 'alter ego', Or you could be less dramatic, and 'Coloured People' [see figure 33] does have elements of to 'hell with this, I am going to party'. Let's dance and everyone looks the same under flashing coloured lights, make it a pool party and he's there, here's to 'life in the rhythm section'. John can be a bit ironic; the figures are from the paper showing people enjoying themselves at various cultural events, I added the coloured lights. Around the same time Gordon Bennett was referencing 'dance' in the late 'Home Decor' works and in the 'Notes to Basquiat' series.

I hope I don't come across as trying to be clever either. I thought they were good questions and they had to make me think about defining John Citizen. I came up with nothing! John Citizen can be described as an abstraction of identity making art about modernism and interior design. He sounds quite different in the description of a person or an identity in himself as described above. I know John Citizen gives Gordon Bennett a chance at other perspectives, like a third space for dialogue between the dualities of self and other, there are many possibilities. At the moment John Citizen is preoccupied with furniture and home decor, and doesn't show much interest in any overt dialogue with Gordon Bennett. So I agree with the idea that you express in the last paragraph.

This has given me a good opportunity to begin to talk about John Citizen. From this I can try and broaden some ideas for John Citizen, like the irony aspect. The 'dumb' flatness of his 'Interiors' show the role of art and modernism as interior design. If I had 'Aboriginal' art on the walls the works would be defined differently than with the more 'general' art of colourfield abstraction. John Citizen did two paintings in October 1997 using paintings of Gordon Bennett's 'Home Decor' series within his own composition called 'flatland' but moved away in a slightly other direction with the 'Coloured People' series back to paintings within paintings work of 2005.

OK now I am rambling, but I guess it all helps. I hope my responses are helpful.

Regards,

Gordon Bennett

❖ This previously unpublished letter is from Bennett's personal archive. Multi-national curator and essayist Ihor Holubizky had previously sent research questions regarding Bennett's artistic alter-ego John Citizen's involvement in the 2006 Museum London, Ontario, exhibition *Radical Regionalism: Local Knowledge and Making Places.* Bennett's answers informed Holubizky's contribution to the accompanying exhibition catalogue. The exhibition toured to Kelowna Art Gallery in Kelowna, British Columbia, in 2009.

understand yourself & your relationships to others

Consciousness is like casting a net out over the unexplainable in order to explain it and to understand it. The problem lies in that it's explanation and it's understanding are thus understood only in terms of the net & what lies inside it. The task is to look ~~[illegible]~~ outside the .

Part Three: In conversation

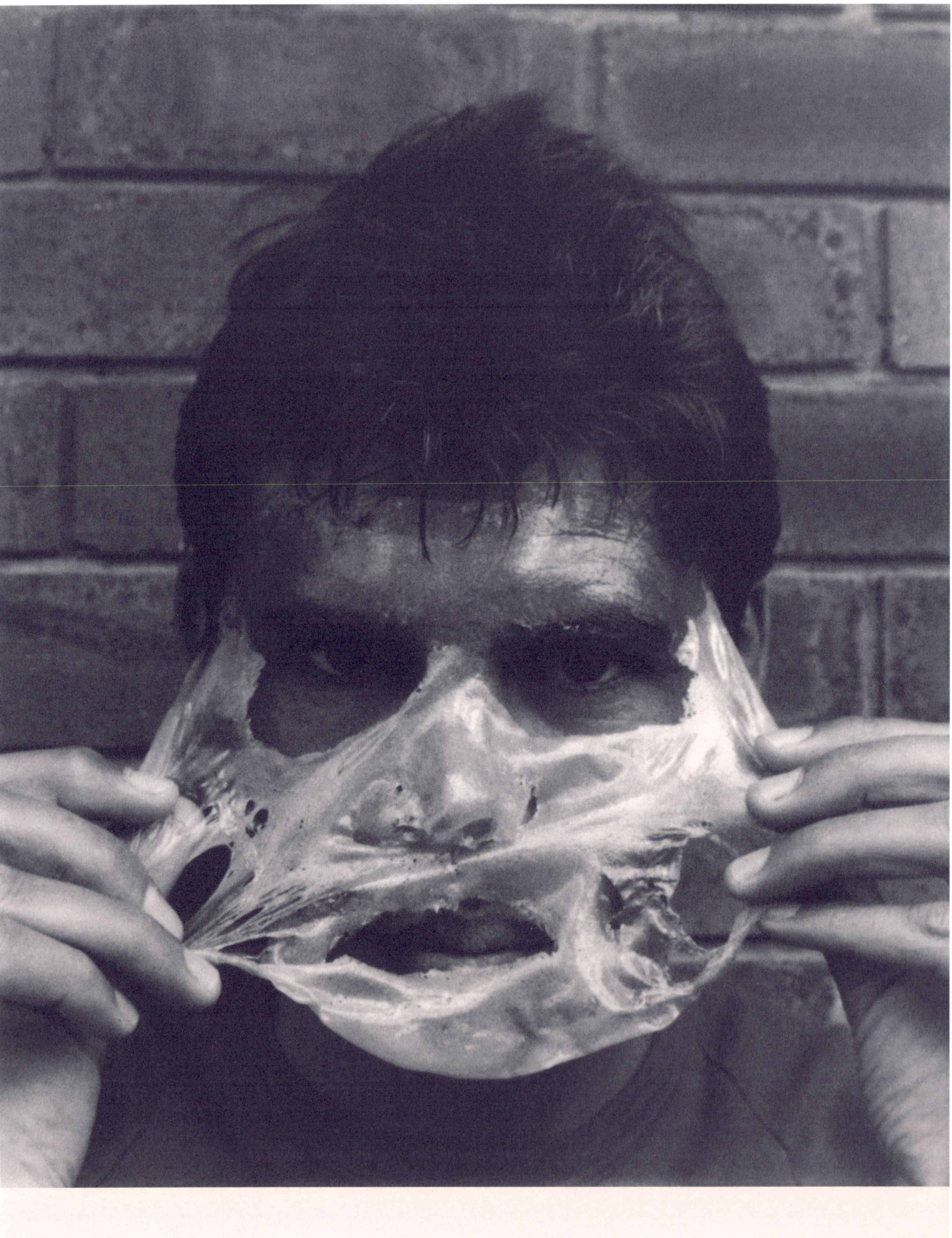

Interviews

These interviews with Gordon Bennett track the broadest time span of his artistic career—from 1989 to 2007. They give potent insight into how his ideas evolve over this time period, especially those around identity. Including a range of interlocutors—from fellow artists to critics, curators, and educators—these interviews offer a complementary perspective on Bennett's practice.

In 1989, the year after he graduated from Queensland College of Art, Bennett was interviewed by one of his former lecturers, Pat Hoffie, which was recorded on video, as well as broadcast via satellite to regional Queensland schools (p. 114). In the interview, Bennett describes his empathy for the Dutch post-impressionist Vincent van Gogh, his interest in the work of fifteenth-century artist Fra Angelico, and his engagement with Western Desert dot painting through the work of non-Indigenous Australian artist Tim Johnson.

In that same year, University of Queensland academic Bob Lingard interviewed Bennett for *Tension* magazine (p. 120). It was in this interview that Bennett began to voice concerns about the role his Aboriginality played in the reception of and engagement with his work, also discussing his conception of his large-scale 'history' paintings. Lingard would go on to write a key article on Bennett's early art with fellow academic Fazal Rizvi entitled '(Re)membering, (Dis)membering: 'Aboriginality' and the Art of Gordon Bennett' for the international journal *Third Text*.[1]

New Zealand/Australian curator Anne Kirker interviewed Bennett for *Artlink* in 1990 (p. 123), providing him with an opportunity to reengage with ideas discussed in the *Tension* interview, as well as to expand on the autobiographical context of his 1989 *Triptych: Requiem, Of Grandeur, Empire*. Bennett also provides valuable context in his discussion with Kirker on his initial engagements with the work of New Zealand artist Colin McCahon, specifically the late artist's use of text from which Bennett drew particular inspiration.

Five years later, Christopher Chapman interviewed Bennett for *Artonview*, the National Gallery of Australia's magazine, where the artist discusses his 1994 exhibition *Mirror Mirror (The Inland Sea)* and his early, experimental video work *D.U.H! (Down Under Homi)* of the same year, presented in an installation-like environment that included a vast floor-painting on canvas (p. 126).

Bennett's discussion with Chris McAuliffe in 1993, first published in 1996 in *What is Appropriation?: An Anthology of Writings on Australian Art in the 1980s and 1990s*, covers his strategies of appropriation, his opinion on how his appropriative method differs to that of his contemporaries, and the conception of his *Non-Performance* work, begun in 1992 (p. 129).

Concluding this section is Bennett's last published interview, with the late Australian curator William (Bill) Wright in 2007 (p. 135). The occasion elicited a rare discussion about Bennett's alter ego, the Australian 'everyman' John Citizen, as well as two bodies of work not discussed in the other interviews: the 'Stripe' series (2003–08) and the 'Figure/Ground (Zero)' works (2003), in which Bennett engaged with neocolonialism through the prism of the Western military presence in Iraq at that time. Though Bennett describes to Wright in this interview that his broader postcolonial project culminated with the 'Notes to Basquiat' series in 2003, it is important to note that he continued making work within this series through until 2007. In addition, though Bennett states that his interest in postcolonial thematics came to an end at this time, subsequent bodies of work, such as the 'Abstraction' series (2011–13), reflect his return to similar subject matter in later pieces.

Like Bennett's letter writing, the interview format also offered Bennett an opportunity to be direct and informal about his perspectives on his art and career. *Non-Performance* was in effect through much of this period, but while there is a gap in his own written reflections Bennett granted interviews to certain individuals he trusted to frame and convey his views.

Though Bennett was shy and averse to being seen as a representative of any particular identity, these interviews, just like his essays and letters, demonstrate that he thrived on a dynamic of exchange. This extended to creative exchanges with artists such as Johnson, Eugene Carchesio, and Imants Tillers. Bennett placed a great deal of trust in intuition as a creative and generative process, but his strongest connections were also built on empathy—a quality that is as visible in his art as it is in his words.

Notes

1. Bob Lingard and Fazal Rizvi, '(Re)membering, (Dis)membering: "Aboriginality" and the Art of Gordon Bennett', *Third Text* 26 (Spring 1994): 75–89.

Urban Aboriginal Art: Pat Hoffie Talks with Gordon Bennett

Pat Hoffie (PH): Good evening and welcome to the *Painting[: Traces of Place]* Program. As promised a few weeks back, we have Gordon Bennett in the studio again with us.[i]

Good evening, Gordon, and welcome back.

Gordon Bennett (GB): Hi Pat.

PH: Now, when I had Gordon on those few weeks ago, it was to discuss the way in which urban Aboriginals cope with a divided history, a history of white written history and an oral tradition that often has been neglected. So, the two people that I was speaking to at the time [were] Ron Hurley and Gordon, and I've had several requests that I have Gordon back on the show because we didn't actually have time to run through all of his work. So, tonight we'll move straight on to looking at Gordon's work, and unfortunately because this is a pre-recorded show, there won't be any opportunity for those of you watching to ring in. However, if you want to get in touch with Gordon, you could write to me care of the Australian Fine Arts School and I'll pass any messages on to Gordon, but let's have a look at the first slide, which was—as those of you who've been watching will know—produced while Gordon was at college, in his last year in 1988, and the name of this particular image is *Outsider*.

It's a large painting—it's 290 x 180 centimetres—and it's done with acrylics on canvas. Now, this image is a very different type of an image to the later works that you've been producing, but would you like to talk a little bit about the types of symbols that you've used there because you're directly alluding, it seems, to particular artists from history.

GB: Specifically [Vincent] van Gogh [...] I've used one of his paintings of his bedroom [*Bedroom in Arles*] which he painted in 1888, which coincidentally was Australia's centennial year, where Aboriginal people were paid to come along to the celebrations—so I read in my history book. And it's about displacement really and a feeling of ... just relating to van Gogh and his predicament at that time; it was a happy period in his life when Gauguin was coming to set up the artist colony. So, I had in mind that feeling of happiness that was later to be destroyed through the incidents that did occur, leading to him cutting off part of his ear, et cetera.

So, I was interested in that pain and that frustration that occurred, [I have] kind of an empathy for that, really.

PH: So this image was taken from the particular image that van Gogh produced of his bedroom but you've superimposed and interceded with different other images.

GB: Yes. Well, the sky is from his *[The] Starry Night* [1889] painting, which I think was done while he was in the asylum and I've just integrated those two with the decapitated Aboriginal person, displaced in this bedroom, with the blood spurting out and turning into the spirals of the sky.

PH: So we've got a violent image but one which isn't melodramatic. You've got an image with no head; you've got bloodied handprints on the bedroom wall; you've got what begins as blood becoming the spirals, as you said, of a night-time scene; and on the bed, you've got two heads from classical antiquity, it looks like.

GB: Yes. I guess he's looking for a head to replace his missing one. It's a kind of transplantation of culture in a way.

PH: Right, now, the hands in that particular image are almost transparent—it seems that way in the slide. Is that not the case in the painting?

GB: No, that is the case; they are transparent. I drew them in from looking at my own hands—I painted them in, rather—and decided that, aesthetically, that looked better than actually [filling] them in, so I decided to leave [them].

PH: [Rather] than filling them in? So that decision to leave those hands as they are seems to be one where you were deciding what style to opt for as you go along, so that you've got a particular style of painting [which] is the one that van Gogh used with broken colour, sitting on the same canvas surface as a very classically painted illusion—that is, the heads lying in the bed. Now, there is a jarring there, yet you've somehow synthesised them together. This thing of pulling apart different parts of history, sitting within one frame—is that intentional?

GB: Yes, it is very much. In my own mind, in this particular painting, I made the relationship [reflect] the period—this painting [*Bedroom in Arles*] was painted in 1888, the

[i] Bennett had joined Pat Hoffie and the late artist Ron Hurley in an earlier interview in the *Painting: Traces of Place* series, as part of the fifth episode, entitled 'Urban Aboriginal Art with Ron Hurley and Gordon Bennett'. In this episode, Hurley's work is the dominant focus, with Bennett providing only limited contributions to the discussion.

centennial—and what was happening in Australia as well as what happened to van Gogh in his own particular situation. The hands are really just one of those aesthetic decisions that you make while you're making a painting and there was no actual thought to interpreting it at the time because I mean, if you're doing a painting [and] you're always continually thinking 'How are people going to interpret this?', you'd never do anything; you'd be too tied up, too tight.

PH: That's right. So that statement that Kandinsky, I think it was, made—'The artist knows all but only after the artwork'—do you think that's true?

GB: Very much, I think.

PH: But still going, it seems as though you're making these—I hesitate to use the word—'intuitive' decisions, but you're very much informed by history, by politics, by a whole number of subjects. How do you marry those two awarenesses, the subconscious and the conscious?

GB: Well, again, I think it is intuition. I read a lot, but I don't remember a lot in the sense of being able to recall and regurgitate what I have read sentence by sentence, you know, like repeat it, parrot-fashion. I make a lot of connections within my mind and when I see an image, it just clicks, so I decide to use it, or I might be watching television and I'll see this image in my head; it's like a waking dream kind of thing, or daydream ...

PH: And there's a sense of rightness about that image.

GB: Yes, very much. Even when I do start the actual painting, it may change from the image I do have in my head but you have to let go—you can't be too pedantic about it; you have to let things flow, I guess you could say.

PH: [So] that that image directs you in its development.

GB: Yes.

PH: Let's have a look at the next slide called *Virgin Dreaming*, which again was produced in 1988. It's mixed media on canvas and we had a look briefly at this image in the last program, but we can see again the broken colour in the background, similar to a divisionist technique or a post-impressionist technique coupled to, again, a Renaissance feeling with the head behind the pilasters. And Gordon, you explained this in the last program that it was about the expulsion [of Adam and Eve from the Garden of Eden], but you've transplanted that very Western mythology into Aboriginal terms.

GB: Yes. The painting I have referred to is by Fra Angelico from the fifteenth century and I think it's called *The Annunciation of Cortona* and it's about the archangel Gabriel coming down and announcing to the virgin that she is to expect a child. The archangel is on the television set in the back room.

PH: Now, in that TV set—we can't see a detail here on the slide—but is that a painted section?

GB: No, it's actually a colour photocopy. This is the mixed media part of it—it's a colour photocopy of the work [from] the reproduction in a book.

PH: So you haven't attempted to get a squirrel brush and paint with three hairs; you've just put that colour photocopy right down on that work and said, 'This is it.'

GB: That's right.

PH: You haven't tried to hide that.

GB: No. Well, I think it relates to the idea I'm trying to get across in that television is a reproduced image made up of dots, [as is] the photocopy, which is also a reproduced image made up of dots.

PH: And how did you arrive at the heads—the grinning death's heads?

GB: I can't remember actually. I think I saw this ... Well, they're laughing clowns, and I really had in mind when I did that kind of the game where you try and win something but you're trying to cheat death at the same time, so it's the kind of capitalist outlook or Western European outlook in that you have to get as much as you can before you die—that kind of thing. So the Virgin Mary is now a person working in this sideshow; the whole thing has become a sideshow.

PH: And in the background [are] the two figures that have been expelled from the Garden of Eden.

GB: Yes. That was in the original painting, but I've schematised it and changed Adam and Eve to black people.

PH: And the style that you're using in the background there is in the style of ...?

GB: The Western Desert painters. This is the first time I've used dots; this was the first painting where I did actually use them.

PH: Were you influenced by anyone in particular to use dots?

GB: Yes, well I was [previously] steering clear of using dots in particular—I was at a bit of a loss as to how to relate my work to Aboriginality in fact—until Tim Johnson came out to the [Queensland College of Art] and gave a lecture one day and I found it very stimulating.

PH: Tim Johnson—just to explain to the viewers—is a well-known painter who's originally from Sydney, who spent a great deal of time working with the Aboriginals in the Western Desert areas, particularly I think Papunya.

GB: Yes, specifically, yes.

PH: And his wife [Vivien Johnson] also has written a great deal about Aboriginal Western Desert painting and [Tim] uses the dot in his own work.

GB: Yes, he does.

PH: And he also works collaboratively.

GB: Yes.

PH: So, you felt after having spoken to Tim that it was quite legitimate for you to use this particular method of painting?

GB: Certainly, yes. He explained to us that the dots were a very recent development in Aboriginal art; the main reason I was steering clear of using them was I didn't want to appropriate any Aboriginal imagery because of moral reasons. Being Aboriginal myself, some people may think that I have more right to do that than many others but many of us don't see it that way because we're actually breaking tribal law by doing that.

PH: Well, how about the appropriation of Western art forms? How do you feel about that?

GB: Well, it's very risky as it's against the law if a person decides to prosecute, but I certainly don't see it as having the same handed-down sacred ... the same sort of thing as in Aboriginal ...

PH: You don't think that the spiritual integrity of the Western imagery that you're drawing from is perhaps as heavy as the Aboriginal culture?

GB: I think it's lost, to tell you the truth. I think that spiritual integrity is something that belonged to the fifteenth century and it is no longer valid in this culture.

PH: That's an interesting point. I think it's one that could require a great deal of debate because, certainly, appropriation is a risky business—you're taking someone else's image and recontextualising it and calling it your own image. When does that become breach of copyright or infringement of just private rights, of ownership? And there's a lot of appropriation being used at the moment in painting. Do you have any ideas about why appropriation is being used at the moment—why people are using images from the past so frequently?

GB: Yes. Well, I think they're basically recontextualising paintings from the past; say, they [the paintings] might be sitting in a gallery somewhere in Europe. Now, most people can't see them, so all we ever see is reproduced images and they don't have that power anymore because they're reproduced so often that that sort of lessens the feeling about them. So, when you do appropriate something, you recontextualise it and you give it new meaning—meaning that is appropriate to the present time, especially if you do change the context of it. Say, you put it next to another image, juxtapose it with another image—well, those two images then interact and the meaning shifts. ... By the way, the meaning of a painting that was done 500 years ago is going to have a completely different meaning now anyway. And I mean, the meaning that you may read about that particular painting in a book is probably a misinterpretation as to what it meant back then anyway.

PH: So you're suggesting that there are layers of meanings in painting and a multitude of ways to approach that meaning?

GB: That's right, yes.

PH: And that the individual artist has license to do what he or she wishes with those images?

GB: I guess you could say that.

PH: But not with Aboriginal imagery?

GB: No, certainly not, because I don't think they are ... Aboriginal imagery is handed down through tribal affiliations and family affiliations; it's part of their lore and part of the culture and it's certainly not that way in Western European culture at all. I mean, Fra Angelico—that particular painting—he doesn't have ancestors who are alive today who have exclusive rights to the painting, that particular painting, or that particular message, so therein lies the difference.

PH: It's interesting though that many living European artists can in fact trace their lineage through their teachers to heritage back as far as the Renaissance; certainly, that's very able to be done with people who have had an art school training in Britain. So that sense of your own particular dreaming, or history, exists for these people as well.

GB: Yes, but in a different way.

PH: Certainly. Let's move on to ... *Echo and Narcissus* [1988], which we've looked at as well before, and the image of the waterhole reproduced from [a] Western Desert type of image.

GB: Yes, the concentric circles which in the Western Desert painting—this particular abstract image can mean different things in relation to other abstract images within the particular painting, so it's a kind of changeable abstract symbol. In using it, I'm not appropriating any particular part of any particular painting. I mean, it's a fairly universal image, like targets et cetera. So I've used it as a ... the tiny 'U' shape is generally the ...

PH: Squatting haunches.

GB: Yes, like the legs in a cross-legged position. So this figure is sitting next to the centre or waterhole or place that may be anywhere the culture is—like a home or something like that—and this pool, which also in Western imagery can be a symbol for the unconscious, perhaps. This is a very private painting, in fact; this is about the two halves of myself and it's about [them] coming together really.

PH: I think it's interesting that we've just spoken to [Australian printmaker] Ron McBurnie [b. 1957] and that point at which art becomes most personal is sometimes something that we shy away from and yet, paradoxically, you can sometimes hit that kernel that's most personal to you and then it enables you to speak on the most broad terms.

GB: Yes.

PH: It's also interesting that a number of people—artists, and certainly some people who rang up after the last program I did with you—were talking about this sense of purpose that many Aboriginal artists feel they have at the moment, where there's this reawakening to this history that has been discounted for so long and that energy is something that's a great carrier through. Certainly, it's been waited for for a long time, but it has a particular ambience; it has permeated a lot of work—the best work that's being done currently. And a lot of these white artists are feeling that they don't have that same sense of purpose, that the type of ... that energy that I've just described, that point at which a whole race is discovering and restating its own history throws others of us who are very much displaced into a kind of a state of limbo and thinking, 'Well, where do I draw my history from?' But, at that point, I threw that just open for people to think about that because I think we do all share a very important personal history that we have to, sort of, do our own little archaeology, private archaeology to find out about.

We'll look at the last image from the 1988 paintings [...]

GB: [...] *Seer.*

PH: Oh yes [...] *Seer.* You'd really turned a corner then with this one.

GB: Yes, I have. Well, there's quite a few paintings in between the last two, before this one, but I'm starting to look at history a bit more here rather than [at] personal responses to things. I'm standing back a bit more from my own personal history and other history and the emotional heartfelt thing.

PH: It's interesting that you're adopting that cooler stance because, in fact, the canvas and the topic, the concept, the image, is on that verge of being close to highly dramatic work, so that you need to get that cooler distancing perhaps to achieve that balance.

GB: Yes, I did. I felt that I did anyway, although this has got a lot of red paint dripping all over it.

PH: Yes.

GB: So, it's a kind of ...

PH: It's a bit like a ...

GB: A wider move.

PH: A Hermann Nitsch [Viennese Actionist, b. 1938] bloodbath.

GB: Yes. [...] I did this after I'd seen his work.

PH: [Antonin Artaud's] *The Theatre of Cruelty* [est. 1932] and the whole bit.

GB: Yes. I mean it's dribbled all over [with] dots, which really basically stands for Country and the image there, the black image, is projected from a history book, the kind that children were given in the 1950s or late 1940s to learn about history. And it's the ships entering Sydney Cove, I imagine, with the Aboriginal people in the foreground, just watching it come in. And the diagram on the right-hand side is a perspective diagram from a Renaissance book on perspective.

PH: And, of course, it is one-eyed.

GB: Yes, that's right and that's why I called it *Seer*. It also relates to the act of seeing plus seeing into the future, but I mean this relates to the bloodbath, I suppose you could call it.

PH: And the red is a glaze in fact, a highly—

GB: Yes, there's quite a few layers of paint on that.

PH: We'll move onto the next in this series produced in 1989 called *The Plough*, where Gordon's using acrylic as well as oil, and the image is a large one—it's 130 x 260 centimetres—[are you] still using that perspective idea?

GB: Yes. It actually has A, B, C, D, E, F, [...] on those little cubes. I'm using the language there—the basis of language is the alphabet because that is how Europeans, or anyone, constructs their world views, through language—so, the A, B, C, D also can stand for 'Abo', 'Boong', 'Coon' and 'Darkie', which are very derogatory terms that I've grown up with, and so I thought that was quite strange how they sort of correlated. But, the other image on the left-hand side of the plough is—

PH: Hans Heysen.

GB: [...] Yes, it's actually a little etching that's only about two inches square, so when it's blown up to about 1.5 metres square, it takes on a whole new meaning.

PH: Isn't it powerful?

GB: Yes, very much.

PH: And you've used that in a couple of your paintings. It's a really powerful image and you've done it with dot painting again and, of course, they're ploughing the land and underneath the land are literally [the] painted bones of a race.

GB: Yes. That can relate to previous ownership and it also can relate to the massacres and poisonings that went on in order to appropriate the land—or steal it.

PH: We'll move onto the next painting, called *The Betrayal* or *Pieces of Silver* [*The Betrayal (Pieces of Silver)* 1989] which is a much smaller painting—it's 38 x 123 centimetres—and in it, Gordon's juxtaposed four canvases, butted straight up against each other. The canvas on the left is actually a photocopy.

GB: It's an actual poster.

PH: A poster itself?

GB: That I bought from the art gallery [Queensland Art Gallery], yes.

PH: Do you want to speak about what's happening in that poster? The image is from ...?

GB: That's from the so-called first Australian history painting. I think it's from Tasmania done by [English painter Benjamin] Duterrau [1768–1851] and it shows G. A. Robinson, who was supposedly the saviour of the remaining Aboriginal people, who rounded them all up and stuck them on Flinders Island, where of course they died one by one because he wouldn't let them practice their own culture and he tried to make Christians out of them. Basically, [he] made them learn the scriptures off by heart and the women did needlework.

PH: And Truganini [c. 1812–1876] is in there as well.

GB: Yes.

PH: But on top of that poster, Gordon has painted with dots [...] again, and then you've got the feet walking across, leading to a Union Jack. Then we've got in the next canvas, an actual artist's palette, a physical palette—not a painted thing, so the paint's really quite encrusted on that.

GB: Yes.

PH: And in the fourth and final panel?

GB: It's another picture of a plough from the history books I told you about before, and the landscape this person is ploughing is actually a section of a cadaver, so it's a dead body—and I thought looking very much like landscape and very appropriate I think because the landscape is now dead. It's not alive with the spirit of Aboriginal people or their ancestors.

PH: So, we've got four different ways of painting. In fact, we've got the tools of the painter included in the final product and they've just been butted together to tell their own story but not in a narrative sense—certainly in an associative sense.

GB: Sure. It's more a conceptual sense, I think, like the palette relates to how a picture is constructed through paint and this image on the left, of Duterrau which Tasmanians like to believe in, was actually painted by someone and it's basically a lie.

PH: Let's move on to the painting called *Frame* [1989], which is one of ... it's a detail actually isn't it?

GB: Yes, it's a detailed postcard that was current in the early 1900s, showing supposedly the Australian natives in their natural environment and it's actually a posed photo in front of a painted backdrop.

PH: You've used text as well as image there.

GB: Yes, well the word 'Frame' [relates] to this idea of the photographer setting the people up and then framing them with his camera and depicting them in a certain way.

PH: So that the framing device actually is referred to as well, as is the next one, which is called *Double Take* [1989] [. . .] Again, a small painting, 30 x 30 centimetres.

GB: Yes. This again is referring to Tasmania. This is the pictographic poster that was used by Governor [Thomas Davey], I think, to speak about justice for Aboriginal people. Now we all know that that didn't actually occur, so what I've done is changed it—in the bottom row where the white person has killed the Aboriginal person, supposedly, the white person hangs for it. Well, I've put them hanging another Aboriginal person because throughout history, if an Aboriginal person retaliated and killed say, a shepherd or some twenty sheep or something, the army or the local people would go out and slaughter Aboriginals all over the place.

PH: Gordon, the image on the bottom, beneath the text that says Doubletake [. . .]

GB: That again is a body, a cadaver.

PH: We'll move onto *Requiem* [1989], which is a much larger image, 120 x 120 centimetres, and that in fact is part of a triptych that Gordon will be exhibiting later this year at *Perspecta*, which is [...] an Australian national survey show at the Art Gallery of New South Wales. We might move onto the next image too [*Of Grandeur*], which is part of the same triptych.

GB: That's right, that's the middle section.

PH: Right. Now, could you talk about this image here?

GB: Yes. There's a little photograph in a gold frame on the right-hand side there that comes from a *Pix Post* magazine from the 1940s and it shows my mother in a missionary school when she was 14, polishing the stairs.

PH: So it actually is your mum?

GB: It is my mother, yes, and so I've lifted that image and painted her in this perspective construction and it's speaking about how history is constructed, how [the] image is constructed and the actual receding corridors where she is cleaning forms a Cross, and I've just lifted two arms from a crucified Christ by [German Renaissance painter Matthias] Grünewald [1470-1528], so these are another two fragments of history.

PH: Let's have a look at the third panel of this triptych and we can then see how Gordon's imagery is drawing from history—it's personal and private. This image is called *Empire*.

GB: Yes, and that is the Arch of Titus, which was built in Judea and it was actually a monument to the Roman conquest of Judea. It's framing another Aboriginal person from a postcard, which is speaking basically about the framing of the idea of the noble savage, which is how people generally see Aboriginal people today.

PH: And the image of the person within the frame?

GB: Yes, that's the person from the postcard. It's actually the same backdrop that was used for the other ones; it's the same natural environment.

PH: So you've used an image—the first image that we looked at of the triptych, was that an image of your mum in that?

GB: No, that's Truganini.

PH: That was Truganini; so you've got Truganini, you've got an image of your mother, and then you've got the postcard image in this triptych, which is talking about history—[both] personal and private.

GB: Yes, and the construction of it.

PH: Well, Gordon, I think that the viewers will have to agree that the work's extremely powerful and drawing as it does from private and public sources, you've got a package that hits home in more ways than one. Is your work moving in any particular direction at the moment, towards larger work or ...?

GB: Basically about the same size but very different in that I'm making paintings that are basically just gestural brushstrokes and dots that up close, you can't really see what they are; they're basically totally abstract but, as you move back, or if you squint at them, they'll form an image from history—I'm using images like Captain Cook or an archetypal sailing ship, things like that [see figures 13 and 14].

PH: Sounds interesting. Well, we look forward to your next show which will be ... your next one-man show will be in Brisbane next year?

GB: Yes, probably about March next year.

PH: Terrific. Well, thanks very much for coming into the studio. I hope you enjoyed it as much as I did tonight, and I look forward to seeing you all next week. Good night.

❖ This interview was originally conducted as a satellite broadcast for *Painting: Traces of Place* (Brisbane: TSN 11 Multi Media Productions, 1989). This transcript of the original video interview is reproduced courtesy of Pat Hoffie and Flying Arts, Brisbane.

A Kind of History Painting
Interview with Bob Lingard

Bob Lingard (BL): Gordon, when I was in Sydney recently at the [Art Gallery of New South Wales], looking at your work in *Perspecta* [*Triptych: Requiem, Of Grandeur, Empire*, 1989], I listened to a guide talking to a large group of people about your work. He seemed to me to be coming to grips with the work, but then a middle-aged woman asked him whether the artist (you) was Aboriginal or not. He answered very confidently that you were not Aboriginal; the woman protested that you had to be, given the content of your work. Would you care to comment about this?

Gordon Bennett (GB): I find that very interesting. Even in the *Perspecta* catalogue it does not come out and say that I am an Aboriginal person. Perhaps it doesn't look like the way Aboriginal work is supposed to look? I suppose you're beginning to raise questions about the stereotyping of Aboriginal art and artists. But what about the content? This woman seemed to perceive the work as a statement about Aboriginality in contemporary Australia. I find that particularly interesting. That she was perceptive and interested enough to argue the point is great.

BL: Just staying on that *Perspecta* triptych for a minute. In it there is a photo of your mother and a painting of her. I have also seen her in other works of yours. Could you comment on the importance or significance of that inclusion?

GB: She showed me once that photo of her which was in, I think, a *Pix People*, in the 1940s. People tend to keep a photo like that when it is in a magazine. That photo's part of my personal history and my mother's, something that I hadn't known about her life at that stage. What struck me particularly about that picture was the associated text: it said something like 'picked out in gold the arches and ornamental pillars lend an old world touch'. I started to think about just what was implied by the term 'old world'. I thought of past empires like the Roman one with their pillars and temples and so on and thought how they were built on slavery. I then began to reflect upon my mother's position and my own position and the position of Aboriginal people.

BL: So out of an individual experience you were coming to a more general point?

GB: Yes, all of my work in a way is me attempting to come to grips with my own socialisation. Of course, the way my mother was socialised had a big impact on the way I was socialised. So that is another reason why I was interested in that photo.

BL: Would you comment briefly then on your own biography?

GB: Fairly uneventful I suppose, as far as overt racism goes. I didn't know about my own Aboriginality until I was about eleven. I learnt about Aborigines at school through Social Studies, just like any other child. I didn't know about my heritage, I was seeing it from one side of the fence you might say; from that I was in a very good position to see how white Australians had been conditioned to see Aboriginal Australians.

BL: You've actually used some Social Studies textbook images in your work.

GB: Yes I have. I think I am in a very good position to deconstruct some of that Eurocentric conditioning. I attempt that in my work, but it is also a way to deconstruct the erroneous construction of myself. I grew up to be ashamed of my Aboriginality and these are the reasons I grew up to be ashamed of it. I remember my work (I left school at fifteen) sitting around at smoko and listening to 'boong' jokes—there was no way I could identify myself to be the butt of those jokes. I became very aware of the negative perception a lot of people had, a perception of Aboriginal people born[e] out of ignorance and of subscribing to popular belief systems that stem back to the eighteenth century.

BL: Coming to your recent work: one thing that strikes me is the sophistication of the art references. You seem to be quoting from a variety of sources, quoting art history.

GB: Again, I see art history linked to general history. This is particularly the case before the invention of the camera; sketches of Captain Cook, for example, which are reproduced in history and Social Studies textbooks. We can look at history through a history of images. Transplanted European culture in Australia has its own history of images going right back to Ancient Greece. So there's the link: art history is related to general history, images constitute part of the cultural memory and reflect its construction.

BL: Given that's the case then, how does your work relate to what is happening in contemporary Australia? Say specifically in relation to Aboriginal people?

GB: I see my current work as a kind of history painting. I am attempting to place into an 'historical continuum' images which should have been placed in a lot earlier. Unfortunately, many events and situations were written out.

BL: As has occurred in historiography with Aboriginal people being written back in?

GB: Pretty much, but I think I am providing more than that. I am attempting to make it clear in my work that these are constructed images. I am trying to make the way of seeing in the picture obvious with the use of perspective lines: how perspective constructs images as well as histories.

BL: Has this got anything to do with the way history and the cultural world are selectively constructed?

GB: Very much. That's got a lot to do with the inclusion of the alphabet (the ABC)—the way you build up your cultural world view from basic units, the way it is constructed and ethnocentrically biased. By doing that, I'm coming to see the way I learnt to see myself as an Aboriginal person.

BL: Sociologists, in talking about art, would raise factors affecting the production of art, such as biography, where the artist fits into the social structure, even down to materials available, and so on. They also talk about social factors impinging upon the reception of the art. You've touched upon how your Aboriginality relates to the production of your work. Would you say a little more about that? And secondly, how do you think your Aboriginality relates to how the pictures are read? Is that important? Is your Aboriginality important for somebody standing in front of the pictures and trying to come to some sort of understanding of them?

GB: I think people knowing my Aboriginality does have a large bearing on how they read the work. I don't know whether that's fortunate or not. It's just a fact of life that these things do have an effect. I think you're touching on a question which worries me a little: it's just a questioning of myself. My quick success has something to do with my Aboriginality and that worries me. Let's face it, Aboriginal work is flavour of the month. It was interesting what you were saying before about the guide not appearing to know. I quite like that in a way.

BL: It is a difficult question, isn't it? I mean on the one hand, support for Aboriginal art is a positive thing, given the history of black/white relations in this country. On the other hand, you want people to regard your work in the way they regard any other artwork, I suppose?

GB: I think, like anyone, I would like my work to be appreciated for itself, rather than because of who I am. It also interests me what you said about the middle-aged woman who saw my work as work by an Aboriginal person. I think that's good too.

There's a lot being written now about how the art market positions people and chews them up and spits them out. I'm just a bit worried about that. There's a problem about Aboriginal art in general being treated that way. I'm really new to all of this, just stumbling my way through.

BL: You went to art college a bit later than is usually the norm. Do you think that has had any impact? Right from the outset, your work didn't look like student work—it appeared much more sophisticated. Had you painted before you went to art college?

GB: Only part-time. I went to some art courses at night time. That gave me a portfolio I could take to college. I hadn't done any artwork after I left grade 10 until 1984. I worked for fifteen years before going to art college and that gave me a lot of time to read and think about things. I had reached a stage at Telecom where I just had to get out—I didn't relate to people there. Art college was something I had thought of because I thought I had some capacity to paint. I put myself under a lot of strain at college. I worked my bum off. I went to college to learn as much as I could and that's all I was interested in.

BL: I understand that you recently travelled to Maningrida in the Northern Territory and spent a short time with the Aboriginal people there. I wonder if you would comment upon that experience, its impact upon you, and perhaps its longer term impact on you as an artist?

GB: I went up to Maningrida for two weeks with Michael Eather [b. 1963]. It was very interesting. One of the things that struck me was the difference in culture and I felt very much unable to get below the surface. It really brought me to question my work and what I'm doing. My work has until now been about socialisation and coming to see Aboriginal people in a particular way. I found by going up there, I came into contact with a lot of my white conditioning. Like the tidy house syndrome that European people have. That had been instilled into me and that was one of the things I was trying to shed when I was up there. I realised how very different tribal Aboriginal culture is to the way I've been brought up. The experience brought me face to face with my own cultural conditioning. People must realise that there is stereotyping of what the background of urban Aboriginal artists is and what their art should be like. My position was highlighted for me by going to Maningrida. I've basically been conditioned to the Anglo-Australian worldview. My perception of Aboriginal culture has come in the same way as it has for most white Australians—through school, newspapers, general public comment. It is that which I've been trying to come to grips with and deconstruct in my work. This is very hard for me! Going to Maningrida was coming face to face with what my work has been about. There was a lot of turmoil for me personally.

BL: There was a question I was going to ask you later about appropriation of Aboriginal art. There are two questions: what is the relationship between your work and that of more traditional painters such as those at Papunya and Yuendumu and where do you stand in relation to the appropriation of that work? Secondly, how do you feel about the appropriation of that work by non-Aboriginal artists like Tim Johnson?

GB: That is a very difficult question. I can only speak for myself. I can't say what is appropriate for other artists. In late 1987/early 1988, I actually appropriated a Mimi spirit figure by a person called Guningbal [Crusoe Kuningbal, c. 1922–1984] in Maningrida in Arnhem Land. I didn't think I was breaking any copyright law because I did my figure from a photograph of a three-dimensional figure. I decided to do it because I like the Mimi spirit figure so much; it felt very powerful. This particular work of mine was shown in the National Aboriginal Art Awards in Darwin. The Mimi spirit dancers came in and saw it and this upset them very much. Thankfully, the situation was explained to them by people there who knew my work. Recently when I went up there, I spoke to the relatives of Gunin[g]bal, his son in fact [Crusoe Kurddal], who has inherited the rights to the design. I won't be appropriating any more Aboriginal images because I now more fully understand the situation.

You have to understand my position of having no designs or images or stories on which to draw to assert my Aboriginality. In just three generations that heritage has been lost to me. Dots are my bridge to my Aboriginality. They connect to their obvious relationship to the Western Desert paintings and in their relationship to reproductions and representation (the photos of my grandmother and mother). I am continually searching for ways to connect, to express by Aboriginality, and dots obsess me for now.

I won't appropriate any Aboriginal images and as far as Tim Johnson is concerned, he won't either. He uses dots and dots are fairly universal. As I understand it, dots are only a fairly recent development in Western Desert painting anyway. As far as people like Imants Tillers who appropriated Michael Nelson Jagamara's [b. 1949] work directly, I would never do that. Yet I don't condemn him. I think it's quite a good painting, but it does raise all of these issues. The people that really annoy me are those who put them on t-shirts—that really disgusts me. I have to tread lightly because I appropriate all over the place. But in relation to the appropriation of Aboriginal images, first you must understand the deep differences between the two cultures before you make any equivalences. There is also a big lack of understanding of Aboriginal culture—people don't really know what they're doing when they appropriate.

BL: Getting back to your work, I've seen slides of your early work. It seems to me that it was much more expressionistic, while your later, recent work is much more analytical. Is that a development?

GB: I guess you could say that. I came into college not knowing one thing really about art history. I came into college when new-expressionism was all the vogue. That depressed me really because that was the way I wanted to paint. I found that alchemy too was something people had been using forever. So I had to find new ways. Being interested in psychology too, I found my work very cathartic. I needed to work like that at a particular time, having just left a safe, secure job. For the first time I was coming out and letting people know about my Aboriginality. It was a very hard thing for me to say I was Aboriginal. My work helped me as a kind of emotional release. When I started using words like 'Abo', 'boong', 'darkie' on my paintings, it was a very hard thing to do. Since then my work has changed. It is more analytical. Having come to terms with that, I'm exploring now how language operates (those derogatory terms)—the references they carry and the emotions. So the language aspect was there from the beginning and it's still there.

BL: Would you comment on the politics of your work?

GB: I guess my work is political in that it deals with how Australians have come to see themselves and how they have come to see Aboriginal people. This Australian collective image has a big effect on how people relate to Aboriginal issues such as land rights. If they don't understand the Aboriginal relationship to the land, they will have no sympathy for land rights, for instance. My work is political in that it focuses on some of these issues, attempting to deconstruct the Eurocentric view of Aboriginal people.

❖ This interview was originally published in *Tension* 17 (1989): 39-42, and is reproduced courtesy of Bob Lingard.

Gordon Bennett: Expressions of Constructed Identity Interview with Anne Kirker

Anne Kirker (AK): Gordon, I first became acquainted with your painting in February last year at the time of your first solo exhibition, at Bellas Gallery in Brisbane. Like others who saw the show, I was impressed by the confrontational, sophisticated meshing of imagery which spoke of the tensions of identity within contemporary Australia, particularly in relation to Aboriginal people. Could you briefly describe the biographical factors which led up to these polemical works?

Gordon Bennett (GB): My history was quite ordinary in that I grew up in a working-class context and I was taught about Aboriginal people, like everyone else, at school. Later when I discovered my Aboriginal heritage, I was ashamed of it because of what I'd been taught and what I had experienced of general opinion living in a Eurocentric society. Then when I was aged about thirty, I started the hard task of coming to terms with my identity.

AK: You went to art college at this point after years of working for Telecom. The images you started producing were very expressionistic and what you have referred to as 'grotesque'.

GB: It was natural for me to paint that way, given the anger I harboured. It still is, but I'm using another language now, a cooler more directed one. I read something about theories of the grotesque and there's a quote that I have always kept:

> The characteristic themes of the grotesque, The Temptation of Saint Anthony and The Apocalypse, to name a few, jeopardise or shatter our conventions by opening up into vertiginous new perspectives characterised by the destruction of logic and regression to the unconscious—madness, hysteria or nightmare. For an object to be grotesque it must arouse three responses. Laughter and astonishment are two; either disgust or horror is the third. [ii]

I feel that by breaking a frame of reference, by introducing the novel or unexpected, the spectator may be jolted out of accustomed ways of perceiving the world. I think my work *Outsider* is a good example.

AK: Yes, I agree. You painted *Outsider* while still at Queensland College of Art, in 1988, and it partly parallels a painting van Gogh did in 1888 of his bedroom at Arles. You quote art history sources quite often.

GB: Certain people's work strikes me at certain periods of time. There is this element of synchronism happening. In the case of van Gogh, I started with the central figure and then looked for pictures of bedrooms and just happened to find this one. So things happen by coincidence but it's a meaningful coincidence, which I recognise. For instance, someone saw me using writing and suggested I should look at McCahon's work so I found a book in the library and liked it so much that I used some of the texts. I did a painting paralleling his *Valley of Dry Bones* [1947] and *The Promised Land* [1948], wishing these bones would come back to life and tell their story in relation to the massacres of Aboriginal people. It was a lament.

AK: Your reading at the time included [Thomas] Keneally's *The Chant of Jimmy Blacksmith* [1972] and recently you've made reference to critical texts like *Inventing Australia* by Richard White [1981]. It seems to me that they parallel the shift of emphasis in your work from overt expressionism to a more analytical approach. Would you agree?

GB: I've always read all over the place. Before I went to college, I was following theoretical texts as well as science-fiction and fantasy novels, but most of the analytical texts I was reading had to do with psychology. As well as this I was in analysis and doing workshops in rebirthing, gestalt theory, etc. However, my 'expressionism' was always informed by reading, including analytical texts. This notion of the purely emotional response of the expressionist embodied in the gestural brushstroke is a myth.

AK: In a recent interview with Bob Lingard for *Tension* magazine, you stated that you saw your current work as a 'kind of history painting'. Could you explain this?

GB: During the bicentenary, I was looking at how certain images are presented over and over again to reinforce a particular Australian collective self-image. There is a lot of misunderstanding about Aboriginal people because the historical perspective is either absent or misleading. This has made it easy for even intelligent people to accept the stereotype of an incompetent group. This history of abuse comes out in my painting *Web of Attrition* [1989], a gradual wearing down of self-esteem in people through being framed by racist beliefs. I remember watching a television news clip, supposedly about the Royal Commission on deaths in custody, which suddenly flashed to a night scene by the side of the street with two Aboriginal guys drinking. I believe it was put in there, out of context, to reinforce the stereotype. But getting back to history painting, I took images of Captain Cook and the 'first' landing which have become part of our conditioning and our Australian identity and I decided to make some pictures that show the other side of this identity. There's a good deal of anger in that I have been somehow duped into seeing myself in a negative way. It's been a process of going back and looking at the points of view the stories were written from. You always have to take into account the position of the observer. For instance, Cook came here and looked at the coast and named it New South Wales because it reminded him of South Wales. Aboriginal people thought the ships looked like floating islands and the sails like billowing clouds. You understand new experience from what you already know.

AK: Your large triptych hung in *Perspecta* 1989, divided into

[ii] Geoffrey Harpham, 'The Grotesque: First Principles', *The Journal of Aesthetics and Art Criticism* 34, no. 4 (Summer 1976): 463.

panels titled *Triptych: Requiem, Of Grandeur, Empire* [1989], brings in these concerns and images which you repeatedly use. Would you like to comment on some of these?

GB: Sure. I like to use religious iconography and symbols which have a wealth of meaning attached to them such as the crucifixion. In the centrepiece of the triptych, I have taken the dislocated arms and hands from [Matthias] Grünewald, which are very expressive of suffering but it is also part of a perspective diagram where the so-called receding arches (which also come out at you) start from a point at the back and gradually build up and so this event becomes larger than life. The photograph on the bottom shows my mother as a 14-year-old cleaning the stairs in this missionary training college for Aboriginal people. The landscapes came from a book that I have on anatomy and they're actually dissected cadavers. I thought of the landscape as no longer alive with the spirit of my ancestors but also I was interested in the Baudrillardian idea of the landscape as dead, an area which we traverse between two cities. Landscape is something you look at through the window of a speeding car, see on TV or in reproduction. The majority of people have never experienced the landscape that forms a large part of our Australian identity. Similarly, most people have never met an Aboriginal person and yet many have very strong opinions about Aborigines.

AK: For me, the triptych highlights the way you work by conceptual and visual oppositions. You appropriate images from found sources, such as photographs or illustrations from text books, and you set them in opposition to each other.

GB: Yes. I see it a bit like watching a television documentary or an advertisement where although the image is a moving narrative it is actually a construction of juxtaposed stills happening at twenty-five frames a second. If I put a particular image against an alternative, they are going to rub off on one another and the meaning shifts.

AK: You also use abstract formulas, including rules of perspective and language which structure information.

GB: Systems of belief and how they're constructed. I used to hate perspective because it was so artificial. Now I'm analysing how it was used in the Renaissance to create a false harmony. Everything was open, no secrets. The 'truth' was represented as a self-contained whole.

AK: And language is so crucial in moulding our perceptions.

GB: Yes, it is, but it's pretty crude and very limited. I used words in paintings at art college which were derogatory of Aboriginal people—Abo, boong, coon, darkie, heathen, nigger—most of which I grew up with and which contributed to the construction of my self-image.

AK: Could you comment on your use of dots which feature strongly in most of your paintings now?

GB: I was avoiding using dots because of the appropriation problem. Then I realised the links with Western art and dot screens in reproductions, after a talk given by Tim Johnson. I also discovered projectors at that time. In the series 'Notes on Perception' [1988–90] I made a connection between the topographical dot paintings from the Western Desert and the use of gestural brushmarks or European painting. I saw the images partly as 'psychotopographical' maps. Certain images became landmarks in how I perceived my identity. I'd photocopy images of Australian Aborigines, some taken by Baldwin Spencer [1860–1929], enlarge and break them up, inserting dots in the gaps.

AK: I realise how wary you are of appropriating traditional Aboriginal symbolism and that historical photographs of the Indigenous peoples and the dot matrix is as far as you will go.

GB: I'm actually taking more and more of my own images these days, like angels from cemeteries.

AK: Yes, there is one in *Ancestor Figures* [1989], which has been selected for the next Moët & Chandon travelling exhibition.

GB: That was the first time I used them. I was struck by the desecration of gravestones and statues, and also by a feeling of melancholy and loss. I photographed this angel and decided to use it in a painting alongside my grandmother's wedding photo.

AK: You're represented in another show, *Balance* 1990 at the Queensland Art Gallery with a group of small watercolours, which you produced with Eugene Carchesio last year [p. 16]. How did this happen?

GB: Well, Eugene approached me after seeing a work I did

relating to Albert Namatjira. It showed [Namatjira] in jail with an angel. He liked the pathos and asked me to do a collaborative piece with him.

AK: Except for the Aboriginal flag, which is evident in a number of the watercolours, it's virtually impossible to determine who was responsible for what.

GB: I like that! I used the flag obviously because of its Aboriginality, but also because of the abstract qualities of a black and a red bar with a yellow circle. With one of them Eugene started out with using Kandinsky's *Black Relationship* [1924]. It was the first. Another one, *Daddy's Little Girl* [1989], is based on an old gas heater commercial from the 1940s which shows a little girl in the living room with building blocks putting together words like 'abo' and 'darkie'. It tied in with using the grid as a model of consciousness and speaks of the transmission of racism from parent to child, from one generation to the next.

AK: Are there points that we haven't covered which you would like to close on?

GB: Well, the bottom line of my work is coming to terms with my Aboriginality. By deconstructing the way I've come to view Aboriginal people through a white perspective, I feel I act as a measure for how racism has been built up and how Australian identity is constructed. Perhaps by becoming a more whole person through accepting rather than denying this part of myself, I can help towards integrating some of the perspectives of Aboriginal people into the greater Australian context. Perhaps Australia, on a collective level, can become a more whole, more mature country by accepting the 'skeletons in its closet' instead of denying they ever existed. Denying the history of abuse means not being able to face it and thus not being able to understand current issues such as land rights in their full context, or in the clear light of reason, free of guilt. Until Australia comes to terms with itself and its fabricated identity based on the false ethnocentric notion of *terra nullius*, it will only ever be half a nation. I would like to think that my art can play a role in its growth.

❖ This interview was originally published in *Artlink* 10, no. 1 & 2 (1990): 93-95, and is reproduced courtesy of Anne Kirker and *Artlink*.

A Discussion with Gordon Bennett: The Inland Sea Interview with Christopher Chapman

Christopher Chapman (CC): I'm interested in the spaces between the works themselves and the systems that they operate in. Painting makes claims for all representation—it constructs certain points of view and is often exclusionary. If it's not exclusionary it's based upon certain hierarchical languages. In this case Western colonialism.

Gordon Bennett (GB): It comes back to that binary construction that the West has based its knowledge on. The black/white and primitive/civilised distinctions with no space in between. It's about abstraction, believe it or not. *Mirror (Abstract Field)* [1994] is probably one of the key works in this exhibition. With the organising principle being language—and language is taken for granted, like it's God-given (that's white God-given)—Western cultures structure things in a hierarchical way. Anything other is positioned further down the scale.

CC: The way that you have alerted the viewer to these systems has been through the use of Western perspective, used to point out the way that [it] operates—that it is a constructive device that's not universal nor is it necessarily even representative of the objective world. Could you tell me about the use of the mirror? In some of your installations, you have used actual mirrors. In *Present Wall* [1994], you mirrored the text so that it subverted and altered. In these paintings you have used Lichtenstein's mirror, and actual mirrors in *The Aboriginalist (Identity of Negation: Flotsam)* [1994]. The video operates as a kind of mirror as well. Could you say something about that? Why did you use the Lichtenstein mirror?

GB: I used that mirror image in 1991 in a piece called *Abstract Mirror*. It was paired off with another piece called *Interior (Abstract Eye)*. The eye is an organ which receives data from outside the body. It sends impulses to the brain in such a way that we 'see' the world. We then take that to be a very true picture of what we call reality, when it really is quite a constructive process that happens in the mind. The world is constructed using language and also knowledge which is actually learned experience and memory. We then forget that it is a kind of constructed thing that we're looking at. The actual image on the eye I believe is upside down, and eyes actually wobble to and fro all the time. So I'm really interested in that space between the thing out there and the eye, and then the space in between where the signals are received and how they're interpreted and organised in the mind, and how that relates to specifically Aboriginal people and to myself.

CC: It's an assumption even to say that what happens between the world and the eye is a given. It really comes down to certain languages, to the way that we're taught to perceive.

GB: Yes, how we gain knowledge. Which is then not questioned. For instance, we have this whole concept of primitivism where Aboriginal people are represented in one sense negatively but in another sense positively as being like the lost childhood of Western culture: as a sensibility or something that Western culture has lost, a spiritual connection to the earth or whatever. These are all very abstract notions. The whole business of perception is to me about abstraction, so I am interested in how it related to me as I grew up and was taught these things that shaped me as a person—while not knowing that I had an Aboriginal heritage. Then I find myself going to art college and somehow coming out at the other end as an Aboriginal artist, when that was never my intention. And then this continued looking at what that means, and how I'm positioned ...

CC: In between.

GB: Like so many people I am 'in between', in that conceptual space where categories overlap and permeate each other, but I constantly find myself being, I don't know, like told who I should be almost. My identity is imposed, projected on to me on the one hand, like my body is an inert surface onto which is projected the animating gaze of the 'European' eye.

I am like the tree that fell in the forest when no-one was there to observe [it].

Because of the Aboriginal adjective, people make assumptions about me that really aren't relevant and I find that disturbing. My interest lies in trying to turn it around and make myself the focus of the work in a way that disturbs the gaze. It's like foregrounding my own body as the reflection of the viewer. There's a strategy to make people see their other in a way that makes them own it. I'm not sure if it works. As for myself, I'm sort of light brown. If I stay out in the sun for a while, I get darker, but not black, and I'm interested in the white/black dichotomy, how there is no middle position within that narrow structure of the binary world; and so in the 'Body Print' paintings [1992-95] I painted myself as black and then printed this black body onto the white canvas. When I place it as a reflection in the mirror works, it then becomes the viewer looking at a reflection of themself.

The first body prints that I did made particular references to rock art and hopefully the whole idea of primitivism. Rock painting is supposedly the beginning of art.

CC: We were talking about the dots the other day, and all of these paintings use a screen of dots in one form or another, even these body print paintings. In a sense, these are mirror images as well, but a much closer view of the mirror or Lichtenstein's abbreviation of the mirror, so it still signifies the mirror.

GB: I wanted to refer to reproduction and how that figures representation. The dot screen of reproduction has its role in representation and vision. And Lichtenstein's mirrors are certainly about abstraction.

CC: What about the relationship between the dot screen and the use of dots as it signifies Aboriginality?

GB: Well, it's making a kind of cross-reference to it. Two of my major influences have been Tim Johnson and Imants Tillers in both their use of received images and the dot screen—using it as a signifier. I like to use styles as signifiers. Ways of applying paint can be as much a signifier as what you paint. For me, they both have to do with representation, but the hand dotting refers to a style of Aboriginal painting, Western Desert painting, and that too is a representation of a particular world view. The concentric circles are abstract and conceptual and can have different meanings and different relationships often within the same painting.

I use different images in a similar way, as sites that are brought together, that float across the dot screen and form relationships with each other and the viewer.

CC: So they also constitute a field. The *Panorama* [1991-93] paintings in the National Gallery [of Australia] operate in that way. In those paintings, the field acts to destabilise panoramic, linear, historical models.
GB: [This] makes them more fluid in the process, not static.

CC: The skeins of paint under the black ground operate in a similar way. Is that how you think of them?

GB: I was interested in Pollock's work because of the way it was art historically positioned and constructed. In my own mind I related the performance aspect of Pollock's painting process to Aboriginal ground painting being a reaffirmation of culture and identity through the ceremony of painting. I was interested in the abstract field of Pollock's paintings, and how people continually saw images in there, because our mind seems to have a need to construct and order things and thus we 'see' things materialise within the field. So it was a field pregnant with possibilities where images could be brought together; and in fact I think Tillers wrote in one of his essays that *Blue Poles* [1952] acted like a vortex that drew all images into it. I find that quite fascinating. It can become a field upon which images can come together. Also the fact that when one's mind did project and see a shape within this coloured, chaotic matrix, it was formed out of memory because these skeins of paint would look like something, and for it to look like some 'thing', you must already have the idea of what this 'thing' might look like. Where things are torn apart or dismembered, which is how Aboriginal cultures are treated, pulled apart ... parts can come back together or be remembered. With the video work, I liked the performance aspect of Pollock's 'dance', and the dance aspect of ground painting. My choice was to dance to modern music, rap music, and there is a very strong message coming through from that. It acts as a kind of black networking. The political repression of African Americans is conveyed through music and language. There is a certain solidarity coming across that I find influential and also disturbing because of the implied violence.

CC: Conceptually, Pollock's paintings exist in space before they exist as a painted image, and so in that video in a sense you inhabit this space which almost has to exist as an imaginary—the mythological 'moment' before the paint hits the canvas.

GB: The television that I set up in the foreground establishes perspective because of the way the wide-angle lens gives a sense of receding space. But I have organised it in such a way that it looks like I'm dancing on top of the TV—but then I also come around to the front which disturbs even that illusion.

CC: So it disrupts perspective.

GB: Plus the changing dot pattern on the mandala pattern is based on concentric circles. Again, it's the role of suggestion where I'm bringing these things together. There's a serious element in it but there is also a lot of punning and a bit of humour in there, I would hope. Then setting them up as TV to TV monitor, like one was reflecting the other which reflects the other, reflects the other—it goes on. Like the 'mirrors' in the exhibition. Things are made more complicated and strange.

CC: The motif of the sinking boat appears quite often in these paintings: what's the story behind that?

GB: I haven't been able to check that, but sometime during my readings and my art training, I remember that the boat was used as a metaphor for the conscious, rational mind. It was seen as a man in a small boat bobbing on an ocean which represented the unconscious.

CC: So the inland sea could be the nation's unconscious?

GB: In a way, yes, and certainly the Aboriginal succour given to the successful explorers of the inland has been consciously repressed. The 'inland sea' is an important aspect. As an idea it was created because Europeans figured that rivers that ran inland must go into a sea. It was like a European rational organisation of what they knew projected onto what was unknown. So it represents an inability to come to grips with the 'essence' of this country. After all, most of us live on the coastal regions with our backs to the inland. We always look back to Europe for our positive reflection of ourselves.

CC: Or for our knowledge.

GB: And also for approval.

CC: To enter the installation which comprises the videos and paintings, people have to walk across the black canvas on the floor which then forces them to enter a field.

GB: They're actually walking on black skin.

CC: The backdrop in the video is then used as the floor that people walk on.

GB: In the video I dress up in a tuxedo, which is also like a black skin, with a white shirt and gloves. It's a bit like performing a ceremony in the painted field and investing it with energy and then painting over it and then having people walk into that space—it's an energy field. I like the idea of people removing their shoes and actually feeling the cold floor and hopefully feeling the ridges in the painting through their socks or stockings. I wanted the tactile experience to be part of an aesthetic experience; and because it would be through the feet, which are not usually part of any aesthetic experience, I thought it would have a disturbing or disorientating effect on the viewer which would implicate the viewer very strongly in the production of meaning in the work, a work that the viewer was lured inside of.

The work itself is heavy with violence, which is both visually present in the form of small paintings and implied in the floor piece. The dancer was meant to act almost as a comedy relief, a joker or trickster figure that would offer some relief to the seriousness of it all. I mean, there is humour there and when humour and seriousness come together, it becomes a very strange and powerful force for catharsis. The work is a grotesquerie.

❖ This interview was originally published in *Artonview* 1 (1995): 38-42 and is reproduced courtesy of Christopher Chapman and the National Gallery of Australia, Canberra.

Interview with Gordon Bennett
Chris McAuliffe

Chris McAuliffe (CM): Do you think that people come to your work with a set of expectations, having heard a term like appropriation or Aboriginality?

Gordon Bennett (GB): I think they do; mostly the Aboriginal preconceptions. I'm not so sure about appropriation. I don't see myself as an appropriation artist really.

CM: So when you say 'appropriation artist', you're assuming that there's a particular kind of artist who's self-conscious about lifting and manipulating imagery.

GB: Yes, appropriation as a particular strategy in itself that they base their entire practice on. I've heard that term used but I've never seen myself as that. While I do use images that already exist, it's not what I do all the time; it's something I do when I feel it's necessary.

CM: When is it necessary—for particular shows, or to make a particular point?

GB: The strategy I am employing is a re-reading of images that exist within the pages of history books or school texts or just images that have kind of been put to sleep in a way and now exist between pages on library shelves. Images which people rarely see but which have become part of the visual referencing of how Australians see themselves.

CM: White Australians or black Australians?

GB: Well, most of us went through a school of some sort so it's immaterial what colour, as it's things that are within the education system, that are circulated through television, through art magazines or history texts; works that have become fixed in place and exist with a relevant label at the bottom of the picture which explains what this particular picture means and people never go beyond that meaning; it's like it's fixed within that frame of reference and illustrates a particular text that informs people of Australian history, which in turn informs a sense of Australianness. My strategy using appropriation has been to dig these images out and either recontextualise part or all of them in some way so that they can be re-read in the present context ... It's like bringing them back to life, resuscitating them, and exploring their meanings given what we know about Australia now.

CM: When you say 'dig them up', do you stumble across them or do you actively look for them, or remember them from childhood or ...?

GB: Mostly I stumble across them. I'll just be browsing in the library and open a book and find some illustrations that are interesting because of their initial impact on me, in coming at them from a questioning point of view, not just an accepting point of view. For instance, the illustrations of Cook raising the flag and taking possession. Anyone who gazes at more than one of these images will see that they're different and that they're all interpretations. But I know that before I had an art education, I would see these as being like photographs and not question them, the fact that they are constructed.

CM: So you're finding these images and you're recognising that the image itself is constructed and that by extension history and Australianness are also constructed. But if you bring the image back to life, you're manipulating too just as the original artist did ...

GB: And in doing that I'm trying to show that that's what I'm doing. I'm not trying to say, 'It wasn't that but it is this'. I don't want to say that because I can't. It's about questioning. It's not about giving alternative absolutes, but about finding other possible perspectives.

CM: When you're resuscitating and manipulating, how do you show that you're doing that? You talked about the originals concealing their constructedness, but how do you show you're constructing when you're making a picture?

GB: I guess that in the visible layering of the images one can see that it's being put together. Because there are these things that jar and don't feel right being there. I've used strategies of overlaying perspective on top of the picture, and making the picture very flat and not using tonal gradation to give the illusion of space, but when I overlay the perspective, it actually gives it depth and you can see why it's giving it depth; it's not hidden. It's like exposing the framework or the skeletal structure of the image itself.

CM: I was also thinking, say, of a painting like *Prologue: They Sailed Slowly Nearer* [1988], the way it was a layering of imagery; a cartoon strip of Captain Cook's voyage of discovery, with cubes in perspectival construction adjacent to it. You were mapping out these positions rather than nesting them inside each other.

GB: I was trying to make the means of the illusion quite visible and placing them so that there was this jarring or not-quite-fitting-together properly, so you could see where they were coming from. The images came out of a kind of comic book history book, from around the 1950s, made for kids to understand easily.[i] So it was already flat; there was no illusion [of space], it was just black and white. I guess the dot screen comes again from the whole idea of appropriation art, if I can call it that, in Australia, with the Benday dot screen and receiving images via reproduction, and conflating that with the Aboriginal dot screen from Western Desert paintings.

CM: The comic strip was not done in the dot technique in the first place—it was a line drawing—so the dot screen that you laid over it doesn't belong to the image you've lifted. It belongs to the idea of reproduction, and that separation of the two made it clear that you weren't just talking about the image itself but also the means of its circulation and, broader yet, the culture in which it was circulating.

GB: And also trying to say something about its repetition, as a site of reference. The particular image being a site of reference for the construction of one's identity. So in that image there's a roundel that makes reference to the Western Desert paintings in that it's a site, a reference to cultural renewal ... and Captain Cook's discovery is the first sighting. The sighting of the eyes becomes the site of reference now, and you find even on television—particularly during the bicentennial [of the first white settlement of Australia, 1988], which was my last year of art college, when I did that picture—it was very noticeable how certain images were repeated and other things completely left out. And that's part of the story, bringing those things that were left out back to the forefront ... saying, well, you have to take the good with the bad and how does that change your point of view of the pioneers. The pioneers did such atrocious things to other human beings. I'm just trying to examine how those Aboriginal people were seen to be less than human, through ways of naming them. Names that are still in use today.

CM: Events like the bicentennial are so visual, primarily spectacular, and maybe something like that upped the ante on appropriation art. Obviously people are so conscious that the circulation of the image is the primary site of meaning these days.

GB: I think that what's often forgotten is that these things operate outside of the art world. For instance, if you watch people doing re-enactments of the landing, raising the flag, it's like they're staging something that they've already seen. Where did these images come from that they're relating back to in their minds in order to stage this re-enactment? It's like images become part of the Australian unconscious. They're buried, and this is a way of bringing them back into memory, but remembered in a different way from the way that I was taught, looking at them from a different angle and looking at how they work, where they came from

[i] According to Leanne Bennett, Bennett refers here to *The Australian Children's Pictorial Social Studies* (Sydney: Australian Visual Education Pty Ltd, 1958). The series of 25 books is based on the Social Studies curricula of all Australian Education departments and aims to tell a complete story of some important parts of Australian history.

initially, and how these images still support contemporary stereotypes, etc.

CM: You say that this has an effect outside of the art world. This seems to be where your borrowing and redeploying imagery differs a little from other appropriators in Australian art of the 1980s; so much of what was being done there seemed to operate within the idea of art. Imants Tillers is the most obvious example; he was talking about the possibility of being a contemporary artist in Australia, whereas your work is considerably different from that.

GB: My focus is outside of the art world, and I guess that comes from where I grew up. I went to art college late, at thirty, after fifteen years of work experience listening to people's views about Aborigines, and there's this sense of trying to communicate to these people that the way they have been taught to see the world, and to see Aborigines, is not God-given. It's not absolute; it's relative. There are different ways of seeing things. And most of my work has layers of meaning that can be approached by anyone who doesn't have an art background, there is this level of communication to uninformed or lay people.

CM: Maybe there's a parallel with some of Juan Davila's [b. 1946] work because he's looking beyond art as well, whereas Lindy Lee [b. 1954] or Mark Titmarsh [b. 1955], whose work is much more about a tragic view of art history, or a sense of loss—it's more poetic in their case. Your citations, a lot of the time, seem to be much more anonymous citations, not about recognising the art historical sources.

GB: I do use details and I'm not trying to make the source so apparent. The point is that the detail can be changed, that it doesn't really matter where it came from because it can be changed. And I have found that when people ask me where did it come from and I tell them, that it somehow defeats the purpose of actually taking the detail. For instance, if I use an image that has the black police, the part I use may not have the body of the policeman, just a hand holding an axe. That says something entirely different than if people know it's actually the black police involved. I'm not sure why; on this one superficial level, there's this romantic belief that 'Aborigines shouldn't kill each other', but white people do it all the time so what's the difference? It's about people hurting each other, not black and white.

CM: It's not as if you're appropriating in order to engage in a debate with another artist. There have been occasional instances, but most of the time you're talking about narratives of discovery, the discourse of colonisation, the discourse of historical re-enactment.

GB: I guess the idea of the project is to put things on the agenda and to draw things out of these notions, to keep it on the agenda too, keep it in people's minds, keep the questioning there. My experience of people is that they have hard and fast opinions on Aborigines, never having met any but only having seen them through the media [via] repeated images, but only certain kinds of images—whether it's drinking or violence or something. So there's always that sense of being informed by the world outside, which I live in. Because I live in the suburbs of Brisbane. So there's something very real about me looking through an art-historical text and seeing an image and having the night before had an argument at a barbecue. The art theory is there but it's more something to play with than something serious for me. There's a sense of layering and historical layering as being a text; parts of it can be re-interpreted and the citation is working in a similar way to writing where you cite another author's point of view. So if I use Pollock drips or a pastiche of Pollock, I'm referring to him and the work then takes on board some of the meaning of how his work was interpreted and his historical position. And that forms a layer which I then project other images onto. So if you see that as a metaphor for unguided, unconscious chaos or something, there's this ordering going on when you project an image onto it, as is the case when people 'see' in images in Pollock's work. And for me that sort of relates to mirroring and how images rise up as sites where you locate the sense of self. So I use Cook's landing, and I use ships as the idea of exploration, and arrival and even the convict thing and slavery—a ship can have all these different meanings. And if, for instance, it's a ship imposed on a Pollock-like drip surface, in one sense it can refer to the romantic exploration of the heroic artist and modernist progression.

CM: There's almost an assumption that the audience itself is going to be adept at using these multiple languages as well. It's as if appropriation art assumes more of the viewer and gives the viewer a good deal more authority.

GB: By using images that people know, it's also a way into the work. With a lot of work, you can't get past the surface of it—perhaps that's the intention—whereas with my own work this layering thing's important. I relate to what I know of Western Desert painting and Aboriginal artists. There is a public layer to any of the works that the people within the group can all relate to, a part of the story. Then there are different layers below that level, according to one's level of 'initiation', that you can understand. So in a way I do see the images I find as Dreamings and the site is the Dreaming site, that site of memory that you draw on for your sense of Australianness. It's about not being complacent about the image. It's about possibilities for forging new levels of understanding.

CM: Your early work seemed to me to be much more angry, making that point emotionally. Was there a point at which you started to feel your work becoming less emotional and becoming more contemplative?

GB: That was in my last year at art college, it was probably more to do with the theory-based subjects I was doing plus trying to cool the work down. The anger was still there. Part of the reason I'm using projectors too is to remove myself to the point at which I become like a printing press. I'm not painting what I feel, I'm tracing it on the surface of the thing. I went to art college with a lot of bottled-up anger and I still have it, I've just learnt to channel it in different ways.

CM: The reason I'm asking is that it seems to go back to what you were saying earlier about not being too specific because if you made a very expressionistic, immediate, angry work, it's easier for a threatened audience to dismiss it as just one angry young man, it's his problem, let's hope he works it out ... rather than it being the viewers' problem as well, or a problem that viewers can't localise.

GB: My so-called 'expressionist' work was always conceptually based on the idea of the grotesque, and it was so strong that I felt it could work against communication in an audience. It was a matter of education for me. I guess I went to art college as an artist, but I didn't have the language to say what I wanted to. I was prompted to that by the theory aspects. I was reading [Jean] Baudrillard and [Roland] Barthes and Walter Benjamin [1892–1940], also John Berger. Mainly particular readings that were part of the course. I did [the course] Postmodernism in my second year. I found Communication Studies very interesting, I got a lot out of that. I'd already been reading in that area before I went to art college as part of my own personal growth, and in courses that I went to, just trying to pull myself out of a rut.

CM: We've been using the words 'appropriation artists'. Was there a point where you came across someone like that, where you thought, this is what it means, this is what they're talking about?

GB: Yes, I was interested in photography as well, and Sherrie Levine [b. 1947] was someone we looked at in my first year. And I probably read about it in some of the art magazines. And Richard Prince as well was very interesting. I was doing a bit of appropriating of people's landscape photographs out of books and matching my own images, collage-like, and re-photographing that and altering it again, and re-photographing and re-photographing. It wasn't directed with content so much, there was content there, but I couldn't really pin it down as to what it was.

CM: It was the process that was more interesting?

GB: At the time. At a point in my Postmodernism classes, I realised that there was a lot of fitting things into prescribed theories. During my time in college, appropriation was something that was in the air, as well as neo-expressionism, which was not something I followed. It just happened to coincide with my way of painting; I'd always been interested in the expressionists anyway, the German expressionists, German art in general ... appropriation was something that we'd been taught, and it was in the magazines. I guess I just came into it naturally because I could see the possibilities ... It was another art strategy that was totally accepted within a Western context, and able to be drawn upon as much as abstraction was or different ways of applying paint.

CM: This was in the second half of the 1980s?

GB: Yes, in the late 1980s.

CM: What is often forgotten is that appropriation has its own minor history, and in the late 1970s/early 1980s, it did seem to be a very radical thing to be doing; it seemed to marry pop and conceptual art in a way that could then be turned against neo-expressionism to very good effect. And in Australia, people like Paul Taylor [1957-1992] added another level to it by using it as a metaphor for the historical condition of the white Australian artist. By the time you get to the later 1980s, it's just another text, just another system, that art students work through. And people forget how much art school is about trying things out.

GB: Certainly, I try to keep that attitude about trying things out all the time. The layering that I do is part of that. Pastiche for me was about learning how to paint as well as referring to other artists' work. And I have this weird thing where I can't paint twice in the same way in the same day. I certainly do not have this wish to get my signature style down.

CM: That's the burden of the appropriation artist because as soon as the appropriation artist develops a signature style, then she or he is appropriable.

GB: I've always seen styles as being as much about meaning as images or words for that matter. Words can have different meanings and references in relation to their context. The Expressionist brushstroke has a set of meanings that have been accrued, and that can be used also like a reference. It's like the entire history of Western art—and other art for that matter—is like a book on a library shelf that you can draw from, so there's no need to have your own style because all these styles have virtually been done with the exception of new technologies; but even that becomes something that you can integrate into a text, a visual text.

CM: The Italian take on appropriation, Achille Bonito Oliva's 'Transavantgarde', claimed that all of history was available because of reproduction, because of historical self-consciousness, but one engaged with it at a very superficial level as a consequence. And Baudrillard, too, suggested that you're just playing with the pieces, you've got all these fragments and you just shuffle them around. It was like a really crude nihilism: we can do anything, but it's going to be nothing. That doesn't seem at all what you're doing.

GB: I relate to that attitude, but it always comes back to my everyday life and trying to negotiate human relationships. So I can't divorce my art practice from my life. I know that Imants Tillers' practice is based very much on this shuffling things around, but he does rely on intuitive ways of putting things together and I think that there are issues in his work, although he might deny that. Again, I think it might come down to the work of artists being appropriated by critics and theorists to meet their own ends. Pollock was appropriated to fit the agenda of critics like Clement Greenberg, which he went along with, of course, and it made him very famous, but it was not of his making. He was doing his work and his work just happened to fit this particular niche ... And it was the same with Paul Taylor's 'Popism—The Art of White Aborigines' [1982]. I think it's a mistake when artists start to believe all that stuff and start calling themselves 'White Aborigines', and really taking that stuff seriously.

CM: I think a lot of people prefer the written version of an artwork because it's more assimilable. Do you feel that's been done to your work?

GB: I think so, yes. I'm very conscious of being appropriated to fit whoever's particular theory about Aboriginality or even postcolonialism. I have been trying to argue my point, but I've found that what I say doesn't matter. So I decided to stop saying it. For the five years from 1992, I'll put a 'non-performance' clampdown on giving public talks. My work is often seen as about exploring my identity in order to secure it, like I'm searching for it, like I've lost it somewhere, which is the total opposite to what I'm doing. Sure, I'm exploring identity, but I'm trying to make it obvious about how open it is; how it's a process of the negotiation of these different sites of memory, human relations. It's all those other things, and it shouldn't be closed off. It shouldn't be a thing that constricts nor should it be an imposed thing, from outside oneself, like a prison.

CM: That openness ... does that leave you adrift? There's this problem of subjectivity, identity, whatever you want to call it. If it's open and mobile the way you say, doesn't that leave you insecure and uncertain?

GB: It has its negative side. I think the way Foucault describes freedom is the clue—to what I think I'm doing anyway: we need to cut ourselves adrift from the historical narratives that have informed our sense of self of feeling and identity. I feel the only identity you need is really a human one, you're a human being in the world. Sure all those things—I'm an Australian, I'm an Aussie and all that stuff—it's safe, but it's not free. And I think freedom is about not being tied down by those things; the feeling's scary, but freedom is about being uncertain and even insecure.

CM: We were talking earlier about the way that a lot of your appropriated imagery is very much historical, either literally quite an old source image or it's an image that was always within an historical context. Have you ever considered looking at the kinds of historical representations and even quite specific representations of Aboriginal culture that you get within recent white Australian art? I'm thinking of [Russell] Drysdale [1912-1981], [Noel] Counihan [1913-1986], [Yosl] Bergner [1920-2017]. Have you ever looked at that 1940s and 1950s work?

GB: I have but not too seriously because mainly that's too recent, and those artists were generally empathising with Aboriginal people as human beings. I'm working through historical stuff. Maybe I've got the feeling too that that's too art specific, too closed off. But I'm not sure because you can get into the area where any representation of an Aboriginal person by a non-Aboriginal artist is problematic. Perhaps it's also that I haven't come across those images in the context that I'm interested in as historical illustrations, things that more directly feed our sense of cultural position and that position Aborigines as a negative other.

CM: The dominant Australian culture has been profoundly uncertain about itself since World War II; it's always been a sub-text in Australian art—who are we? And appropriation, in the hands of quite a lot of Australian artists, actually gave an answer ... well, we're this weird hybrid, we're this postmodern, postcolonial layering. And there was almost some security in the uncertainty.

GB: It's like trying to find an identity in a non-definite field. It's like trying to transcend your self-identity before you know what your self-identity is.

CM: It's a real fudge that almost says: 'I articulate this postmodernity, this profound uncertainty, and out of this I forge this profoundly modernist notion of an identity that can speak about itself knowingly, an identity that can say, I name myself.' It seems to me that with appropriation that's where it differed a little in Australia; from what I read that's what often happens in South America and Latin America as well. Appropriation is used to speak about being a coloniser and a colonised; to speak about, as you suggest, becoming postmodern before you've even worked out your modernity; coming up with a myth of nation at the very moment when you know that myths are what you're supposed to be questioning. Which is so different from the American appropriationists who seem much more concerned about the author at a theorised level, or mechanical reproduction at a theorised level. We've talked on another occasion about the appropriation theory that goes into a kind of infinite regress, that argues that there never was an original, that it was always already a copy. Is there any originality available to you?

GB: I think there is. I put things together in an original way and from a different perspective, and I'm conscious of the positions I'm placed in. I play with those and I realise my work is appropriated by people who are looking for, critics and art historians who are looking for, someone to appropriate for their own ends. That's the way it's always worked and I'm conscious of that, so I'm not naïve in the sense I believe I can recapture some essence of identity that colonisation has denied me, some sense of an original identity that only I can speak of and defend. However, paradoxically, I do keep insisting on defining myself, but in ways that are creative and fluid and not static and essentialist. One of my strategies is constantly to take issue with imposed names such as 'urban Aboriginal artist'. There is an inherent violence in such naming, in its confining limits, which is reflected in my work. Imants Tillers once said to me that I should become more 'pataphysical'. He didn't realise that I couldn't possibly become more pataphysical than I already am. He failed to see he was creating me with his own preconceptions of the 'Aboriginal'. Paul Taylor appropriated Aboriginality to create his 'white Aborigines', but of course what he actually referred to was not an 'original' but a Western construct; he copied a copy, in other words. By being aware of this, and by being aware of my own position in relation to the construction of an Aboriginal identity within Western cultural parameters, I think I can lay claim to some sense of originality.

CM: It seems to me the way out is an acute awareness

of context. Because you're talking about studio practice, education, your life experience, your position within the art industry, your position within a culture that's trying to figure itself out in relation to others. Within all of them, those competing and interacting forces, to say that there's no difference between your image and some other image just doesn't work. At the theoretical level, a lot of the language-based discussion of appropriation or the lack of originality tends to use the French models, which are interested in the play of language, as opposed to the Americans, whose linguistic theory is much more pragmatic. The Americans talk about the operation of language; they're saying, let us look at how it works in this instance rather than how it plays at the level of theory.

GB: There are some things you can't describe with language. I guess that's what the whole idea of metaphor and what allegory is about, about trying to describe something that is other than what you have in front of you. In a lot of ways, I'm trying to do that. I'm very self-aware of many things about myself. But I'm too self-aware to want myself to be pinned down, or to pin myself down to one thing—Aboriginal or something like that. That I am human is about the most anchored I could get, but that's really open to question too, I guess.

CM: But you've chosen a particular discourse—the humanist discourse.

GB: I don't even know that I've chosen the humanist discourse because that's kind of ... it's a way of circumscribing things, pinning them down. A sentient being might be another one ... Things are in flux, it's a negotiation type thing. Like one day you might be one thing and make a stance, and the next day, after reading more information, you might totally change your mind ... and that's what people do. It's not about taking a stance and fighting for it until the bitter end. It's much more creative in relation to the context of any given moment or set of ideas.

In my Camerawork essay ['Re-Writing History', p. 18], I tried placing myself in a fluctuating text or, rather, a historical narrative ... It consisted of all quotes, just to embed myself in an ongoing discourse. Where I put a statement by a person from the nineteenth-century next to one from February 1993, you could see that there's very little difference between the opinions. Some of the criticism of my work is that it's all about the past and that it doesn't relate to the present. But I'm trying constantly to point out that the past is always with us and that it informs our present and also our concepts of the future. So it's important and I guess that's why I call myself a history painter sometimes ...

Most of my artist's statements now consist of quotes that I juxtapose. Because I'm interested in the gaps between words and the gaps between quotes that speak about us sometimes. I guess they're allegorical; it's in the gaps where the meaning becomes more profound. If you put together two juxtaposing statements, they change each other and that area where they're changing, that field of interpretation, is interesting.

❖ This interview was conducted in September 1993, during Gordon Bennett's time as artist-in-residence at the University of Melbourne. It was originally published in *What Is Appropriation? An Anthology of Writings on Australian Art in the 1980s and 1990s*, ed. Rex Butler (Sydney: Power Publications and Institute of Modern Art, 1996), 271-279. This interview is reproduced courtesy of Chris McAuliffe, the Power Institute Foundation for Art and Visual Culture, University of Sydney, and the Institute of Modern Art, Brisbane.

Conversation: Bill Wright Talks to Gordon Bennett

Bill Wright (BW): Most people familiar with your work have observed that a significant shift occurred several years ago. After fifteen intensive years, the project you once aptly referred to as 'postcolonial' came to an end. This extensive body of work, in its central iconic disposition, dealt with issues of iniquity and injustice and the endemic abuses and manipulations of power in the human realm. It is the work by which you are widely known and most respectfully identified in Australia and beyond.

So this stage in your creative working life seems to usher a new beginning, as an abstract painter; a shift from explicit visual content to overt visual phenomena. This could be understood as representing a point of perennial dilemma for many artists at different times, between representation and embodiment, of the very nature of the artist's engagement in his or her profession as a painter, a maker of material images. What led you to what appears to be such a radical change?

Gordon Bennett (GB): There are a number of reasons why I began painting abstract paintings that focused on 'overt visual phenomena' as opposed to 'explicit visual content'. One reason is that I felt I had gone as far as I could with the postcolonial project I was working through. This culminated in the 'Notes to Basquiat' series in 2003. The content of the work was getting to me emotionally. So, painting in an overtly 'abstract' manner was a way to go silent on the issues involved and yet still keep painting. It was a way forward for me.

Another reason was to make people aware that I am an artist first and not a professional 'Aborigine'. I found people were always confusing me as a person with the content of my work. While it is true that most of my work has been autobiographical, I'm still separate from it. There is a conceptual distance involved in the making of my work, and my work was largely about ideas rather than emotional content emanating from some stereotype of a 'tortured' soul.

So, the overtly 'abstract' work is a way of distancing myself from the work so people can see me as separate from it. I'm placing inverted commas around the word 'abstract' because I believe all my work has been abstract in one way or another. I can't explain this sense of the abstract in my work properly, so I won't try, but I know all my work to date has been about 'abstraction'. The work I'm making at present is more 'overtly' abstract in that it fits the conventional meaning/look of 'abstract' painting.

Finally, I've never been one to make art about art before. There was always some sense of social engagement. I needed to change direction ... at least for a while. Art about art seems appropriate for the time being. The 'Stripe' series [2003–08; figure 34] of abstract paintings represents a kind of freedom for me as an artist.

BW: The points you make about conceptual distance and not being a professional Aborigine are clearly important in addressing a fundamental misconception about who you are, the nature and meaning of your personal history and identity, as well as the conceptual impetus of what you do as an artist. I remember our first conversation a decade or so ago; you talked about the nature of what you referred to as cultural baggage, which I took to mean baggage received, or imposed, from both of your inherited cultural camps.

Of course, irrespective of stereotypical misapprehension, the real matter of your achievement as an artist, your work, is beyond its misreading. But while it may be either a valid insight or a projection, in conversations in recent years about your work, people have seen the abstract 'Stripe' paintings as invoking a sense empathically connected to Aboriginal visual traditions, more than to the European traditions, often polemically referenced in earlier works.

GB: I see the 'Stripe' paintings as coming primarily from a Western tradition rather than an Aboriginal one. Perhaps such assertions that the 'work invokes a sense of Aboriginal visual tradition' is an example of imposing cultural baggage. It's in the eye of the beholder. Personally, I don't see the connection other than to stripes as body art. I looked to both camps to develop this series of paintings, but I think the work owes more to the European tradition than any Aboriginal one. Cultural baggage is a problem in that one can't see clearly past one's expectations. If a person expects an 'Aboriginal' artist to make Aboriginal art, then that is what they will find or read into the work.

BW: As you say, your work is largely autobiographical, but what also interests me is the indivisible capacity you indirectly refer to when you say that people confuse you as a person with the content of your work. I take this as meaning, beyond stereotyping, the failure to acknowledge your singular capacity to independently exercise ethical or aesthetic choice and make radical historic and moral connections, when so much of your work is essentially 'about ideas'.

I'm intrigued by the idea that this notable independence may also be in part due to the other side of the misconception (quite widely known but perhaps not understood) that race, hence racism, was not initially a key part of your awareness but was thrust upon you at a vulnerable early stage in your individual social development, and later identified in a personal way as 'baggage' adopted purposefully; taken up by you as an important source of polemical insight, a core critical part of your living dialectic.

GB: Yes, my work is largely autobiographical. I use my own experience as a source or starting point to develop a stream of thoughts about broader issues of race and identity. My own upbringing and cultural socialisation was the basis for many ideas used in my earlier work. I recognised my individual social development as an important source of ideas.

I agree with your interpretation of my comment about people confusing me as a person with the content of my work. People tend to focus on the emotional aspect rather than the conceptual when interpreting my work, and that bothers me. Even if the starting point for a work is an emotive one, I believe I conceptually examine the ideas behind the emotion and extrapolate from there.

BW: In the context of the last century in Western art, the term 'abstract' has had various shades of meaning for different groups and individuals working under its aegis in Europe, America and here in Australia. For example, while too often gratuitously lumped together, there was a seldom referred to but profound difference between the apolitical Greenberg identified American 'Second Generation' abstract artists and politically engaged precursors like [Mark] Rothko, [Barnett] Newman, [Robert] Motherwell [1915-1991] and [Philip] Guston [1913-1980], who, in their formative development, shared an abiding commitment to social action, as well as a growing disposition towards non-literal imagery.

In another sense, there are as many kinds of abstraction as there are artists 'abstracting'. Would you talk a little more about the nature of the abstraction that you refer to as a constant in your work, as well as the more recent approach: would it be possible at this stage in your work to describe the experience of commonality and difference between these two approaches?

GB: I believe everything to be more or less an abstraction. The way we as human beings experience the world we live in is through the senses. The eyes 'see' the world upside-down on the lens of the eye, this information is electrochemically transferred to the brain where it is interpreted by comparing what we 'see' with previous experiences. Language here is an important factor in interpreting what we 'see'. Words have accumulated meanings that come from somewhere and are culturally relative and biased. All this seems very abstract to me, and is, in a nutshell, what I mean when I say my work has always been about abstraction.

BW: I would find it hard to envisage your abstract work as being entirely divorced from the experiential dimension informing your earlier work. To engage and extend into other areas or layers of consciousness by such means as you are now employing seems to involve a different non-referentially intuitive kind of approach. You refer to the present work as 'art about art'; will this prove to represent divorce or, as you imply it might, some kind of transient separation from the emotionally demanding societal critique that encompassed your creative life up to this recent turning point?

GB: The recent work does represent a transient separation from the emotionally demanding societal critique of my earlier work. I guess I would relate it more to an existential experience of the paint being dragged across the surface of the canvas rather than to a continuation of any 'Aboriginal' art traditions. People will always read into a painting what they expect to see. The 'Stripe' series relates more overtly to what most audiences think of as abstract art—not so much about ideas of abstraction. Basically, what you see is what you get—less about underlying layers of meaning. This current series is about paint on a surface, colour and composition. The contemplation of the object in itself is nothing more than what one sees before one's own eyes. There is nothing to hinder the viewer from having the aesthetic experience and becoming 'the pure subject of will-less knowing'.

BW: While, as you say, this work is about paint on a surface, colour and composition, and you've identified all your works as in some way abstract, you have also referred to the new 'abstract' works as being different in kind. I'd like to get a closer sense of how the internal dialogue with this work is different beyond these formal attributes, to what particular experiential dimension these hold for you that is different?

GB: I guess the work is different for me in that I concentrate on the act of painting in itself rather than as a means to an end. Whilst painting, I am totally consumed by the act of dragging the brush down the surface of the canvas, by the act of keeping the lines/stripes even and as straight as possible. There is something very existential about this act of painting.

BW: How did you respond to Ian McLean's seemingly contradictory point in his introduction to your 2004 Greenaway Gallery exhibition,[1] about the abstract works being the culmination of your desire to circumvent Aboriginalisation by shifting your imagery to a more internationalist arena, noting, of particular relevance here, that the first of these were consistently also appropriations: in the particular instance of politicised late 1960s abstractions, such as the works of the archetypal production materialist Frank Stella [b.1936]?

GB: I gave Frank Stella as a major influence in making the 'Stripe' paintings simply because he was, among others, a major influence. The question of my desire to circumvent Aboriginalisation by shifting to a more internationalist arena is true, but I guess I failed in that respect, given your conversations with people regarding the 'Stripe' paintings' emphatic connections to Aboriginal visual traditions rather than to European traditions. People will always bring their preconceptions to the work. Emily Kame Kngwarreye was just as influential when I made the 'Stripe' paintings as Frank Stella, but if I had put her name forward before Stella's I wouldn't be circumventing Aboriginalisation. Furthermore, I don't see the reference to Stella as appropriation, which I understand as the use of another artist's work directly, rather than as a starting/reference point of departure.

BW: The proto-artist John Citizen is a presence we could discuss as equally relevant within the framework of your current practice.

I recently received notification of a coming exhibition by John Citizen that included images of his recent works. John Citizen is one of the more confounding presences in the contemporary visual art field. In conversations I've had about his work he has been variously described as a redneck, social climber, vandal, errant alter-ego, even a National Party voter. Where will the invective end and a true picture of this talented emerging artist begin?

GB: John Citizen is an abstraction of the Australian 'Mr Average', the Australian 'everyman'. John Citizen is a work in progress that allows me to follow other streams of thought in my practice. He serves as a counterpoint to Gordon Bennett, his 'Other', and yet we are one and the same. When Gordon Bennett is labelled an 'Aboriginal artist' he is 'othered' as an Aborigine and all the preconceptions that entails. John Citizen lets me take my Australian citizenship and cultural upbringing back from the netherworld of the imagined 'Other'. As far as pinning down who John Citizen actually is, I'm not interested in doing that. His identity must remain fluid. He is in a sense all things to all people. He can be anything the viewer wants him to be—white, black or any shade in between, as is true of Australian citizens in general in our multicultural country. No longer is citizenship seen solely as the province of the white Anglo-Saxon Protestant, which was the image of white Australia I grew up with.

BW: It would be more appropriate to simply ask you (as I now do) how this alter ego came into existence; what necessity caused you to invest this productive second, often seemingly antithetical, artist and to share your working time in the production of his very different worldview and artistic output; to what extent he is the projection of a self or pure fabrication, a fiction. Whichever, he seems to be of sufficient importance in your total schema to have occupied a lot of your productive attention. Are there imaginary conversations between the artists Citizen and Bennett, or a state of tension, as between two divergent yet inseparable aspects of personality and what if any are their (your) commonalities?

Latin has a word, *habitus*; habit; a habit like a coat that one wears. [I]t occurs to me that John Citizen is perhaps such; a persona, one assumes? One whose creative disposition is possibly as relevant as the abstract painter in the process of extending or redefining your vantage?

GB: John Citizen is a projection of myself, and yet to others he is pure fiction, and that is fine with me. I had thought of doing a series of conversations between John and myself, but I let that slide. John Citizen is indeed a persona that I assume allows me to follow other directions in my practice. I purposefully kept John Citizen out of any postcolonial debate, after initially toying with the idea, because I wanted to maintain the freedom he gives me.

BW: I'd like to ask you about artists, including [Jean-

Michel] Basquiat, who have inspired you or provided valuable insight along the way?

GB: My initial influences at art college were Komar and Melamid. They painted in any style they found suitable, on small component canvases that amounted to creating visual texts. That interested me a great deal. After that, I was influenced by too many artists to mention. It was like everyone gave me ideas. Sigmar Polke [1941-2010], George [*sic*] Baselitz, Ad Reinhardt, Edvard Munch, Vincent van Gogh, to name just a few. I'm always open to influence and usually get ideas from anywhere. I don't really have artist 'heroes' so I can't discuss any one artist over another. Sometimes I empathise with an artist, such as Vincent van Gogh, Jackson Pollock and Jean-Michel Basquiat. So it becomes the artist's life as much as the work that interests me. With Basquiat's work, it was again the creation of visual texts as well as the historical/contemporary content of his practice and his positioning in a white art world.

BW: Of course, as the title of your postcolonial project indicates, there are postcolonial discourses that inform and intersect with its highly polemical content. Who were the writers, theorists and dialecticians who most affected your ideas during the time of the project?

GB: John Berger's *Ways of Seeing* was a seminal text for me in its focus on the nature of perception and the importance of the reproductions of the 'original' seen in different contexts giving rise to different interpretations. Walter Benjamin's 'Art in the Age of Mechanical Reproduction' [1935] was another influence. Again, with the focus on the reproduction as opposed to the 'original', all of which led me to appropriation and the recontextualising of images into visual texts. Semiotics was important here. There were many postmodern theorists such as Jean Baudrillard, Frederic [*sic*] Jameson [b.1934], [Gilles] Deleuze [1925-1995] and [Félix] Guattari [1930-1992], and Jacques Derrida [1930-2004], all names I retrieved from my Postmodernism college folder, but whose theories I can't expound verbally. I operate intuitively. I read and I get ideas. My mind makes the connections to what I've previously experienced, through reading. I can't explain it.

BW: Your generation was exposed to a very different range of theoretical propositions to the prior generations—poststructural theories and the influence of postmodernism. In several respects your work took on strategically postmodern attributes, specifically using appropriation as a weapon in the war on past and present misrepresentations and iniquities. How did postmodernism enter your field of awareness thence creative means?

GB: Postmodernism was my best theoretical subject at art college. It was an elective I decided to take because it sounded interesting and had a strong psychology base, which interests me. It proved to be fruitful. Among other things, I learnt about deconstruction and semiotics, which I applied to my art practice.

BW: You were born in Monto, a place that doesn't conjure myriad associations of a creative cultural order, but nevertheless there must have been experiences in your early life there that have stayed in your mind as connected in important ways to later insights and developments.

GB: I may have been born in Monto, but I did not live there. The family was passing through as it were, with my father's job as an electrical linesman. We lived on site in caravans and tents. When it was time for my mother to give birth, Monto was the closest town with medical facilities. My early life, from age four to eleven, was spent in Victoria where I learnt at school about Aborigines as 'Other' to me. I was like all the other children; I didn't see myself as any different. Issues of race never surfaced for me, though my mother was aware of race issues. She told me later in life that people thought of her as being of Indian [descent]. She did nothing to correct them. I remember watching movies and documentaries that dealt with racism, and being appalled at the injustice of it all. I remember thinking, I'm glad I'm not black. In fact, watching movies and documentaries and reading books were my main influences during this pre-art college period.

BW: Such involvements at this stage of life invariably live on and colour one's experience, hence the tenor of one's work. I'm curious to know if and in what ways, other than this early experience of racism, any of these movies, documentaries and books may have had lasting repercussions on your understanding and sensitivities.

GB: There was an English documentary series called *The Real Thing* [1980] that comes to mind. It was essentially about human consciousness, the way the mind works, how language works, etc. It gave me real insight into the way we see/perceive the world. Also influential was a documentary produced by John Pilger called *The Secret Country—The First Australians Fight Back* [1985], which I found very inspiring. It told of the 'white' lies of Australian history. These sources have been an integral part of my practice. A publication called *Blood on the Wattle* [Bruce Elder, 1988], which I read while at art college, also exposed similar colonial stories.

BW: Before you decided to become an artist, what other points or sources of influence have remained with you? What circumstances influenced your decision to become a visual artist?

GB: The decision to pursue a career in art grew out of psychoanalysis. I was looking for a new direction in life as I was very unhappy with the career path I had chosen. The idea/advice was to find my talent and develop it. Art was my best subject throughout junior high school, so I began taking art classes in the evening. This gave me a representative portfolio to apply for a Bachelor of Art degree at art colleges within Brisbane. Competition was fierce in 1986 and I recall scraping in by the skin of my teeth. Once enrolled at the Queensland College of Art in Brisbane as a mature-age student, I began to excel and became one of a handful of students to complete the course with honours in every subject over the three years.

BW: In the past, you have spoken positively about the importance of your time of tertiary education at the Queensland College of Art. For many artists, the importance of this period of their development tends to be under-stressed—it is often even denied—yet, for most, it is in fact an important time of critical transition. How did it directly benefit you?

GB: Art college was a revelation. I found a world of ideas and possibilities at my fingertips. Learning to paint better was only a small aspect. The humanities subjects, for example—'Postmodernism', 'Aboriginal Art and Culture', and 'Classicism'—were very important to me. Postmodernism in particular seemed to confirm the way I had been feeling about the world. The postmodern condition I learnt about was what I had been living through. Things just seemed to fall into place. I learnt to articulate my ideas through images—a language I felt competent with, unlike verbal speech. I had found a way to articulate these ideas through painting.

BW: Clearly the die of your social-critical awareness had been cast early on, in your youth, but how did it come about that you came to make those first and, as it turned out, definitive decisions to confront racial issues as the core content of your artistic practice?

GB: They came about as part of a process of psychoanalysis. I was examining my life, my self-worth and self-esteem and realised the affect racism had on me. I decided to examine the root causes of these perceptions as a process of self-healing.

BW: Having parted company with the postcolonial project, I imagine you will have now gained sufficient 'distance' to talk about it in the light of hindsight, starting with the *Notes to Basquiat*, a body of works in homage to a fellow artist, which through its appropriation and identification provided expansive ground for critique. How did the identification with his work come about and develop?

GB: I first became aware of Jean-Michel Basquiat in my first year of art college. In May 1994, I did my first painting in response to him entitled *Ideal (Basquiat and I)* [figure 15].[2] It was a work on paper that depicted arms reaching out of a black rectangle (really a square that was partly off the page), towards an oval shape with the word 'Ideal' written in it. In this work, I attempt to identify with Basquiat as an abstraction of 'Blackness' as positioned by a white Western point of view—he the 'Black' American artist, and me the 'Aboriginal' artist (also black).

The series 'Notes to Basquiat' began in 1998 with an invitation to show at the Gramercy Park Hotel Art Fair in New York. I sent a series of works on paper consisting of various notations and quotes of Basquiat's work. These were juxtaposed with imagery of my own. I tried to translate my work into 'American' so that an American audience could relate more easily to the issues of racism and its history that were common to both our cultures. Being somewhat 'jacked off' with Australian politics at the time, I decided to continue and expand the series as a way of focusing my attention outside of Australia.

BW: Following this, your work took a different direction with the 'Figure/Ground (Zero)' [2003] works, which I first saw exhibited at Sherman Galleries in 2003. These works seemed to offer multiple avenues of interpretation in relation to the politics of Western (American, British and Australian) military presence in Iraq. To me, the postcolonial critique—of another Western-instigated neo-colonial outrage—resonated quite implicitly within this work with its hybrid Western military, camouflage and Saddam Hussein images—another example of colonial dominance. What did you feel when you painted these works?

GB: The 'Figure/Ground (Zero)' series was realised as a response to the government-generated paranoia surrounding Iraq, Saddam Hussein, and the so-called 'weapons of mass destruction'. The series was very short lived as I preferred not to involve myself in world politics. In fact, by that time, I had had my fill of politics and was getting depressed about Australia and the world in general. It's true the work was about colonial dominance. I took no definite position on the issues, other than to mix them up so people would at least think about and examine them, in hopefully new ways, and more critically.

❖ This interview was originally published in *Gordon Bennett* (Melbourne: National Gallery of Victoria, 2007), 96-105, and is reproduced courtesy of the Estate of William Wright AM and the National Gallery of Victoria, Melbourne.

Notes

1. Ian McLean, 'Gordon Bennett's Abstract Art: The Aesthetics of Commitment and Indifference', *Gordon Bennett: New Work* (Adelaide: Greenaway Art Gallery, 2004), n.p.

2. This work is held in the collection of The Wesfarmers Collection of Australian Art, Perth.

net - to understand it from other perspectives - from inside other nets in order to broaden our understanding - a more wholistic net - a bigger net. This not only expands our awareness of ~~the~~ whats in the net but also expands ~~our~~ awareness of self as caster of the net and the interpretor of its contents.

JB. 24-1-90

Colour plates

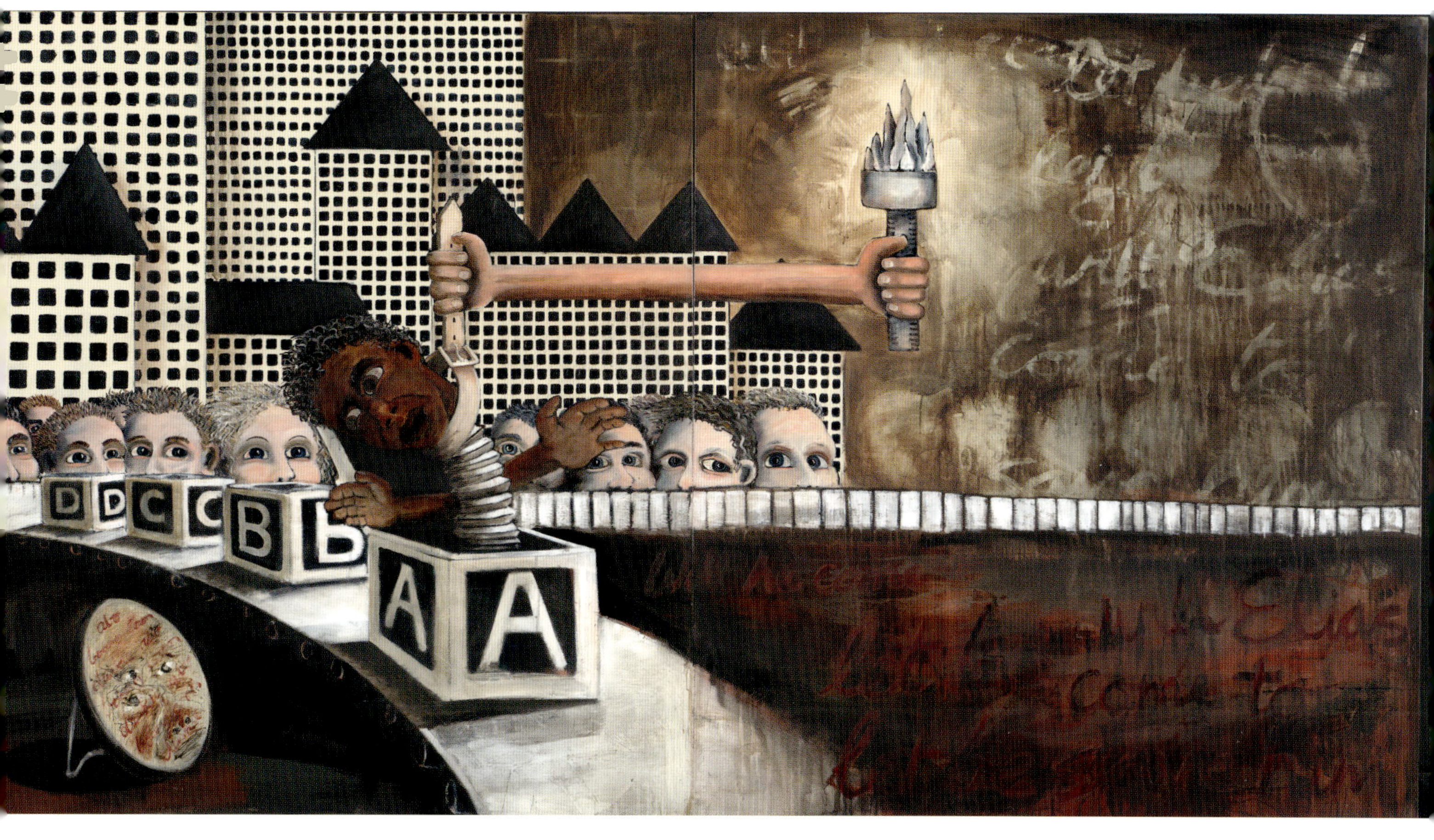

Figure 1

The Coming of the Light 1987
Synthetic polymer paint on canvas
Two parts: 152 x 137 cm (each); 152 x 274 cm (overall)
Gift of Leanne and Caitlin Bennett in memory of and admiration for Gordon Bennett through the Queensland Art Gallery | Gallery of Modern Art Foundation 2016
Donated through the Australian Government's Cultural Gifts Program
Queensland Art Gallery | Gallery of Modern Art, Brisbane
Photo: Natasha Harth, QAGOMA

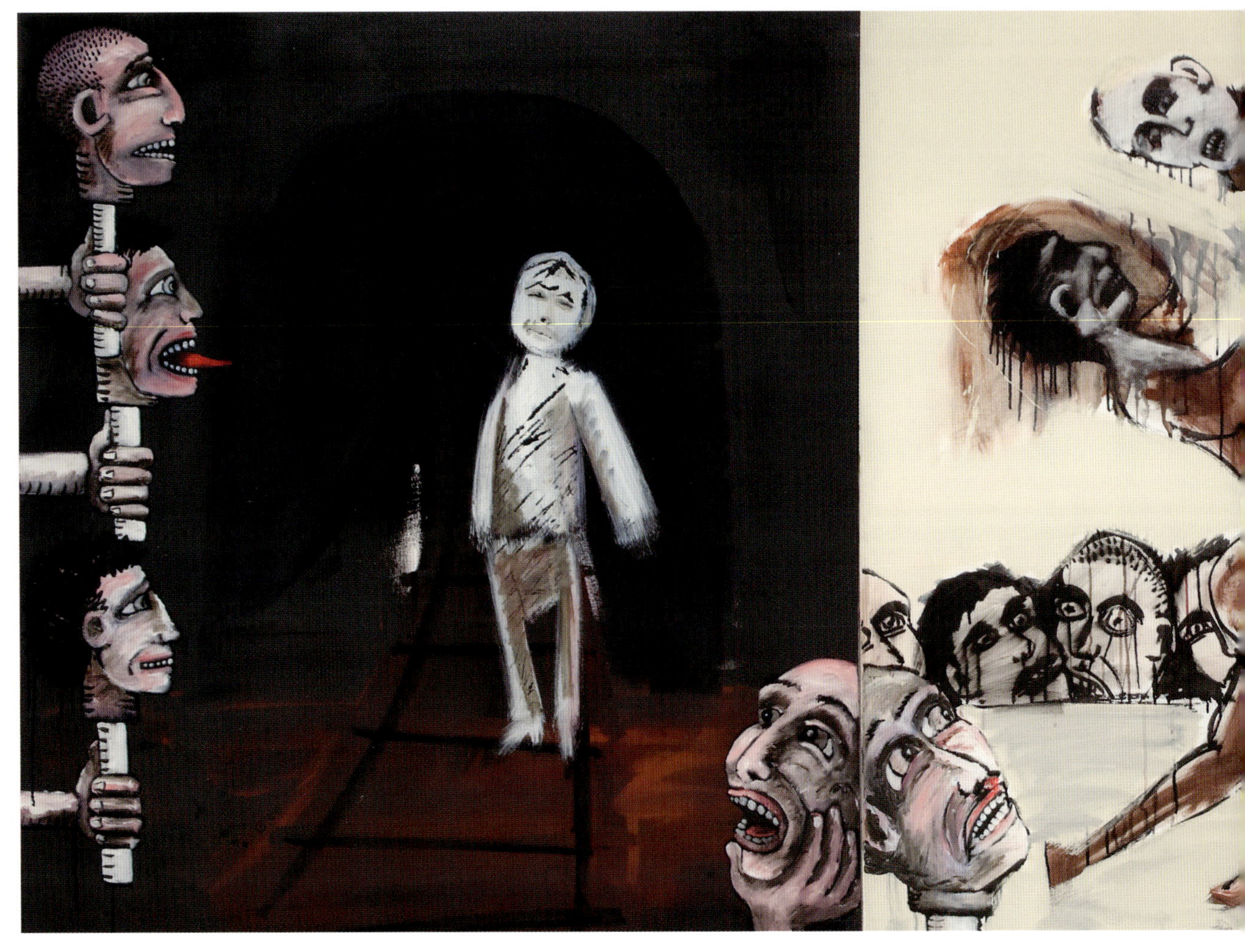

Figure 2

The Persistence of Language 1987
Synthetic polymer paint on canvas
(a,c) 152.3 x 137 cm, (b) 152.1 x 137 cm, 152 x 411 cm (overall)
Purchased 1989, State Art Collection, Art Gallery of Western Australia, Perth

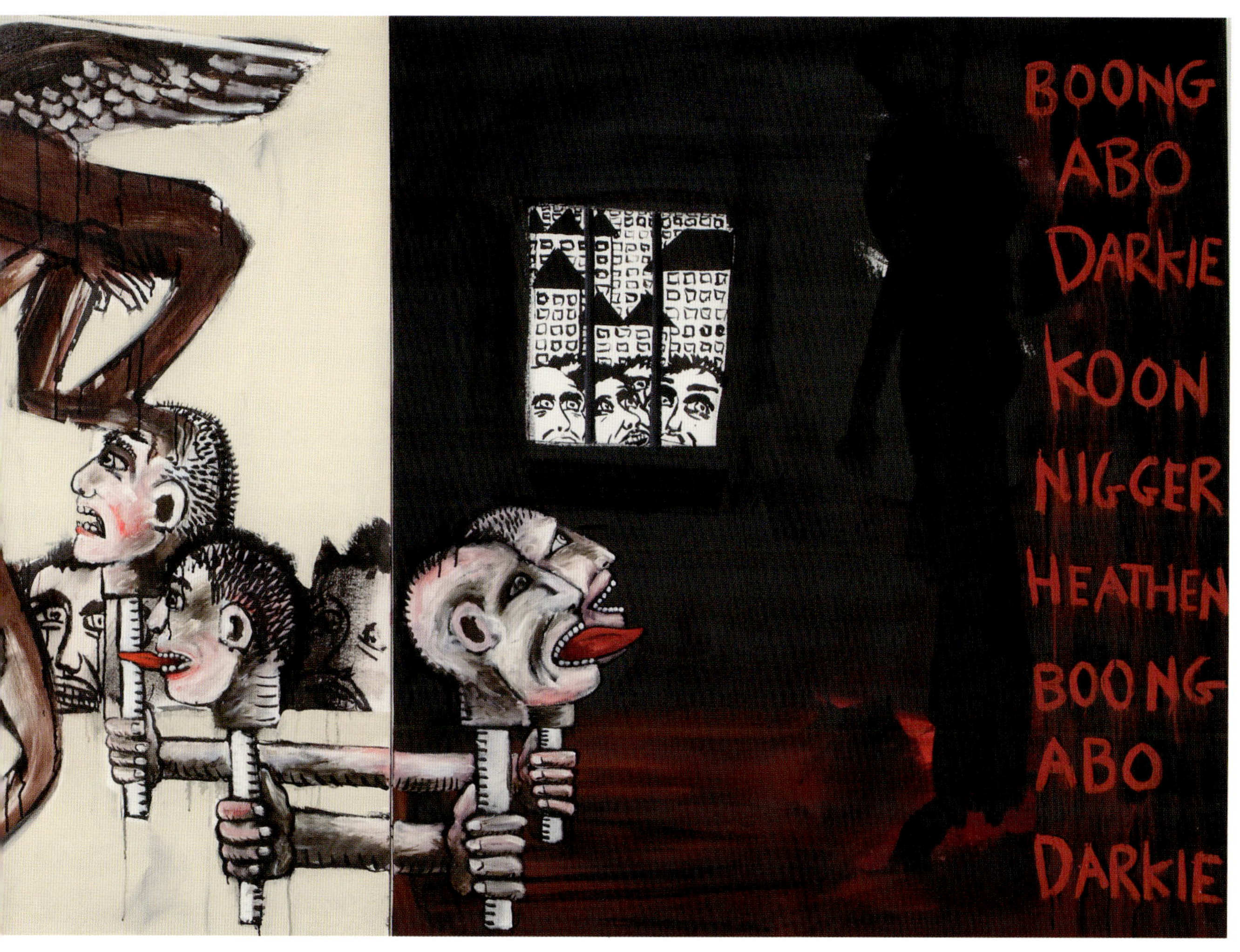
BOONG
ABO
DARKIE
KOON
NIGGER
HEATHEN
BOONG
ABO
DARKIE

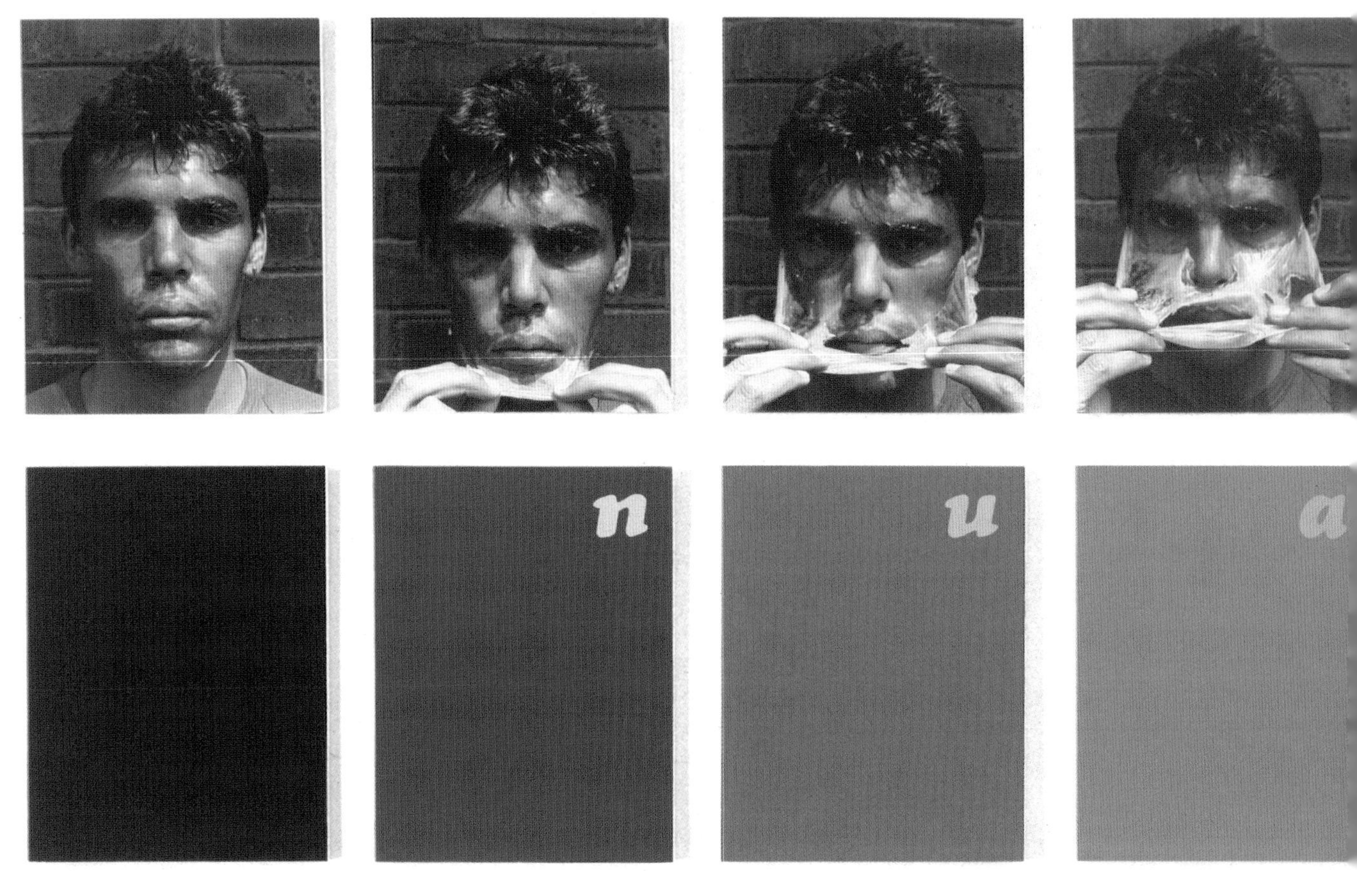

Figure 3

Untitled (Nuance) 1992
Photographs and synthetic polymer paint on foamcore panels
Sixteen panels, 85 x 275 cm overall
Private collection
Photo: Natasha Harth, QAGOMA

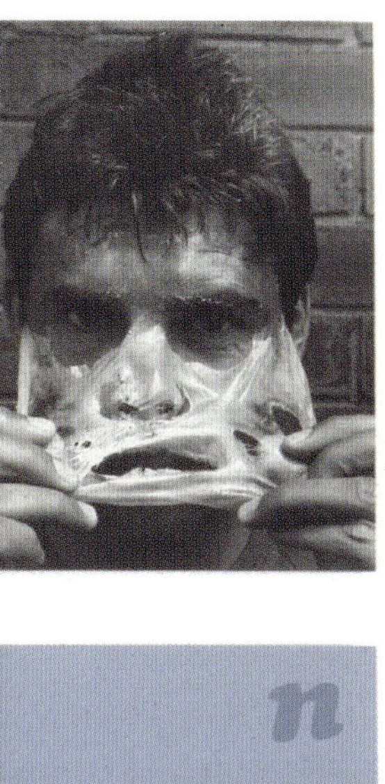

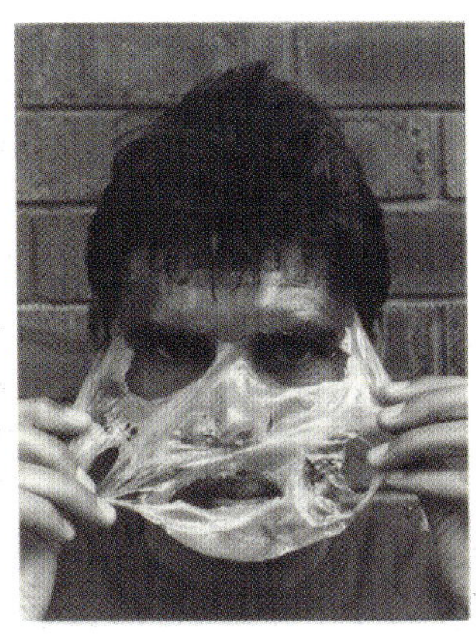

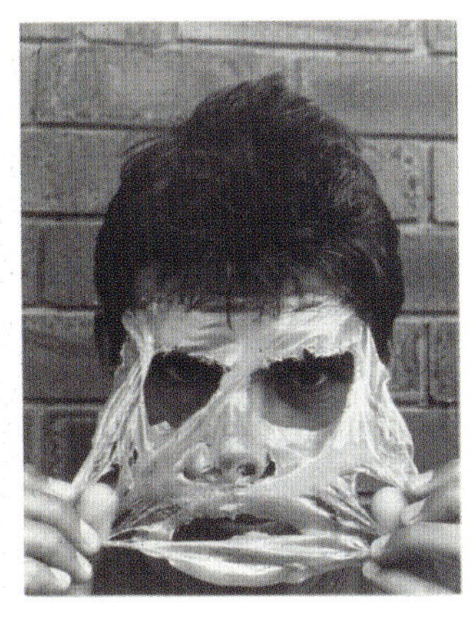

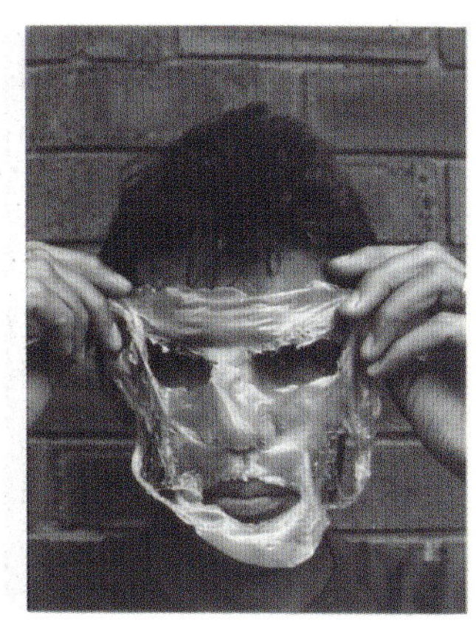

n

c

e

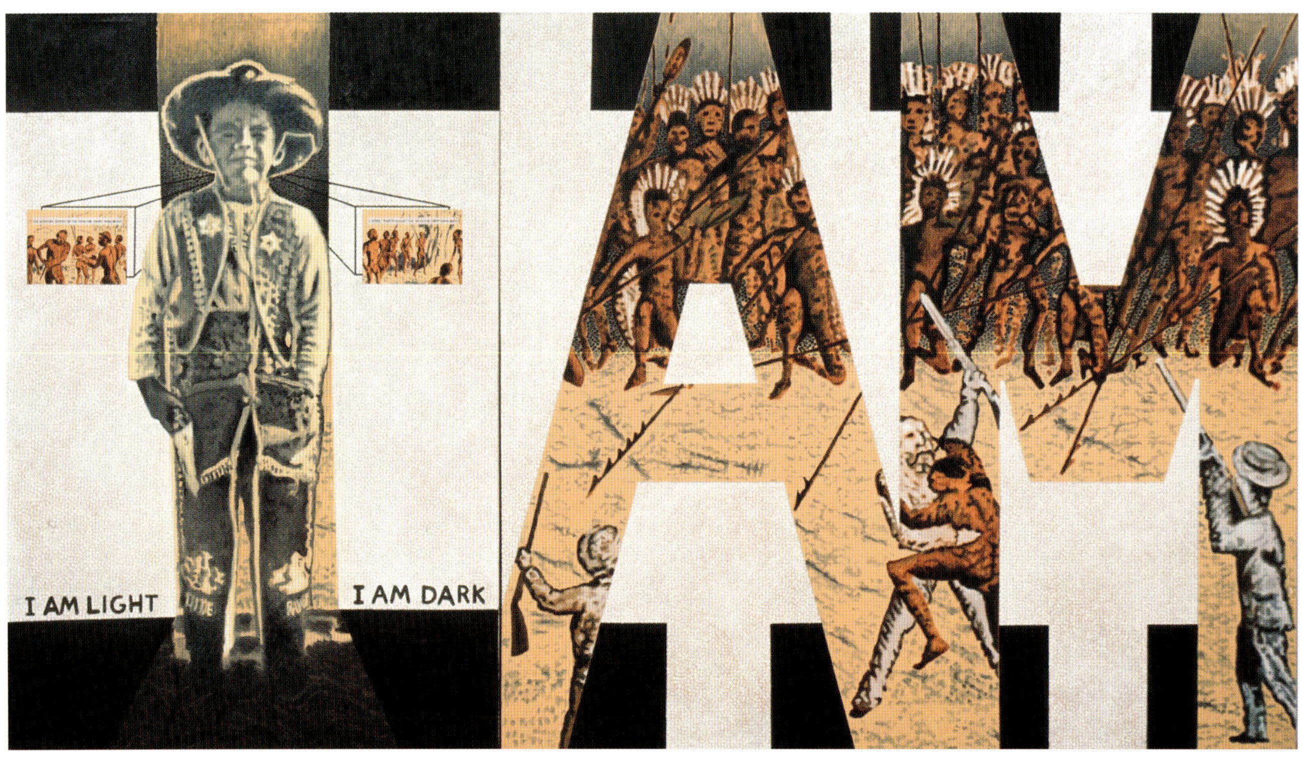

Figure 4

Self Portrait (But I Always Wanted to be One of the Good Guys) 1990
Oil on canvas
150 x 260 cm
Private collection, Switzerland

Figure 5

'Bounty Hunter' series 1991
(Clockwise)
Valley of Dry Bones (To the Sound of Cicadas);
Valley of Dry Bones; *Bounty Hunters*; *Cornfield (With Scarecrow)*
Watercolour, photocopied images and gouache on paper, 37 x 27 cm (each, sheet size)
Gift of Dr Paul Eliadis through the Queensland Art Gallery | Gallery of Modern Art Foundation 2013
Donated through the Australian Government's Cultural Gifts Program
Queensland Art Gallery | Gallery of Modern Art, Brisbane

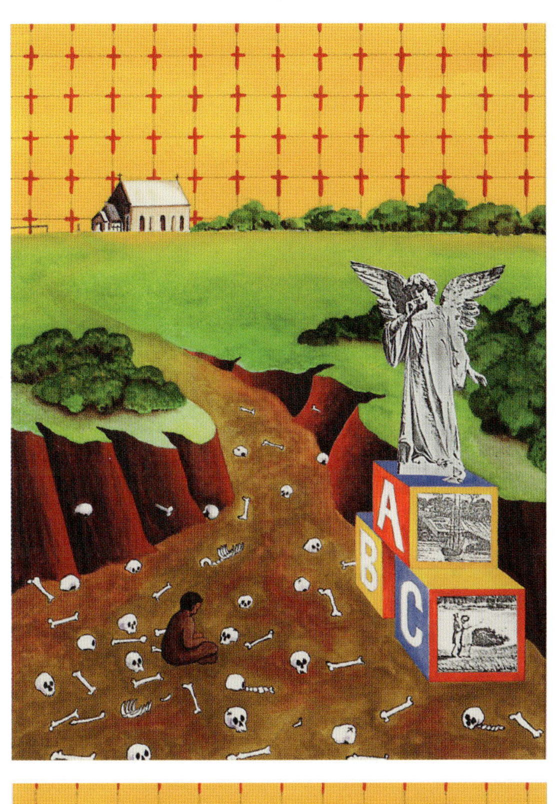
A
B
C

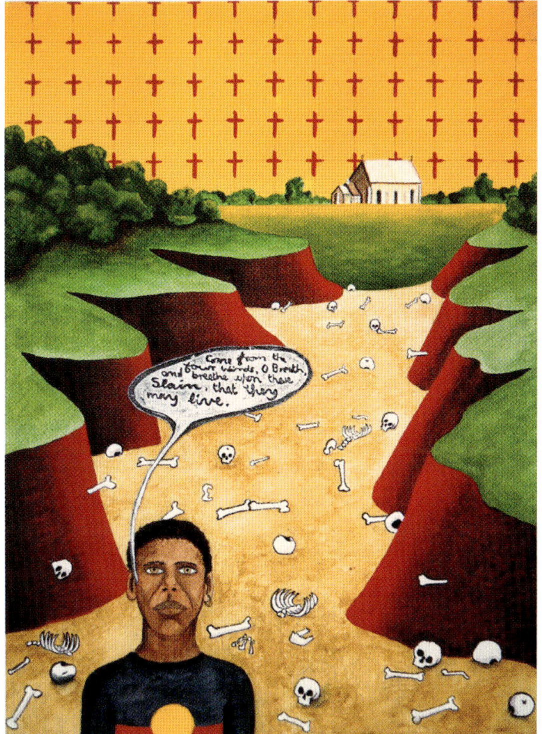
Come from the four winds, O Breath, and breathe upon these Slain, that they may live.

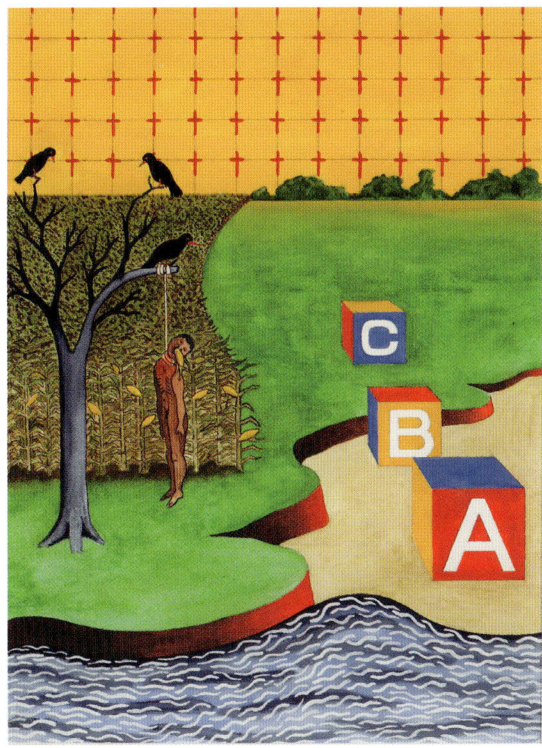
C
B
A

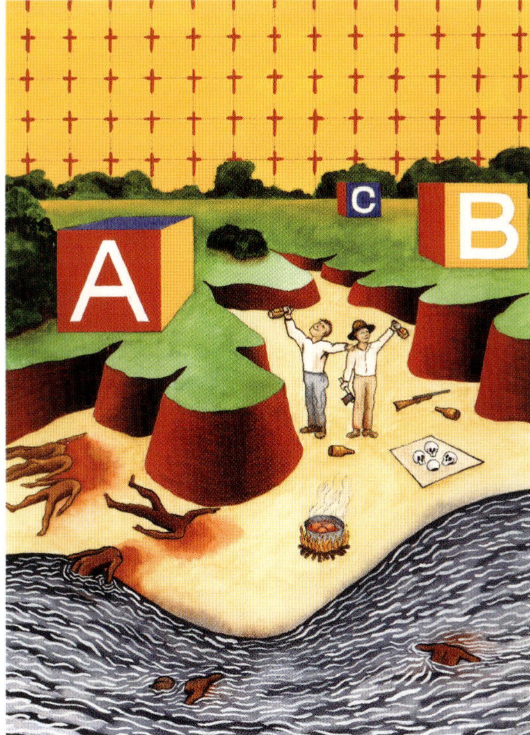
A
C
B

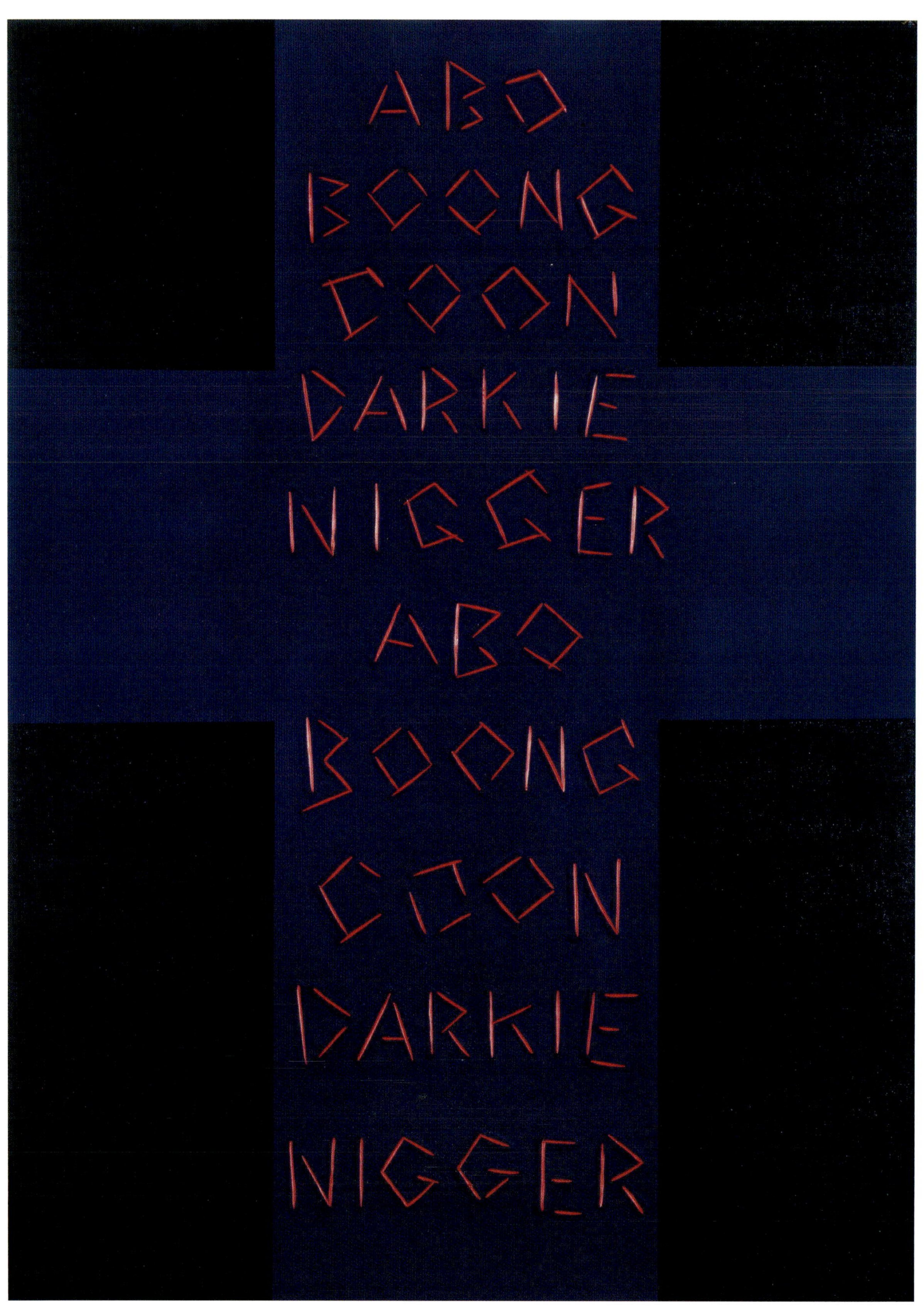

Figure 6a

History Painting (Excuse My Language) 1992
Synthetic polymer paint and flashe on canvas
92 x 65 cm
Collection of Janet Holmes à Court
Photo: courtesy Heytesbury

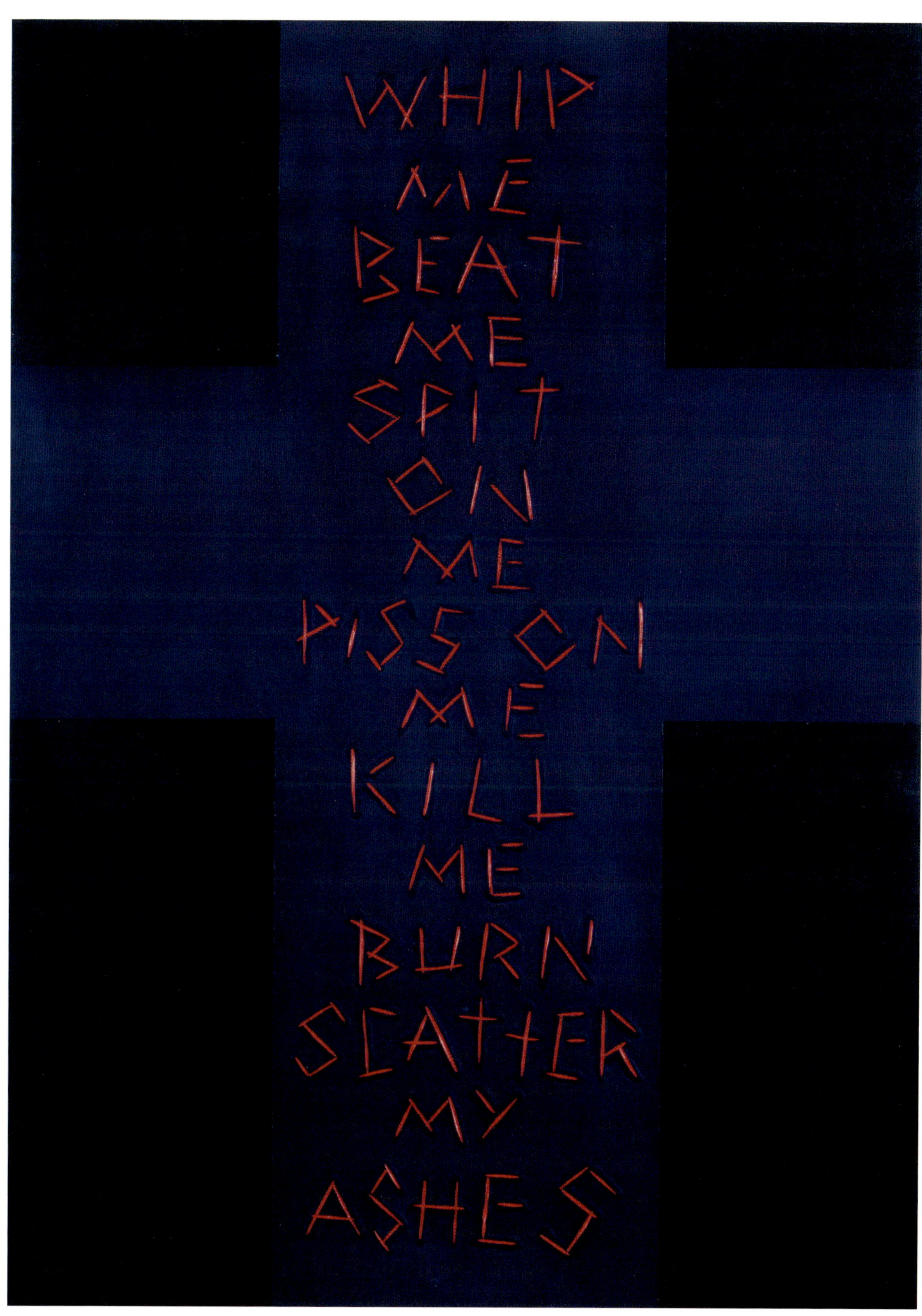

Figure 6b

History Painting (Burn and Scatter) 1992
Synthetic polymer paint and flashe on canvas
92 x 65 cm
Collection of Janet Holmes à Court
Photo: courtesy Heytesbury

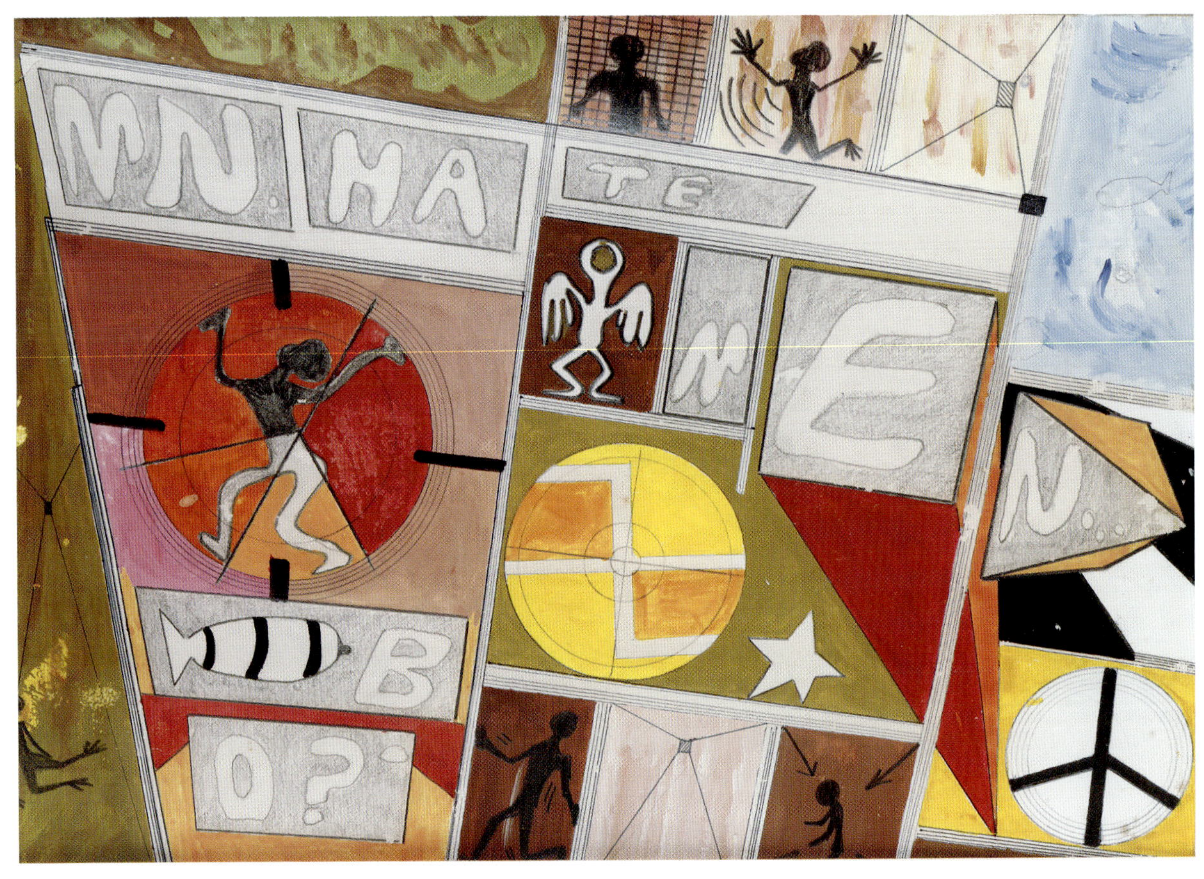

Figure 7

Untitled (Men Hate Men) c. 1968
Mixed media
26 x 35.5 cm (image), 47.6 x 55.7 cm (framed)
The Estate of Gordon Bennett

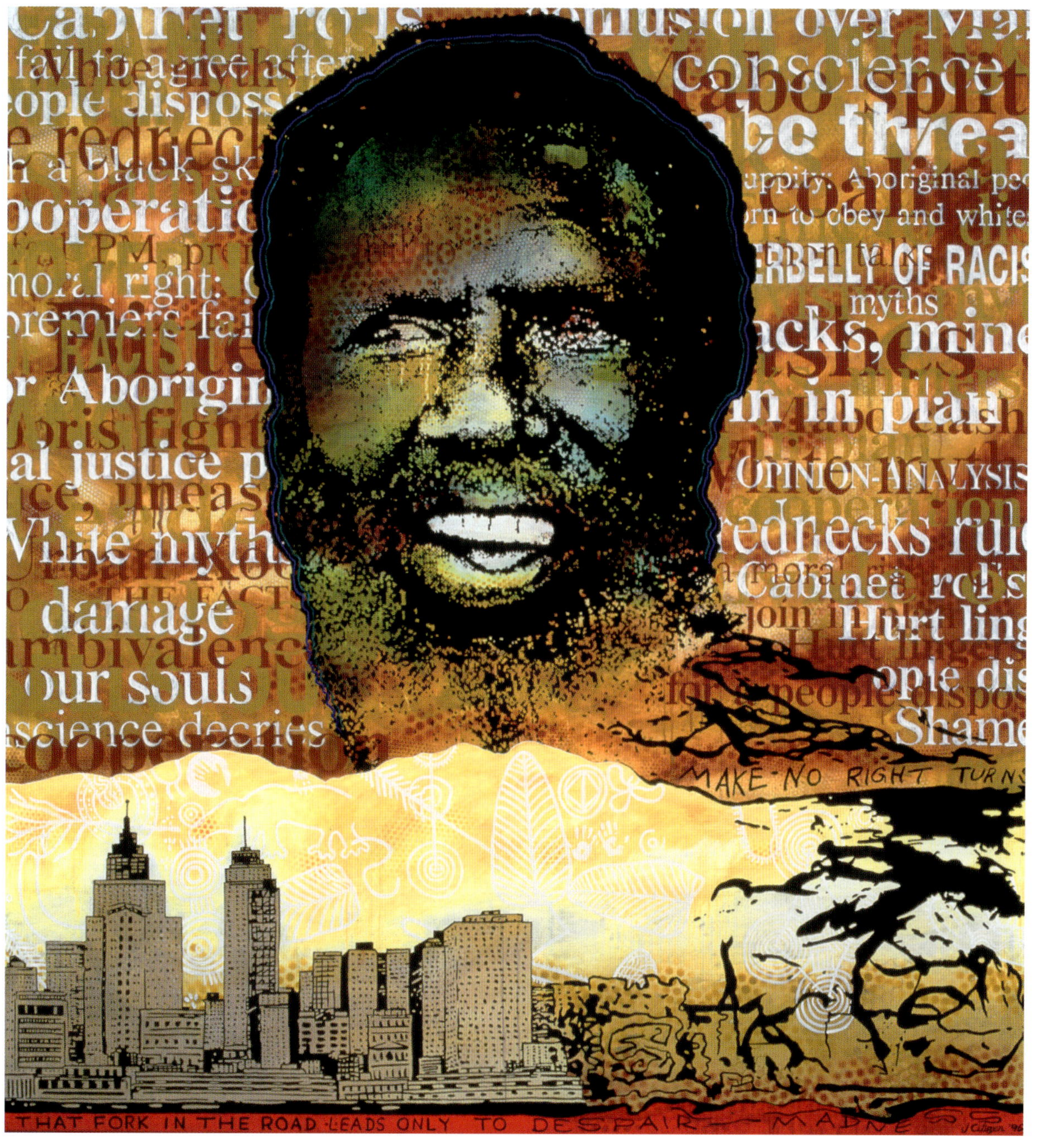

Figure 8

John Citizen

Eddie Mabo (after Mike Kelley's 'Booth's Puddle' 1985, from Plato's Cave, Rothko's Chapel, Lincoln's Profile) No.3 1996

Synthetic polymer paint on canvas

168 x 152.5 cm

National Portrait Gallery, Canberra

Purchased with funds provided by L. Gordon Darling AC CMG 1999

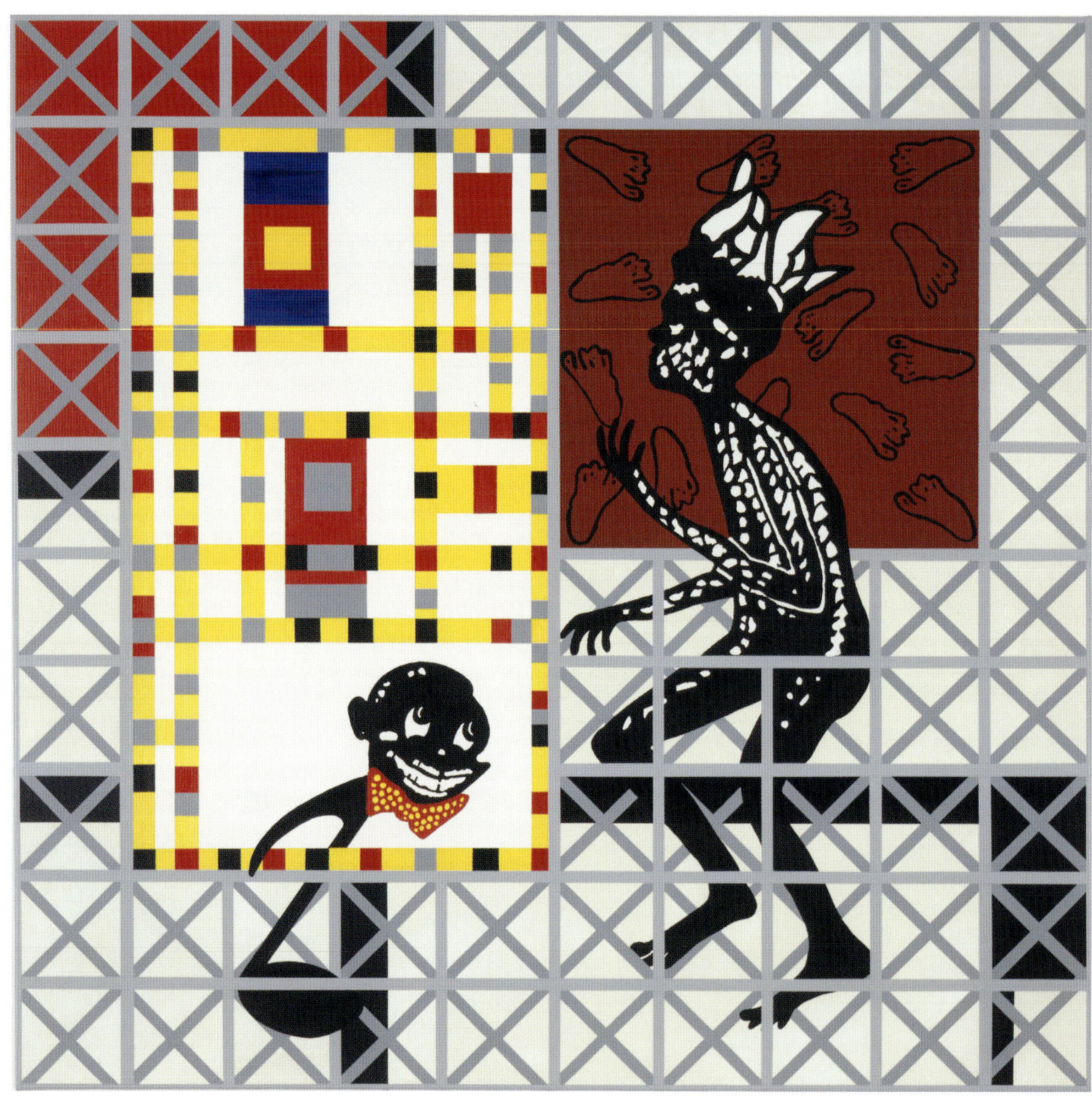

Figure 9

Home Décor (Preston + De Stijl = Citizen) Life in the Rhythm Section 1996
Synthetic polymer paint on canvas
100 x 100 cm
Private collection, Melbourne

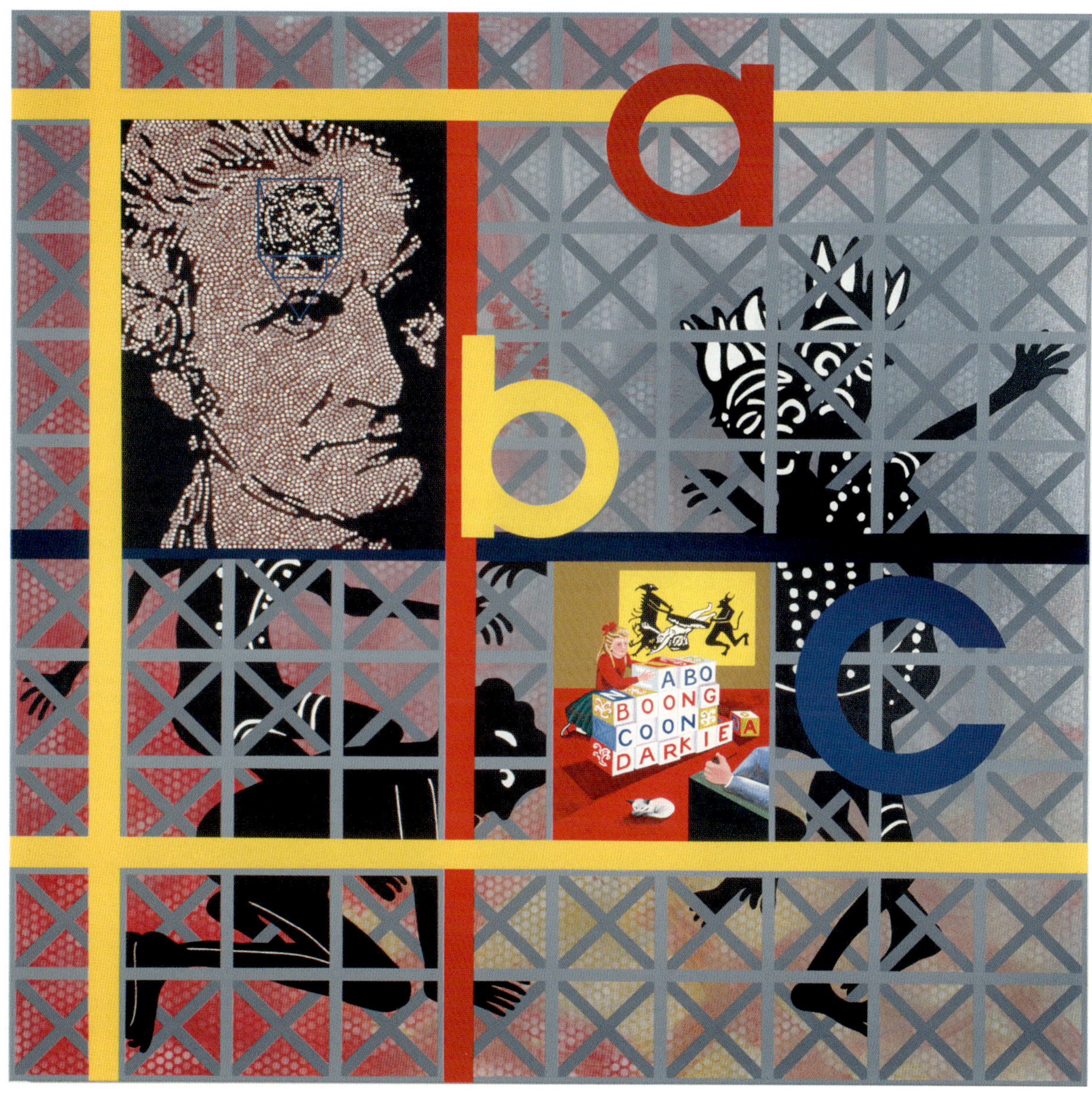

Figure 10

Home Décor (Algebra) Daddy's Little Girl 1998
Synthetic polymer paint on linen
182.5 x 182.5 cm
Private collection, Melbourne

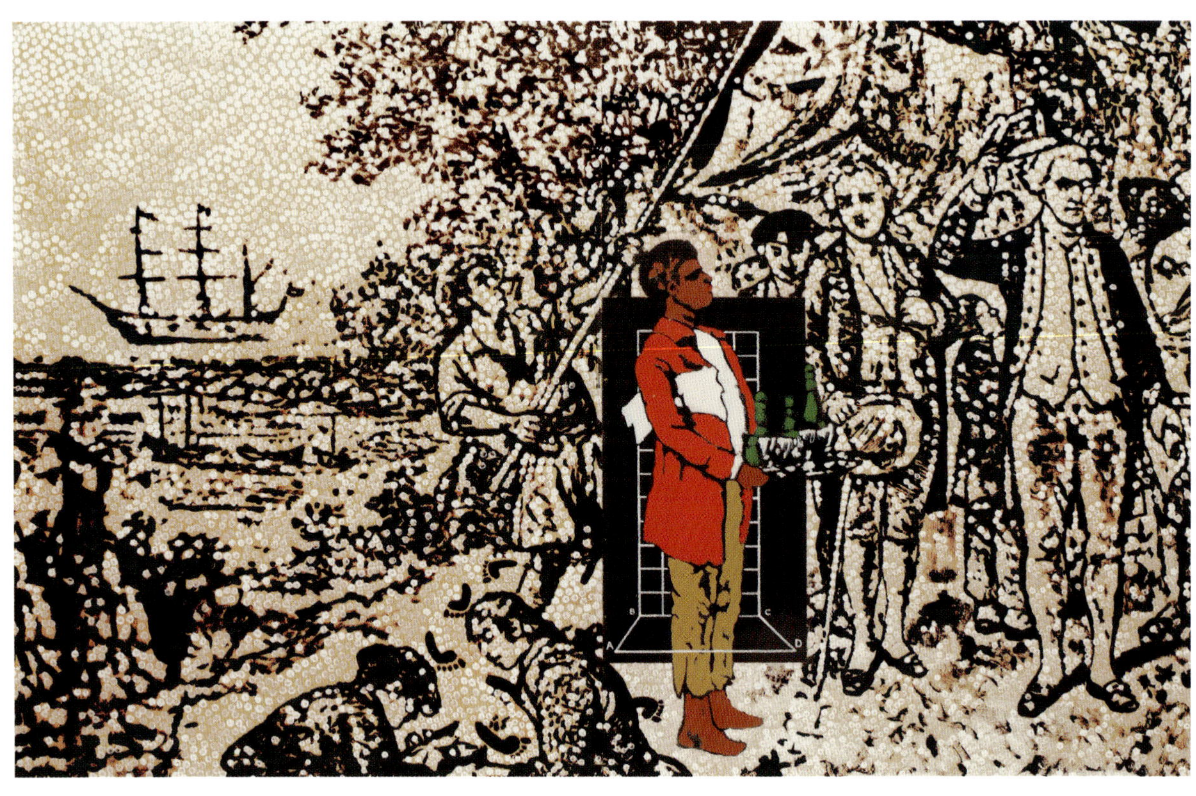

Figure 11a

Study for Possession Island 1991
Oil, synthetic polymer paint and gouache on illustration board
65 x 100 cm
Collection of Wavell State High School, Brisbane
Photo: John O'Brien

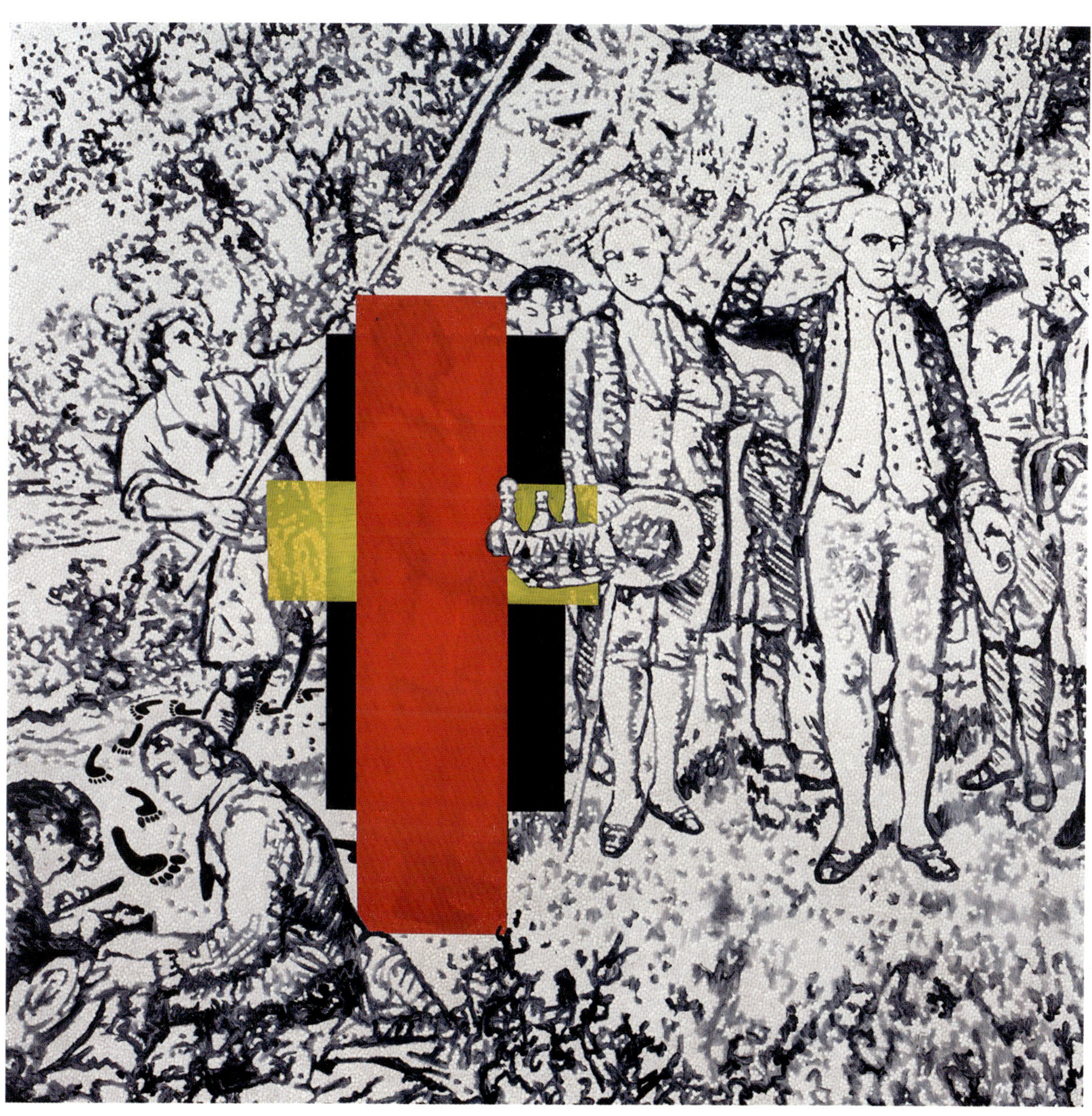

Figure 11b

Possession Island (Abstraction) 1991
Oil and synthetic polymer paint on canvas
184.3 x 184.5 cm
Museum of Contemporary Art Australia, Sydney, and Tate, London
Purchased jointly with funds provided by the Qantas Foundation 2016

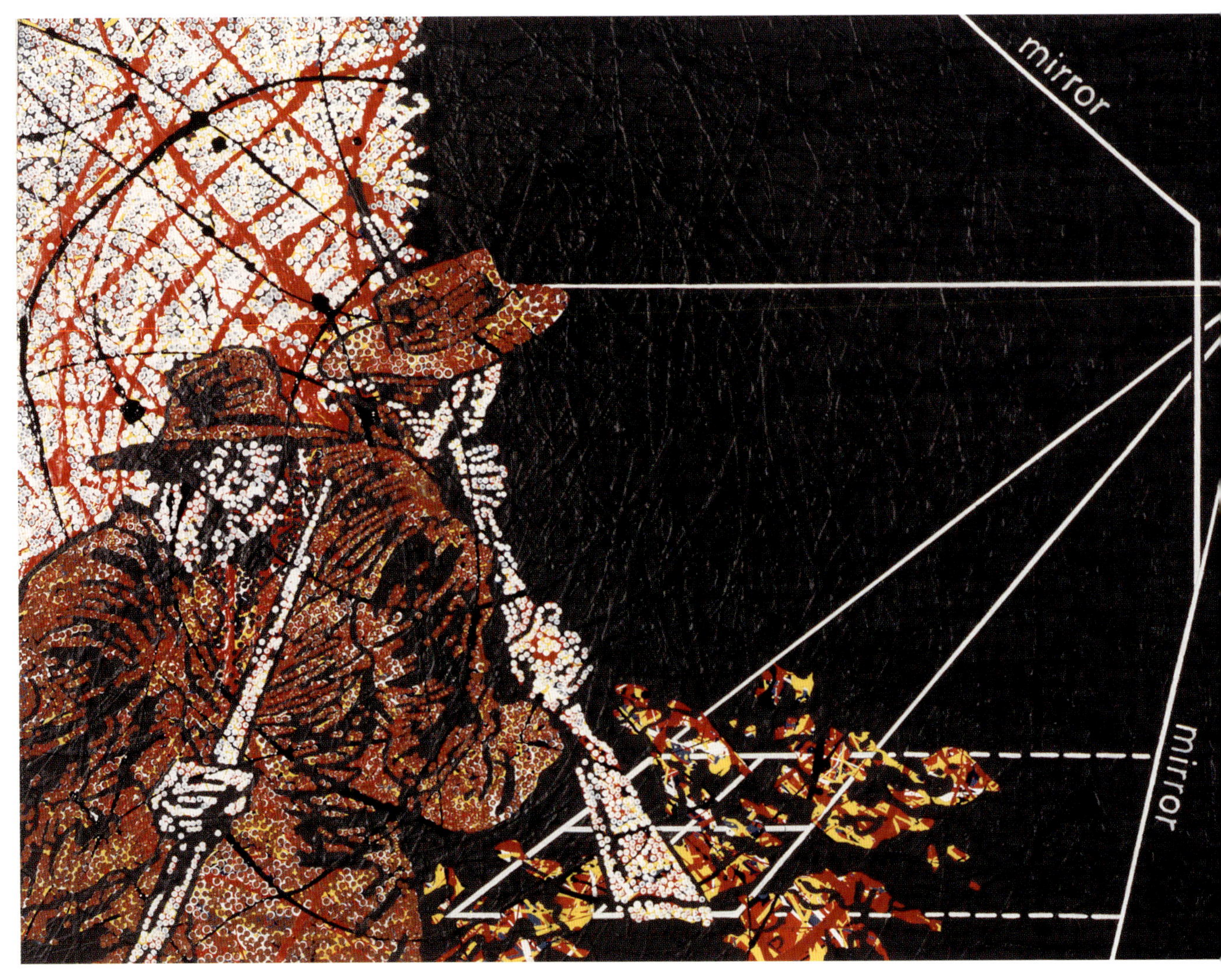

Figure 12

Men with Weapons (Corridor) 1994
Synthetic polymer paint on linen
89 x 232 cm
Collection of Carey Lyon and Jo Crosby, Melbourne

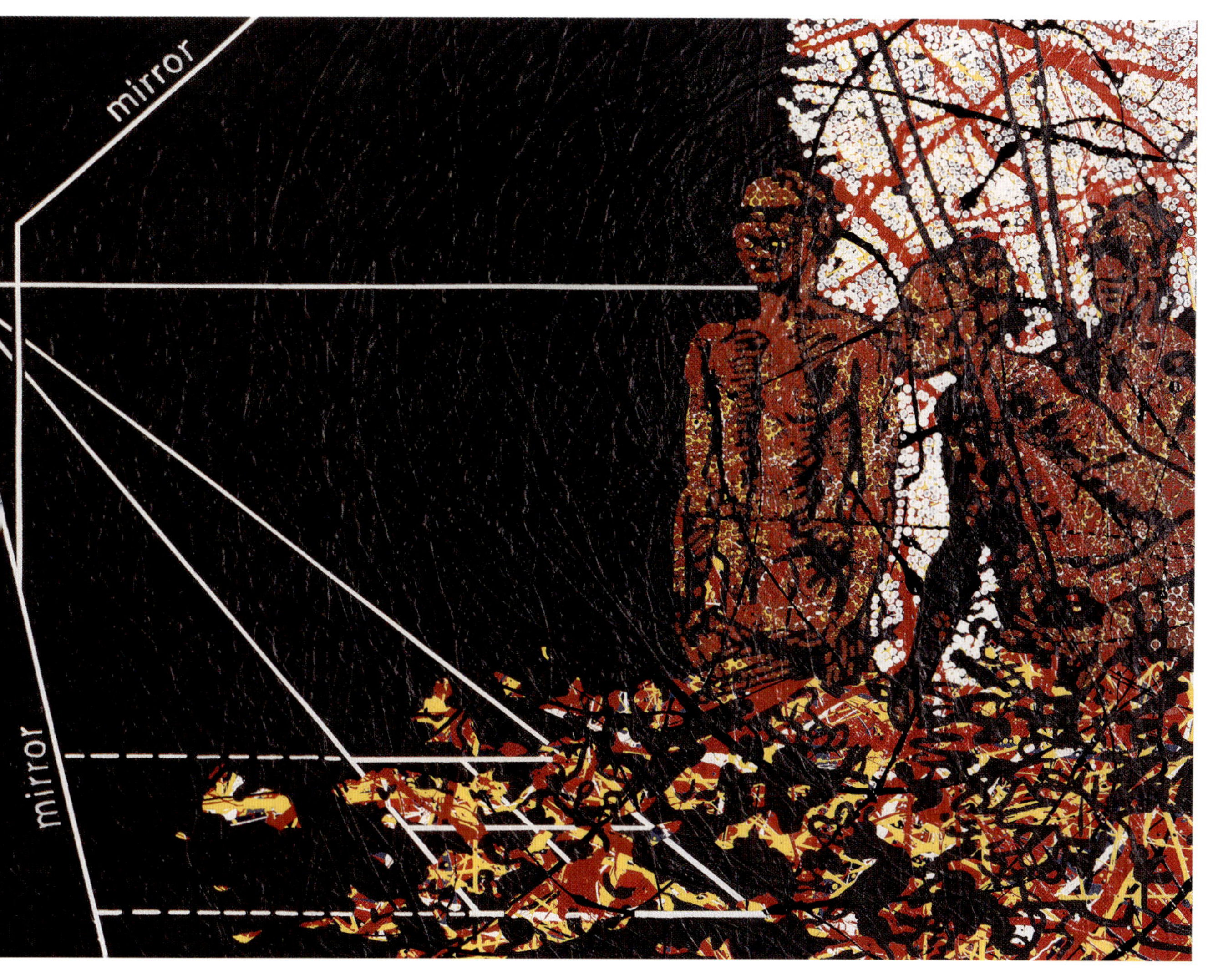
mirror
mirror

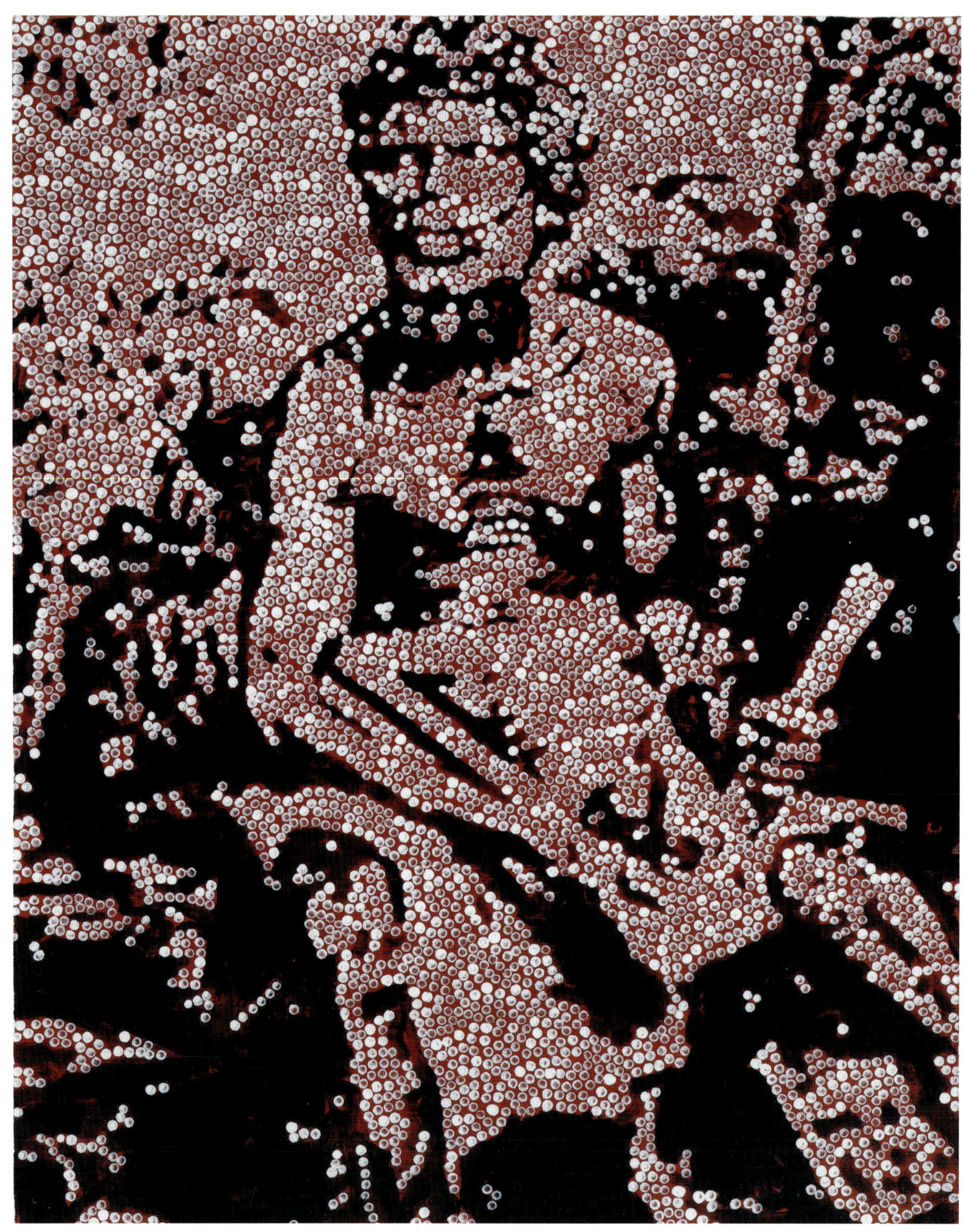

Figure 13

Australian Aborigines (Notes on Perception no. 2) 1989
Synthetic polymer paint on paper
67 x 51.5 cm (image) 88 x 72.5 x 2.5 cm (framed)
Griffith University Art Collection. Purchased 1989

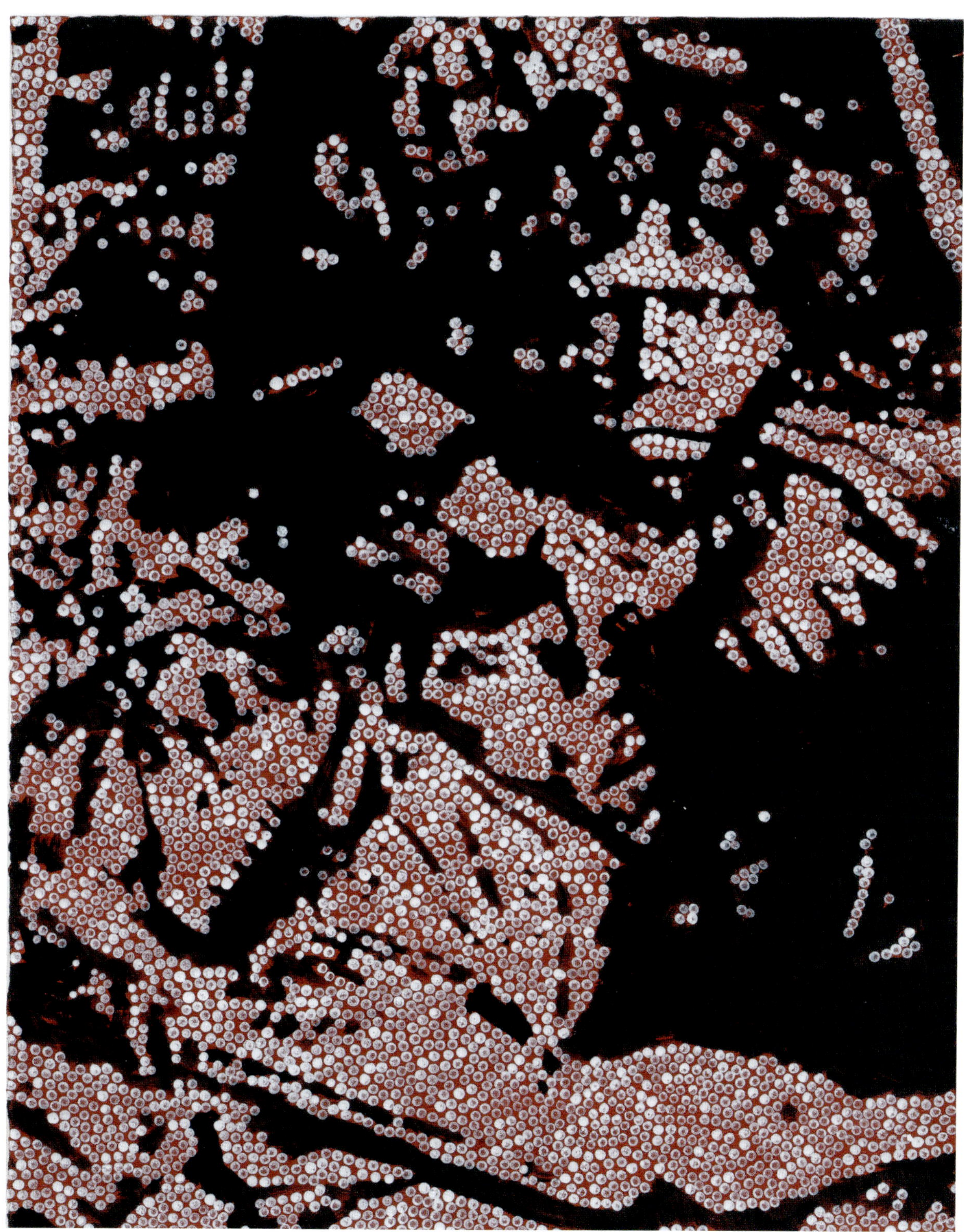

Figure 14

Australian Aborigines (Notes on Perception no. 3) 1989
Synthetic polymer paint on paper
67 x 51.5 cm (image) 88 x 72.5 x 2.5 cm (framed)
Griffith University Art Collection. Purchased 1989

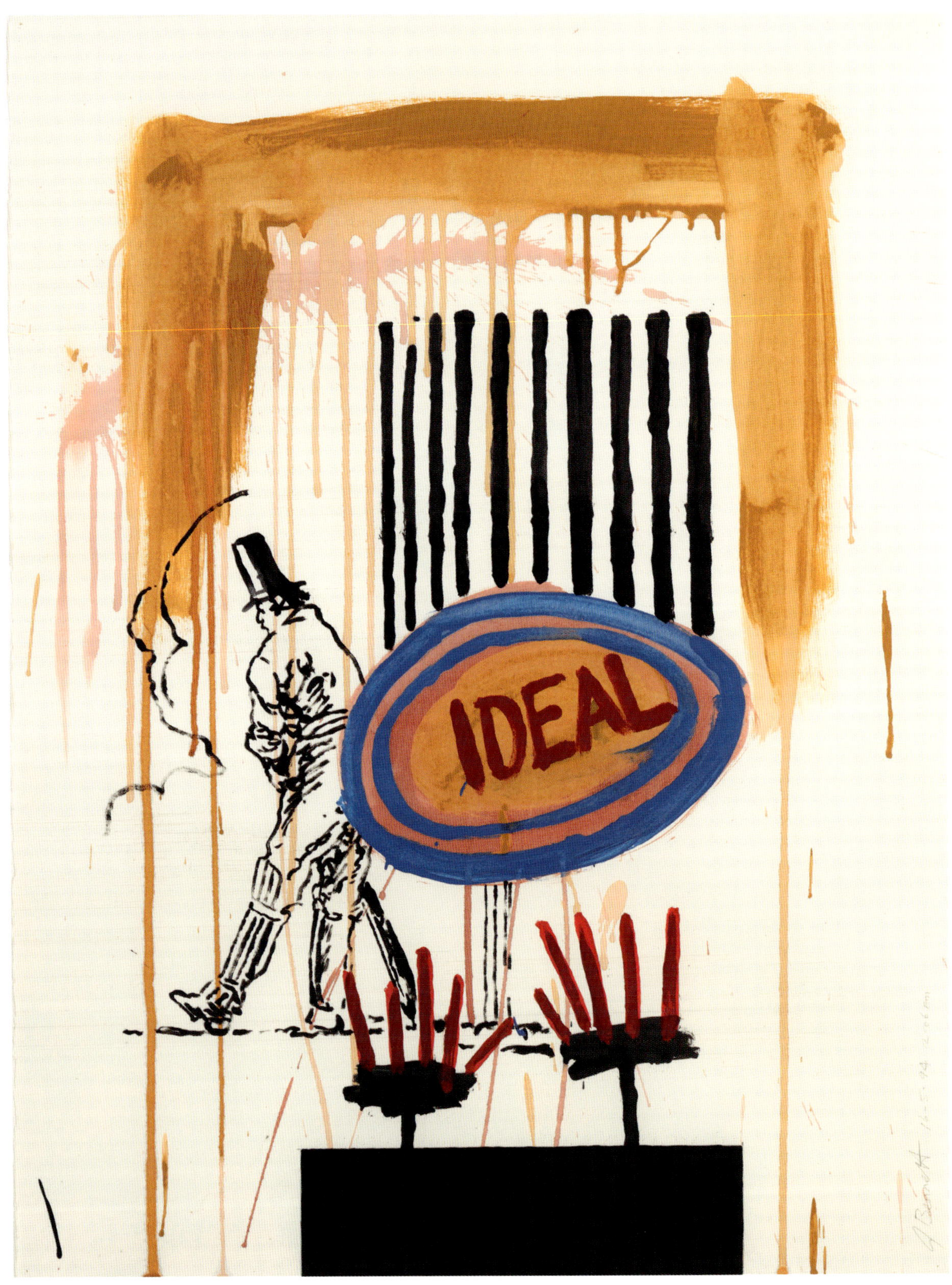
IDEAL

Floating throbbing violence
staring red glowing embers –
that dismember internal
organs – I envision my brain
slowly turning racing it's
own shadow through
streaming tunnels of vacuous
excrement in the abstract
land of mind – turning slowly
turning slowly, ever slowly
elated in the burning fire
of castrating dragons to sing
– "Having a wonderful time
wish you were here" –
gleefully giggling to a
hideously unnamed
joke.
all the best Gordon
Lenne. xxx

© Réunion des musées nationaux, Paris, 1988 Imprimé en France MAAO 3651

Kongo
Congo

Statue de magie
Bois, fer, cornes, cauris, graines, tissu, miroir, plumes
55 cm
Cliché J.M. LABAT/C.F.A.O.

Musée national des arts africains et océaniens

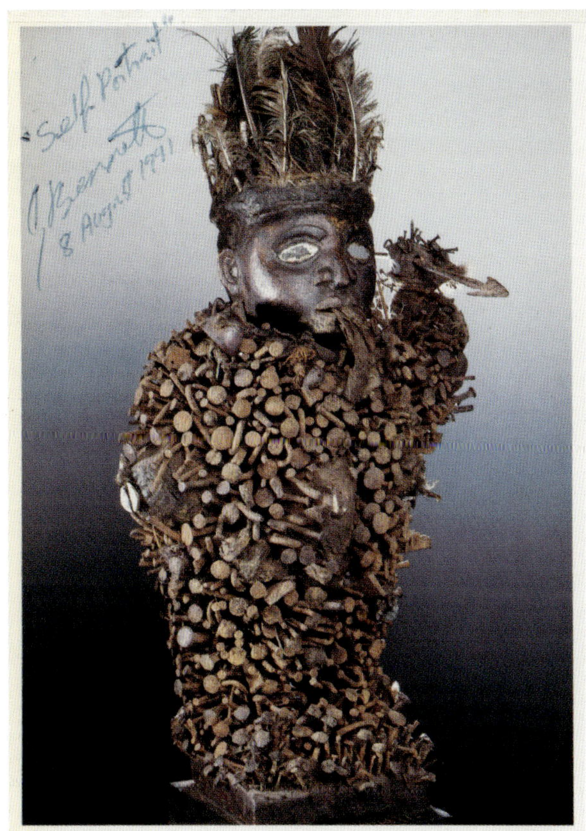

Figure 15

Ideal (Basquiat and I) 1994
Synthetic polymer paint on paper
76 x 56 cm
The Wesfarmers Collection of Australian Art, Perth

Figure 16

Self Portrait 1991
Ballpoint pen on paper postcard
14 x 9 cm (image) 31 x 24 cm (framed)
Private collection, Brisbane

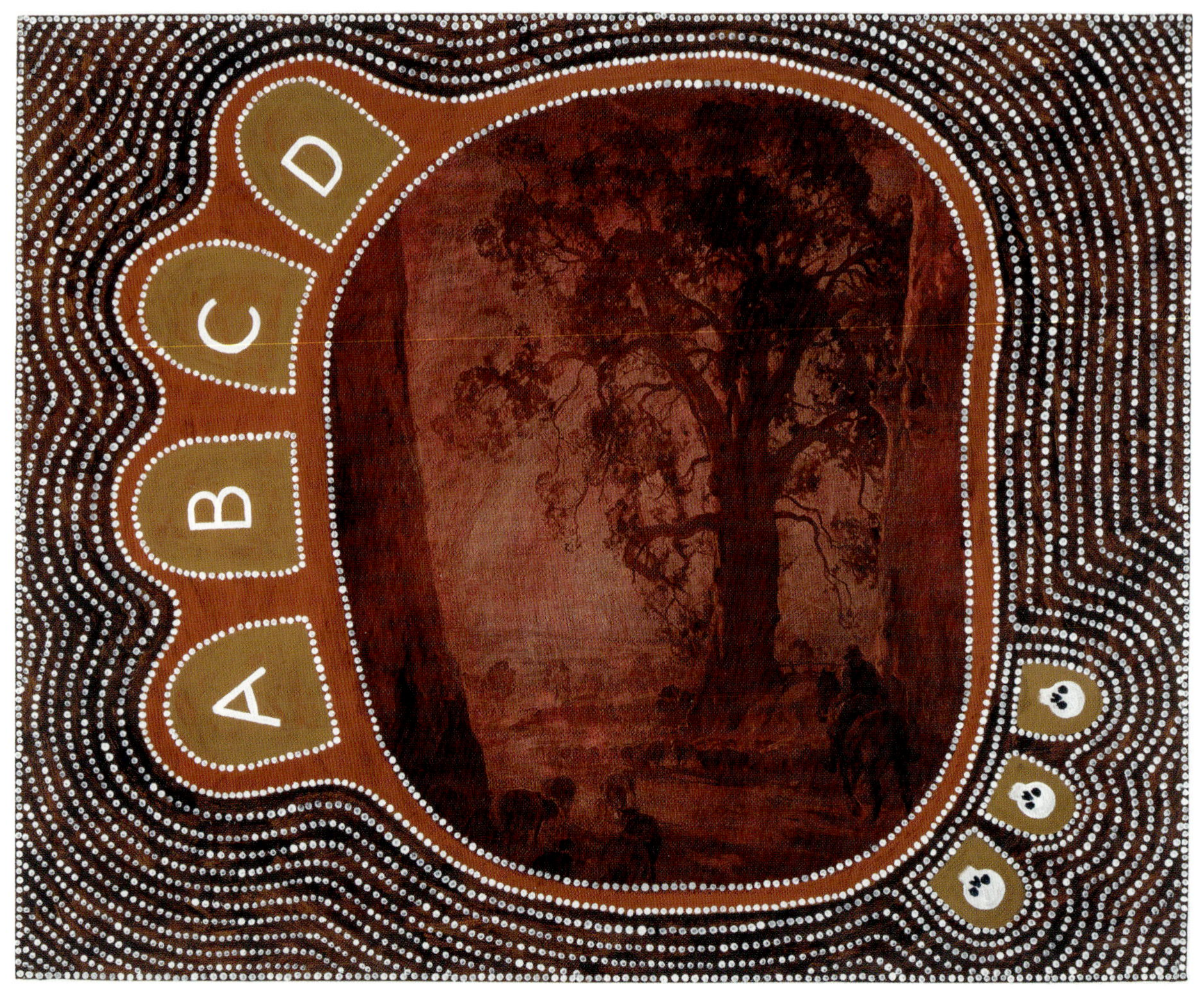

Figure 17

Psychotopographical Landscape (Pastoral) No. 11 1990
Synthetic polymer paint on 'Hans Heysen' print
70 x 86 cm; 94 x 108 cm (framed)
The Estate of Gordon Bennett

Figures 18–19

Ricochets; Manifest Destiny (A Painting for the Distant Future: 2001); and Window Onto a Shadow Universe (detail) 1993
Mixed media installation
Dimensions variable
The Estate of Gordon Bennett

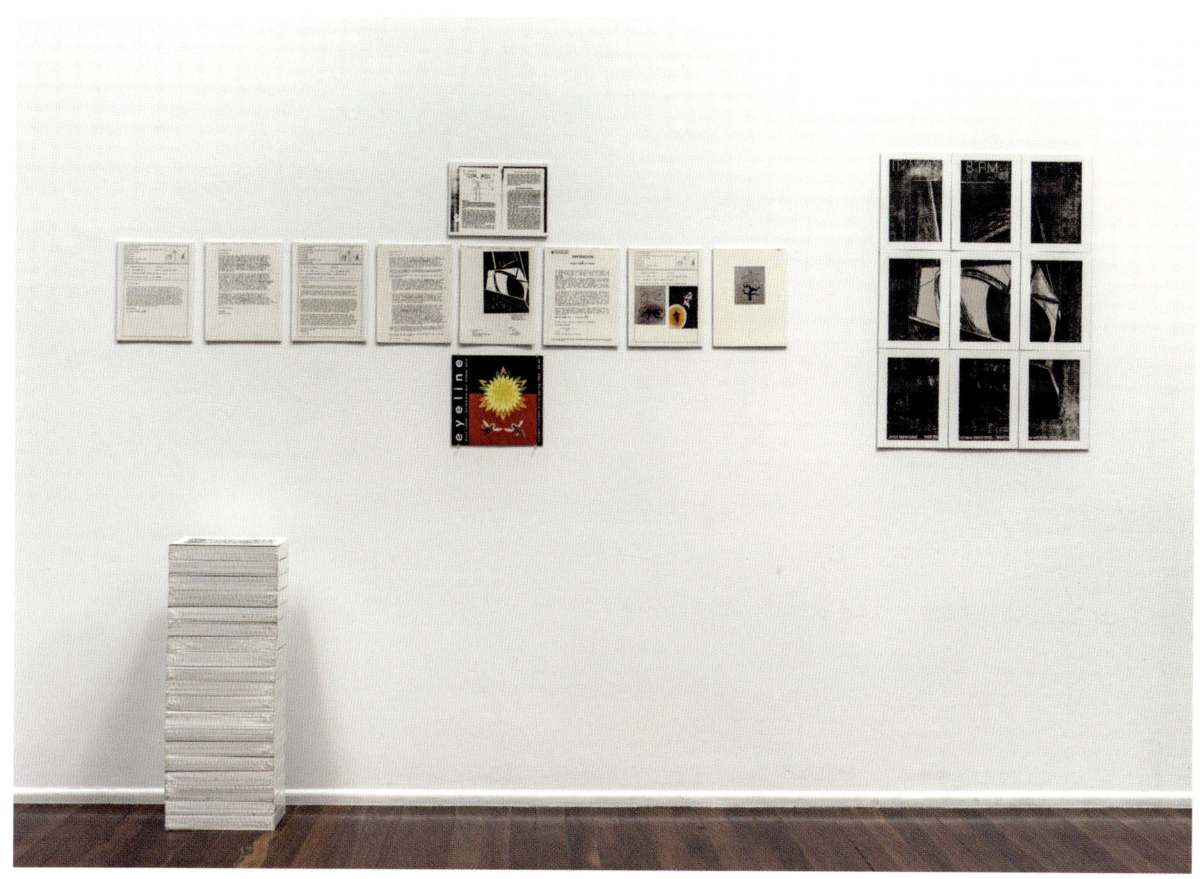
eyeline
8 PM

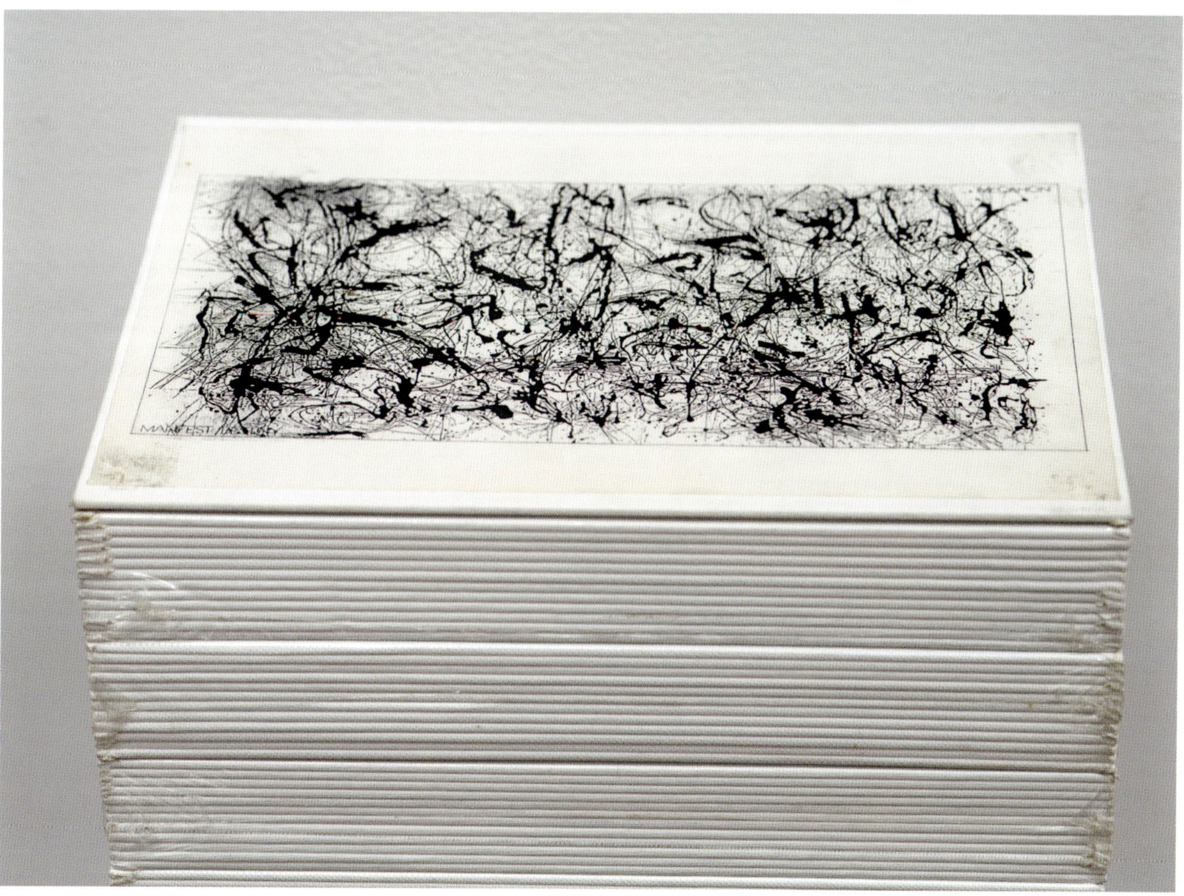

GORDON BENNETT
FAX: (03) 499 1381 Temporary until October 1993
C/- BELLAS GALLERY
49 James Street
Fortitude Valley
QUEENSLAND AUSTRALIA 4006
PHONE: (07) 257 1608

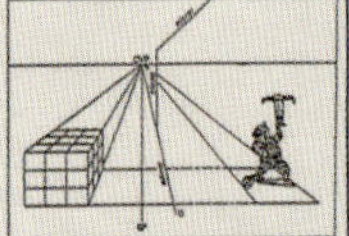

TO: Imants Tillers ATTENTION:

FAX NO.: 02 698 1170 DATE: 2 August 1993

TOPIC: Collaborative Work I.M.A. show

NO. OF PAGES (including this cover sheet): 1 (one)

Dear Imants Tillers,

I've thought about your proposal for a work based on an image received telepathically from myself. I need to know more information before I can agree to your proposal. I want to know details of the image and your ideas concerning it etc.. My idea of a collaborative work is one that is produced on an equal basis. Your idea just seems a little too convenient and I must say a little patronising as well. I want to know more about your telepathy idea as I am concerned about its reference to romantic ideas surrounding Aborigines (it belongs in Crocodile Dundee). {by the way I was driving throught the Central Desert between Yuendumu and Papunya at 1.30pm 27 July} If we can't come to some agreement on an equal basis then I suggest we forget about the whole idea and the exhibition - the rush for the catalogue publication is not a concern and is only a fault of the organizers of the exhibition; a blank page would suit me. Your suggestion requires a tremendous amount of trust (or gullibility) on my part so please forgive me if my fears are unfounded but the fact remains that I don't know you...

Yours Sincerely,

Gordon Bennett

SENT BY:LEWIN TZANNES | 2- 8-93 2:53PM | 026981170→ 03 499 1381;# 2

2nd August 1993

Dear Gordon,

Thank you for your fax. I appreciate your concern regarding an image received telephatically by me from you, when you were not even aware of sending it (although you were"driving through the central desert between Yuendumu and Papunya" at the precise time of its reception by me). It is perhaps expecting too much trust on your part to have my resulting work "PAINTING FOR CLOSED EYES" as part of the "Commitments" exhibition, although part of my enthusiasm to have it inthis context was that it suggested an alternative approach to the idea of collaboration where "collaboration" can be carried out without the conscious knowledge or indeed volition of the other party.

By the way this is not the first time I have collaborated in this way with another artist i.e. by mental telepathy. The other recent occasion was with Sigmar Polke in May 1991 and this resulted in my work for the Museum of Contemporary Art in Sydney - "PURE BEAUTY" but that is another story. Also I mentioned to you the case of your own work "THE NINE RICOCHETS" which while quoting specifically from one of my works ("PATA-PHYSICAL MAN") and making reference to my practice in general also inadvertently (or by mental telepathy !) included 2 other direct quotations (i.e. the small red superimposed panel and the large axeman with axe at the right of your picture) from particular works by me which youwould probably not be aware of.

While realising that you do not seem keen about this kind of collaboration I would nevertheless like to send you a study for my larger painting. I am quite relaxed if you do not wish to be associated with this work and do not wish it to be exhibited in the "Commitments"context or any other for that matter. I will respect your wishes on this. Also I am quite open to the idea of a more conventional collaboration, sometime in the more distant future. Let me know your feelings on all this.

With best wishes,

Imants

Imants Tillers

GORDON BENNETT
FAX: (03) 499 1381 Temporary until October 1993
C/- BELLAS GALLERY
49 James Street
Fortitude Valley
QUEENSLAND AUSTRALIA 4006
PHONE: (07) 257 1608

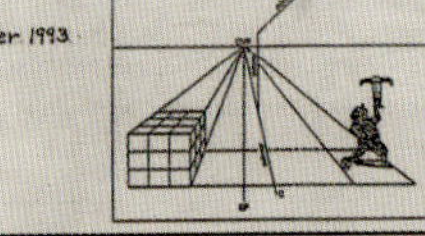

TO: Imants Tillers ATTENTION:

FAX NO.: 02 698 1170 DATE: 4 August 1993

TOPIC: "Commitments" exhibition collaboration

NO. OF PAGES (including this cover sheet): 1 (one)

Dear Imants,

Thankyou for sending me the study of our collaborative work "Painting for closed eyes" - via the more conventional means of a fax machine ! However one piece seems to have gone missing.

I have considered your proposal and have decided that I am also quite relaxed about this sort of collaboration and I would be happy to have "Painting for closed eyes" exhibited in the "Commitments" exhibition, but I would ask that you grant me as much trust as I have extended to you.

The faxed study of "Painting for closed eyes" has a piece missing, whether you intended this to happen or not I do not know but I consider this to be a sign that the work itself wishes me to have some input. As part of my contribution to the "Commitments" exhibition I propose to reconstruct the study from the faxed version. Most of the detail has been lost in transmission so it would be an electronically distorted shadow of the larger work. (I would simply glue photocopies to canvas boards.) I would insert the missing piece also. Furthermore I would like to include, as a piece referring to our negotiating process, these few faxes to be hung along side the "shadow" piece I am proposing. Imants, would you be relaxed enough to endorse my above proposal?

I am interested to hear that my work "The Nine Ricochets (Fall down Black Fella, Jump up White Fella)" also contains two other quotes from works by you. It is even more interesting to note that the specific quotation from your work "Pataphysical Man" that I chose contained an image I had kept close to me since 1983, an image that I was keeping for use in the right painting at the right time. I was very excited to find this small grostic symbol of a snake nailed to a cross revealed to me, during the painting process, situated precisely where I wanted it ! Maybe there is something in mental-telepathy after all ! For the moment I will rely on the Fax machine

I look forward to hearing from you soon regarding my proposal for a "shadow reflection" of "Painting for closed eyes".
Kind Regards,

Gordon

02698117Ø→ 03 499 1381;# 1

6th August 1993

Dear Gordon,

Thank you for your fax of the 4th August. Firstly, in answer to your questions - NO! I did not intend to send you an incomplete image of the study for "PAINTING FOR CLOSED EYES" and YES! I am happy for you to proceed with your "shadow" version of my painting and to exhibit our faxes. Most of all I amglad you are warming to the idea of a work (an interchange) precipitated by an act of mental telepathy. By the way the full version of the title for my work was going to be:

PAINTING FOR CLOSED EYES: AN EXPERIMENT IN THOUGHT TRANSFERENCE FROM AN IMAGE RECEIVED TELEPATHICALLY FROM GORDON BENNETT AT 1.30PM ON JULY 27, 1993.

Also there are several other bits of essential information that might amuse you:

1. AT THE MOMENT I am reading a book on "SUPERSTRINGS" by F.DAVID PEAT which happens to mention the existence of "the shadow universe"as a definite possibility at the level of sub-atomic particles. (See enclosed copy). Furthermore this shadow universe extends to the macro scale as well, why not also to the level of our day-to -day experience as well? It is also interesting to compare his diagram on the facing page in relation to your cover image for the EYELINE magazine, winter/spring 1992.

2. After I received your fax on the 4th August I also, literally straight away, received an invitation to participate in an exhibition "SHAMAN SUMMER IN FINLAND" at the Aino Art Museum in Tornio. I am invited to PARTICIPATE BY FAX-MACHINE. So I suggest we both participate in the form of our faxes. This would be our joint work. Almost uncannily, it is exactly what is called for ! (See enclosed copies).

3. Also yesterday I started to notice for the first time a very strong visual correspondence between your cover image on the winter/spring 1992 issue of EYELINE magazine and my source image for "PAINTING FOR CLOSED EYES" ie Giorgio de Chirico's painting "GREETINGS OF A DISTANT FRIEND" 1916. While both images refer to eyes, lines and have mysteriously similar triangles and ellipses the most striking similarity, which is unfortunately lost in the monochrome of a fax, is that they have near identical colour schemes - a very powerful combination of BLACK, RED and YELLOW. While your image does not have the powerful eye of de Chirico's it is integrated with the design of the cover to such an extent that the word "EYELINE" seems to become part of your image. (See if you can find a reproduction of the de Chirico in colour somewhere.)

I am very excited because our collaboration (by mental telepathy) seems to be triggering off many more "events"- unexpected relationships and correspondences than we could ever have expected if we'd pursued a more conventional line.

This is all for now. I have also sent the missing panel (Top Left Hand corner) in this despatch.

Best wishes, Imants

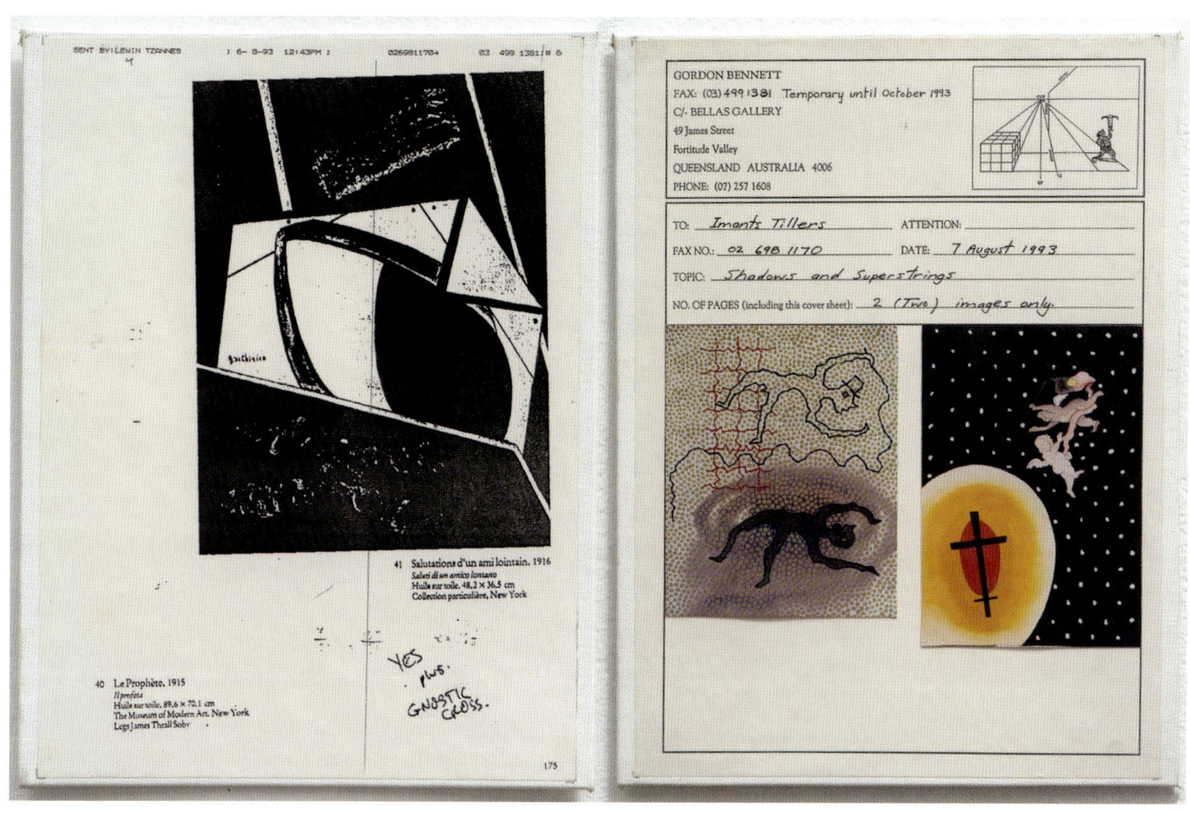

Figures 20–21

Ricochets; Manifest Destiny (A Painting for the Distant Future: 2001); and Window Onto a Shadow Universe (detail) 1993
Mixed media installation
Dimensions variable
The Estate of Gordon Bennett

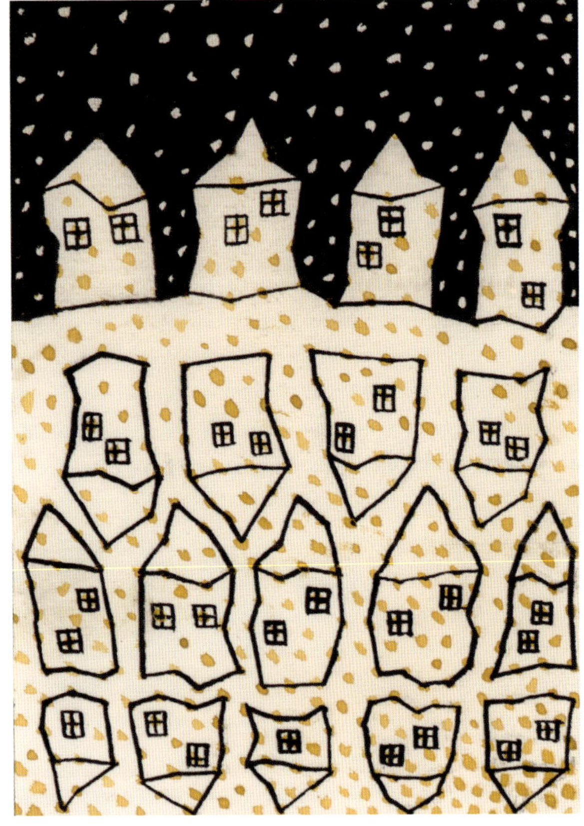

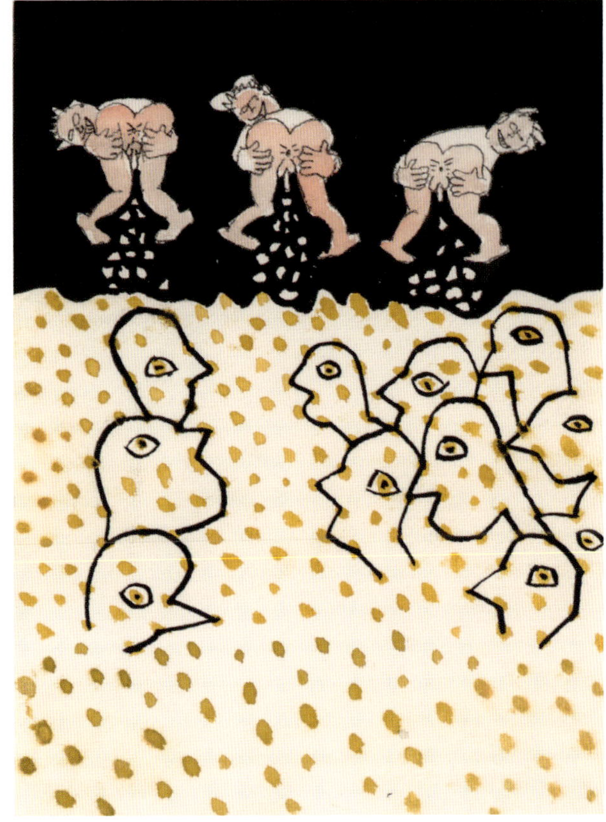

Home sweet home 30·9·93 10·37am

Please excuse me I don't mean to offend. I was just reflecting on the "great Australian dream". Leanne and I own our house in the outer northern suburbs of Brisbane. We saved like crazy to pay it off. All that time getting up in the morning and going to work, coming home, going to work, coming home, going to sleep and getting up again, like clock-work toys. Spending weekends in the garden, mowing, maintaining the house. We put a lot of time and effort into it – but for what? So I could go to the back yard barbie with the neighbours, have a sense of community, have children, get drunk, watch T.V. I think it was the barbeques that got to me in the end. The party talk both at work and around the neighbourhood. The subject of Aborigines always came up. It was then that I felt an outsider. I could not fit in The bloody boongs, the fucking coons, abo's, niggers – put them in a house and the first thing they do is burn it down. Try and imagine what it's like, sitting quietly, listening to this shit while your stomach turns in knots – try to fit in, keep the peace, after all you live right next door, right? Who needs to be a target for all that bullshit – life's tough enough as it is. So, there I sit, in a quiet rage, hoping no-one will notice my tan, my nose, my lips, my profile, because if I start trouble by disagreeing, then that would be typical of a damn Coon wouldn't it? G Bennett 10·54am.

Suburban Boyz have brown eyes too 22·9·93 11·47am

Please excuse me, I don't mean to offend but I was remembering some of the things my friends would do as teenagers – some things I guess a "shrink" would call "ego development". I used to hear about this thing called "chucking a brown eye". It was performed as a kind of expression, usually out of speeding car windows aimed at no-one in particular. While I never actually participated myself, (perhaps I was ashamed of my bum – I don't know), I did see it performed a few times. However the extent of my participation never went as far as exposing myself. I did indulge in the yelling of certain statements out of car windows. Some of these statements were aimed at the male partners of pretty girls walking along the street. "Fuck her mate, we did!" or "Spit her out mate, you never know where she's been!" were two of the most popular. Everyone would break up in laughter. If a lone girl was unlucky enough to be on the street when we drove by, she would get, "drop your pants" accompanied by loud wolf whistles and howls of laughter. I don't recount these teen memories with any fondness, in fact I am very ashamed of some of the things I did in order to fit in with my peers, and like any young person I did so want to fit in. I guess it was the same for many teenagers growing up in the suburbs of Brisbane. I feel compelled to add that I'm not talking about Aboriginal Teenagers here, all my friends were "white" – I was the only Boong on the block. G Bennett 12·05pm.

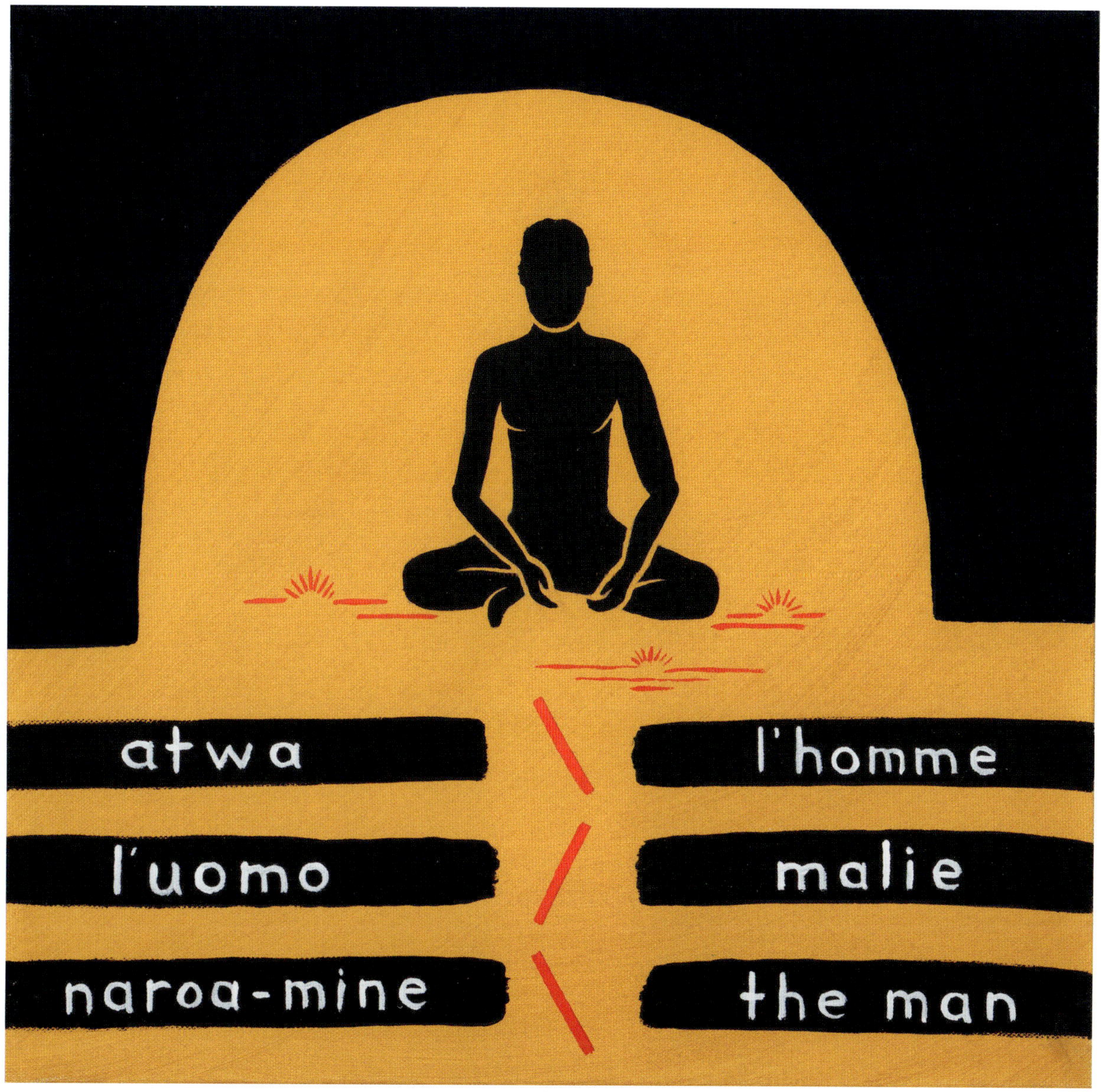

Figure 22

(left, top and bottom)
Home Sweet Home from the 'Home Sweet Home' series 1993–94
Watercolour and pencil on paper
27.5 x 19 cm each (sheet), 78 x 40 cm overall (framed)
Griffith University Art Collection. Donated through the Australian Government's Cultural Gifts Program by Dr Paul Eliadis, 2011

Figure 23

(right, top and bottom)
Suburban Boyz Have Brown Eyes Too from the 'Home Sweet Home' series 1993–94
Watercolour and pencil on paper
27.5 x 19 cm each (sheet) 78 x 40 cm overall (framed)
Griffith University Art Collection. Donated through the Australian Government's Cultural Gifts Program by Dr Paul Eliadis, 2011

Figure 24

Relative/Absolute (Man) 1991
Synthetic polymer paint and flashe on canvas
40 x 40 cm
The Estate of Gordon Bennett

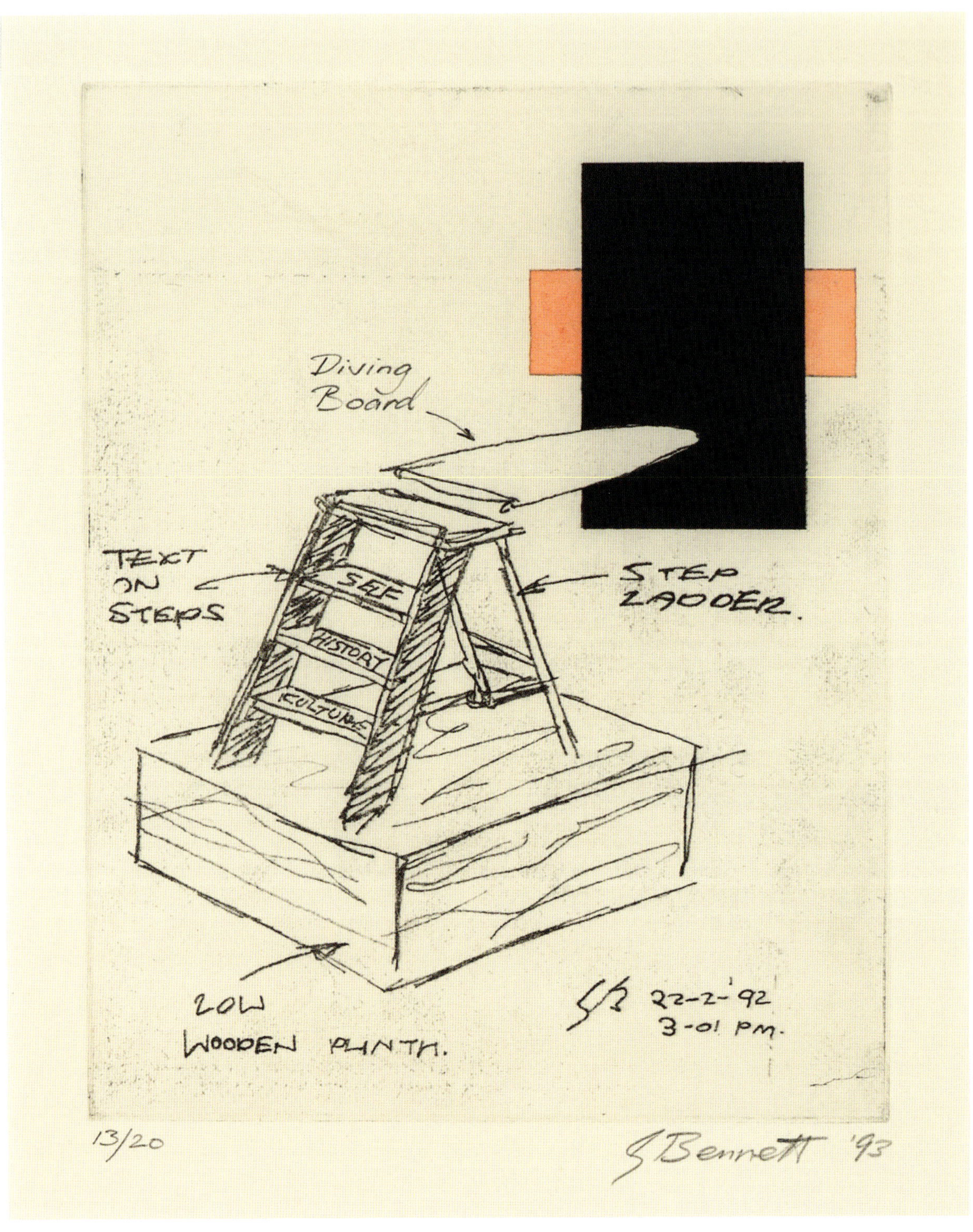

Figure 25

Through the Void (Diving Board) 1993
Soft ground etching, hand coloured, on paper
Edition of 20, 20.5 x 15 cm (image) 69.3 x 48.3 x 3 cm (framed)
Griffith University Art Collection. Donated through the Australian Government's Cultural Gifts Program by Gordon and Leanne Bennett, 2008

Figure 26

Created by Flux 1993
Soft ground etching on paper
Edition of 20, 31 x 19.8 cm (image) 69.3 x 48.2 x 3 cm (framed)
Griffith University Art Collection. Donated through the Australian Government's Cultural Gifts Program by Gordon and Leanne Bennett, 2008

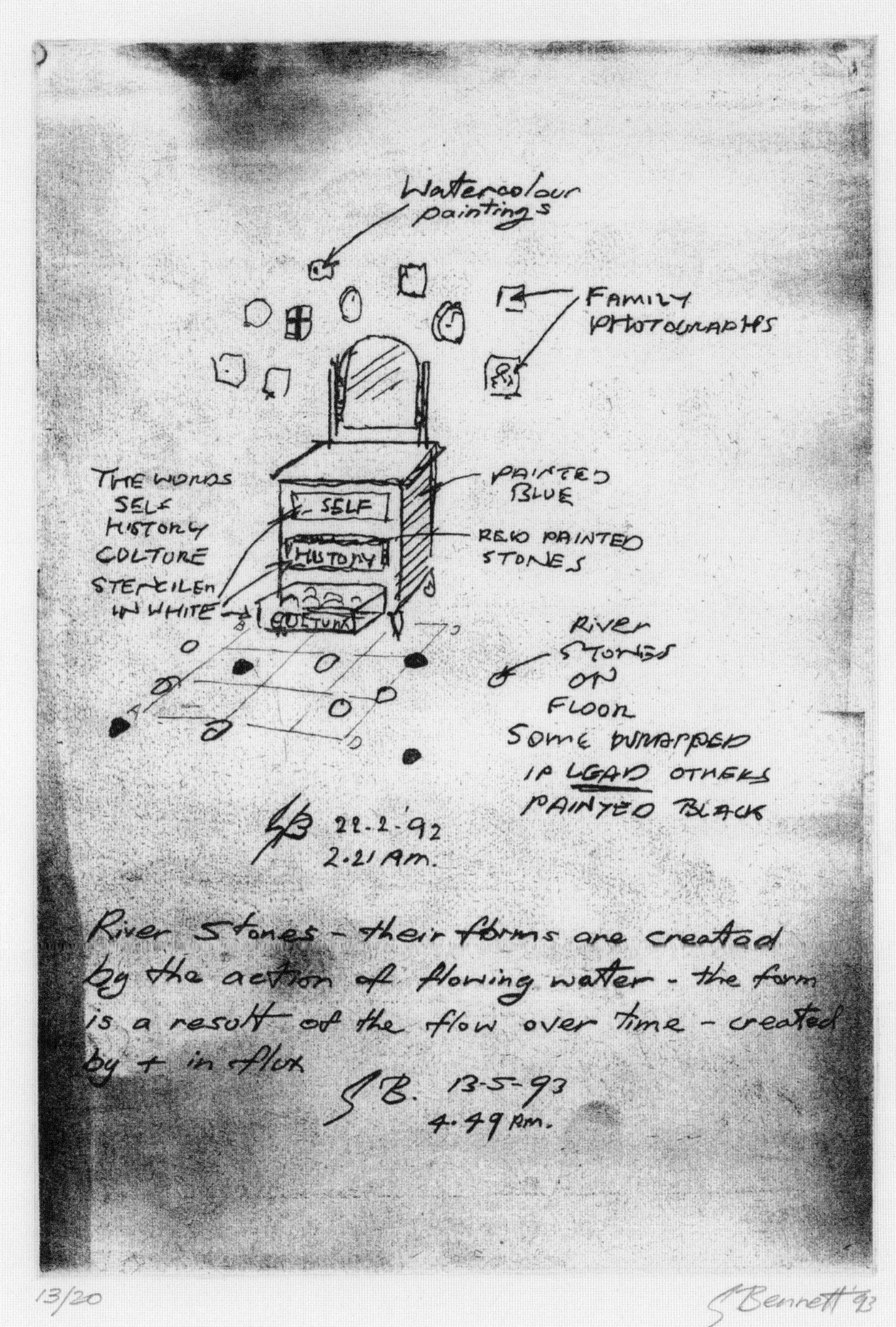
Watercolour paintings
FAMILY PHOTOGRAPHS
THE WORDS SELF HISTORY CULTURE STENCILED IN WHITE
PAINTED BLUE
SELF
HISTORY
CULTURE
RED PAINTED STONES
River STONES ON FLOOR SOME WRAPPED IN LEAD OTHERS PAINTED BLACK
SB 22-2-'92 2.21 AM.
River Stones - their forms are created by the action of flowing water - the form is a result of the flow over time - created by + in flux
SB. 13-5-93 4.49 PM.
13/20
S Bennett '93

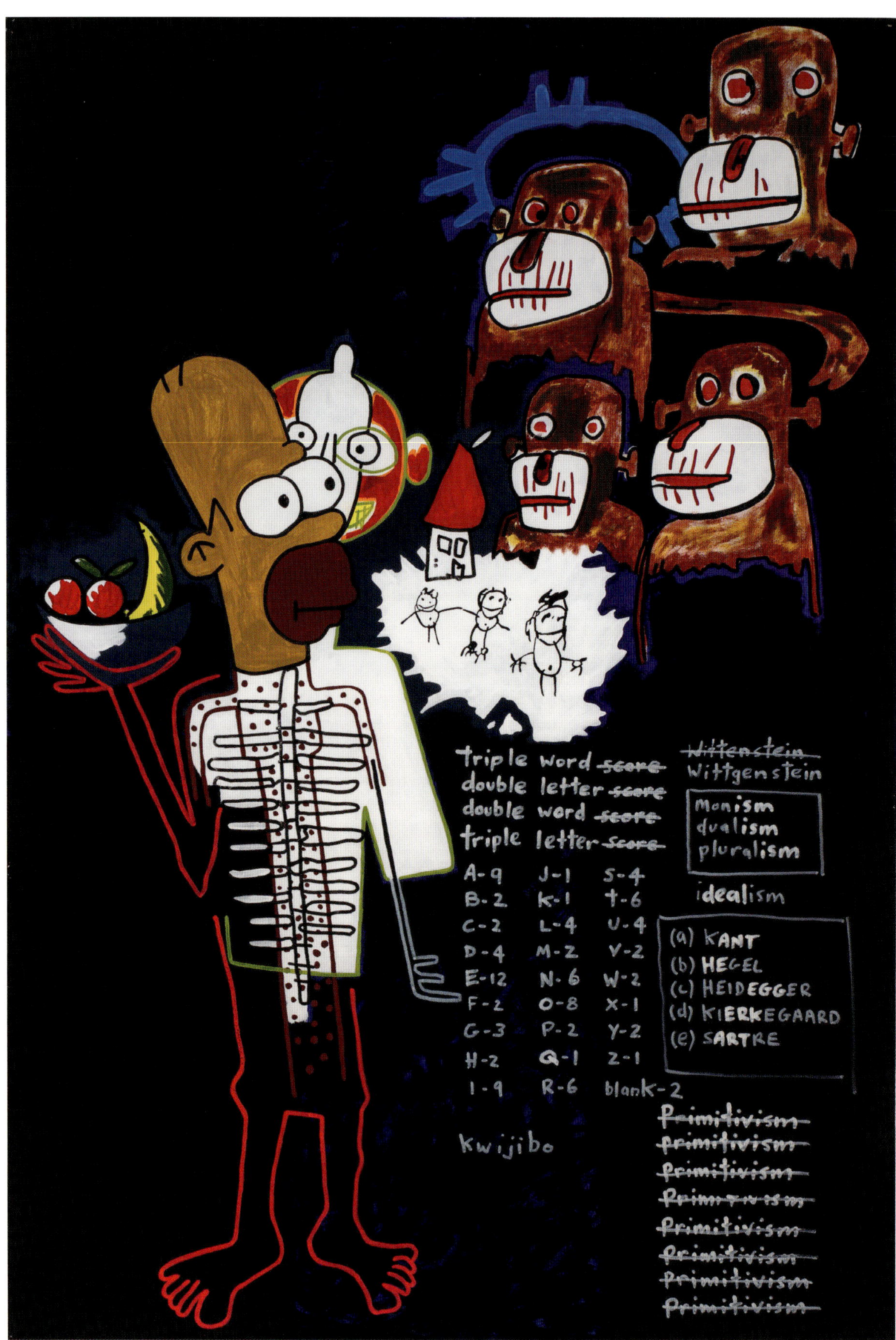

Figure 27

Notes to Basquiat (Kwijibo) 1998
Synthetic polymer paint on paper
120 x 80 cm (image); 136 x 94.5 cm (framed)
Griffith University Art Collection. Donated through the Australian Government's Cultural Gifts Program by Dr Paul Eliadis, 2011

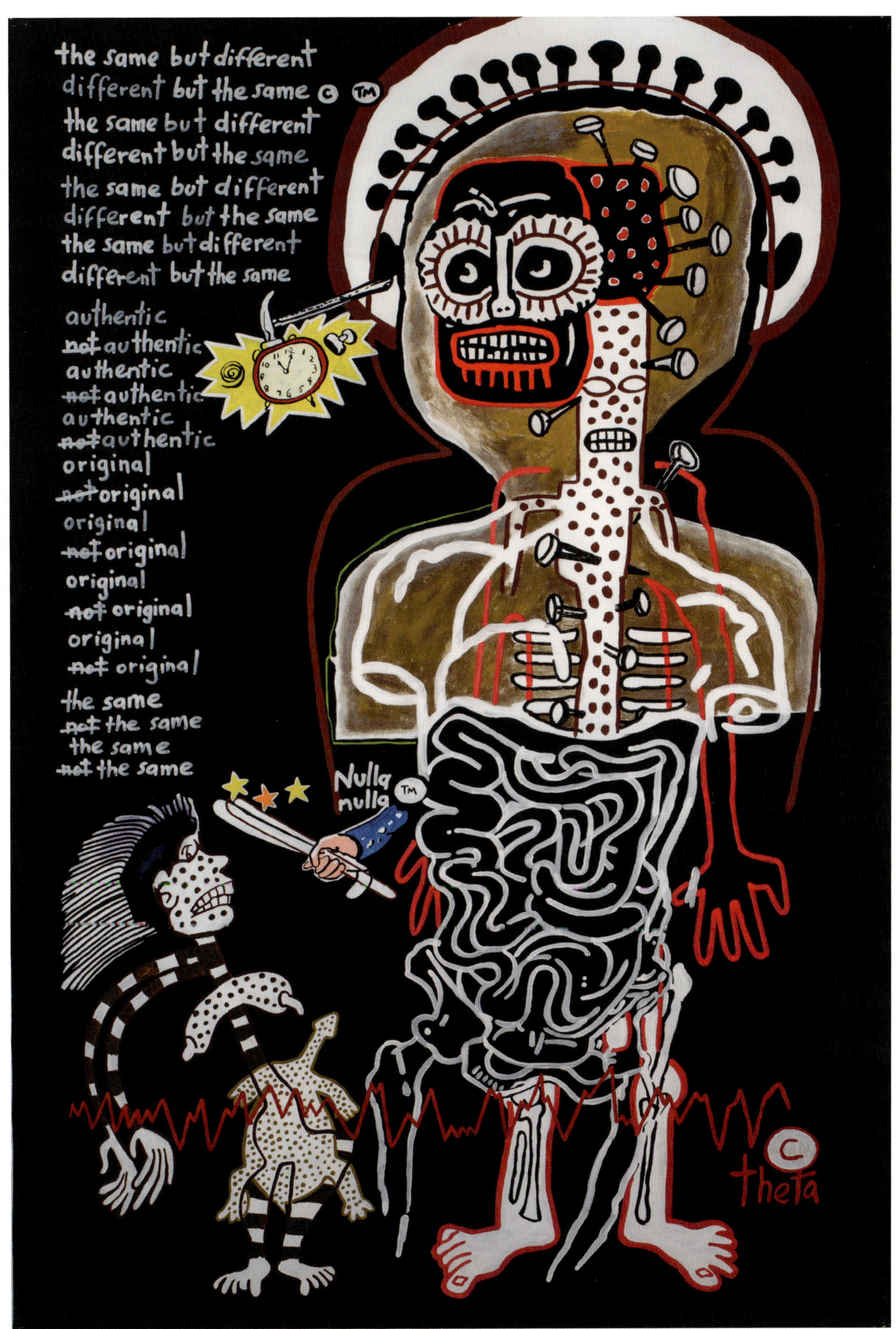

Figure 28

Notes to Basquiat (Ab)original 1998
Synthetic polymer paint on paper
120 x 80 cm (image); 136 x 94.5 cm (framed)
Griffith University Art Collection. Donated through the Australian Government's Cultural Gifts Program by Dr Paul Eliadis, 2011

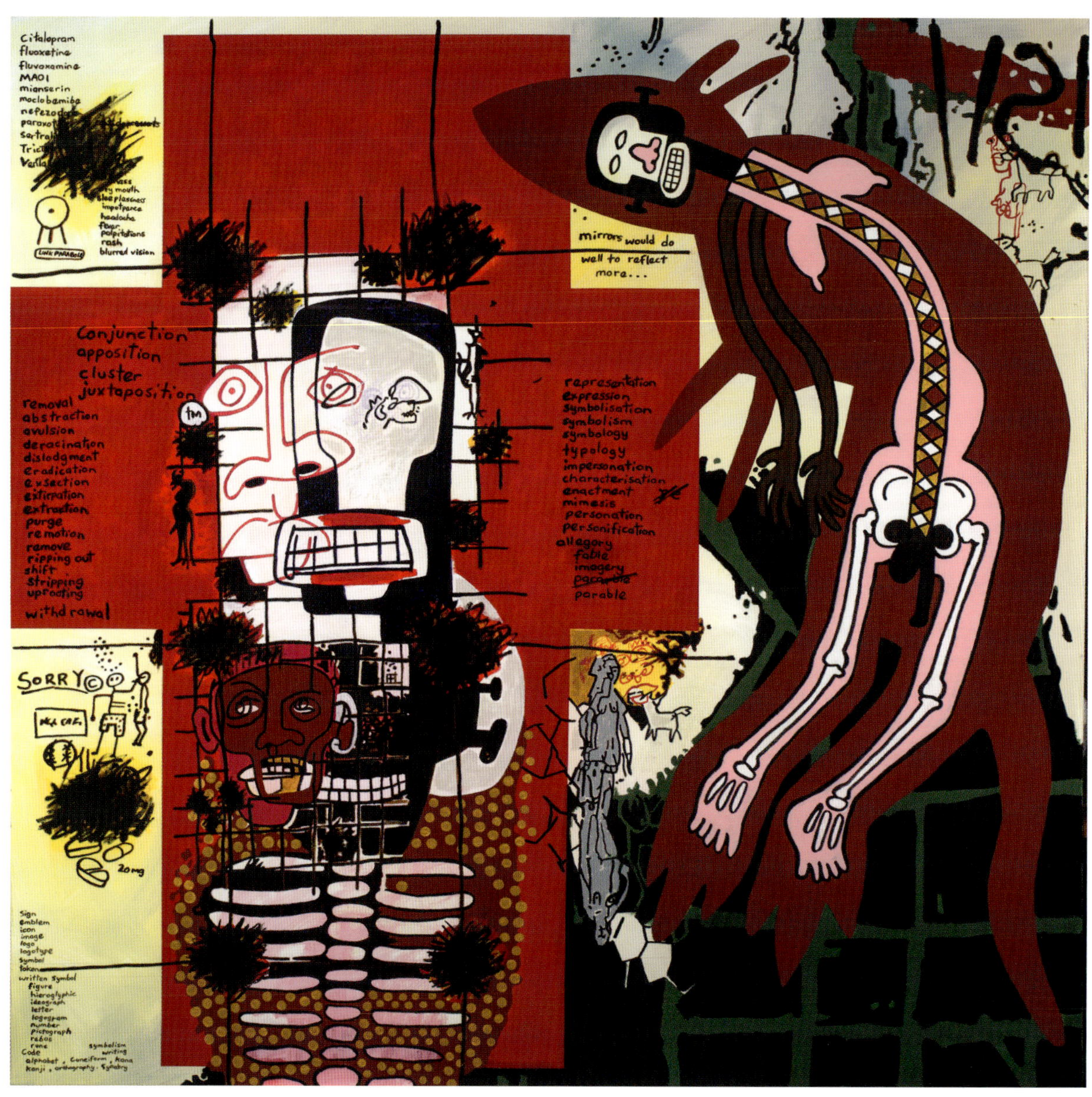

Figure 29

Notes to Basquiat: Haunted 2000
Synthetic polymer paint on linen
152.2 x 152 x 3.5 cm
Griffith University Art Collection. Purchased 2000

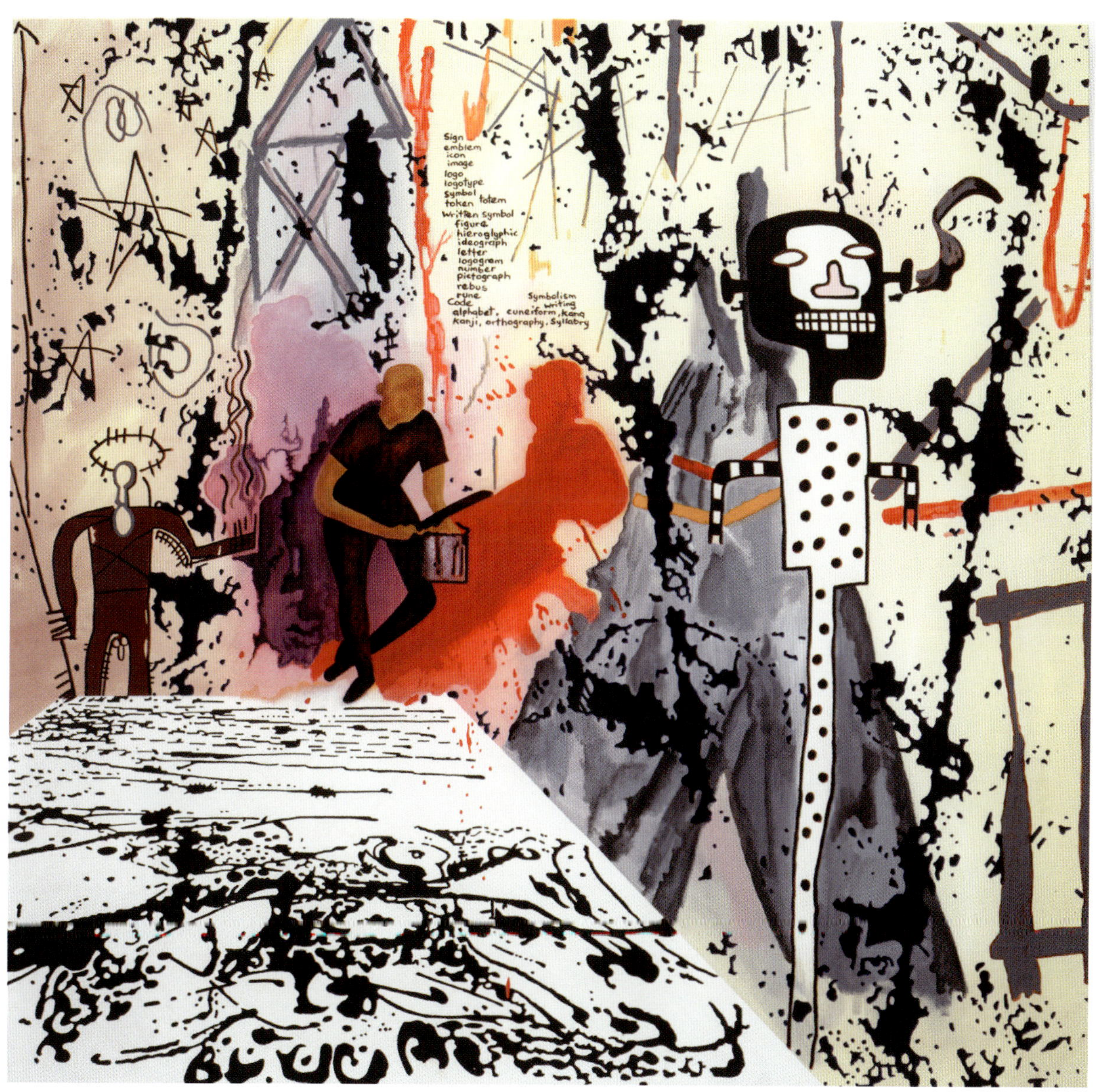

Figure 30

Notes to Basquiat: Totem Lesson 2001
Synthetic polymer paint on linen
152 x 152 cm
Private collection, Sydney

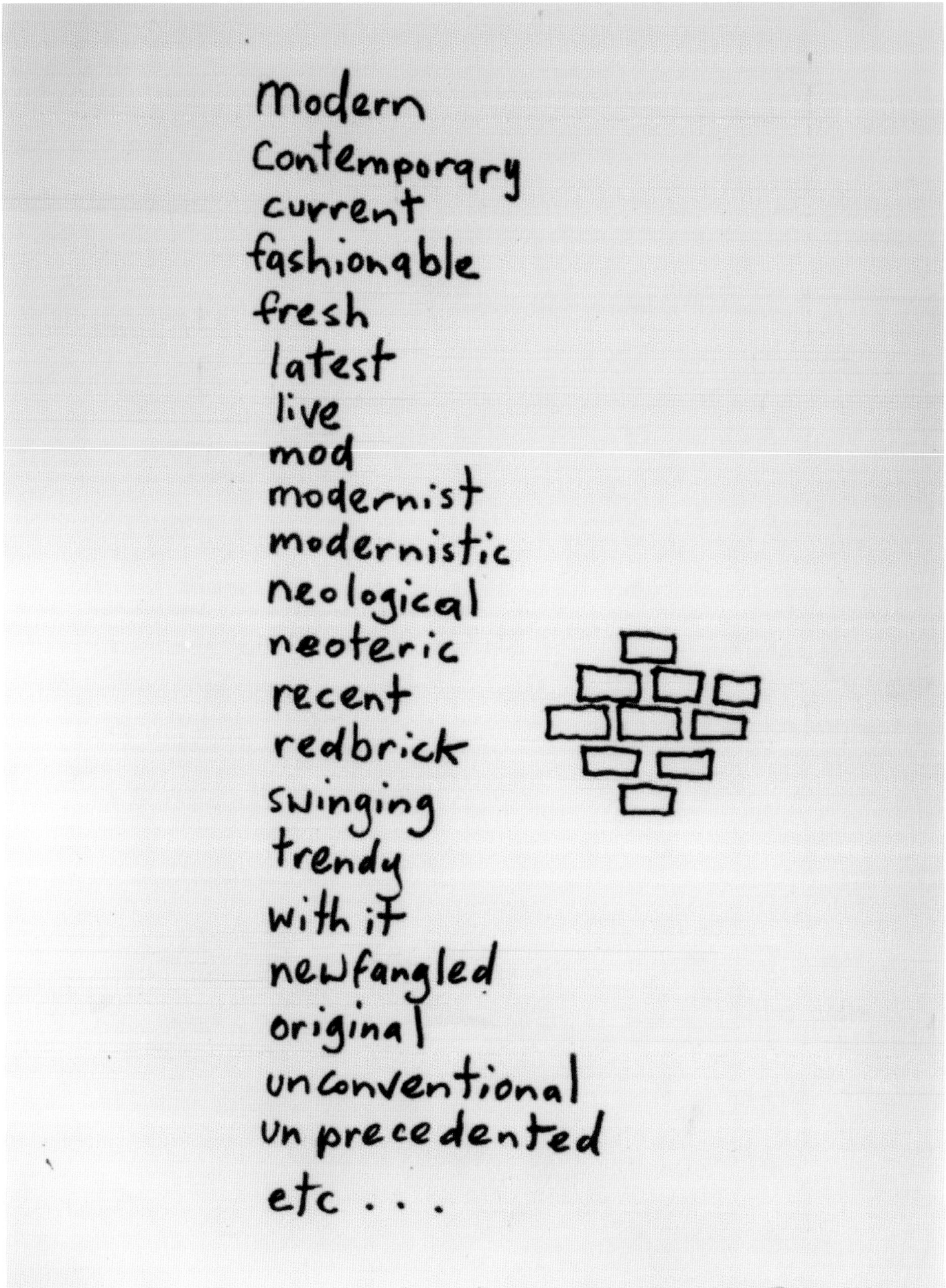

Modern
contemporary
current
fashionable
fresh
latest
live
mod
modernist
modernistic
neological
neoteric
recent
redbrick
swinging
trendy
with it
newfangled
original
unconventional
unprecedented
etc . . .

A/P "modern" G Bennett '04

Figure 31

Modern from 'Notes to Basquiat' series 2004
Inkjet on paper 26.3 x 20.4 cm (image) 29.7 x 21 cm (sheet)
Griffith University Art Collection. Donated through the Australian Government's Cultural Gifts Program by John Citizen Arts Pty Ltd, ATF The Bennett Family Trust, 2007

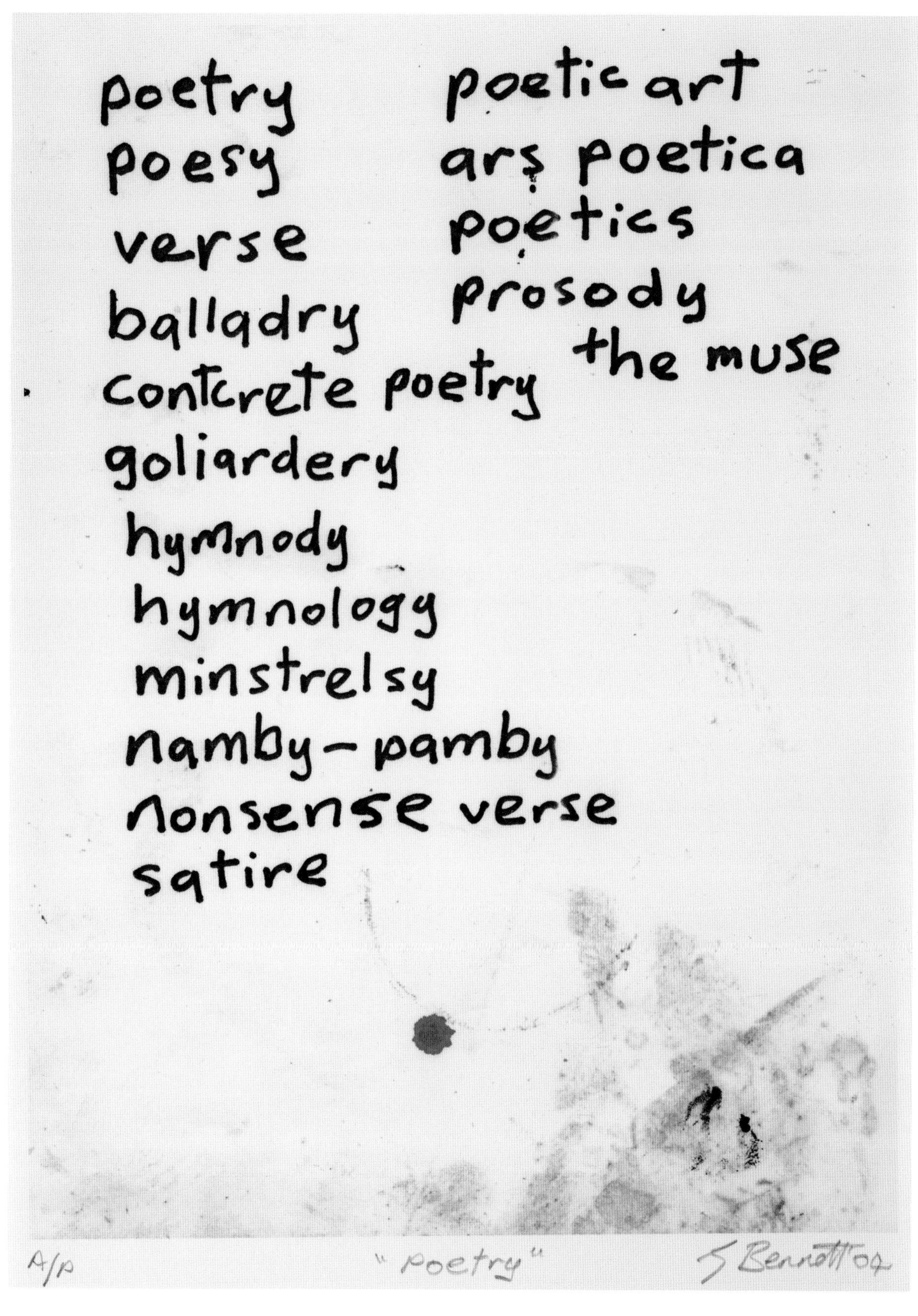

Figure 32

Poetry from 'Notes to Basquiat' series 2004
Inkjet on paper 26.3 x 20.4 cm (image) 29.7 x 21 cm (sheet)
Griffith University Art Collection. Donated through the Australian Government's Cultural Gifts Program by John Citizen Arts Pty Ltd, ATF The Bennett Family Trust, 2007

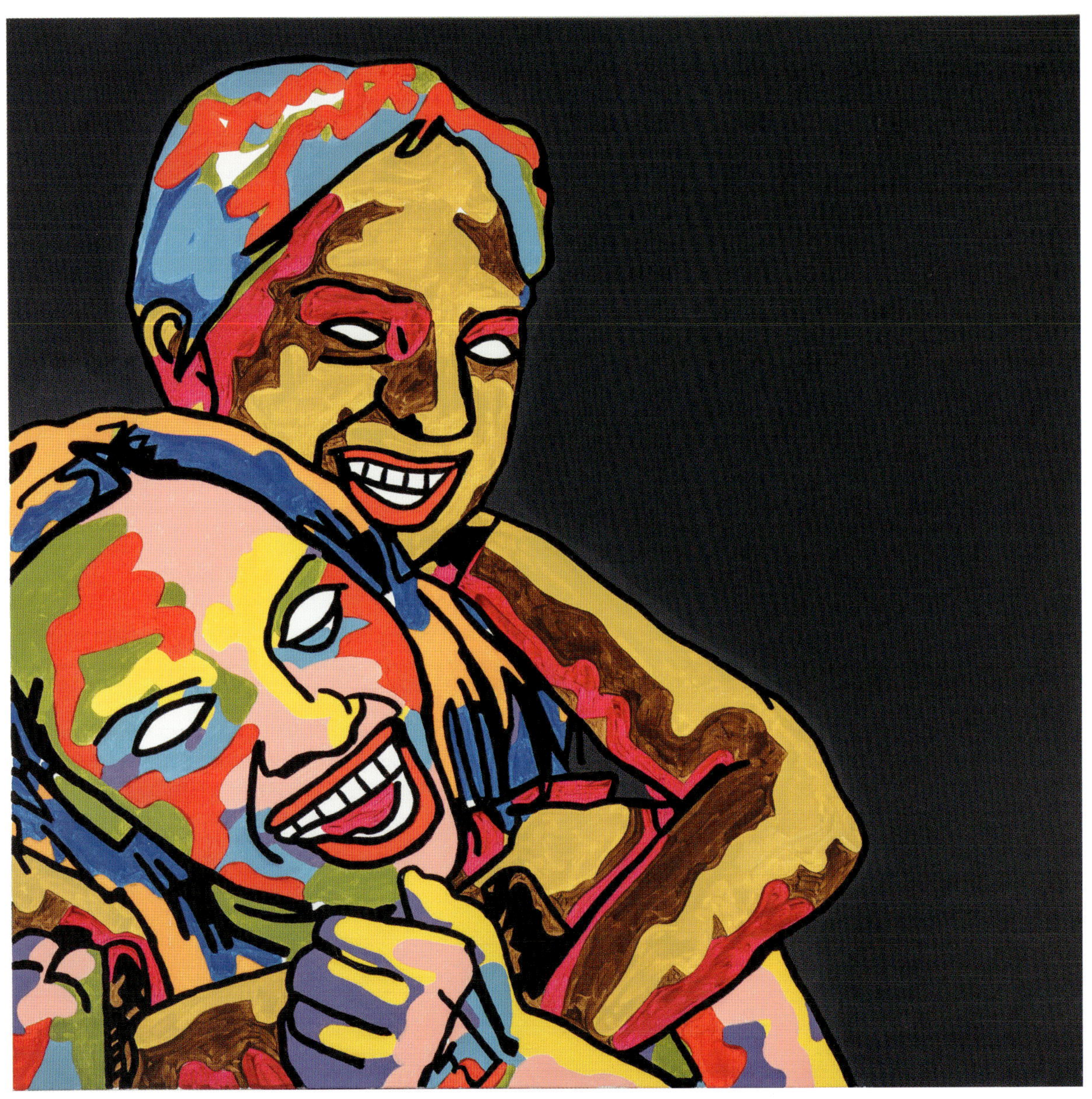

Figure 33

John Citizen
Coloured People No 37 2008
Synthetic polymer paint on canvas
101 x 101 cm
The Estate of Gordon Bennett

Figure 34

Number Twelve 2003
Synthetic polymer paint on linen
182.5 x 152 cm
Museum of New Zealand Te Papa Tongarewa, Wellington
Purchased 2016

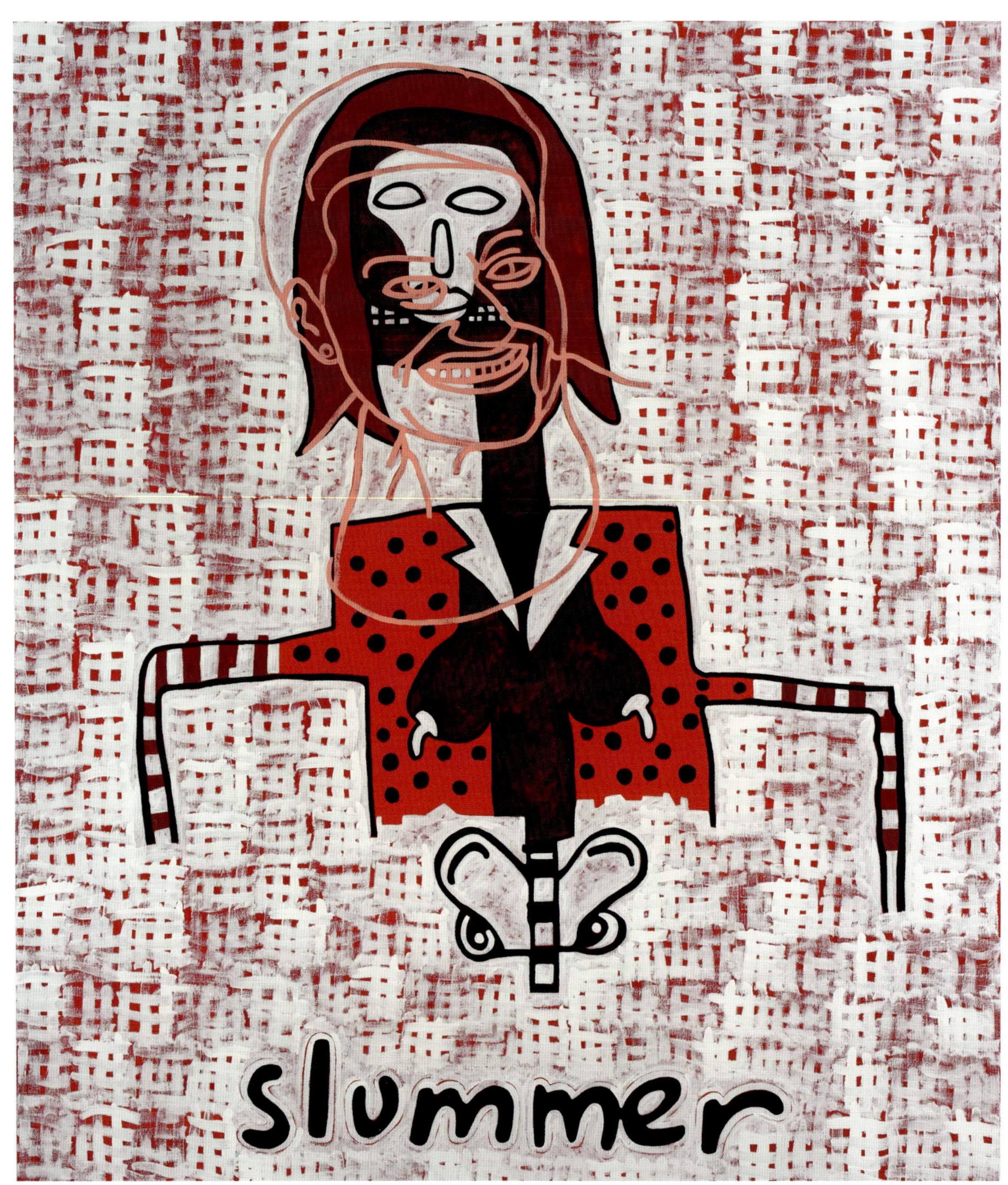

Figure 35

Abstraction (Slummer) 2012
Synthetic polymer paint on linen
182.5 x 152 cm
The Estate of Gordon Bennett

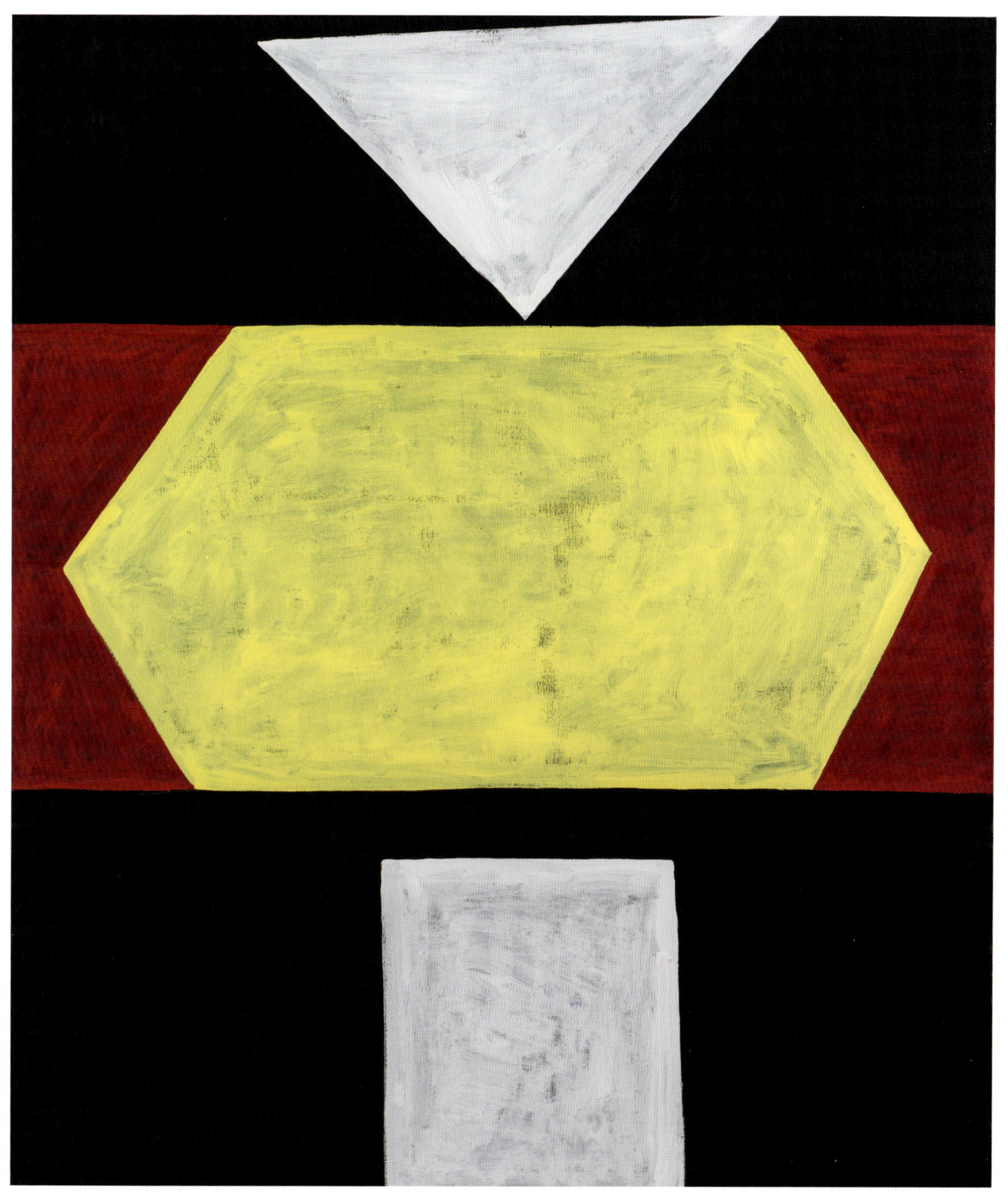

Figure 36

Home Décor (After M. Preston) #21 2013
Synthetic polymer paint on linen
182.5 x 152 cm
The Estate of Gordon Bennett

I won't be an uppity nigger no more. I won't be an uppity nigger
no more. I won't be an uppity nigger no more. I won't be an uppity
nigger no more, I won't be an uppity nigger no more I won't be an
uppity nigger no more, I won't be an uppity nigger no more, I won't
be an uppity nigger no more, I won't be an uppity nigger more,
I won't be an uppity nigger no more, I won't be an uppity nigger no
more. I won't be an uppity nigger no more, I won't be an uppity nigger
no more, I won't be an uppity nigger no more, I won't be an uppity
nigger no more. I won't be an uppity nigger no more
I won't be an uppity nigger no more, I won't be an
uppity nigger no more I won't be an uppity nigger
no more, I won't be an uppity nigger no more, I
won't be an uppity nigger no more, I won't be an uppi
nigger no more. I won't be an uppity nigger no mo
I won't be an uppity nigger no more, I won't be an uppity nigger n
more, I won't be an uppity nigger no more, I won't be an uppity
nigger no more, I won't be an uppity nigger no more, I won't be
an uppity nigger no more, I won't be an uppity nigger no more, I wo
be an uppity nigger no more, I won't be an uppity nigger no more
I won't be an uppity nigger no more, I won't be an uppity nigge
no more, I won't be an uppity nigger no more, I won't be an uppit
nigger no more, I won't be an uppity nigger no more, I won't be an
uppity nigger no more, I won't be an uppity nigger no more, I won
be an uppity nigger no more, I won't be an uppity nigger no more,
I won't be an uppity nigger no more, I won't be an uppity nigger
no more, I won't be an uppity nigger no more, I won't be an upp
nigger no more, I won't be an uppity nigger no more, I won't be
uppity nigger no more. I won't be an uppity nigger no more, I don
be an uppity nigger no more, I won't be an uppity nigger no more
I won't be an uppity nigger no more, I won't be an uppity nigger no
more, I won't be an uppity nigger no more, I won't be an uppity
nigger no more, I won't be an uppity nigger no more. I won't be a
uppity nigger no more, I won't be an uppity nigger no more, I won
be an uppity nigger no more, I won't be an uppity nigger no more
I won't be an uppity nigger no more, I won't be an uppity nigger
more, I won't be an uppity nigger no more, I won't be an uppity
nigger no more, I won't be an uppity nigger no more...

Part Four On reflection

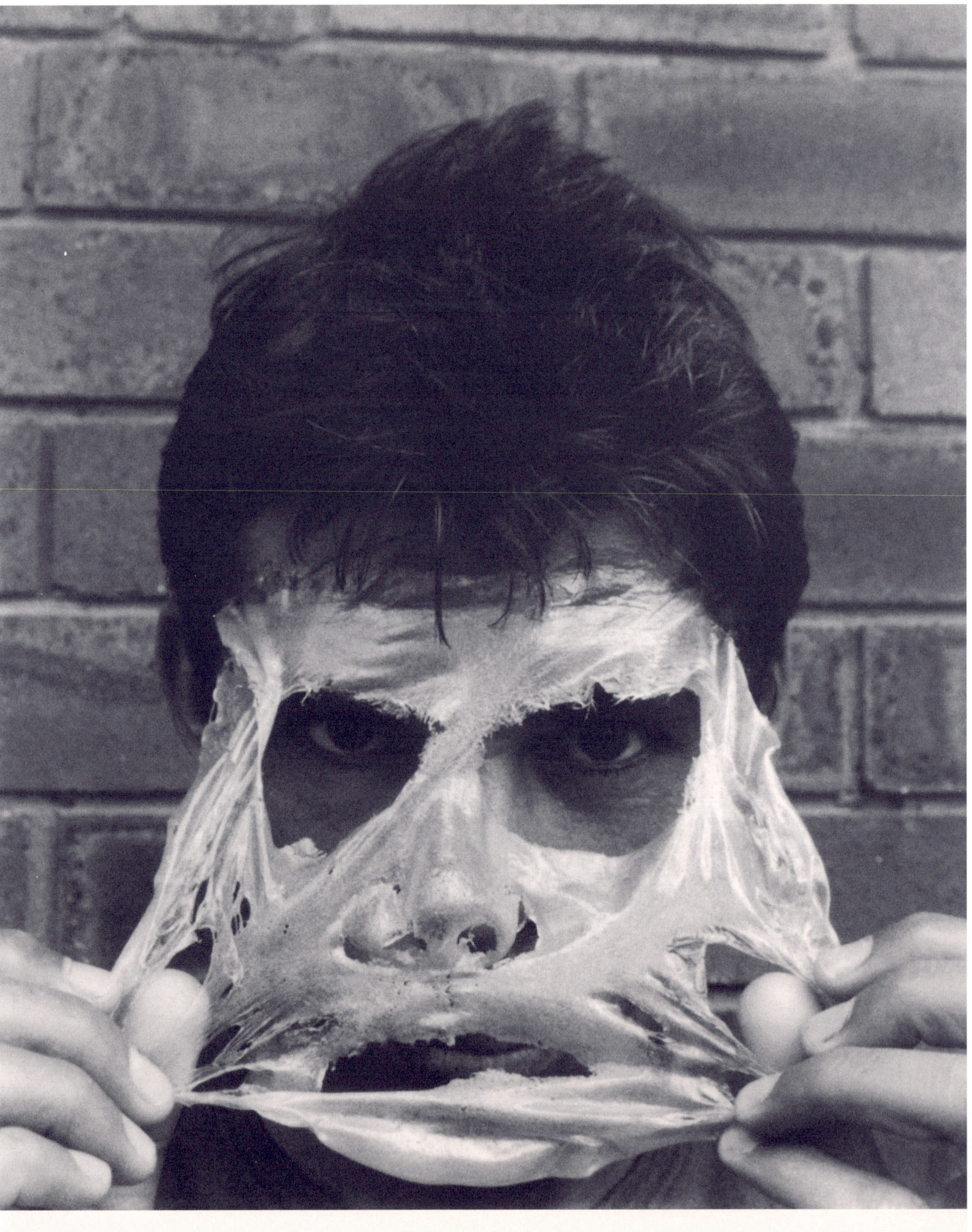

Uncertain Words: The Writing of Gordon Bennett

Tim Riley Walsh

> *Writing can be so uncommunicative sometimes. How can one write in order to transmit the depth of feeling one feels inside? Words appear so sterile, so trite. Or maybe they only appear that way to me. More specifically maybe only my words appear sterile and trite.*
>
> —Gordon Bennett, 11 October 1986[1]

This opening quote from Gordon Bennett's art college journal, penned in the artist's distinctive handwriting two days after his thirty-first birthday, expresses his deep sense of uncertainty over language's capacity to communicate emotion. This quality of uncertainty belies the central role language came to inhabit in Bennett's art and writing, yet it also tempered his engagement with it—particularly in his writing practice. Bennett's experimentation through and with language, and his investigation of its effects and structures, became characteristic of his diverse oeuvre. Despite this interest, he also remained deeply critical of language. As the selected texts presented in this book have shown, Bennett's relationship with the written word evolved alongside his artistic practice. And though his public writing exists only in the first half of his nearly thirty-year-long career, his interest in and use of text was sustained in his private writing and in his art. This persistent discursive presence is reflected best in the experience of viewing much of his art: Bennett's art is equally traversed by reading as it is by looking.

From Bennett's art school days onwards—as his most dedicated and sensitive interlocutor, Australian art historian Ian McLean, describes—language persisted and 'became a central theme of [his] art'. Bennett's work frequently 'probed the grammar and alphabet of the two principal forms of visual language or signs in the modern world—writing and pictures'.[2] Whether operating separate to or working in unison with images, words were crucial tools of his ongoing and ardent analysis: a critical examination into the colonial and racist abuses of Australia's past and their impacts on the present. Like his artworks, Bennett's words in his private writing and public essays presented in this publication challenge the complacent 'pop history' of this country—a dominant Euro-Australian historical narrative that sustains its fiction through the processes of education and socialisation. Though his art questions and subverts dominant (Western) social and cultural structures, it does so by embracing their very forms. Bennett utilised Anglophonic text and Euro-American images in a process of creative contradiction: a simultaneous critique of and creative dependence on Western language. At times, this double bind of being inculcated within the system and actively critiquing its limits has led viewers to misinterpret Bennett's irony for sincerity. But importantly, he recognised himself as an already colonised subject, in both mind and body, and so used this position to speak from within the system, weaponising its very vocabulary for his work.

Bennett may have begun his creative journey thinking his words were 'sterile and trite', but they became a generative force for his artistic practice: a vehicle for emotive communication and critical engagement, but always tempered by a sense of modesty. The texts published in this book reflect the developmental, even iterative quality of Bennett's writing practice. It is not unusual to note in his art the reintroduction of an image, motif or even an entire earlier work within a new piece, a technique which curator Kelly Gellatly relates to Bennett's sense of his art's 'interconnectedness', its ability 'to fold back on itself while forging new ground'.[3] Similarly, Bennett often repurposes earlier texts in subsequent writings, expanding on his initial argument with a new perspective, or reiterating a particular position as a means to remind readers of his personal context. At times, this demands from the reader some patience as Bennett returns to an earlier idea; while Bennett's technique may initially seem like repetition, close reading reveals subtle developments in his thinking. Regardless, Bennett's writing played a crucial and critical role in communicating his ongoing focuses: his investigation of institutionalised racism, and his theorisation of a space of 'freedom' outside of categorisation or identity. As this collection of writings has demonstrated, Bennett conducted these formally through his public essays and artist's statements, as well as informally through correspondence with close friends, as a way to process his thoughts and perspectives emerging from his studio practice.

Both Bennett's art and writing appear prescient today because of their forceful interrogation of Western hegemonies and for their expansion of the terms and structures of identity. In its critical stance, Bennett's writing embodies his long-held desire for an uncertain space outside of identification, definition, and binary thinking.[4] This desire for a fluid, expansive understanding of identity is visible most overtly in Bennett's relationship to language, which similarly echoes the oppositional qualities of Bennett's art and the positions he took. Though his paintings appropriated the work of other artists, he did not see himself as an appropriation artist.[5] Though he made work that investigated his Aboriginality, he did not identify strictly as Aboriginal.[6] Though his life experience informed much of his work, he considered his art and life as distinctly separate.[7] In his 1994 letter to 2UE Radio broadcaster John Laws (p. 90), Bennett penned an impassioned and emotive text advocating the recognition of Indigenous freedom fighters in Australian history, while at other times he 'wrote' essays, such as 1992's 'Re-Writing History' (p. 18), constructed of entirely pre-existing, competing quotations, lifted from historical sources and Bennett's own artist's statements, reconceived as a conceptual gesture. For over twenty-two years, Bennett refused to speak publicly as part of his *Non-Performance* (1992-2014), though continued to conduct email interviews in rare circumstances. Bennett was precise about this position of radical uncertainty, where he evaded categorisation—a quality that his work mirrored, seemingly never being reflective of a particular style for any extended time. This state of flux was an ethos that Bennett not only embraced in his art as a means of avoiding classification, but also expressed in his writings, as embodied through their variety, repetition, refusals, absences, and experimentations.

The Persistence of Language: Text in Bennett's Art

While this publication has focused on Bennett's texts as conducted on the page, it is crucial to investigate the prevalence of language on the canvas or within his artwork more generally, as the two were closely connected. Though Bennett wrote for much of his career, he saw himself as an artist first and foremost, and this dynamic was established early on. At art school, he found 'the language in which I was most articulate to be the visual language of painting', stating that 'it was through painting that I found a voice'.[8] Bennett's probing of language and text initially became evident in his early college works, in particular 1987's *The Persistence of Language* (figure 2)—a vast expressionist triptych that traces the process of colonisation across its three panels, depicting the arrival of language, religion, and then, in the final canvas, a black figure hanging in a cell from a rope.[9] This reflection on black deaths in custody is framed at its right edge by a litany of racist taunts scrawled in blood-red paint. In an artist's statement for the work (p. 16), Bennett describes the title as relating to the persistent repetition of these words in his mind and their 'common usage persistently directed at Aboriginal people'.[10]

Bennett was approached around this time by a fellow student who encouraged him to explore the work of New Zealand artist Colin McCahon.[11] He borrowed books from the library and began engaging with and appropriating some of McCahon's words. *The Coming of the Light* (figure 1), a two-panel work also from 1987, incorporates text from McCahon's 1959 'Elias' series of paintings—'Will he come/let be/let be/will Elias come to save him'—in a cursive script in the background of the right panel.[12] On the left, a monochromatic set of children's alphabet blocks approaches the foreground of the image on a conveyor belt in their familiar succession of A, B, C, and D. An Indigenous figure stylised as a Jack-in-the-box has been pulled from the A block's dark interior by his neck, strangled by a belt. The belt is grasped by one of two conjoined hands, the other hand holding the light of liberty, and Enlightenment, aloft.

These same blocks return in the 'Bounty Hunter' series (1991, figure 5), now interrupting depictions of the Australian landscape. Here they are painted in a bright, playground palette, a style which Australian art historian Terry Smith describes as 'a way of communicating with a directness which presumes no prior literacy, as in children's books'.[13] Far from child-like in their content, the works depict the massacres of Indigenous peoples, rape and bodily abuse, and half-buried mass graves, signifying the atrocities overlooked or ignored amid the march of colonisation. The ABC blocks—repeated in varying combinations—stand as mute monoliths among the violence. In one of the works from this series, *Valley of Dry Bones (To the Sound of Cicadas)*, they become the stacked plinth for a classical, angelic sculpture, a monument to Western 'civilisation' and religion, looking benignly down toward a young Indigenous figure who mournfully contemplates a skull within the titular valley—its name and rough composition borrowed from McCahon's 1947 work of the same name.[14] In the final work of the series, a young Indigenous figure in a t-shirt emblazoned with the Aboriginal flag stands before the valley of dry bones, declaring words from the Old Testament, also incorporated into McCahon's original: 'Come from the four winds, O Breath, and breathe upon these slain, that they may live.'

In 'Home Sweet Home' (1993-94, figures 22 and 23), a series of seven graphic watercolours depict scenes of racist and sexual violence, accompanied by corresponding handwritten letters examining abuse in its psychological and more casual guise as Australian larrikinism. These letters (p. 88) relay how Bennett, having settled into suburban life with his young family in Brisbane, saw through the thin veneer of this idealised environment. They describe its dark, emotional landscape—how Bennett, after spending weekends labouring over the garden and house, was rewarded with navigating the caustic racism emerging from his neighbours after a few beers. The text's tone drips with a biting, discordant sarcasm encapsulated in the repeated phrase 'Please excuse me, I don't mean to offend . . . '. These letters recall in their formatting and style much of Bennett's private correspondence—often recorded with the date, his distinctive signature, and occasionally their time of writing. In 'Home Sweet Home', his letter writing takes on a form of radical public address: their recipient is left purposefully unnamed, allowing their moral invective to inhabit a space of wide-ranging social critique of the 'great Australian dream'.[15]

In his 1993 work *Ricochets; Manifest Destiny (A Painting for the Distant Future: 2001); and Window Onto a Shadow Universe* (figures 18-21), Bennett expanded his interest in written correspondence as a component of his artworks, incorporating faxes exchanged with Latvian-Australian artist Imants Tillers. Presented on individual canvas boards and accompanied by a tall, precarious stack of the same boards on the floor, the work expands upon their artistic sparring established with Bennett's rapprochement of Tillers in his 1990 painting *The Nine Ricochets (Fall Down Black Fella, Jump Up White Fella)*.[16] Their correspondence, heated at times, discusses the prospect of their potential collaboration, with the work itself incorporating images and artworks drawn from their practices.

The early to mid-1990s was a time of both growth and regression for Australia's public discourse, fluctuations that Bennett felt deeply and channelled into his work. Bennett's methods of processing during this time of social and political change—making, writing, speaking publicly—were increasingly tested.

Positive events included Paul Keating's Redfern speech and the Mabo decision in 1992, as well as the *Native Title Act* of 1993, which built on the Mabo case's victory. By 1996, however, the mood had shifted considerably, with John Howard's conservative Coalition government in power and Pauline Hanson sitting as an Independent in the Queensland Parliament, despite her openly racist views. The *Native Title Act* and its hard-fought victories for Indigenous Australian land rights were partly repealed by Howard's *Native Title Amendment Act* of 1998, commonly known as the Ten Point Plan, which reprioritised mining, farming, and governmental use of land over traditional owners'.

As Bennett's painterly compositions at this time matured, so his use of text within his art grew increasingly more complex. Interested in exploring other creative avenues that he saw as sitting 'outside' the artistic purview of his typical work, in the mid-1990s, Bennett began conceiving of a separate practice: that of John Citizen's. In these works, Citizen was free to explore new streams of thought and to develop his own separate artist CV and oeuvre. In Bennett's own practice, new experiments were taking place in the 'Home Décor' series. In the dense webs of floating images and grids typical of this series, such as 1998's *Home Décor (Algebra) Daddy's Little Girl* (figure 10), images from Bennett's past return and jostle with new, increasingly international imagery. Some works also incorporated previous text works, such as his 1989 collaboration with Eugene Carchesio, *Daddy's Little Girl*. Gellatly's description of the 'interconnectedness' of Bennett's art is exemplified here through this process of reintroduction. This technique produces new meanings through juxtaposition: reincorporating his work of the past, such as *Australian Icon (Notes on Perception No 1)* (1989), with his present subjects—in this case, the appropriated works of Australian modernist painter Margaret Preston (1875-1963) and the Dutch abstractionist Piet Mondrian. This process was described by Bennett as a way of 'reviewing my own work in the context of new images and possible "meanings"'.[17] The A, B, and C return, now aligned stylistically with De Stijl's primary colour palette, their symbolism deepened through the title and the painting's three-letter allusion to algebraic variables, which links back to the mathematical formulae present in the titles of many works of this series: Preston + De Stijl = Citizen. As McLean notes, algebra is utilised by Bennett for its dual meanings as 'both an abstract calculus of symbols, and ... its Arab derivation meaning "reunion of broken parts"'.[18] According to McLean, Bennett here attempts a sort of unlikely reconciliation via the pairing of Preston and Mondrian—a stylistic 'fugue' that may become the basis 'of a virtuous Australian republic'.[19]

Bennett expanded on his thinking about the 'Home Décor' series in a private letter sent to McLean and a separate artist's statement, both included in this publication (p. 102 and p. 61, respectively). The series, as Bennett describes, represented a visual response to the political context of the mid-1990s—in particular, to the influence of figures such as Hanson and Howard.[20] The process of taping up his canvases and painting the sharp Mondrian grid lines, as he described to McLean, 'became like basket weaving, something to do, a way of keeping going until I felt better, when I felt like just stopping work altogether'. Bennett's engagement with the political climate of the country, and investment in issues of reconciliation, had begun to weigh on him. Rather than stopping entirely, as he desired, Bennett accelerated his painterly process with the series 'Notes to Basquiat' (1998-2007), a heady mix of scrawled text and imagery drawn from the painting practice of the late Jean-Michel Basquiat.

This new series built on Bennett's initial experimentations with mimicking Basquiat's distinctive style that he began in 1994 (figure 15), though Bennett's admiration for the artist extended even further back. Basquiat, who was an American artist of Haitian and Puerto Rican descent, died of a drug overdose in Bennett's last year at art college. He had been an early inspiration during Bennett's studies, considered as 'one of a small group of "Black" role models'.[21] Basquiat's distinctive canvases are frequently punctuated by phrases and word lists, and Bennett's work in the series continued this technique (figure 27). Bennett identified with Basquiat's life as an artist of colour who had, like him, achieved significant success in the art world and found the resulting attention difficult to bear. Describing the series to McLean, Bennett saw it as 'a kind of communication to Basquiat, much like this letter is to you, only pictorial'.[22]

Bennett's 1998 'Letter to Jean-Michel Basquiat' (p. 101) accompanied many of the series' public presentations, including their first exhibition at the 1998 Gramercy International Art Fair in New York City. This heartfelt text provides a clear rationale for this series, illustrating the empathic nature of Bennett's appropriation. Towards the end of his text, Bennett includes a quote from the African-American writer Greg Tate: 'to be a race-identified race-refugee is to tap-dance on a tightrope'.[23] Following this, Bennett communicates his empathy for Basquiat's precarious position, reflecting 'you lost your balance, I feel I can understand why'. As part of this empathic engagement with Basquiat's life Bennett considered his own emotional state during the production of this series, trying to communicate in his letter and in the works 'a sense of tension, like a fit almost'.[24] A heightened quality of emotion pervades these works, which Bennett expressed through particular imagery and motifs. The brain wave pattern, visible in *Notes to Basquiat: (Ab)original*, 1998, figure 28) and other works of this series, 'was of a kind that is normally found in children (Theta waves), but when found in an adult is indicative of extreme emotional stress'. This state of distress, emotional and psychological, is applied by Bennett to communicate a sense of apprehension and foreboding, a feeling he related to the end of the millennium.[25]

A similar psychological tenor emerges in the word lists and text that appear within works from this series. In *Notes to Basquiat: (Ab)original*, the text takes on the appearance of white chalk on a classroom blackboard, a kind of traumatic repetition. The words are similar to those Bennett described as racing through his head during the painting of *The Persistence of Language* or the A, B, C, D of *The Coming of the Light*: 'The same but different, different but the same' and 'authentic, ~~not~~ authentic' echo over and over, line by line. In other works, word lists function as synonymic records. Beginning with one word that relates to the work's subject or feeling, Bennett utilised a thesaurus to list similar words 'linked by nuances of meaning'.[26] The resulting texts read 'something like spoken-word lyrics or poetry'. In later works such as 2004's *Modern* and *Poetry* (figures 31 and 32) these lists became the main subject matter of the work. For Bennett, the importance of the poetic is that it 'doesn't seek closure on its meaning. I think it seeks to go beyond the words on the paper into a world of metaphor, allegory, images and ideas in order to say "something".'[27]

By around 2003, Bennett had reached an impasse in his artistic practice. Reflecting on this in 2007, he stated: 'I felt I had gone as far as I could with the postcolonial project I was working through ... The content of the work was getting to me emotionally.'[28] This emotional toll and the weight of responsibility Bennett felt keenly as a high-profile artist guided him frequently to periods of silence. From 1992 he stopped speaking publicly in Australia as part of his *Non-Performance* and from 1999 he no longer published his writing. Despite exploring ways to manage expectations projected on him by limiting his public speaking and writing, Bennett's position of significance nationally, and increasingly internationally, meant he could not escape art altogether. With his next series, he sought a way to translate this desire for silence through his art.

From 2003, this same desire for silence that powered his *Non-Performance*, as I have argued elsewhere,[29] informed his 'Stripe' series (2003-08): non-objective, abstract paintings of bands of colour (figure 34) inspired by the 1950s' 'Black Paintings' of American artist Frank Stella. Bennett's repeating lines and crisscrossing knots, generated as tangential strokes on a Y- or X-axis, were not dissimilar in form to the 'basket weaving' lines of his 'Home Décor' series. Gellatly, in her brief engagement with the 'Stripe' works at the end of her seminal 2007 text 'Citizen in the Making: The Art of Gordon Bennett', states that this series:

> almost sever[s] itself from the work of the artist's earlier career ... Bennett sought a form of release ... a means of stepping away from ... the frameworks through which both the artist and his work have been contained and perceived throughout his career.[30]

Reflecting further, Gellatly adds that the 'denial of information' these works depict through their abstraction reflects a 'refusal to "communicate"'.[31] As Bennett noted himself, painting in an 'overtly "abstract" manner was a way to go silent on the issues' of his earlier work 'and yet still keep painting. It was a way forward for me'.[32]

From 2008 until his untimely passing in 2014, Bennett returned to postcolonial critique, and text returned too—albeit briefly—in his 'Abstraction' series (2011-13, figure 35). Conflating Bennett's exploration of abstraction in the 'Stripe' series and his engagement with Preston in 'Home Décor', Bennett's final series of works, 'Home Décor: After M. Preston' (2008-13), functioned as a sequel of sorts to the earlier series of the same name. Bennett exhibited a suite of these paintings at 2012's dOCUMENTA(13) in Kassel, Germany—which were exhibited alongside the very works that inspired Bennett's series: Preston's appropriations of Aboriginal designs of baskets, mats, and predominantly shields, a selection of which were featured in *Art in Australia* in 1925.[33] In 2013's *Home Décor (After M. Preston) #21* (figure 36), a sense of closure permeates the composition: a bright yellow hexagon framed on its right and left with blood red appears compressed from above and below by bands of black, pinched together by a white triangle at the top and a white square at the bottom.[34] No text features in this final body of work, but Bennett had reached a point where what he wished to communicate need not be dependent on written language: what was being said was strongly imbued and expressed through colour and shape alone.

Public/Private: The Journey of Bennett's Written Voice

Bennett's writing has a direct and empathic quality that is often more disarming and personal than the precise manoeuvres of his paintings, and his art more generally. Though Bennett never dropped his guard, he lowered it in his essays, letters, and interviews. His art and writing were responsive to changes within his life—new influences in his personal or professional circumstances. Text was a conduit between Bennett's public and private lives, a site for expression and for making meaning. His writing also evolved with his changing perspectives on Australian society and his place within it, as well as his interest in postmodern and poststructural theories.

Like Bennett's drawing practice, explored in the Institute of Modern Art's 2016 exhibition *Gordon Bennett: Be Polite* and its accompanying publication, the immediacy of these texts show a very different side to his paintings, which were products, as McLean describes them, of 'a highly polished, thoughtful performance'.[35] Often coexisting on the same page, the practices of writing and drawing provided a sense of freedom for Bennett. Similar to the 'sanctuary or space in which he could work things through' that drawing provided,[36] writing allowed Bennett space to analyse and process his thoughts.

From 1990 to 1999, the written word in its formal mode was a way for Bennett to articulate his ideas, feelings, and opinions to the public in a different tenor from his artworks. He published artist's statements and essays, and was the subject of many interviews. Informally, he wrote frequently as part of his studio practice from 1986 onwards, and the handwritten notes that fill his archive describe in close detail his internal dialogue and thinking. In his letter writing especially, a practice which continued past 1999—the year that Bennett ceased publishing his writing—a close and personal vantage point on Bennett's thinking and fierce intellectualism is provided. The power of these letters are not only to be found in their philosophic moments, but in their ameliorative desire. This drive to right wrongs and heal particular divides extended to Bennett's correspondence with members of the public, outside of the art world's inner circles, as well as to close confidants and more public figures. In these more old-fashioned forms of communication, a softer side of Bennett is sometimes exposed—for example, in his series of letters to one of his longest collaborators, fellow Brisbane artist Eugene Carchesio—while, in others, he strongly asserts his position on particular issues, such as in his letter to John Laws, mentioned above.

Bennett's correspondence with members of the public included detailed and heartfelt responses to Judith Hugo, a volunteer guide from the Art Gallery of Western Australia (p. 72), and Rose Johnson, a student at Flinders University, Adelaide (p. 97). This willingness to engage with the public also extended to those more well known in Australian society. In the 1994 letter to Laws, Bennett fiercely and passionately admonished the radio announcer for his opinion piece in the *Sunday Telegraph* on 29 May of the same year. In his letter, Bennett reminds Laws in precise detail what Indigenous Australians have lost and fought for since British 'settlement', but tempers this fire with a tone of compassion: '[there] cannot be "reconciliation" without recognition of both our fight for our country and our aid in its development. There can never be reconciliation while ignorance is fostered. This is not to "pick at old wounds" but to *heal* wounds that have festered. Please, try and understand that.'[37]

In Bennett's letters to Carchesio written in the early months of 1992, he describes his life abroad in Hautvillers, France (p. 82). Travelling to Europe in 1991, Bennett was the winner of that year's Moët & Chandon Australian Art Fellowship for an eleven-month residency in the French town. To Carchesio, he describes his recent trip to Paris to see a retrospective of the Belgian artist Marcel Broodthaers and details his immediate attraction to Broodthaers' 'museum',[38] the shortened parlance for the artist's 1968 *Musee d'Art Moderne, Département des Aigles* (Museum of Modern Art, Department of Eagles), which Broodthaers named after announcing that he was no longer an artist, appointing himself instead as director of a new institution.[39]

Like his artistic practice, it was not unusual for Bennett's writing to often inhabit experimental or conceptual forms, and his text 'Re-Writing History' is an important example of these same tendencies. Initially commissioned by Camerawork, London, Bennett chose to 'write something that would basically allow others to speak for me'.[40] The resulting 'essay' is constructed from competing quotations appropriated from a mixture of historical and current sources. Through this process, Bennett reveals the evolution and perpetuation of institutionalised racism within Australia, offering quotes from his personal writings on his art and life in response as a form of comparative panacea. This gesture's power also lies in its acknowledgement of the reiterative quality of the narrative Bennett had established by this point in his career—a quality most noticeable when reading his texts consecutively in this publication.

The reworked and repurposed text in Bennett's writing was indicative of the demands frequently placed on him to justify his position. 'Re-Writing History', then, stands as a powerful critique of the 'echo chamber' that he found himself in, both in Australia and abroad. Bennett was caught between history's influence on perception and society as embodied in the Australian public's behaviour towards Indigenous

Australians and his repeated attempts in his own writings to redefine his identity in relation to it, which the public, the media, and the art world frequently overlooked.

The juxtaposition in 'Re-Writing History' was further developed in his more famous, long-form essays that followed: 1993's 'Aesthetics and Iconography: An Artist's Approach' (p. 27) and 1996's 'The Manifest Toe' (p. 37). These essays combine autobiography and theory in a more traditional style, revealing how postmodern, postcolonial, and poststructural thought informed Bennett's art and life, and establish how language manipulates our view of the world and the words we use to frame our views of others. Championing Bennett's voice in this publication, especially through his writing, is not only important because he had such vital things to say, but also because doing so highlights the entrapping qualities of language, the racial bias that prioritised Euro-Australian voices, and the tendency for words to be appropriated and abstracted by those in positions of power.[41]

Though Bennett found that writing helped to formalise his perspectives and positions, as evidenced by its very vital presence within his archive, he was particularly conscious of its role in shaping our perception of the world as a system of representation. Bennett's relationship with language, and therefore text, was one accompanied by a level of scepticism. This hesitancy was fuelled, no doubt, by his interest in postmodern and postcolonial theory, as well as the work of poststructuralists such as Michel Foucault. At school age, Bennett's attitude towards his socialisation in language seems to recall German media theorist Friedrich Kittler's description of learning the alphabet as a form of 'structural violence'.[42]

In his 1993 text 'Aesthetics and Iconography: An Artist's View', Bennett recalls receiving demerits in the classroom for misspelling a word he had written phonetically. The young Bennett, confused, asked himself 'why that spelling rather than this one? Why this sound rather than that?'[43] Only with the threat of lower marks and physical punishment did his questioning stop: '[and] so it is that as children we become socialised into a particular societal structure; a network of relationships to, and ideas about, the world that is constructed by language'. This internalised contract that Bennett so eloquently reflects on—and as Richard Harland describes it in his book *Superstructuralism*, relating this idea to the work of Swiss linguist Ferdinand de Saussure (1857-1913)—is one that no individual gets the chance to evaluate before signing. Harland elaborates:

> The individual absorbs language before he can think for himself: indeed, the absorption of language is the very condition of being able to think for himself. The individual can reject particular knowledges that society explicitly teaches him, he can throw off particular beliefs that society forcibly imposes upon him—but he has always already accepted the words and meanings through which such knowledges and beliefs were communicated to him. Words and meanings have been deposited in the individual's brain below the level of conscious ownership and mastery. They lie within him like an undigested piece of society.[44]

As Bennett described, language is like a 'cement that binds and maintains the social organisation of a particular society or cultural group'.[45] This pre-existing structure, which holds such influence on people, contributing to their ingrained perceptions of others, frequently occupied Bennett's thinking and clearly framed his conceptual development. Though language is a system of representation, the boundaries of which define and by effect limit our understanding of the world, Bennett believed that its restrictions could be disrupted through art.[46]

Non-Performance: Retreat and Refusal

After the publishing of 'The Manifest Toe', both Bennett's formal and informal writing practices began to slowly retreat. Instead of writing freely in notebooks, reflecting on ideas or work, Bennett started to type out texts—though some examples of handwritten text are still visible into the 2000s. After the publication of a pre-existing text in 1999 reflecting on his 'Notes on Perception' series of the late 1980s, *Australian Icons: Notes on Perception* (p. 65), Bennett stopped publishing too. This decision, though not discussed in Bennett's writing, echoes similar periods of self-enforced silence in his past.

One such period of silence was Bennett's *Non-Performance,* discussed briefly earlier. Inspired by Broodthaers, Bennett proposed a new project in his 1992 correspondence with friend Carchesio—a 'non-action' of five years duration that he would begin when he returned to Australia in mid-1992. Over this five-year period, Bennett intended 'to say nothing about my work, other than what I have already said in the past', since talking about his art had already 'become a matter of saying the same things in different ways anyway so nothing will be lost in this practice'. Bennett decided that his future artistic statements would 'constitute quotes by other people and myself juxtaposed or ordered in a particular way'.[47] On 2 March 1992, Bennett writes in reply to a new letter received from Carchesio and includes a copy of his new essay: 'Re-Writing History'. After arriving home from France in mid-1992, Bennett stopped speaking publicly within Australia, a conceptual development of the 'non-action' that he described to Carchesio. This project, his 'Non-Performance' as Bennett titled it, was extended globally in 1994 after his presentation of 'The Non-Sovereign Self: Diaspora Identities' at the then Tate Gallery, London. Not included in this publication due to its close similarity in content to his later essay 'The Manifest Toe', Bennett received predominantly positive responses from the audience, though fielded some negative feedback from a high profile African-American artist. Confronted by his criticism, Bennett extended his *Non-Performance* internationally to stop speaking publicly altogether.[48] By the end of the 1990s, Bennett had firmly refocused his attention to his art—that trusted mode in which he had found a voice.

Bennett's retreat from writing and public speaking was due to a number of complex reasons. British art historian Linda Goddard considers the predicament of the painter 'who is obliged to use words to defend the autonomy of the visual'.[49] Bennett's position was doubly charged in that his writing and his art were and continue to be called upon to defend the autonomy of his identity. An artist of Aboriginal and Anglo-Celtic descent, Bennett was unaware of his Aboriginal ancestry until his early adulthood. His texts were often the site where his family history was explored in descriptive and emotive fashion. These include his mother Grace's upbringing within the mission system in regional Queensland under the auspices of the State Government's *Aboriginals Protection and the Restriction of the Sale of Opium Act* of 1897 and its succeeding acts. They too recorded his own experiences of institutionalised racism in its many insidious guises.

As Bennett was a notably shy person, his quick ascendance in the Australian and international art worlds often sat uncomfortably with him. He worried about the influence his Aboriginality may have on viewers' readings of his work and perhaps on his success—emerging during Australia's 1988 bicentennial 'celebrations' of the country's 'peaceful settlement': a time of significant pain, but also increased visibility for many Indigenous Australians. In his 1989 interview with Bob Lingard (see p. 120), Bennett discussed his concerns:

I think people knowing my Aboriginality does have a large bearing on how they read the work. I don't know whether that's fortunate or not. It's just a fact of life that these things do have an effect. I think you're touching on a question which worries me a little: it's just a questioning of myself. My quick success has something to do with my Aboriginality and that worries me.[50]

Bennett would build on this 'questioning' to a point where he began to articulate a position of post-identity, embracing a state that avoided essentialist positions between binary oppositions such as white/black, civilised/savage, self/other, categories enmeshed within a discourse of hierarchies that he fought to transcend, inspired by poststructural theorists such as Foucault. Bennett's refusal to be categorised was a position that he spoke of widely in his art and writing. Despite his advocacy for a wider representation of his ancestry and conception of identity, others continued to overlook his attempts at self-determination: often he was described as an 'Aboriginal artist' despite his constant description of both his Anglo-Celtic and Aboriginal ancestry. The irony of this predicament, working with visual, verbal, and written language to articulate his position between its innate categorisation was not lost on Bennett—in fact, he made his career out of turning the tools of his entrapment into mechanisms of criticism.

McLean describes Bennett as a 'Foucauldian historian: he examined the relationship between discourse (knowledge and language) and power, thus focusing on the epistemological basis of historical shifts, and in particular the epistemological assumptions and language of racism'.[51] In discussing Foucault in 1993, Bennett explained that the French theorist 'talked of a concept of "critical community" where something "intolerable" is found in a system of identification. It is characterised as a refusal to participate in this system of recognition and thus "problematises" identity and makes of "subjectivity" an open and endless question, at once individual and collective.'[52] A similar refusal to participate took on an expanded and powerful role with Bennett's conception of his *Non-Performance*.

Confusion from the public and media around Bennett's identification reached a critical stage during his residency in France. The artist was obliged to participate in several promotional interviews with visiting journalists from Europe and Australia, interrupting his studio time and often resulting in misrepresentations of him and his work.[53] On 23 May 1992, just prior to returning to Australia, he wrote a short note where he described the term 'Aboriginal' as 'an abstraction as I also find the term Australian an abstraction'.[54] Instead of subscribing to either, he stated '[for] now I identify as a human being only and as neither of the above ... although I am both. I am both and I am neither. I am both outside and inside both terms, both categories used to classify human beings.'[55] Here Bennett marshalls his contradictions, utilising his disidentification as a healing, even radical, space of uncertainty. This moment of reflection could be further interpreted as Bennett enforcing his position as part of Foucault's concept of a critical community, which John Rajchman describes as 'not the community of those a society excludes in order to function' but rather 'all those who start to refuse their part in maintaining the specific form of thinking that defines it and them, of those who depart from it, taking their identities or forms of experience in new directions outside its compass'.[56]

In *Non-Performance*, Bennett articulated Foucault's notion of refusal through his active rejection of demands to speak, to identify, and began exploring new approaches to framing and discussing his work. Describing the context of his decision to Australian art historian Chris McAuliffe in an interview conducted in 1993 (p. 129), Bennett stated:

I'm very conscious of being appropriated to fit whoever's particular theory about Aboriginality or even postcolonialism. I have been trying to argue my point, but I've found that what I say doesn't matter.

> So I decided to stop saying it. For the five years from 1992, I'll put a 'non-performance' clampdown on giving public talks. My work is often seen as about exploring my identity in order to secure it, like I'm searching for it, like I've lost it somewhere, which is the total opposite to what I'm doing.[57]

Around that same time, linking back to his desire in 'Re-Writing History' of others speaking for him, Bennett scrawled a quick thought in one of his notebooks:

> One reason for my non-performance period is to explore the possibilities of engaging with people through writing. I hoped to encourage other people to talk about my work, and listen to what they have to say in relation to how they interpret my work. By finding and meeting (and vice versa) intelligent people who are interesting and creative in their fields—who are more educated than I at present and thus are a source for ideas and feedback.[58]

This note, although dated prior to his longest essay, 'The Manifest Toe', highlighted a significant shift in Bennett's public writing and speaking. Key academics and writers were invited by Bennett to elucidate his perspectives and thoughts, especially his friend Ian McLean, who began writing on Bennett's work in 1993. By the end of the 1990s, this dynamic was firmly established, and Bennett stopped publishing his own words.[59]

The contradictory nature of this position—growing resistant to others' interpretation of his art and life, but increasingly relying on friends and colleagues to represent his practice—was perhaps informed by the stubborn resistance Bennett's attempts at changing society through his art and writing had met, or the burden of representation as a 'named Aborigine'.[60] McLean sees Bennett's refusal as recognising how 'the artist's word easily becomes a straightjacket, taken as a truth';[61] by being overly attentive to the artist's voice, we deprioritise the artwork's. In this trade off, the ambivalent quality of the artwork—its own experience and fluctuation of meaning across time—loses out in a desire to define interpretation. For McLean, Bennett's desire for his work to be 'an ever-contemporaneous critique that opens discourse to its otherings' meant putting down his pen.[62] He had been right all along about language, his uncertainty consistent: doubting its strict regulations at primary school, questioning its capacity to communicate the true depth of feeling in his first year at college, and recognising its entrapments as an adult. Despite this, his writings offer the reader deep insights into Bennett's art, life, and thinking. But it was through painting that Bennett had found a voice, and thus where his trust, like language, persisted.

Uncertain and Insecure

As the contents of this publication have traced, Bennett's writing provided a crucial space for developing and testing his beliefs in a space of radical uncertainty. Through writing, Bennett came to discover that he did not need to write or speak publicly to appease the expectations of society: his position evolved to a point where the strict parameters of language struggled to contain or represent him. He found comfort in the 'spaces between words and what they attempt to describe', an uncertain space, seeing the gaps within language as 'the common reality we all share'.[63] At the very end of his interview with McAuliffe, he elaborated on the powerful feeling of leaving things undefined:

> I feel the only identity you need is really a human one, you're a human being in the world. Sure, all those things—I'm an Australian, I'm an Aussie and all that stuff—it's safe, but it's not free. And I think freedom is about not being tied down by those things; the feeling's scary, but freedom is about being uncertain and even insecure.[64]

He devoted his energy and words to a language to which he remained consistently faithful: painting. While text continued to appear in his art and to play a profound role in its research and production, Bennett's role as a writer in the public sphere eventually followed the maxim of his *Non-Performance*: he chose not to participate. And, in that action, he spoke volumes.

Notes

1. Gordon Bennett, handwritten notes, Communication Studies journal exercise, 11 October 1986 (Saturday, 9am), Personal Archive of Gordon Bennett, Brisbane. In his first year of art college, Bennett was set the task of keeping a journal, and was required to write at least one entry per week. Bennett, along with his fellow students, were encouraged to work towards a loose 'collection of disparate perceptions, experiences and observations ... you are experimenting consciously with language as a means of expression and communication'. 'Communications Studies (UG1001) Journal', Queensland College of Art typed course task sheet, undated (c. 1986), Personal Archive of Gordon Bennett, Brisbane.
2. Ian McLean, 'Everything You Ever Wanted to Know About Drawing', in *Gordon Bennett: Be Polite*, ed. Aileen Burns and Johan Lundh (Brisbane and Berlin: Institute of Modern Art and Sternberg Press, 2016), 131–32.
3. Kelly Gellatly, 'Citizen in the Making: The Art of Gordon Bennett', in *Gordon Bennett* (Melbourne: National Gallery of Victoria, 2007), 9.
4. Gordon Bennett, 'The Manifest Toe', in *The Art of Gordon Bennett* (Sydney: Craftsman House/G+B Arts International, 1996), 10–12.
5. Chris McAuliffe, 'Interview with Gordon Bennett', in *What Is Appropriation? An Anthology of Writings on Australian Art in the 1980s and 1990s*, ed. Rex Butler (Brisbane: Institute of Modern Art and Power Publications, Sydney, 1996), 271.
6. McAuliffe, 'Interview with Gordon Bennett', 278.
7. Bill Wright, 'Conversation: Bill Wright Talks to Gordon Bennett', in *Gordon Bennett* (Melbourne: National Gallery of Victoria, 2007), 97.
8. Bennett, 'The Manifest Toe', 27.
9. Gellatly, 'Citizen in the Making', 10.
10. Gordon Bennett, artist's statement to *The Persistence of Language*, handwritten notes, undated [1990], Personal Archive of Gordon Bennett, Brisbane.
11. Anne Kirker, 'Gordon Bennett: Expressions of Constructed Identity', *Artlink* 10, no. 1 and 2 (1990): 93.
12. As Rex Butler observes, 'many of the works from [McCahon's] *Elias* [series] are simply made up of lines taken from the Book of Matthew, in which Christ's words on the cross to God, '*Eloi, eloi, lama sabachthani*', are misheard as referring to Elijah [Elias], a prophet of Israel, with nearby spectators wondering whether Christ is calling upon Elijah to come and save Him. The point of the parable is that responsibility for the welfare of Christ must be understood to lie not with his heavenly Father but with those who are alive here on earth'. Rex Butler, 'Victory over Death: The Gospel According to Colin McCahon', *ABC Religion and Ethics*, 25 July 2012, https://www.abc.net.au/religion/victory-over-death-the-gospel-according-to-colin-mccahon/10100406, accessed 24 February 2020.
13. Terry Smith, 'Australia's Anxiety', in *History and Memory in the Art of Gordon Bennett* (Birmingham and Oslo: Ikon Gallery and Henie Onstad Kunstsenter, 1999), 11.

14. Colin McCahon *The Valley of Dry Bones*, 1947, oil on canvas. Collection: Te Papa Tongarewa Museum of New Zealand, Wellington.
15. Gordon Bennett, *Shadow Monsters from the Id*, 1993, from the 'Home Sweet Home' series, watercolour and pencil on paper. Collection: Griffith University, Brisbane.
16. Tillers and Bennett's artistic dialogue, at times fractious, has been profiled widely in other texts. See Terry Smith 'Australia's Anxiety'; Helen Hughes, 'Skin Deep: The Anatomy of Images in the Art of Gordon Bennett' in *Gordon Bennett: Be Polite*, ed. Aileen Burns and Johan Lundh (Brisbane and Berlin: Institute of Modern Art and Sternberg Press, 2016), 29-48; Ian McLean 'Philosophy and Painting: Gordon Bennett's Critical Aesthetic', in *The Art of Gordon Bennett* (Sydney: Craftsman House/G+B Arts International, 1996), 73-94; and, Rex Butler, 'Two Readings of Gordon Bennett's *The Nine Ricochets*', *Eyeline* 19 (Winter/Spring 1992): 18-23.
17. Gordon Bennett, letter to Ian McLean, 'Notes to Basquiat: Modern Art', typed letter, 4 April 2001, Personal Archive of Gordon Bennett, Brisbane.
18. Ian McLean, 'Gordon Bennett's Home Décor: The Joker in the Pack', *Law Text Culture* 287 (1998): 292-93.
19. McLean, 'Gordon Bennett's Home Décor', 293.
20. Bennett, 'Notes to Basquiat: Modern Art'.
21. Gordon Bennett, 'Letter to Jean-Michel Basquiat', *Gordon Bennett*, exhibition pamphlet (Sydney: Sherman Galleries, 1999), 4.
22. Bennett, 'Notes to Basquiat: Modern Art'.
23. Bennett, 'Letter to Jean-Michel Basquiat', 4.
24. Bennett, 'Notes to Basquiat: Modern Art'.
25. Bennett, 'Notes to Basquiat: Modern Art'.
26. Bennett, 'Notes to Basquiat: Modern Art'.
27. Bennett, 'Notes to Basquiat: Modern Art'.
28. Wright, 'Conversation', 97.
29. Tim Riley Walsh, 'A Transient Separation: Gordon Bennett's Abstract Art', in *Unfinished Business: The Art of Gordon Bennett* (Brisbane: Queensland Art Gallery | Gallery of Modern Art, 2020), 138-145.
30. Gellatly, 'Citizen in the Making', 24.
31. Gellatly, 'Citizen in the Making', 24.
32. Wright, 'Conversation', 97.
33. Margaret Preston, 'The Indigenous Art of Australia', *Art in Australia*, 3rd series, no. 11 (March 1925): 41-55.
34. This particular work draws from a later article by Preston that includes sketches of hers inspired by two designs, 'one an Aboriginal one from Mandated New Guinea [today's Papua New Guinea]'. Margaret Preston, 'The Application of Aboriginal Designs', *Art in Australia*, 3rd series, no. 31 (March 1930): 60.
35. McLean, 'Everything', 126.
36. McLean, 'Everything', 126.
37. Gordon Bennett, letter to John Laws, 3 June 1994, handwritten letter, Personal Archive of Gordon Bennett, Brisbane.
38. Gordon Bennett, letters to Eugene Carchesio, handwritten letter, 28 February 1992, Personal Archive of Gordon Bennett, Brisbane (see p. 82).

39. Francesca Wilmott, 'Marcel Broodthaers', *Museum of Modern Art*, New York, https://www.moma.org/artists/795, accessed 19 February 2020; Bennett, letters to Eugene Carchesio (pp. 82-85).
40. Gordon Bennett, 'Re-Writing History' in *Southern Crossings/Empty Land: In the Australian Image*, ed. Helen Sloan (London: Camerawork, 1992), 28-29. See page 18. 'Re-writing History' was commissioned for the *Southern Crossings/Empty Land: In the Australian Image* exhibition catalogue, which accompanied the exhibition *Southern Crossings/Empty Land (Parts One and Two)* featuring *Untitled (Nuance)* (1992, figure 3), a new photographic work by Bennett at London's Camerawork art gallery in 1992.
41. McAuliffe, 'Interview with Gordon Bennett', 277.
42. John Armitage, 'From Discourse Networks to Cultural Mathematics: An Interview with Friedrich A. Kittler', *Theory, Culture and Society* 23, no. 7 (2006): 24. Kittler states, 'when I got an invitation to attend a big conference in Berlin a few years ago, an extremely famous literary critic got very angry with me personally for stating that we are literally taught the alphabet through a sort of structural violence. For him, the idea that we are inscribed in this way was unbearable. But I cannot see it otherwise. How else would I have learned the alphabet? I certainly would not have learned it on my own accord.'
43. Bennett, 'Aesthetics and Iconography: An Artist's Approach.' In *Aratjara: Art of the First Australians*, 85-91. Cologne: DuMont Buchverlag, 1993, 85.
44. Richard Harland, *Superstructuralism* (London: Routledge, 2003), 12-13. Bennett's personal library includes a copy of Harland's *Superstructuralism*.
45. Bennett, 'Aesthetics and Iconography', 85.
46. Bennett, 'The Manifest Toe', 53.
47. Bennett, letters to Eugene Carchesio, Personal Archive of Gordon Bennett, Brisbane.
48. Leanne Bennett, email to the author, 20 February 2019.
49. Linda Goddard, 'Artists' Writings: Word or Image?', *Word and Image* 28, no. 4 (Oct-Dec 2012): 409, https://doi.org/10.1080/02666286.2012.740191, accessed 19 February 2019.
50. Bob Lingard, 'A Kind of History Painting: Gordon Bennett', *Tension* 17 (1989): 41.
51. Ian McLean, 'The Eternal Return of Irony: Gordon Bennett 1955-2014', *Discipline* 4 (Spring/Summer 2015): 172.
52. Bennett, 'Aesthetics and Iconography', 87. See also John Rajchman, *Truth and Eros: Foucault, Lacan and the Question of Ethics* (New York and London: Routledge, 1991), 102.
53. Leanne Bennett, email to the author, 20 February 2019.
54. Gordon Bennett, untitled handwritten note on paper, 23 May 1992, Personal Archive of Gordon Bennett, Brisbane (see p. 213).
55. Bennett, untitled note, 23 May 1992.
56. Rajchman, *Truth and Eros*, 106.
57. McAuliffe, 'Interview with Gordon Bennett', 277.
58. Gordon Bennett, untitled handwritten note on gridded paper, 29 June 1994, Personal Archive of Gordon Bennett, Brisbane (see p. 213).
59. From this point, Bennett very rarely conducted any interviews with the press, occasionally agreeing to respond via email to questions. Around the time of his 2007 survey exhibition at the National Gallery of Victoria, Bennett agreed to an interview with the late curator William (Bill) Wright. This interview is included in this publication (see p. 135).
60. McLean, 'Eternal Return', 175.

61. McLean, 'Eternal Return', 175.
62. McLean, 'Eternal Return', 175.
63. Gordon Bennett, untitled handwritten note on paper, 7 September 1991, Personal Archive of Gordon Bennett, Brisbane (see p. 208).
64. McAuliffe, 'Interview with Gordon Bennett', 277.

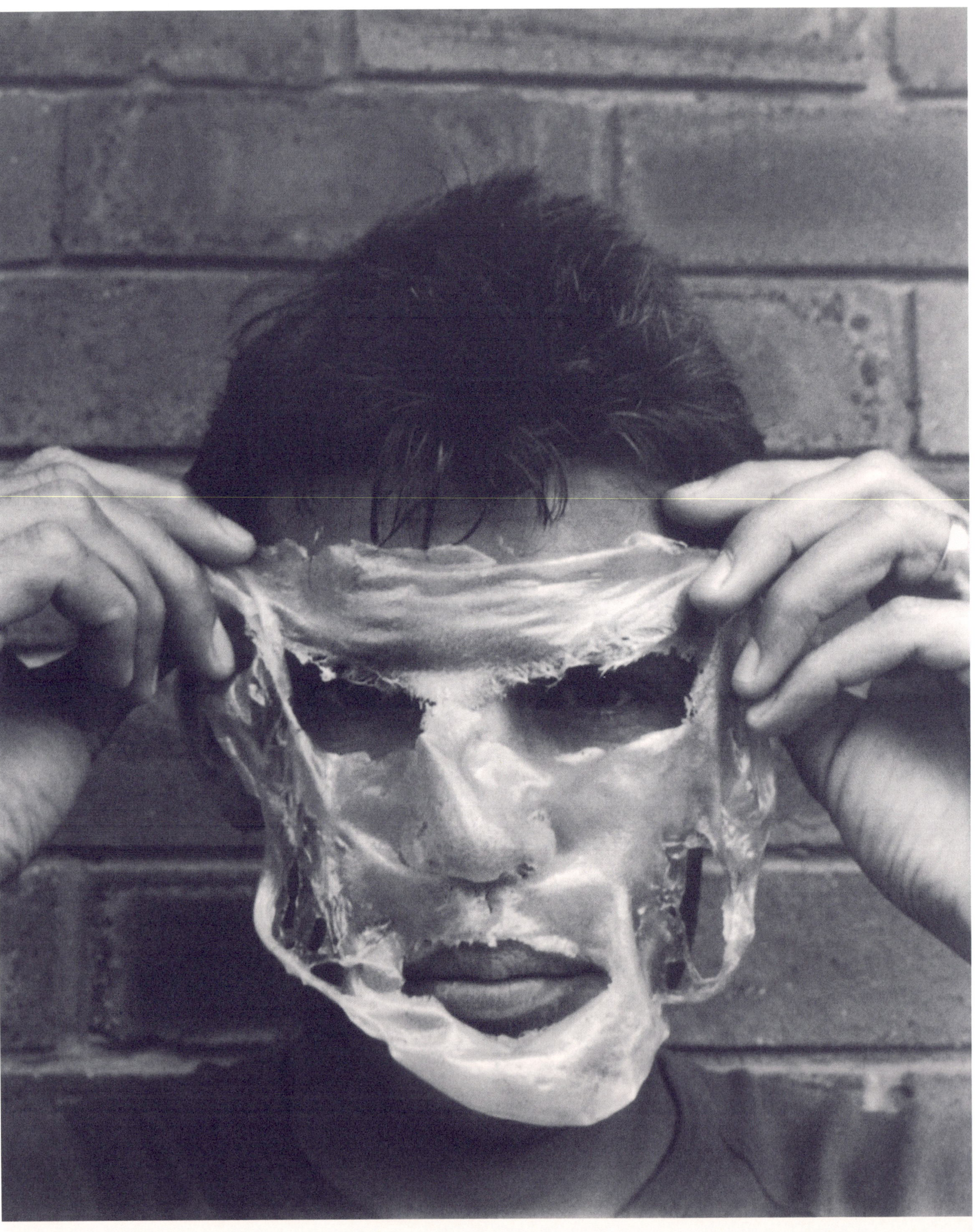

Index

Artist's bibliography

Index

I am interested in the spaces between words and what they attempt to describe. In that space is the common reality we all share. that which exists in relation to our own existence. It vibrates with us - and we all try to capture this reality in the net of languages - to understand it to grasp it & know it & thereby know ourselves and then outside our spectrum exists other worlds other possibilities.

SB 7-9-91

Artist's bibliography

1990

'"The Coming of the Light" Artist's Statement.' In *Balance 1990: Views, Visions, Influences*, edited by Janet Hogan, 46–49. Brisbane: Queensland Art Gallery, 1990.

1992

'Re-Writing History.' In *Southern Crossings/Empty Land: In the Australian Image*, edited by Helen Sloan, 21–29. London: Camerawork, 1992.

'Artist's Statement.' In *Southern Crossings/ Empty Land: In the Australian Image*, edited by Helen Sloan, 43. London: Camerawork, 1992.

'On Double Standards: An 'Other Perspective.' *Art Monthly Australia* 47 (1992): 26–27.

'Ästhetik und Ikonographie: Die Annäherung Eines Künstlers.' *Art Vector* 10, no. 1 (June 1992): 11–16.

'Artist's Statement.' In *Strangers in Paradise: Contemporary Australian Art to Korea*, exh. cat., 22–25. Sydney: Art Gallery of New South Wales, 1992.

'Artist's Statement.' In *Tyerabarrbowaryaou: I Shall Never Become a White Man*, exh. cat., 14. Sydney: Museum of Contemporary Art, 1992.

1993

'Artist's Statement.' In *Identities: Art from Australia*, exh. cat., 53–55. Taipei: Taipei Fine Arts Museum, 1993.

'Artist's Statement.' In *Confess and Conceal*, exh. cat., 26. Perth: Art Gallery of Western Australia, 1993.

'Artist's Statement.' In *Fifth Australian Sculpture Triennial Vol. 1*, edited by Sally Moss, 32–33. Melbourne: Melbourne International Festival of the Arts, 1993.

'Aesthetics and Iconography: An Artist's Approach.' In *Aratjara: Art of the First Australians*, exh. cat., 85–91. Cologne: DuMont Buchverlag, 1993.

1995

'Myth of the Western Man (White Man's Burden).' In *Inner-Land: Exhibition of Australian Contemporary Art*, exh. cat. Tokyo: Lumani Gallery, 1995.

'Artist's Statement.' In *Zero One – Digital Shifts*, 8. Noosa: Noosa Regional Gallery, 1995.

'Altered Body Print (Howl).' In *A Selection from the Downlands Art Collection: Toowoomba Regional Art Gallery*, exh. cat., 19–20. Toowoomba: Downlands College, 1995.

1996

'The Manifest Toe.' In *The Art of Gordon Bennett*, by Ian McLean and Gordon Bennett, 9–62. Roseville East, NSW: Craftsman House, 1996.

1997

'Cloud Gazing.' In *Breaking Borders*, exh. cat., 37–42. Winnipeg: St. Norbert Arts Centre, 1997.

1999

'Australian Icons: Notes on Perception.' In *Double Vision: Art Histories and Colonial Histories in the Pacific*, edited by Nicholas Thomas and Diane Losche, 252–56. Cambridge: Cambridge University Press, 1999.

'Letter to Jean-Michel Basquiat.' In *Gordon Bennett*, exh. cat., 4. Sydney: Sherman Galleries, 1999.

2002

'Australian Icons: Notes on Perception.' In *Readings in Indigenous Religions*, edited by Graham Harvey, 311–16. London: Continuum, 2002

2006

'Aesthetics and Iconography: An Artist's Approach.' In *The Anthropology of Art: A Reader*, edited by Howard Morphy and Morgan Perkins, 513–19. Oxford: John Wiley & Sons, 2006.

liberty
autonomy
freedom
freeness
independence
self determination
individualism
arbitrariness
nonconformity
unconventionality
licence
familiarity
outspoke~~ness~~ness
spontaneity
spontaneousness
unrestraint
abandon
anarchism
anarchy
incontinence
indiscipline
inordinacy
irrepressibility
wildness
wantonness

Gordon Bennett: Selected Writings

Published by Power Publications and Griffith University Art Museum

Editors: Angela Goddard and Tim Riley Walsh

Designer: Michael Phillips

Editorial Assistant: Mandy Quadrio

Copy editing: Evie Franzidis and Marni Williams

Photographer: Carl Warner, unless stated

Colour management: ColourChiefs

Print: 1010 Printing International

ISBN: 978-0-909952-01-3

A catalogue record for this book is available from the National Library of Australia.

This publication was produced on the traditional lands of the Gadigal, Yuggara and Turrbal peoples.
The editors and publishers of this book acknowledge the traditional custodians of these lands, pay respect to their Elders, past and present, and extend that respect to other Aboriginal and Torres Strait Islander peoples.

ACKNOWLEDGEMENTS

Professor Carolyn Evans,
Vice Chancellor, Griffith University

Professor Scott Harrison,
Pro Vice Chancellor (Arts, Education and Law), Griffith University

Professor Elisabeth Findlay,
Director, Queensland College of Art, Griffith University

Carol Ha, Carrie McCarthy, Kylie Spear, Michael Barnett, Naomi Evans, Ross Manning, and volunteers, Griffith University Art Museum

Leanne Bennett and Caitlin Bennett
Ian McLean
Josh Milani and staff
Peter Bellas
Irene Sutton and staff
Kelly Gellatly
Andrew McNamara
Mandy Quadrio
Terry Smith
Rex Butler
Jane Devery
Eugene Carchesio
Pat Hoffie
Bob Lingard
Chris McAuliffe
Christopher Chapman
Ihor Holubizky
Anne Kirker
Hilarie Mais
Barry Keldoulis
Gene Sherman
Kerryanne Farrer, Flying Arts
D'Lan Davidson
Lauraine Diggins Fine Art staff
Megan Patty, National Gallery of Victoria
Eve Sullivan, Artlink
Eric Meredith and Tracey Dall, National Gallery of Australia
Michael Fitzgerald, Art Monthly Australasia
Liz Nowell, Institute of Modern Art
Jacinta Sutton, State Library of Queensland
Aileen Burns and Johan Lundh
Megan Tamati-Quennell, Museum of New Zealand Te Papa Tongarewa
Chris Saines, Simon Wright, Judy Gunning and Zara Stanhope, QAGOMA

The Estate of Gordon Bennett is represented by Milani Gallery, Brisbane, and Sutton Gallery, Melbourne.

SUPPORTERS

John Citizen Arts Pty Ltd,
ATF The Bennett Family Trust

This project is supported by the Queensland Government through Arts Queensland.

Power Publications
Power Institute Foundation for Art and Visual Culture
University of Sydney
NSW 2006 Australia
powerpublications.com.au

Griffith University Art Museum
artmuseum@griffith.edu.au
Telephone: +61 7 3735 7414
Fax: +61 7 3735 7932
PO Box 3370
South Brisbane, QLD 4101
Australia
226 Grey Street
South Bank, QLD
griffith.edu.au/art-museum

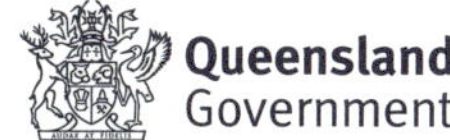

POWER PUBLICATIONS

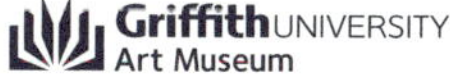

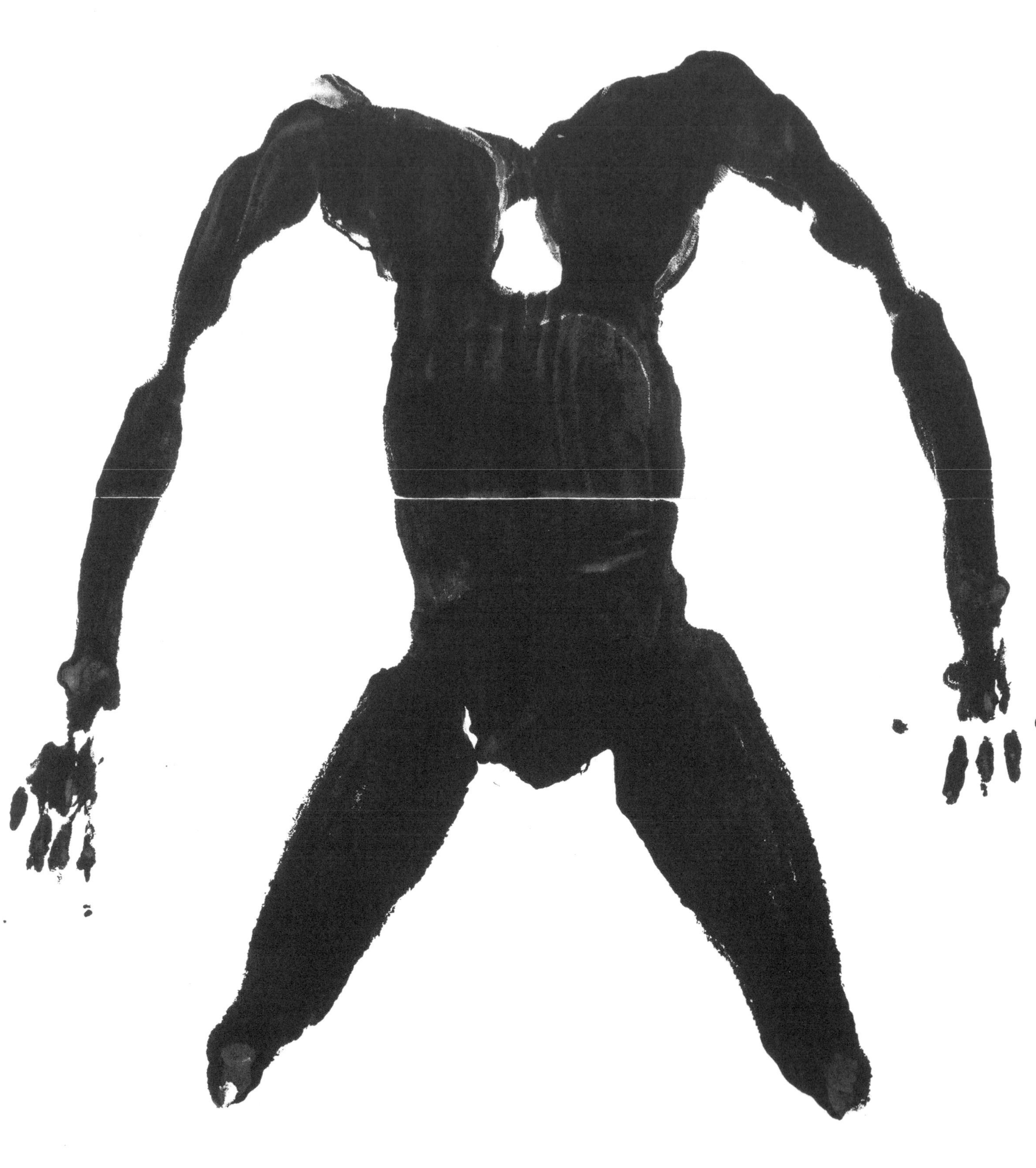

As far as the question of being Aboriginal goes. I find the term Aboriginal an abstraction as, I also find the term Australian an abstraction. For now I identify as a human being only and as niether of the above (Aboriginal or Australian) although I am both. I am both and I am niether. I am both outside and inside both terms, both categories used to classify human beings. As an outsider to both classifications I am liberated to explore them in a detached manner, like a biologist dissecting a specimen. As an insider I understand what I find as it is my being I am dissecting, as a specimen I feel every prod, every cut + I know where it hurts the most, where the healing needs to begin.

G B. 12.59 AM
23-5-'92

Of course all this begs the question of what is a human being and I'm stupid enough to ask it. But for now I'm content with looking in a mirror + seeing one of them there. 10.10 AM
23-5-92.

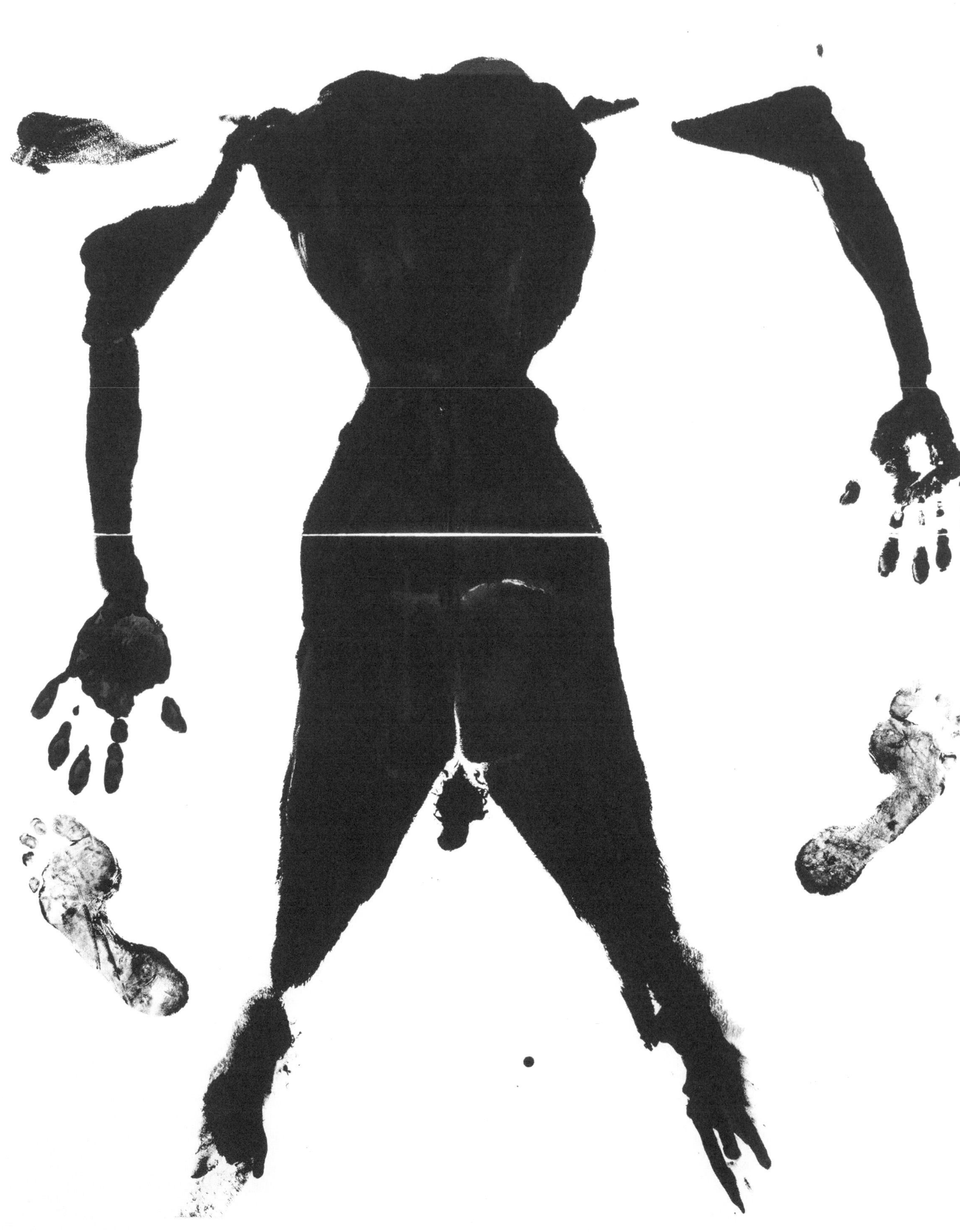

Sometimes I wish I could have all my bodily orifices sewn shut including my ears & eyes so I would not hear, see or be able to respond to the stupidity of racism I now see & hear around me nearly every day. I would be in paradise. The thing is though I know that won't stop it. It will go on, it will seep through the gaps in the stitches & find it's way inside & since I've already been soaking in it for 36 years now it's already inside anyway so it will recognise itself!
With this thought I would explode if I did not tear the stitches out & spit on the nearest canvas I could find.

GB 11-12-91
9-56 AM.

Additional plates

pages 1, 2, 4

Untitled notebook drawings (detail), undated
Felt-tip pen on paper
The Estate of Gordon Bennett
Note: the drawing on page 2 is a collaboration with Caitlin Bennett

pages 6, 8, 10, 14, 70, 112, 186, 202

Untitled (Nuance) (detail) 1992
Photographs and synthetic polymer paint on foam core panels
Sixteen panels, 85 x 275 cm overall
Private collection
Photo: Natasha Harth, QAGOMA

page 12

Untitled note, 23 January 1990
Handwritten note on paper
The Estate of Gordon Bennett

pages 13, 69, 111

Selected details of Gordon Bennett's personal notebook covers, undated
The Estate of Gordon Bennett

page 26

Photocopied page from Bruce Elder's *Blood on the Wattle*
with handwritten annotation by Gordon Bennett, undated
The Estate of Gordon Bennett

page 36

Self Portrait (Gone Primitive) (detail) 1992
Book, photograph, plastic, cord
23 x 15.5 x 2 cm
Collection of Michael Phillips

page 60

John Citizen
Home Décor 1–9 (after Margaret Preston) 1995
Watercolour on paper
27 x 19.5 cm each
Private collection, Melbourne

page 62

Photocopied page from Gordon Bennett's personal
archive with cardboard framing tool, undated
The Estate of Gordon Bennett

page 68

Untitled note, 23 January 1990
Handwritten note on paper
The Estate of Gordon Bennett

page 100

Ideal (Basquiat and I) (detail) 1994
Synthetic polymer paint on paper
76 x 56 cm
The Wesfarmers Collection of Australian Art

page 110

Untitled note, 23 and 24 January 1990
Handwritten note on paper
The Estate of Gordon Bennett

page 142

Untitled note, 24 January 1990
Handwritten note on paper
The Estate of Gordon Bennett

page 184

Untitled notebook drawing, c. 1995
Ballpoint and felt-tip pen on paper
The Estate of Gordon Bennett

page 208

Untitled note, 7 September 1991
Handwritten note on paper
The Estate of Gordon Bennett

page 210

Untitled word list from notebook, 29 April 2000
Felt-tip pen on paper
The Estate of Gordon Bennett

page 212

Body Print C1 1995
Synthetic polymer paint on two sheets of paper
160 x 120 cm (image), 167.3 x 128.2 x 5.6 cm (framed)
Griffith University Art Collection. Donated through the Australian
Government's Cultural Gifts Program by John Citizen Arts Pty Ltd,
ATF The Bennett Family Trust, 2007

page 213

Untitled note, 23 May 1992
handwritten note on paper
The Estate of Gordon Bennett

page 214

Body Print D 1995
Synthetic polymer paint on two sheets of paper
160 x 120 cm (image), 167.3 x 128.2 x 5.6 cm (framed)
Griffith University Art Collection. Donated through the Australian
Government's Cultural Gifts Program by John Citizen Arts Pty Ltd,
ATF The Bennett Family Trust, 2007

page 215

Untitled note, 11 December 1991
Handwritten note on paper
The Estate of Gordon Bennett

Dust jacket–Front

Subject Matter from 'Notes to Basquiat' series (detail) 2004
Inkjet on paper
26.3 x 20.4 cm (image) 29.7 x 21 cm (sheet)
Griffith University Art Collection. Donated through the Australian
Government's Cultural Gifts Program by John Citizen Arts Pty Ltd,
ATF The Bennett Family Trust, 2007

Dust jacket–Back

Original from 'Notes to Basquiat' series (detail) 2004
Inkjet on paper
26.3 x 20.4 cm (image) 29.7 x 21 cm (sheet)
The Estate of Gordon Bennett

Cover

Untitled notebook drawings, undated
Felt-tip pen on paper
The Estate of Gordon Bennett